TINDERBOX
East-Central Europe in the Spring,
Summer, and Early Fall of 1956

Tinderbox

East-Central Europe in the Spring, Summer, and Early Fall of 1956

First Edition

John P. C. Matthews

Fenestra Books

Tinderbox: East-Central Europe in the Spring, Summer,
and Early Fall of 1956

All rights reserved.

Copyright © 2003 by John P. C. Matthews

Publisher's Cataloguing-in-Publication Data

Matthews, John P. C.
  Tinderbox : East-central Europe in the spring, summer, and early fall
of 1956 / John P. C. Matthews. — 1st ed.
  p. cm.
  Includes bibliographical references and index.
  LCCN: 2002112796
  ISBN: 1-58736-140-X (hardcover)
  ISBN: 1-58736-141-8 (paperback)

  1. Europe, Eastern—History—1945-1989. I. Title.

DJK50.M38 2003
943'.0009045

Published (2003) by Fenestra Books™

610 East Delano Street, Suite 104, Tucson, Arizona 85705, U.S.A.
www.fenestrabooks.com

Cover art by Amelia Carling

Book design by Atilla Vékony

To Verna, without whom . . .

Contents

Acknowledgements

The author would like to thank the many people who played roles—some of them significant—in bringing this book to its present form:

In the United States: Cynthia Crippen, Rita DiFiore-Czipczer, István Deák, Patricia Gilchrest, Marczenia James, Stephen and Kasia Jerzak-Larsen, Mark Kramer, Verna D. Matthews, August Molnár, Károly Nagy, Ladislav Němec, Jan Nowak (Jezioranski), Richard Rowson, Margery Cuyler Perkins, Charles E. Townsend, Atilla L. Vékony, Leslie H. Whitten, Jr. and Ralph C. Woodward.

In the Czech Republic: Muriel Blaive, Maggie Evling, Lechosław Gawlikowski, Jan Havránek, Zdeněk Herman, Michael Heyrovský, Karel Kaplan, Saša Mangel, Petr Mareš, Jiří Pernes, Jiří Pešek, Jiří Skopek, Eva Strnadová, and Michal Svátos.

In Slovakia: Jozef Jablonický and Juraj Marušiak.

In Hungary: Csaba Békés, András B. Hegedűs, Erika László, György Litván, András Mink, Trudy Peterson, László Rajk, Jr., István Rév and Jiřina Šmejkalová.

In Poland: Aleksandra Banasiak, Aleksander Berger, Robert Gamble, Andrzej Górny, Konstantin Górny, Pawel Machcewicz, Jan Sandorski, Zofia Trojanowiczowa and Jan Wieczorak.

Introduction

The year 1956 is remembered for many things. In this country it was the year Dwight Eisenhower defeated Adlai Stevenson for the presidency for the second time. This election campaign, however, took place against a background of even more memorable events overseas, the twin crises of Suez and the upheavals in Eastern Europe, particularly the revolution in Hungary. (Because no outbreak of violence was involved, people tend to forget that the "Polish October," which put in place a seemingly anti-Soviet régime in Poland, was taking place simultaneously with the Hungarian Revolution.) People remember that revolution less for the exhilaration it brought than for the anguish that swept around the world when it was brutally crushed by Soviet tanks.

Both the Suez crisis, brought on by Nasser's nationalization of the Suez Canal, and the revolution in Hungary were manifestations of the cold war that had built up between the two superpowers, the U.S. and the U.S.S.R., after World War II.[*] The way these two crises were resolved seemed to alter forever the course of world history. The fast-declining British and French empires were dealt a deathblow by U.S. opposition to their action at Suez, and U.S. cold war policy was dealt a deathblow by its inaction in Hungary. The seemingly unstoppable expansion of communism and communist influence also was destroyed in Hungary by the revelation that only military might held the Soviet empire together and that belief in communism, in the heart of the communist empire, was dead. The reluctance of both superpowers to engage in direct military confrontation—despite the full outbreak of military hostilities in both of these crises—revealed the true state of affairs: nuclear stalemate.

---

[*] It is ironic that Eisenhower's secretary of state, John Foster Dulles, was more responsible for bringing on each of those crises than any other man alive at the time and that the American people, quite unaware of this irony, and fearful of *any* crisis abroad, gave Eisenhower a far larger plurality than pollsters just two weeks before the election had predicted they would.

Introduction

While some in the West were convinced that the Soviet empire could never recover from a full-scale revolution which had completely toppled its régime in Hungary, and that it was, in fact, the beginning of the empire's end, in reality both sides were so fearful of what they had seen that they were content to settle for the status quo. As a result the cold war lasted another thirty-three years.

A number of books have been written about the Suez crisis, nearly all of which include some aspect of its linkages to the crisis in Hungary. Recent archival discoveries have shown that these two crises were not as closely interlocked as it seemed at the time. Unfortunately, we will never know to what extent the Soviet decision to intervene in Hungary was influenced by the Suez events, for "the evaporation of history"[*] leaves us with nothing but archival evidence—and that is not enough.

This book, however, is not concerned with Suez. It is confined to the other crisis and was conceived from the author's conviction that quite enough has been written about Suez and the events which led to it, and that not enough is known or has been written about the buildup to the explosions in Eastern Europe in the latter half of 1956. Thus its focus is on the event that triggered the process: Nikita Khrushchev's secret speech denouncing Stalin on February 24, and the main events that followed: the Czechoslovak student revolt, the Poznań Uprising, the Petőfi Circle meetings in Budapest, the reburial of László Rajk in Budapest, the Poznań Trials and finally the "Polish October."

It is totally arbitrary, of course, to end with the "Polish October," which broke out just five days before the Hungarian Revolution and continued well past the Soviet suppression, but the Hungarian Revolution itself is too vast a topic to include in this volume. It is the author's intention to follow this book with a sequel devoted entirely to that revolution and its impact on the world.

It is equally arbitrary, I suppose, to select just a few main events and try to re-create them as they happened, because they were neither as isolated from one another as I have made them, nor were they the only notable happenings occurring at the time. To give a complete impression of that incredibly fascinating spring, summer, and early fall, however, would take several volumes and deluge the reader with far more facts than he or she could, or would want to, absorb. Instead, I have chosen these particular events because they are representative not only of what was going on in these countries at

---

[*] I am indebted to Timothy Garton Ash for this phrase, which he first used in public, I believe, in September 1996 at the Budapest conference on the Hungarian Revolution in the light of newly discovered archival materials.

that time, but because they are also representative of the countries themselves. I want the reader not only to gain some new facts, but to gain as well some lasting impressions of what these events were like, and to note the difference between Poles, Czechs and Slovaks, and Hungarians, for each event took place within a particular national context.

I come to my topic as an old "cold warrior." I served the Free Europe organization from August 1951 to August 1961, including the period from March 1954 to March 1959 in Munich, Germany. While I had many friends among the "exile" employees of Free Europe during these years and learned much about their national characteristics, I still, like many Americans, tended to lump them all together. (Hadn't I seen all of the régime representatives slavishly follow Andrei Vyshinsky's vote in the UN?) It was not until I began to travel behind the Iron Curtain in 1969 as an employee of IREX (International Research and Exchanges Board) that I became aware of how different these East European countries really are from one another. When I first arrived in Bratislava from Prague, for instance, I was immediately aware that I was now in an entirely different country than the land of the Czechs, despite the presence of the same flag flying from all government buildings.

I come to my topic also as a one-time journalist now obliged to write as an historian. If what follows appears to be more journalism than history, so be it. I have tried to be as historically accurate as possible, but I also want the reader to experience these events as though he or she had actually been there, or had at least read about them in the paper the next day.

In the course of using this approach I had to use many non-English-language sources. I hope, therefore, that some of the materials will be new even for those familiar with Eastern Europe.

My title selection is obvious: Eastern Europe in 1956 was a tinderbox. As early as 1944 and 1945, when the Red Army occupied the countries of this region, the process of stripping these countries of machinery and sometimes dismantling entire factories as war reparations and shipping them to the Soviet Union had begun. Later, when people's republics has been established in each country, the method of milking them of goods and services took the form of "joint companies"—which, of course, continued to move things of value east in return for shoddy goods the U.S.S.R. could not otherwise dispose of, or in exchange for rubles that were unusable anywhere but within the U.S.S.R. There is ample evidence that not long before Stalin died in March 1953, he had plans for all of the people's democracies to be absorbed into the Soviet Union as new republics, much as the three Baltic states had become "Soviet" republics. Soviet economic exploitation of its new satellite states went on long after Stalin's death. And it was not just machinery, commodities, and services that were sucked out, it was the very cultural juices of these once proud and individualistic nations. Hermetically sealed off from the West, with almost all intellectual contact severed, the area became an intellectual vacuum into which the Soviets pumped their version not only of how things were to be done, but also their version of history itself. Not every Novotný, Ulbricht, Bierut, or Rákosi who outdid himself in Sovietizing his native land did so on orders from Stalin. Indeed, orders sometimes came from Moscow to slow down and not overdo the process. But there were never any orders to reverse Sovietization or even to stop it. Not, that is, until 1956 when the Soviets suddenly changed their line so abruptly. By that time the countries of east-central Europe had become almost as much of a cultural wasteland as their Soviet model and their hopelessly centralized economies so locked into that of the Soviet Union that they were incapable of adjusting to local needs, which, in some cases, had reached emergency proportions. The kindling of discontent could be found in almost every situation in almost every land.

Into this dry vacuum both sides, in effect, tossed lighted matches. The Soviets, with their denunciations of Stalin, inadvertently pulled the rug out from under all party leaders from the top central leadership down to the lowest cadre level, for Stalin worship had been the unifying factor of the drives to Sovietize their countries. Heated debates broke out within the national parties and these, of course, soon involved the party press from which it leaked out to the noncommunist masses. The West, but particularly the U.S., threw provocative lighted matches into the area via VOA and RFE broadcasts, particularly whenever they were quoting the president's or the secretary of state's most recent pronouncements of America's policy of "liberation" for Eastern Europe. RFE's sister organization, Free Europe Press, meanwhile, was literally littering Bohemia with balloon-borne leaflets in Czech, as well as launching occasional flights carrying leaflets to Hungary and Poland. The Pentagon was simultaneously sending huge stratospheric balloons with cameras—the U-2 was not yet fully operational—over Soviet air space. Most provocative of all, and still not properly documented because of the CIA's refusal to open its archives, was the steady stream of agents the CIA was sending into Czechoslovakia.

Seen from today's historical distance, it is a wonder that the explosions did not come earlier than they did. Still more puzzling is the fact that neither the U.S.S.R.—the major cause—nor the U.S.—the major provocateur—saw the explosions coming.

It is, I suppose, an old story. Those of us who were on the ground—whether Soviet advisors and KGB agents within these countries, or American employees of Free Europe or VOA—were well aware of the extraordinary changes daily taking place. Yet despite all the frantic up-to-the-minute reporting on both sides via phone, cable and radio teletype, the powers that were in the Kremlin and in Washington simply were incapable of digesting the information fast enough to comprehend what was coming, much less take measures to prepare for it. The intelligence on both sides was there; the leaders simply lacked the intelligence to make proper use of it.

In writing this book I hope to recapture the texture of those cascading events in that extraordinary time at mid-century. Despite frequent flashes of lightning and occasional thunder in Eastern Europe, few people on either side could bring themselves to believe that the storm was actually coming. If the reader gains only an inkling of what it was really like, my purpose will have been achieved.

CHAPTER I

Stalin Denounced: Khrushchev's Secret Speech

The last red rays of sunshine had long since ceased to gleam off the golden onion domes of the Kremlin's several churches by the time the delegates filed wearily out of the great hall in which they had been meeting into the frigid evening air. The first icy gulp that pierced their lungs with its sudden shock was nonetheless a welcome relief from the long hours of inhaling the stale atmosphere of rank body odors and breath that reeked of garlic and cabbage. Despite the hall's high ceiling, air circulation was poor.

It had been a long ten days, but at last the record-breaking Twentieth Party Congress of the Soviet Union, which had begun on February 14, 1956, had come to a close. It was time to prepare for the long journey home. There was definitely a new mood afoot. Collective leadership was now clearly the way of the future and "the cult of the individual"—a phrase that had repeatedly turned up in the speeches of Malenkov, Mikoyan and others—was definitely being consigned to the past.

Though it was the first party congress many of the delegates had ever attended, even the newcomers were veterans of such affairs, for they each had many years of party membership under their belts. Party discipline had earned them their promotions, and along the way each had acquired at such party meetings the *Sitzfleisch* for which Molotov was so famous in the West. One did not answer a call of nature in the middle—or even toward the end—of Comrade Khrushchev's seven-hour speech. Coughing was carefully muffled and whispering to one's neighbor during one of these orations was quite out of the question.

It had not all been listening, however. During the breaks for meals and at the end of each day clots of delegates engaged in animated conversations, swapping impressions and information. No one was so foolish as to challenge anything that had been said from the rostrum. But many sought clarification of what they thought they had heard, or wanted to listen to explanations from those sharper than themselves as to the significance of what had been said. And, over the course of those ten days, a great deal had been said.

Comrade Nikita Sergeievich Khrushchev, first secretary of the party, had led off with his seven-hour "General Report." He covered just about every conceivable domestic and foreign topic. As the text of his speech came chattering off TASS teleprinters around the globe in all of the major world languages, most analysts in the West dismissed it as routine.* They noted, however, that Khrushchev had gone out of his way to quote Lenin as recognizing the possibility of "peaceful revolution" as one way for communist parties in the bourgeois world to achieve socialism.[1] They also noted his virtual silence on Stalin—a figure usually praised to the skies—whom he praised only once.

Khrushchev had been followed by all the members of the politburo; such persons as Bulganin, Kaganovich, Malenkov, Mikoyan, Molotov, and even the new man, Shepilov. All had spoken for many hours, though none for so long as the first party secretary. There had also been speeches from the party secretaries of the individual Soviet republics and even the leaders of the major "fraternal" (i.e., foreign) party delegations, of which there were about fifty with some three hundred delegates, though fewer than a dozen of these got to speak.[2]

Most of the main speakers had referred to the "cult of the individual" (a euphemism for "Stalin worship"), as though it were some virulent disease to be avoided, but only one, Anastas Mikoyan, provided the congress a major jolt when he not only attacked the "cult of the individual" but attacked Comrade Stalin by name. And not just once, either. The repetition of his discourteous remarks about Stalin had clearly been for the benefit of those who had not believed their ears the first time. There had literally been consternation in the hall the second time Mikoyan mentioned the up-to-now holy name "Stalin." It was, after all, only two months before that they had all read in *Izvestia,* on the seventy-sixth anniversary of the birth of the former leader of world communism:

---

* One Western analyst, the author, reported to Radio Free Europe's political advisor, William E. Griffith, in Munich, Germany, that despite all the bombast in the speech, he detected an unusually defensive note, with such frequent references to "the enemies of socialism" and their attacks on the "peace camp" that it amounted to first-hand evidence of the effectiveness of current Western radio and leaflet operations against the U.S.S.R. and its East European satellites.

Great Revolutionary and profound thinker ... The name of Stalin is close and dear to millions of toilers in all corners of the earth. Stalin—great fighter for peace and security of all the peoples. In millions of hearts burns the inextinguishable flame of his word.[3]

Clearly Mikoyan will have to retract his words or pay the consequences. For decades now anyone caught badmouthing the great Stalin has simply disappeared. But how could Mikoyan have dared to attack Stalin by name unless he had cleared it with the politburo of the Central Committee? "Something new is definitely in the wind," thought many of the delegates "and it behooves us to pay strict attention to the printed text—in fact, all printed documents that emanate from this Twentieth Party Congress—so that we get the new line straight."

With such thoughts running through their heads, the Soviet delegates were queuing up for supper at their hotels and hostels, grabbing a bite from food already stashed in their rooms, or simply packing for the next day's journey, when word reached them: "There is to be one more session, a closed session, which the fraternal comrades will not be attending. It starts in two hours. Comrade, if you value your future, be there! And tell no one." Rumors later circulated that some delegates had actually gotten to the main railroad station before the word reached them. With as much fear as excitement they returned to their hotels.

It is nearly 10 P.M. The great hall is full, though not completely so, for the seats in the far back and in the small rear gallery, seats formerly occupied by the fraternal comrades, remain empty. The stale air is not much different than when they left five hours ago, just a bit cooler. And the ill-lit room, twice as dark as it is in daytime with the skylights, is as dim as when they left it. It is a strange hall, neither square nor in the shape of an amphitheater, but a long rectangle. It is two halls, actually, or at least had been before the party connected the two ends in the mid-1930s creating the present inordinately long structure. The Great Hall of the Congresses, with its giant heads of Marx and Lenin in relief behind the wide dais will not be built until 1961.[*]

Some of the delegates are secretly annoyed at having been summoned for yet another session—and without any prior warning too. Others are feeling

---

[*] This great assembly hall was torn down again in 1998, whereas the hall in which the Twentieth Party Congress met was restored to its original two halls the same year.

miffed about having to undergo body inspections by plainclothes KGB agents as they enter. Those who have pads or notebooks confiscated are especially miffed. "It is not permitted," is the only explanation.

For those at the back of the hall, the bespectacled, baldhead that bobs just above the floodlit lectern seems tiny against the gigantic dark statue of Lenin, frozen in forward stride, in the 30-foot-high niche behind the dais. There is nothing tiny about Nikita Khrushchev's amplified voice as he shouts "Comrades!" and then waits for the dying murmurs to reach absolute silence.

"Quite a lot has been said about the cult of the individual ... it is impermissible and foreign to the spirit of Marxism-Leninism to elevate one person, to transform him into a superman possessing supernatural characteristics akin to those of a God ...

"Such a belief about ... Stalin, was cultivated among us for many years.

"The objective of the present report is not a thorough examination of Stalin's life and activity. Concerning Stalin's merits, an entirely sufficient number of books, pamphlets and studies had already been written in his lifetime ... for the party [we are concerned] with how the cult of the person of Stalin has been gradually growing, the cult which became ... the source of a whole series of grave perversions of party principles, of party democracy, of revolutionary legality ... the Central Committee of the party considers it absolutely necessary to make material pertaining to this matter available to the 20th Congress of the Communist Party of the Soviet Union."

First Secretary Khrushchev is as good as the words he has just spoken. During his five-hour harangue, whenever he mentions a particular document from which he is quoting—usually something long suppressed by Stalin— copies of that document are passed out to the delegates.

Khrushchev goes all the way back to a quotation from Marx to prove how antipathetic the cult of the individual is to the idea of communism. He then moves on to Lenin. But first he invokes Lenin against Stalin. Lenin, he says, "detected in Stalin those negative characteristics which resulted later in grave consequences." He quotes a letter "known in the party history as Lenin's 'Testament,' in which Lenin says "Stalin is excessively rude ... this defect cannot be tolerated in one holding the position of General Secretary."

"Comrades!" shouts Nikita Sergeievich, startling the already aroused delegates, "the congress should know about two 'new documents.'"[*]

These are a letter from Lenin's wife, Krupskaya, to Lev Kamenev complaining of Stalin's deliberate insolence to her now that Lenin is on his death-

---

[*] New only to the delegates. Long buried by Stalin, they are widely known in the West at this time.

bed, and a subsequent letter from the dying Lenin addressed to Stalin. "I have no intention," writes Lenin, "of forgetting so easily that which is being done against me, and … I consider as directed against me that which is being done against my wife. I ask you, therefore … whether you are agreeable to retracting your words and apologizing or whether you prefer the severance of relations between us."

A great gasp erupts from the assembly and a stirring (later noted in the minutes as "commotion in the hall") while the speaker pauses to let this sink in.

Khrushchev then goes on to say "Lenin's fears were justified" and he describes Stalin as someone "who practiced brutal violence, not only toward everything that opposed him, but also toward that which seemed, to his capricious and despotic character, contrary to his concepts." Stalin demanded "absolute submission to his opinion." Anyone who brooked him was "doomed to removal from the leading collective and to subsequent moral and physical annihilation."

There is total silence in the hall. "Is he talking about the same man whom we have been taught for so long to revere and even love?" think many of the delegates as they begin to squirm in their seats. "Surely it is not as bad as Nikita Sergeievich is portraying it."

But Khrushchev goes on to cite chapter and verse. His main complaint is that in precisely that time "when socialism in our country was fundamentally constructed, when the exploiting classes were generally liquidated[4] [and] the ideological opponents of the party were long since defeated politically—Stalin originated the term 'enemy of the people' and began to purge the party itself. Mass arrests and deportations of many thousands of people, executions without trial and without normal investigation created conditions of insecurity, fear and even desperation …" says Khrushchev. It was true that Lenin had "demanded uncompromising dealings with the enemies of the revolution and the working class and, when necessary, resorted ruthlessly to such methods … but only in the most necessary cases … Stalin, on the other hand, used extreme methods and mass repressions at a time when the revolution was already victorious …"

It was not just that "many thousands of honest and innocent communists died" due to Stalin's "monstrous falsifications," but he totally disrupted normal party life. During Lenin's life, party congresses were convened regularly. "Was it a normal situation when over 13 years elapsed between the 18th and 19th Party Congresses?… Even after the end of the war a congress was not convened for over seven years. Central Committee plenums were hardly ever called."

A Central Committee commission to study party congresses[5] "determined that of the 139 members and candidates of the party's Central Committee who were elevated at the 17th Party Congress, 98 persons, that is, 70%, were arrested and shot." (Once again the hall erupts with involuntary cries and murmuring.)

"The same fate," Khrushchev goes on, "met not only the Central Committee members but also the majority of the delegates to the 17th Party Congress, 1108 out of 1966, decidedly more than a majority."

Khrushchev then begins to recount long histories of individual high party officials who, it seems, had been framed and eliminated by Stalin. Prominent among them is the case of S. M. Kirov, the party's top official in Leningrad, who was murdered on December 1, 1934. In feigned revenge for this suspicious murder, Stalin had let loose a blood bath. "There are reasons for the suspicion that the killer of Kirov, Nikolaev, was assisted by someone ... whose duty it was to protect Kirov ... When the Chekist assigned to protect Kirov was being brought in for interrogation on December 2, 1934, he was killed in a car "accident" in which no other occupants of the car were harmed. After the murder of Kirov, top functionaries of the NKVD[*] were given light sentences, but in 1937 they were shot. We can assume that they were shot in order to cover the traces of the organization of Kirov's killing." (Once again there is commotion among the delegates and Khrushchev pauses for effect.)

On the very night of Kirov's murder Stalin had induced the secretary of the presidium of the executive committee, Yenukidze, to sign a directive which stated: "I. Investigative agencies are directed to speed up the cases of those accused ... of terror ..." II. Judicial organs are directed not to hold up the execution of death sentences ... and III. The organs of the Commissariat of Internal Affairs are directed to execute the death sentences against criminals of the abovementioned category immediately after the passage of sentences."[6]

Khrushchev points out that Stalin came up with a new formulation at the time to justify his increasing purges: "'The closer we are to socialism, the more enemies we will have.'... The number of arrests based on charges of counterrevolutionary crimes," Khrushchev continues, "had grown ten times between 1936 and 1937."

To make this more graphic for his audience, Khrushchev takes up a number of individual cases of longtime, loyal communists, people who had been party members since before the revolution. Each history ends with so-and-so on such-and-such a date being "shot," or, "Sentence was pronounced on him

---

[*] Acronym for the secret police in 1934.

and in 20 minutes he was shot." Each time the word "shot" makes a visible impact upon the assembled comrades.

To rectify these crimes of Stalin's, says Khrushchev, at least in the case of the military, "from 1954 to the present time the Military Collegium of the Supreme Court has rehabilitated 7,679 persons, many of whom were rehabilitated posthumously."

The Soviet Union, he points out, would have been far better prepared to defend itself against the Nazi onslaught "were it not for the tremendous loss in the cadres suffered as a result of the baseless and false mass repressions of 1937-1938 ... Stalin put forward the thesis that the tragedy that our nation experienced in the first part of the war was the result of an 'unexpected attack against the Soviet Union.' But, Comrades, this is untrue."

Khrushchev then speaks of documents indicating that Stalin had received warning of the impending German invasion, such as Churchill's message as early as April 3, 1941, and a report from his own military attaché in Berlin on May 6. A cable from the Soviet embassy in London warned him again on June 18, just four days prior to the attack. In every instance Stalin regarded it as a trick to provoke him into preparations that would give the Germans an excuse to attack. He gave orders that no preparations to defend the country be made on or near the borders lest they prove a provocation to Hitler. Even as initial reports of the invasion came, he refused to believe them.

"After the first severe disaster and defeats at the front," Khrushchev continues, "Stalin thought that this was the end. In one of his speeches in those days he said, 'All that which Lenin created we have lost forever.'" Later, when he saw that all was not lost, "the nervousness and hysteria which Stalin demonstrated, interfering with actual military operations, caused our army serious damage."

Khrushchev now demonstrates this with a personal reminiscence showing himself at the front in a good light and Malenkov, back at headquarters, in a dubious light. Khrushchev had not been able to get through by phone to Stalin, who had indicated that he should talk to Malenkov instead. Khrushchev had warned of a serious situation that called either for immediate reinforcements or retreat. Stalin, secretly listening in on the conversation, said "Let everything remain as it is." The result? "The Germans surrounded our army concentrations and consequently we lost hundreds of thousands of our soldiers. This is Stalin's 'genius'; this is what it cost us." Khrushchev pauses to let this sink in.

"During the whole Patriotic War," he continues, "Stalin never visited any section of the front or any liberated city, except for one short ride on the Mazhiask Highway during a stabilized situation at the front."

"We should note," says Khrushchev, "that Stalin planned operations on a globe." (The delegates react in disbelief.) "Yes, Comrades," shouts Khrushchev over the din, "he used to take the globe and trace the front line on it." When Mikoyan had later pointed out to Stalin that, judging from the result, Khrushchev must have been right in his warnings, "You should have seen Stalin's fury!"

"After our final victory over the enemy which cost us so much, Stalin began to downgrade many of the commanders who contributed so much to the victory over the enemy, because Stalin excluded every possibility that services rendered at the front should be credited to anyone but himself ... He tried to inculcate in the people the version that all victories gained ... were due to the courage, daring and genius of Stalin."

Khrushchev now pokes fun at the absurd lengths Stalin went to, such as the film he had made called "The Fall of Berlin." In this docudrama there is a scene showing Stalin all alone in a great hall with nothing but empty chairs. He issues orders and the only man who approaches him with a report is Poskrebyshev, his loyal shield-bearer." (Laughter breaks out in the hall.)

"Where is the military command ... the politburo ... the government?" Khrushchev asks rhetorically, and he can see from their faces that emotion is building. "Not Stalin, but the party as a whole, the government, our heroic army, its talented leaders and brave soldiers, the whole Soviet nation—these are the ones who assured the victory in the Great Patriotic War!"

Once again the room erupts with applause, this time so sustained that it ends in rhythmic clapping, like a mighty army marching. Khrushchev is clearly enjoying the response he is getting. He milks the patriotic theme for another five minutes, eliciting several more outbursts of thunderous applause.

Now he returns to Stalin's wartime crimes—the deportations of whole peoples from their traditional homelands. He mentions the Karachai, the Kalmyks, the Chechen and Inguish, but for some reason fails to mention the Volga Germans and the Crimean Tartars.[7] "The Ukrainians," he adds, "avoided meeting this fate only because there are too many of them and there is no place to which to deport them. Otherwise he would have deported them also." (Laughter follows this remark, but it is nervous laughter. Many of the comrades have been involved in these deportations and many delegates are Ukrainian.)

"After the war," Khrushchev goes on, "Stalin became even more capricious, irritable and brutal." His main accomplice was "the abject provocateur and vile enemy, Beria, who murdered thousands of comrades and loyal Soviet people."

There was the "Leningrad Affair," the "Georgia Affair," during which "thousands of innocent people fell victim." And in foreign policy there was the "Yugoslav Affair"—the break with Tito's Yugoslavia. "There was no significant basis for the development of the 'affair,' it was completely possible to have prevented the rupture of relations with that country."

Again Khrushchev demonstrates his firsthand knowledge. "Once," he says, "when I came from Kiev to Moscow, I was invited to visit Stalin, who, pointing to a letter lately sent to Tito, asked me 'Have you read this?' Not waiting for my reply he answered 'I will shake my little finger—and there will be no more Tito. He will fall.' But Tito did not fall."

Last of all Khrushchev speaks of the "Affair of the Doctor-Plotters." This causes yet another stir, for it was only four years ago that the country was caught up in the mounting terror of that mysterious affair. Stalin had not only issued orders for the arrests of many prominent doctors—a majority of whom were Jewish—but he had given the following advice on the investigation and interrogations. He had called in the minister of state security, Comrade Ignatiev, and told him curtly: "If you do not obtain confessions from the doctors we will shorten you by a head." (Again, a wave of disturbance moves through the audience.) Stalin's advice to the interrogators themselves had been "simple: 'beat, beat and beat!' [Then] Stalin told us: 'You are blind like young kittens; what will happen without me? The country will perish because you do not know how to recognize enemies.'

"We felt, however, that the case of the arrested doctors was questionable. We knew some of these people personally because they had once treated us. When we examined this 'case' after Stalin's death, we found it to be a fabrication from beginning to end."

More revelations about Stalin and Beria follow and then a recess is called. The first secretary has been speaking for three and a half hours and even he needs a break.

When the session resumes, Khrushchev speaks of other methods by which the "cult of the individual" had been promulgated. Take, for instance, the *Short Biography of Stalin* published in 1948. This, it turns out, is not a biography, but an autobiography, in that it was written entirely by Stalin himself. Quoting from the book Khrushchev says it speaks of "a core of the party which, after Lenin's death, upheld the great banner of Lenin, rallied the party behind Lenin's beliefs and brought the Soviet people into the broad road of industrializing the country and collectivizing the rural economy. The leader of this core and the guiding force of the party and state was Comrade Stalin. Although he performed his task of leader of the party and people with consummate skill and enjoyed the unreserved support of the entire Soviet people,

Bulganin addresses the public session of the Twentieth Party Congress. Note Malenkov
and Molotov sitting behind Mikoyan, Voroshilov, and Khrushchev at the upper left.
Khrushchev's head is just below the huge statute of Lenin. Purchased from TASS in 1999

Stalin never allowed his work to be marred by the slightest hint of vanity, conceit or self-adulation."

Khrushchev goes on to cite many other examples of Stalin shamelessly blowing his own horn, including even a line about himself, which he had inserted into the national anthem. He assures his listeners that a new text for the anthem is in preparation.

It was back in 1925, says the speaker, that the Soviet government resolved to award "Lenin Prizes" for excellence in educational work. "Until this day there are no Lenin Prizes." But, as the audience wells knows, there have been "Stalin Prizes" galore.

"Stalin separated himself from the people and never went anywhere. This lasted tens of years. The last time he visited a village was in January 1928." Because of this isolation he was completely out of touch with the true situation in the countryside and gave orders which it was impossible to fulfill. Khrushchev then points to the reported achievements in earlier speeches of the Twentieth Party Congress and pledges that the new Five-Year Plan based, he implies, on real figures and reasonableness, "will be accomplished successfully." This provides the comrades with another opportunity to applaud themselves as well as their leader, and they do so with gusto.

"Comrades!" shouts Khrushchev, bringing the room back to order, "Various persons may ask: 'How could it be? Stalin headed the party and the country for 30 years and many victories were gained during his lifetime. Can we deny this? In my opinion, the question can be asked in this manner only by those who are blinded and hopelessly hypnotized by the cult of the individual, only by those who do not understand the essence of the revolution and of the Soviet state, only by those who do not understand, in a Leninist manner, the role of the party and of the nation in the development of Soviet society …

"Some comrades may ask us: 'Where were the members of the politburo of the Central Committee? Why did they not assert themselves against the cult of the individual in time? And why is this being done only now?'

"First, we have to consider that members of the political bureau … initially, many of them backed Stalin … because Stalin was one of the strongest marxists … at that time Stalin gained great popularity, sympathy and support … Later, Stalin, abusing his power more and more, began to fight eminent party and government leaders and to use terroristic methods … Attempts to oppose groundless suspicions and charges resulted in the opponents falling victim to the repression … Bulganin … once said: 'It has happened sometimes that a man goes to Stalin on his invitation as a friend. And when he sits with Stalin, he doesn't know where he will be sent next, home or jail.'"

Khrushchev then goes into a number of intrigues involving politburo members. Stalin, at the Nineteenth Party Congress, had suggested that Molotov and Mikoyan might be guilty of some baseless charge. "Had Stalin remained at the helm for another several months, Comrades Molotov and Mikoyan would probably not have delivered any speeches at this congress. Stalin evidently had plans to finish off the old members of the Political Bureau."

At length Khrushchev pauses to make sure he has everyone's attention and then in a lowered, almost conspiratorial voice says: "We cannot let this matter get out of the party, especially not to the press. It is for this reason that we are considering it here at a closed congress session. We should know the limits: we should not give ammunition to the enemy; we should not wash our dirty linen before their eyes. I think the delegates ... will understand and assess properly all these proposals."

Is he finished? It appears that he is and applause, which becomes prolonged, breaks out. But it seems he is not finished.

"Comrades!" he again intones. "We must abolish the cult of the individual ... condemn and eradicate [it] ..." He now proposes three ways to do this. First to compile "in the immediate future ... a serious textbook of the history of our party ..." Second, "to continue ... the work done by the party's Central Committee during the last years ... by minute observation in all party organizations from the bottom to the top, of the Leninist principles of party leadership ... characterized by the wide practice of criticism and self-criticism. Thirdly, to restore completely the Leninist principles of Soviet socialist democracy, expressed in the constitution of the Soviet Union" (which Stalin had long ignored).

"Comrades!" comes the shout from the podium once more, but this time it is the beginning of a familiar litany which ends all such meetings: boastful slogans of what will be achieved followed by increasingly tumultuous applause until the final "Long live the victorious banner of our party— Leninism!" at which everyone rises to his feet and joins in an ovation of frightening volume and duration.

As the tumult dies down, those with watches note that it is now three A.M.; the speech has lasted a good five hours. It has been twenty hours since most of them have had any sleep. Stunned, outraged and terrified by what they had heard, they also feel overcome by exhaustion. As they grope dazedly out of the dim hall, they brush past KGB plainclothesmen who keep repeating, "Remember comrades, this stays within the party, only within the party." The first shock of cold air this time is nothing compared to the shocks they have absorbed inside the hall. In many respects their world has just been

Delegates vote unanimously in the public session of the Twentieth Party Congress. Note
the balcony in the back where the foreign party representatives are sitting.
Purchased from TASS in 1999.

shattered and will never be the same again, but they are too disciplined to
admit this to one another or to show, in any conversation, how profoundly
shaken they are. As the first hint of light of the coming dawn shows in the
night sky, they mumble monosyllables to those who sleepily let them into the
long-locked hotels and hostels, their homes away from home.

⌒

The foreign guest delegates had been told nothing of the secret session.
But it was only a matter of hours before they found out. "Strictly our own
party business," they were told. "It doesn't concern any fraternal communist
parties, just the Soviet party." Khrushchev, in fact, had been loath to wash the
Soviet party's dirty linen even in front of comrades from abroad.

On second thought, it soon became obvious to the Soviet leaders that
they could not keep their foreign comrades completely in the dark and still
command their respect.

So an oral briefing with the leaders of the delegations was arranged. These leaders in turn briefed their delegations. A written, if thoroughly edited, version of the "report" would be made available as soon as possible at a later date on an "eyes only" basis for very limited circulation within their parties.

Meanwhile, the dangers of letting 1,436 delegates recount what they remembered of that evening—even to the highest party cadres in their districts, became clear to Khruschev and his colleagues. For the time being delegates were to remain silent about the secret session. Meetings of leading party officials by district were then arranged and a single copy of the report was sent by courier to each meeting where it was read, but no note taking was allowed. A few questions were answered, but no opportunity for discussion permitted. The courier then immediately returned the copy to party headquarters in Moscow.[8] No hint of the speech or these meetings appeared in any of the Soviet press. Four months later, when the text of the speech was released to the public by the U.S. Department of State, the Soviet press acknowledged this report of an "alleged" speech, but nothing was ever admitted.

Over the years there have been many reasons put forward as to why Khrushchev gave that secret speech. Early speculation that Mikoyan's having attacked Stalin publicly during the open part of the congress forced Khrushchev into seizing the initiative, or that there was some special collusion between the two of them, was easily dismissed. When one considers all the research involved in turning up all of those documents exposing Stalin and the time it would have taken to get them secretly reproduced, it is clear that it could not have been done at the last minute. Similarly, the supposition that Khruschev acted entirely on his own is most unlikely. He would not have dared to announce that his report was based on a decision of the Central Committee—which had met in January—had there not in fact been such a decision.

The most detailed explanation to date comes from Khrushchev himself in his memoirs, first published in 1970 as *Khrushchev Remembers*. He writes:[*]

> For three years we were unable to muster the courage … to lift the curtain and see what had been hidden from us about the arrests, the trials, the arbitrary rule, the executions and everything else that happened during Stalin's reign. It was as though we were enchained by our own activities under Stalin's leadership and couldn't free ourselves of the psychological after effects of the hysteria which had gripped us during the hunt for enemies of the people. We persisted in believing that we were surrounded by enemies

---

* The memoirs were actually dictated and recorded onto tape.

that we had to do battle against … Then came Beria's arrest and the investigation into his case."[9]

Khrushchev is rewriting history here for his own benefit. Beria was actually arrested in June 1953, three months after Stalin's death, so that the curtain, in fact, began to be lifted then, not three years later as he implies.

Khrushchev goes on to admit that he still admired and mourned Stalin "as an extraordinarily powerful leader." Then he says: "… because of the revelations made during the investigation into Beria's case, I felt the urge to lift the curtain a bit further."

This "urge" of Khrushchev resulted in his finally persuading the presidium of the Central Committee to appoint a commission, headed by Comrade P. N. Pospelov, to uncover the truth about everything Stalin had done. The establishment of the commission, Khrushchev implies, was fought tooth and nail by Voroshilov, Molotov, and Kaganovich, older presidium members who were much more implicated in Stalin's crimes than were Khrushchev and some of the others. Nonetheless, a majority supported it.

Khrushchev again tries to pull the wool over his readers' eyes when he claims that "the evidence gathered by Pospelov's commission came as a complete surprise to some of us." He wants the reader to believe that he and others were not involved with most of Stalin's crimes, whereas the older members were.

Khrushchev claims that on the eve of the Twentieth Party Congress he tried to avoid being the one to give the "General Report" opening the congress (a bit of false modesty) and tried to persuade Molotov, as the oldest member of the politburo, to deliver it. Molotov, who knew a Stalinist maneuver when he saw it, declined this privilege. He was not the only member of the "collective leadership" who was keeping a wary eye on Khrushchev. He and others were alarmed at signs of a new "cult of personality" and were disturbed by how easily Khrushchev was running roughshod over those who opposed his schemes such as the "virgin lands" cultivation scheme.[10] Had Molotov agreed to give the report, Khrushchev could have pulled the rug out from underneath him with the Pospelov revelations in his secret speech. As it was, it took Khrushchev another eighteen months to get rid of Molotov, Voroshilov and Kaganovich, all of whom he managed to purge in June 1957 as "the anti-party group."

In the end Khrushchev accepted the argument that it would look very odd if the General Report were to be given by anyone other than the first secretary. He writes that the report was well received, but

I wasn't satisfied. I was tormented by the following thought: 'The Congress will end, and resolutions will be passed, all as a matter of form. But then what? The hundreds of thousands of people who were shot will stay on our consciences ... In short, the findings of Pospelov's Commission weighed heavily on my mind. Finally, I gathered myself together and during a recess when only the members of the Presidium were in the room, I brought the whole matter up ...

As soon as I had finished speaking everyone started attacking me, especially Voroshilov: 'You think you can bring all this out at the Congress and get away with it? How do you think it will reflect on the prestige of our Party and our country? You won't be able to keep what you say secret. Word will get out about what happened under Stalin, and then the finger will be pointed straight at us. What will we be able to say about our own roles under Stalin?'[11]

Kaganovich chimed in, fiercely opposing me along the same lines ... out of selfish fear for his own hide ... I answered these attacks as calmly and as convincingly as I could ... We are conducting the first Congress after Stalin's death, and therefore we are obliged to make a clean breast to the delegates ... We are supposed to be giving an account of ourselves ... since Stalin died, but as members of the Central Committee while Stalin was alive, we must tell about that period as well. How can we pretend not to know what happened?...

Newly released prisoners will start coming home and begin informing people in their own way about what happened. The delegates to the Congress will rightly ask: 'Why didn't you tell us about these terrible things at the Twentieth Party Congress?'... We won't have an answer. To say we didn't know anything would be a lie. We have Comrade Pospelov's report in hand and now we know everything ...

Various members of the old guard continue to object to his remarks and Khrushchev replies: "It is inevitable that people will find out what happened, they'll already be sitting in judgement over us. I don't want that to happen. I don't want to accept responsibility in that way. I'd rather we raised the matter ourselves."

He then adds: "In the life of anyone who has committed a crime there comes a moment when a confession will assure him leniency if not exculpation. If we are going to make a clean breast of the abuses committed by Stalin, then we must do so now, at the Twentieth Party Congress."

When finally everyone had reluctantly agreed that a report to the Congress was necessary, the question remained as to who should give the speech. Obviously, whoever gave it would draw the most fire, so Khrushchev suggested that the man least implicated, the man who had done the investigating,

Pospelov, give the report. But the others saw this as a typical Stalinist maneuver and they insisted that he be the one to deliver it.

It is more than likely that the above clashes with the presidium, pretty much as Khrushchev describes them, though not so simplified, did take place. What is highly unlikely, however, is that this occured during the "recess" in the congress as Khrushchev would have us believe. It is much more likely that the debate and the decision came a month earlier in the January meeting of the Central Committee and that the presidium's decision was not unanimous, but was decisively enough in Khrushchev's favor to get the Central Committee to rubber stamp it. Possibly the argument about who was to give the embarrassing address was still going on when the congress began and the decision that it should be Khrushchev himself was only reached during this "recess" he refers to.

If, indeed, it was a reluctant Khrushchev who was forced to give the report, he did his best to turn the tables on those who had forced the task upon him by injecting into the body of Pospelov's text many personal anecdotes which showed himself in a good light and others, such as Molotov and Malenkov, in a dubious light.

In general the decision to make a clear break with Stalin grew out of a natural progression of events. De-Stalinization had, in fact, already begun with the rehabilitation of military officers purged by Stalin. There had also been a considerable downgrading of the secret police and the release of many prisoners from the Gulag. But at the rate they were going, they would all be dead long before full de-Stalinization had been achieved. It seemed necessary to speed up the process. Then, too, it seemed obvious to many of his colleagues that Khrushchev was getting too powerful, beginning to stand out above the collective. With Stalin's legacy still in place it would have been all too easy for him to try to step into Stalin's shoes. But none of them, including Khruschev, wanted to return to the terror of Stalinism.

It is possible, too, that the rumors spreading among the simple people and in the lower ranks of the party to the effect that Khruschev and his colleagues had actually murdered Stalin, might, in fact, have been true, or at least might have been perceived by the masses—who still revered Stalin as a god—to be true. It was necessary, therefore, to unmask the monster once and for all for what he had been, so that his elimination, and their perceived part in it, might be justified. It was now three years since Stalin had died. There had been changes, but people had expected more. It was time to free themselves of the ghost, if not yet the corpse, of Stalin.

While Khrushchev probably instigated and certainly pushed for the decision to denigrate Stalin, in the end the decision was surely a collective one.

Only Khrushchev's somewhat reckless character gave the speech its special flavor.

When the text of the speech finally reached the West four months later, "kremlinologist" Bertram D. Wolfe called it "the most revealing indictment of Communism ever to have been made by a Communist; the most damning indictment of the Soviet system ever to have been made by a Soviet leader."

CHAPTER II

The Cold War: A Synopsis Up to February 1956

Few historians would agree on precisely when the cold war got under way. There is no doubt that throughout most of the latter half of the twentieth century a cold war was waged between the world's two predominant powers, or superpowers: the U.S. and the U.S.S.R. While each had allies, Moscow and Washington called the shots. If it was not entirely obvious that this worldwide rivalry was in place when the wartime Allied armies crushed what was left of Nazi Germany in May 1945, it soon became manifest. By 1956 positions were well entrenched on either side of a divided Europe.

How did the cold war spring up so soon after the two powers had been friendly allies fighting shoulder to shoulder against a common foe? When did it actually begin? What was the starting point?

Some might say it began when an outspoken Harry Truman confronted Stalin at Potsdam in July 1945. Others might place it earlier in February of that year when Stalin, as host, pulled the wool over Churchill and Roosevelt's eyes at Yalta, or even earlier at Teheran in 1943. Some historians might say, no: it did not really start until the first actual confrontation of power, when the U.S. in the newly formed United Nations Security Council challenged the Russians to live up to their agreement with Iran and the British to pull their troops out of northern Iran six months after the cessation of hostilities with Germany. Britain had lived up to the agreement. Stalin, in contrast, had engaged in a few weeks of sham negotiations with the Iranians, and had agreed to pull his troops back into the Soviet Union, but did not. Still others might say that the rivalry began as soon as the U.S. opened its embassy in Moscow—the last of the great powers to do so—in 1933.

A majority of Americans who lived through World War II did not become aware of this phenomenon knows as "cold war" until the blockade of Berlin in 1948, though a few had become aware of it in February of that year when the communists, through a coup d'état, took over the government of Czechoslovakia. Yes, the Russians had been behaving badly and had, for instance, even turned down America's generous offer of Marshall Plan aid. But most Americans were still thinking of Stalin as President Roosevelt had pictured him: jovial, pipe-smoking "Uncle Joe." To be confronted with a full-scale war in Europe just three years after Germany's defeat came as a tremendous shock. Yet even the deadly seriousness of the cold war did not come home to most Americans until that war turned "hot" in Korea in June 1950 and the country suddenly began to re-mobilize.

All this, of course, is from an American perspective. What of the other side's perspective, the Russians, or, more properly, those who spoke for the Russians, the Soviet Communist Party that controlled them? It is the author's contention that from the Soviet Communist perspective the cold war began when the Bolsheviks seized power from the Kerensky government in November 1917 and Lenin declared that the capitalist states surrounding Russia were the new régime's implacable enemies. England headed the list of enemies at that time, but by the end of World War II the U.S. has supplanted it. The U.S., as the most powerful capitalist state, had become enemy number one.

From the Russian viewpoint, the invasion in 1921 of Allied armies—which included U.S. troops as well as French and British—only went to prove Lenin's point. Foreign armies on Russian soil had only one purpose, to overthrow the new régime and restore, if not the czar, at least a bourgeois, capitalist state. To Americans this invasion was a minor, insignificant, if lamentable, incident, quickly forgotten. To Russians, who were never allowed by party propaganda to forget it, it was proof that foreigners, who had invaded and devastated Mother Russia three times in the last 150 years, were not to be trusted and were, in fact, "enemies."

This 1921 invasion and later withdrawal of Allied forces took place during the Russian Civil War and *after* the short-lived communist régimes in Budapest and Munich had been put down and the attempt to set up such a régime in Berlin thwarted. The ill-timed venture of the Western powers was such a fiasco that no similar attempt to intervene occurred—until the Nazi invasion in 1941. Despite Trotsky's attempts to foment revolution outside Russia and the establishment of the Comintern (Communist International Bureau) to coordinate world-wide communist actions, the Soviets began to concentrate their efforts more and more on consolidating their power within Russia, culminating in Stalin's slogan: "Socialism in one country."

Stalin's form of socialism turned out to be whatever increased his power as a despotic tyrant, disguised always in communist jargon. This included forced collectivization of the peasant farms, physical "liquidation" of the "*kulaks*" (a term for prosperous peasants, which Stalin ended up applying to any peasant who was fortunate enough to own a single cow), elimination of political rivals through intimidation, outright murder, false arrest, rigged trials and executions, etc. In 1934 Stalin used the excuse of the murder of the top party official in Leningrad, Sergei Kirov, which he had secretly arranged, to begin a purge and blood bath of high party officials he wanted to get rid of. This led to the years of the Great Terror, 1936 to 1938, when vast cadres of party officials, Red Army officers and others were arrested, tortured, made to sign false confessions, and then executed.

While the Great Depression in the United States and Europe caused many Western workers and intellectuals to be attracted to communism and the great socialist experiment going on in the Soviet Union, the rise of fascism in Italy and national socialism in Germany—both declared enemies of communism—caused these Western intellectuals to overlook what was actually taking place in the Soviet Union. They could see the menace of these totalitarian ideologies and they noted that the U.S.S.R., alone among the nations, came to the rescue of Republican Spain when fascists rose up to topple the republic. They were totally unaware that Stalin had seized the private farms of peasants, who fought tooth and nail to defend their homesteads, killing approximately 10 million in the process. Those millions who survived, if they refused to join a collective or state farm, were shipped off to the forced labor camps in the Gulag. The Ukraine, lower Volga, and northern Caucasus had been known as "the breadbasket of Europe." Now the harvest was much smaller, but there was still sufficient grain to feed the local populace. Stalin had it all confiscated. "This famine was organized by Stalin quite consciously and according to plan."[1] Millions more died.

While idealists in the West flocked to the International Brigades to fight for loyalist Spain against Franco (who was backed by Mussolini and Hitler), Stalin, through the Comintern, and behind the façade of genuine shipments of food and arms to the Loyalists, cynically used the opportunity to murder communists outside Russia whom he did not feel were sufficiently loyal to him and to subvert the International Brigades to his own purposes, which included recruiting candidates for the Communist Party.

Western sympathy for Stalin and the great experiment in egalitarian society declined abruptly with the announcement in August 1939 of the Molotov-Ribbentrop Pact, making allies overnight of the hitherto deadly enemies: Nazi Germany and Soviet Russia. What the world did not know, but soon was to discover, was that a secret protocol of the pact divided up Poland, eliminating Poland from the map of Europe and enabling Nazi Germany to invade Poland beginning World War II, while, also in the secret protocol, Soviet Russia gobbled up, in addition to the eastern half of Poland, the three independent Baltic states, Estonia, Latvia and Lithuania, which had been under German protection.

The Soviet attempt in 1939 to seize Finland as well was thwarted by a courageous Finnish army. The world was treated to newsreels of white-clad Finnish ski troops ambushing dark-clad, ill-equipped hordes of disorganized Soviet troops (whose officer corps had been all but wiped out by Stalin's purges). The Soviet Union had to settle for a small portion of Finnish territory before suing for peace. All sympathy was with the Finnish David against the Soviet Goliath.

It was not until the winter of 1941-42, when the Russian armies, filled with patriotic peasants fighting to protect Mother Russia from yet another foreign invader, managed to halt and throw back the Nazi panzer divisions, that the Russians—in the eyes of British and Americans—became "the good guys" again. And, since Russia, over the next several years bore by far the biggest brunt of the war against Nazi Germany, sympathy and aid, in the form of lend-lease arms and food, began to flow to the Soviet Union in ever greater quantities.

By the time Soviet and American armies met on the banks of the Elbe River in the heart of a collapsing Germany, Allied propaganda had made Soviet soldiers into people just like us. It came as quite a shock to the average G.I. who met Soviet troops, therefore, to find that "Ivan" was five or six inches shorter, crude in manner and dress, and that there were women among them, tough fighting soldiers, not nurses or secretaries, and that Ivan had a penchant for "liberating" or trading wrist watches—especially Mickey Mouse ones—because he had never seen a watch before. Everyone was blissfully happy that the war was over; but the Russians, it turned out, were not just like Americans.

Indeed, Soviet behavior during the war had been curious to say the least. Making impossible demands and then haggling over lend-lease aid had made the American and British authorities dealing with them sometimes wonder which side the Russians were on. And then there was that strange affair of the Russian army suddenly stopping at the Vistula River with the bulk of Warsaw on the other side and just sitting, after urging the Polish Home Army to rise up, while the Poles fought valiantly to hold their capital city they had seized back from the Germans. After sixty-six days of house-to-house fighting, the remnants of the Polish Home Army had been forced to surrender to the Germans. And even then the Red Army had sat on the other side of the river while the Nazis dynamited Warsaw block by block until it was rubble.

And why had Stalin adamantly refused to let British and American planes, loaded with supplies for the Poles and with just enough fuel to reach Warsaw, land at nearby Soviet airbases? That refusal alone had doomed the Warsaw Uprising.

Less than a year later, as the war was coming to a close—and just weeks after the Yalta agreement promising free elections in Poland was signed— Stalin pulled "one of the most treacherous plots of all time" when he had his authorities "proposed amicable negotiations" with the Polish Underground Government.[2]

The British and Americans urged the Polish exile government in London to accept the offer. Several meetings then took place during which the Soviets offered to free several Polish underground leaders they had arrested and to facilitate contact between these leaders and their government in exile in London by flying eight of them there in a Soviet bomber. But this was on condition that the entire underground leadership first meet with Marshal Zhukov. The day of the proposed meeting, March 28, the Poles were all driven to a country villa to meet Zhukov. Instead of meeting Zhukov they were all arrested; and the eight, who had been told they were being flown to London, found their plane was flying East. It landed at a Soviet air force base east of Moscow. The Polish government in London knew their representatives had been seized but had no idea what had happened to them. Torture and forced confessions followed. Four months later the Poles appeared in show trials held in Moscow during which all were found guilty. Only one, Zygmunt Stypulkowski, a lawyer and devout Christian who had refused a Soviet lawyer and insisted on defending himself, ever got out of Russia alive. Most of the others were shot.

There was another aspect to Soviet behavior which, during the war and directly afterward, could not be explained until long after the fact. This was the fact that Stalin, despite his isolation, was better informed about what was transpiring between the two Western allies than they were themselves. As a result of an extraordinarily elaborate system of overlapping intelligence systems and the placement of hundreds of spies within Western governments, Stalin knew, or had access to, everything that was going on. His most reliable group of sources was the "Cambridge five" or, as known within the Soviet intelligence community, the "Magnificent Five."[*] These were five idealistic young men who had been recruited at Cambridge University in the early 1930s and who had each risen to a position in which they had access to many

---

[*] Kim Philby, Guy Burgess, Donald MacLean, Anthony Blunt and John Cairnecross.

secret documents in different branches of the British government. Over time they passed hundreds of thousands of secret British and American documents over to the Soviets.[3] At each summit meeting during the war, whether Teheran, Yalta or Potsdam, Stalin had seen Russian translations of most of the same secret British and American documents that Churchill and Roosevelt had been briefed with. At Yalta in the Crimea, being on Soviet soil, Stalin had even read Russian translations of the transcripts of everything Churchill and Roosevelt had said in the privacy of bedrooms the night before. At Potsdam, when President Harry Truman received word of the successful testing of the first atomic bomb in New Mexico and hinted to Stalin that the U.S. now possessed an extraordinary weapon it might soon use, he was convinced that Stalin had not heard him properly, or at least did not realize the importance of what he, Truman, was saying. In fact, Stalin knew all about the American atomic bomb. Spies from more than one Soviet spy ring had penetrated the Manhattan Project shortly after it had gotten under way. He may well have even learned of the successful test before Truman mentioned anything to him. In addition, Stalin took the fullest advantage of what he knew about the two personalities he was dealing with. He knew of Churchill's penchant for "summitry" and for dividing up the map into "Spheres of Influence," and contrary to Churchill's request on his visit to Moscow in October 1944, he carefully did *not* burn the piece of paper on which Churchill had divided up percentages of influence which the West and Russia should have in each east-central European country after the war. And at Yalta, Stalin knew how weak and sick President Roosevelt was and also knew that if he, Stalin, just threw in the word *democratic* and *democracy* enough, Roosevelt would be satisfied to sign and have the details filled in later. "Democratic," of course, turned out to mean "Communist" to Stalin.

He also knew how to bargain. When the United Nations was formed and founded in San Francisco in the summer of 1945, the Soviet Union ended up with three votes in the General Assembly, to every other country's one.[*]

Soviet espionage played a major, if not so successful, role in the United States as well. The penetration of the Manhattan Project by spy rings involving the Rosenbergs and the German-born British physicist Klaus Fuchs were the most well-known. It now appears that the most important information for the Russians was that provided by a twenty-one-year-old graduate student of physics, Theodore Hall. Hall fled the country in 1952 and lived the remainder

---

* The fiction of the Ukraine and Byelorussia being independent states and thus deserving full membership in the UN may have influenced their breakaway from the U.S.S.R. forty-six years later.

of his life in England, undetected and unprosecuted. Shortly before he died in 1999, Hall as much as admitted his role in helping the Russians build the bomb, and still did not regret it.[4]

With one notable exception, the Soviets were far less successful in planting spies high in the American government. That exception was Alger Hiss. Secret encoded cables from the resident head of the NKVD (later KGB) in the U.S.—now known as the Venona decrypts[*]—alerted the F.B.I. to Hiss. They did not have enough evidence to prosecute, but did have enough to force him to resign from his high State Department post. His code name in these cables was ALES.

Hiss, in his State Department capacity, had traveled to Yalta with Roosevelt as part of the U.S. delegation in February 1945 and later that year had been in charge of arrangements at the founding of the United Nations in San Francisco. One of the Venona cables reveals that Hiss, after the meeting at Yalta, traveled to Moscow where he visited the Kremlin and was personally thanked and possibly awarded a medal for his services to the Soviet Union by Andrei Vyshinsky, then in the foreign ministry, but earlier Stalin's prosecutor at the last of Moscow show trials and later to become foreign minister.[5]

Save for a few tight-lipped communists and a few equally tight-lipped members of Western intelligence agencies, none of this was known in 1945. The war was over, Germany and Japan had surrendered unconditionally, and but for armies to occupy the two defeated nations, there was no need to maintain such a huge military establishment—or so it appeared to the Western allies. "Bring the boys back home" was the cry of the day, and between the war's end and 1947 the U.S. returned 10.5 million men and women to civilian life, leaving 1.5 million still under arms. The Soviets, on the other hand, did not demobilize. And while POWs of the Western allies were welcomed home with joyous parades, over a million Soviet POWs released from German camps faced a far different reception on their return to their homeland. Considered by Stalin to be "contaminated" by their exposure to the West and labeled as "traitors" by the fact that they had surrendered to the enemy rather than die for their country, they were arrested and sent off to the labor camps, or, in some cases, tried and given long sentences, or executed if there was any real evidence against them. True, many Soviet soldiers, particularly Ukrainians, had greeted Hitler's troops as liberators from Stalinist terror and oppression. And many of these had fought against the Red Army in an all Ukrainian

---

[*] F.B.I intercepted and deciphered cables from the 1940s, only declassified in 1995.

and Russian division led by General Andrei Vlasov as part of the German Wehrmacht. But most of these POWs had not been in this unit, and not a few had survived death camps like Auschwitz. With the new infusions of former POWs into the Gulag, the population of these slave labor camps, which had been about 2 million in 1932, swelled to over 7 million in 1946. By 1952 the population of the Gulag had reached 12 million.[6]

While American factories made massive conversions to peacetime production and spewed out a stunning array of new consumer goods into a booming American economy—now more than twice the size it had been before the war—in Europe economic stagnation, and in some cases, economic chaos prevailed. The climate was ripe for exploitation by the well-organized communist parties. These, during the German occupation, had frequently produced the most organized and effective underground resistance. In Italy and in France, in particular, the communists were so strong that the coalition governments formed immediately after the war had to include communist ministers in their coalitions if they were to govern at all. The same political situation existed in the countries of east-central Europe, except here the occupying Soviet army lent material and moral support only to the local communists.

The overall European situation was further complicated by massive exchanges and forced expulsions of people such as the Sudeten Germans from Czechoslovakia, Germans from East Prussia and Silesia, and Poles from eastern Poland, which now became part of the Ukraine and Belorussia. In addition to this there were all the many voluntary migrants, people who did not want to go back to Poland, Russia, the Ukraine, or wherever, and who now became DPs (displaced persons). These were herded into temporary camps until they could be settled in countries that would have them.

Following the second session of the Potsdam Conference—in which the new British prime minister, Clement Attlee, replaced the defeated Winston Churchill—a series of meetings of the big four foreign ministers, known as the Council of Foreign Ministers, took place in Paris, London, and Moscow, during which very little was settled. The stumbling block was always Germany. The Soviets were enthusiastic supporters of the wartime Morgenthau Plan—an American plan calling for the total destruction of Germany's industrial infrastructure and the return of that country to a pastoral state of two hundred years ago—but this was never seriously considered. By the time of the Potsdam Conference the Western allies had abandoned such an extreme position, though they did agree with the Soviets on heavy reparations. The Soviets immediately began stripping their occupation zone of whole factories and sending them back to Russia—this after allowing their soldiers to rape as many as 2 million German women. The Western powers, on the other hand, fearful of what the heavy reparations demanded at Versailles after the First World War had done to Germany with the facilitation of Hitler's rise to power, quickly drew back from such a policy. They had responsibility for three-quarters of the population and four fifths of Germany's industrial capacity. One could sympathize with the Soviets; their country had been totally devastated by the Germans. But stripping Germany was not the way to the stability and growth that Europe desperately needed.

Early in 1946 Stalin gave a routine speech on the eve of a domestic event, the "elections" to the Supreme Soviet. It was meant for internal consumption by the party faithful, and he repeated what had long been communist doctrine: that the very existence of capitalist states in the world meant that future war with them was inevitable. His words were reported by Western journalists, causing great alarm in Washington and London. One person in the American embassy in Moscow, George F. Kennan, was dismayed at the ignorance of the Soviet Union which underlay this alarm. He undertook to set his fellow American diplomats and statesmen straight about communism and the Soviet Union in what was to become known as "the long telegram,"[7] a message of some nine thousand words. Because of the importance of this document in shaping American attitudes and policy for most of the cold war, it is appropriate here to quote from it here fairly extensively.

Kennan began by sketching the basic features of the Soviet postwar outlook: capitalist encirclement; and the background of that outlook: "At the bottom of the Kremlin's neurotic view of world affairs is the traditional and insistent Russian sense of insecurity," and the fact that traditionally Russians "have learned to seek security only in patient but deadly struggle for the total destruction of rival power, never in compacts or compromise with it."

He then warned of "the unresolved mystery as to who, if anyone, in this great land actually receives accurate and unbiased information about the outside world ... There is good reason to suspect that the government is actually a conspiracy within a conspiracy; and I, for one, am reluctant to believe that Stalin himself receives anything like an objective picture of the outside world."

Next, Kennan explained the "two planes" of action of Soviet policy, the official and the "subterranean," for which "the Soviet government does not admit responsibility."

> It may be expected that components of this far-flung [subterranean] apparatus will be utilized ... to undermine the general political and strategic potential of major Western powers ... to disrupt national self-confidence, to hamstring measures of national defense, to increase social and political

unrest, [and] to stimulate all forms of disunity ... In general, all Soviet efforts on the unofficial plane will be negative and destructive in character, designed to tear down sources of strength beyond the reach of Soviet control ... In summary, we have here a political force committed fanatically to the belief that with the U.S. there can be no permanent *modus vivendi*, that it is desirable and necessary that the internal harmony of our society be disrupted, our traditional way of life destroyed, the international authority of our state broken, if Soviet power is to be secure. This political force has complete power of disposition over the energies of one of the world's greatest peoples and resources of the world's richest national territory, and is borne along by deep and powerful currents of Russian nationalism. In addition, it has an elaborate and far-flung apparatus of amazing flexibility and versatility, managed by people whose experiences and skill in underground methods are presumably without parallel in history. Finally, it is seemingly inaccessible to considerations of reality in its basic reactions. For it, the vast fund of objective fact about human society is not, as with us, the measure against which one's outlook is constantly being tested and reformed, but a grab bag from which individual items are selected arbitrarily and tendentiously to bolster an outlook already preconceived.

Kennan then adds "certain observations of a more encouraging nature ...":

[One] Soviet power, unlike that of Hitlerite Germany, is neither schematic nor adventuristic. It does not work by fixed plans. It does not take unnecessary risks. It is impervious to the logic of reason, and it is highly sensitive to the logic of force ... it can easily withdraw—and usually does—when strong resistance is encountered at any point ... If the situation is properly handled, there need be no prestige-engaging showdown.

[Two] ... The Soviets are still by far the weaker force ...

[Three] The success of the Soviet system ... is not yet fully proven ...

[Four] All Soviet propaganda [being] basically negative and destructive ... should be relatively easy to combat ...

He followed these points with suggestions as to "how to deal with Russia."

[One] First ... recognize for what it is the nature of the movement with which we are dealing ...

[Two] ... See that our public is educated to the realities of the Russian situation ...

[Three] Much depends on the vigor of our own society. World communism is like a malignant parasite which feeds only on diseased tissue … Every courageous and incisive measure to solve internal problems of our own society … is a diplomatic victory over Moscow worth a thousand diplomatic notes and joint communiqués …

[Four] We must … put forward for other nations a much more positive and constructive picture of the sort of world we would like to see than we have put forward in the past … Many foreign peoples, in Europe at least, are tired and frightened by the experiences of the past, and are less interested in abstract freedom than in security. They are seeking guidance rather than responsibilities …

[Five] Finally, we must have the courage and self-confidence to cling to our methods and conceptions of human society … the greatest danger that can befall us is … that we shall allow ourselves to become like those with whom we are coping …

This long cable galvanized the Department of State. Prior to this no one had expressed the problem and its long-term implications so clearly. Copies were sent to all senior officers of the department and then to all persons of importance in the government. It would be some years, however, before Kennan's views reached the American public, despite his restatement of them a year later in the journal *Foreign Affairs.*

What did reach the public, and only a few days later, was Winston Churchill's speech in Fulton, Missouri, on March 5, 1946. Never one to mince words, and freed from the responsibilities of public office and thus able to speak his mind, Churchill electrified his audience with one ringing statement: "From Stettin on the Baltic to Trieste on the Adriatic an iron curtain has descended across the continent." Ironically, Churchill's own impetuous, late-night dealings with Stalin had contributed to that division of Europe. It was also premature to write off Czechoslovakia, still enjoying democratic freedom; but the term "Iron Curtain" soon took hold and within a few years that border slicing down through the middle of Europe sprouted barbed wire fences, walls, minefields and watchtowers that made the epithet entirely appropriate for the next forty years.

The winter of 1946-47 was the severest in Europe in living memory. Food and fuel shortages in Western Europe were not made easier to endure by the many wildcat strikes instigated by communist-dominated unions on secret orders from Moscow. Not even during the height of the submarine blockade in the war had Britain had to ration bread. Now, to keep people in the British occupation zone in Germany from starving, the socialist government introduced bread rationing.

President Harry Truman, who, just two weeks after taking over from President Roosevelt had called in Soviet foreign minister Molotov and given him a tongue-lashing for having failed to live up to so many agreements between the two countries, now decided he needed a new secretary of state. James ("Jimmy") Byrnes was a fine politician, but Truman felt this skill had made him too accommodating with the Russians. In January 1947 Truman appointed General George C. Marshall—lifelong soldier and former Chief of Staff who had been the architect of the country's victories over Germany and Japan—to the office.

Within weeks of his appointment Marshall was faced with a major crisis. Britain's Labour government, facing economic disaster at home due to the extraordinarily severe winter, had decided it could no longer maintain all of its commitments overseas. In four weeks they would be pulling their expeditionary armed forces out of Greece and could no longer provide military and economic aid to Greece and Turkey. The British government urged the United States to take over its former responsibilities. In Greece, civil war between communist insurgents and the restored, British-backed government had been raging since the end of the war. Both Britain and the U.S. were convinced that Stalin was shipping arms and aid to the rebels (in fact, it was Tito, not Stalin, who was providing this support); and the two counries felt that it was crucial that Greece not fall to the communists as its neighboring countries, Bulgaria, Yugoslavia and Romania already had. Marshall and Truman quickly agreed that the U.S. had to pick up Britain's obligations in the area. On March 12, Truman, before a joint session of Congress, called for $400 million to aid Greece and Turkey, outlining the emergency in black and white terms. Thus was born "the Truman Doctrine," a policy which as much as said, "any country which is directly threatened by a communist take-over will get American aid."

Marshall now journeyed to Moscow to attend his first Big Four Foreign Ministers' meeting. While there he requested and was granted an interview with Stalin. He emerged from the meeting a changed man. Clearly Stalin had no intention of solving any European problem except on his own unreasonable terms and was quite content to wait until the political and economic situation in Western Europe had deteriorated to the point where local communists could seize power.

Indeed, that very thing was to happen in Czechoslovakia just a year hence. Right now Stalin was seeking bigger game by fomenting as much chaos as possible through the large Italian and French Communist parties.

When Marshall returned from Europe, he was convinced, as he explained in a public radio broadcast, that "the patient [i.e., Europe] was sinking while the doctors deliberate." He called in George Kennan, recently returned from Moscow, put him in charge of the department's brand new Policy Planning Staff, and asked him to outline a plan for European recovery. Kennan had just written his famous article in *Foreign Affairs*, which, because of his government position, he had had to sign "Mr. X." The article repeated much of what he had said in the "long telegram" but the main import was in the sentence which stated: "The main element of any United States policy toward the Soviet Union must be that of a long-term, patient but firm and vigilant containment of Russia's expansionist tendencies."[8] "Containment" became the basis of American policy toward Russia for the next 40 years.

Kennan was joined in the assignment Marshall had given him by Undersecretary of State Will Clayton, who had just returned from Western Europe. Clayton saw the problem in terms of saving Europeans from chaos and starvation, Kennan in terms of a long-range goal of saving Europe from the communists. They put together what was to become known as the Marshall Plan. The plan was unveiled by Marshall in a seven-minute speech he gave at Harvard University's commencement, where he was being given an honorary degree. Few American journalists covered the event, and not a single American newspaper carried it on its front page. A BBC reporter, however, sent a full report of it to Britain where Foreign Minister Ernest Bevin became ecstatic. He quickly flew to Paris to see French foreign minister Georges Bidault, and the two drafted an enthusiastic reply to Marshall.

There now began a long, difficult battle to get the plan approved by a Republican-controlled Congress. The European nations were encouraged to form what became the Organization for European Economic Cooperation (OEEC). They estimated that over a period of five to seven years they would need a total of 17 billion dollars. Truman had already managed to get some interim aid for France, Italy, and Austria; but when he submitted the full request to Congress he ran into stiff opposition. In January 1948 the amount asked was reduced to 6.8 billion dollars for the first fifteen months. A month later this had to be reduced to 5.3 billion. Then, in February, came the communist coup d'état in Czechoslovakia, an abrupt wake-up call, for Czechoslovakia had been the only democracy in east-central Europe and had been the virtual creation of Woodrow Wilson and his friend Tomáš Masaryk.

On March 17 Truman again went before a joint session of Congress. "The Soviet Union and its agents," he said, "have destroyed the independence and democratic character of a whole series of nations in Eastern and Central Europe. It is this ruthless course of action, and a clear design to extend it to the remaining free nations of Europe, that has brought about the critical situation in Europe today."[9]

Public opinion swung behind him and on April 3 Congress approved the 5.3 billion of Marshall Plan aid. There was as much self-interest in the vote as altruism; most of the money would be spent in America on American food and goods, further strengthening the American economy.

The Marshall Plan both in conception and offering was intended for all of Europe—the Soviet Union included. Few Western officials thought that Stalin, once he discovered that it was not just an extension of lend-lease, would decline to take part, and that that would be just as well. Nevertheless, it was offered. Western governments were surprised when at the first meeting in Paris Molotov showed up with a large contingent of Soviet economists and bankers. All of the east-central European nations were there as well, including the not yet communist-dominated Czechoslovakia. All, including Molotov were prepared to accept the terms offered when Stalin, who had been reading secret dispatches between the State Department and Foreign Office about what the Americans and British hoped to accomplish and the unlikelihood of Stalin's participating, decided it was a trap. He ordered Molotov to decline the offer. He would not be a party to something that would build up Western Europe and the Western zones of Germany. "Once the capitalists become involved in our economy," he thought, "we will never get rid of them. We'll be subverted." So the word went out to the other countries of east-central Europe that they too should decline the offer; and reluctantly, one by one, each of the foreign ministers withdrew his initial acceptance—all but the Polish and Czechoslovak foreign ministers. After extraordinary pressure from Moscow, the Poles finally withdrew their acceptance. The Czechoslovaks, on the other hand, insisted that there was no danger in their accepting; they knew it would be good for their country and things had gone too far for them to pull out now. Stalin was furious. He summoned the Czechoslovak foreign minister, Jan Masaryk (son of Tomáš) and the head of the Czechoslovak Communist Party, Klement Gottwald, to Moscow. The Czechs at this time were doing their best to maintain their self-described role as "a bridge between East and West." But when Stalin accused them of betraying the Soviet Union by their insisting on accepting Marshall aid, Masaryk capitulated. On his return to Prague he told friends "I went to Moscow as the foreign minister of an independent, sovereign state; I returned as a Soviet slave." Shortly after the communist takeover in February 1948, Jan Masaryk's body was found in the courtyard underneath his open bathroom window. To this day it is not certain whether it was a genuine suicide or whether he was pushed. At the time, most people assumed the latter.

Well before Nazi Germany was defeated, Stalin had begun his plans for establishing buffer states along Russia's European border. From the groups of East European communists who had fled to Moscow in the 1930s Stalin set up puppet governments ready to assume political control as soon as the Red Army had liberated a small portion of any specific country. At first he was forced to accept the leaders of noncommunist parties into coalition governments—in most countries the communists were tiny minorities at first. Where the communists had only a few ministries, they were careful always that these were ministries such as interior, police, or agriculture, through which they could multiply their power. Once sufficient power had been acquired—frequently with the help of the occupying Soviet authorities and Red Army—the noncommunist parties were either forced, like the Social Democrats, to meld with the smaller communist parties, where those unwilling to become communists were purged, or were destroyed by the false arrest and imprisonment of their leaders, or in some cases by outright murder with the culprits never being apprehended. It is significant that even with all of the terror and pressure from the Soviet authorities, no communist party—save in Czechoslovakia where the party in the inter-war period had been strong— ever came close to getting as much as 30 percent of the vote. By 1947 most of the noncommunist ministers, even prime ministers like Stanisław Mikolaj-czik in Poland and Ferenc Nagy in Hungary, had been hounded from their office and even had to flee to the West to save their lives. "Democratic" to Stalin meant "communist," not the "democratic" that Roosevelt and Byrnes meant when they used the term during negotiations at Yalta and Potsdam.

In September 1947 the Comintern, which had been disbanded during the war, was reconstituted as the new Cominform (Communist Information Bureau) when the leaders of all the world's communist parties met in a small Polish village. The Marshall Plan was thoroughly denounced and the policies of the Soviet Union praised, but there were some new policies established as well. Since the late 1930s the Communist parties of Italy and France had been following Popular Front policies, working with other left wing parties. Tito, who had come to power without such tactics, was used by the Soviets to chastise these two Western parties for not taking full advantage of their great strength in numbers. No Western economic recovery plan could succeed if these parties unleashed their full powers against it.

The strikes that followed in France in autumn and winter of 1947-48 nearly brought the French government to its knees. The country seemed poised on the verge of civil war. Not just strikes, but sabotage in the mines and on the railroads began to wreck the economy. In December, when a Paris-Lille express was purposely derailed and twenty innocent people were killed, the French decided they had had enough, and public opinion began to swing against the communists. Washington, which was at the point of giving the French government emergency aid, made it clear that aid would not be forthcoming for a pro-communist government, nor for one unable to deal with the tactics of its domestic communists. Four days after the train derailment, the régime offered to increase the national minimum wage a significant amount. It was not the 25 percent the unions had demanded, but it was sufficient to defuse the situation. The wave of strikes receded, and the economy got under way again.

In Italy the strikes had been less militant. Nevertheless, the party was even larger numerically than in France. When the Italian elections of April 1948 came up, the U.S., realizing that it might take a year for Marshall Plan aid to have any noticeable effect, looked in desperation for some way to prevent the communists from winning. A solution was found in the newly created CIA (Central Intelligence Agency)—descended from the wartime OSS (Office of Strategic Services) which had closed down when the war ended. In its charter it possessed a vaguely phrased function described as "perform such other functions and duties related to intelligence affecting the national security as the National Security Council may from time to time direct." The CIA's legal counsel pounced on this loophole passage, pointing out that the National Security Council could "direct" the CIA to do anything it wanted done—in this case prevent the communists from winning in Italy. With such carte blanche the agency, peopled by old OSS operatives who had done many illegal things during the war, immediately began pumping money into the noncommunist parties in Italy and began pulling every trick they knew to subvert the Italian Communist Party. The U.S., now operating on the same subterranean plane the communists had always operated on, was now clandestinely interfering in the politics of another democratic state. On the overt and official level the U.S. government warned that a communist-elected government would receive no Marshall Plan aid, and it also organized a massive letter-writing campaign of some 10 million Italian-Americans to their relatives in Italy. It was an aroused Vatican, however, that was probably most responsible for the stunning defeat the communists received at the polls on April 18. Its organization, with churches in every hamlet in the country, was vaster than that of the communists, and had deeper pockets. When the votes were counted, the Christian Democrats had a clear majority—the only time they ever achieved it.

Massive and imaginative[10] as it was, Marshall aid was only a few drops in the bucket of the total of West European economies. What it did, by forcing prioritizing and cooperation upon the Europeans, was to jump-start their economies, to prime the pump of nations that already had most of their economic and industrial infrastructure, albeit damaged, in place. The aid lasted from 1948 to 1952, by which time all of Western Europe, save Spain and Portugal, which were under dictatorships and therefore not eligible, had begun to prosper, including the three Western zones of Germany.

In 1948 Germany, despite very different things going on in the western and eastern halves, was still under nominal four-power control, with Berlin itself still divided into four zones. The old Reichsmarks were still in circulation, a huge black market was in operation and inflation was running ever higher. But by this time cooperation on Germany with the Soviets had become impossible. The Soviet zone, while not yet as Sovietized as the other satellites, was becoming more and more like a vassal state. Its large Social Democratic Party, having been forced to merge with the much smaller Communist Party into the new Socialist Unity Party (SED), as happened in all of the other East European countries, was no longer in opposition, but giving vitality, money, and recruits to its former enemy.

The Western allies, who had already merged the economies of their three zones on June 1, 1947, now wanted to integrate their zones politically so that the Marshall aid could be more efficiently received and distributed. An economically healthy portion of Germany, integrated into the West, was seen as a strong bulwark against communism. Knowing the Soviet ability to frustrate and delay anything they attempted in Germany, the Western allies turned to secrecy.

They met in London with the Benelux countries to plan the future of an emerging west German state. The news of the communist takeover in Czechoslovakia made them more determined in their purpose. The only way to wipe out the black market and high inflation was a sudden, unannounced currency reform.

Stalin, of course, knew everything that was going on, including the plans for the currency reform. He had his foreign minister, Molotov, denounce the London conference, accusing the Western powers of "transforming Germany into a strongpoint." All of the decisions that may be taken at the conference, he said, are "invalid" because they do not include the Soviet Union. Then he had the Soviet member of the Allied Control Council in Berlin, Marshal Vassily Sokolovsky, press his British and American counterparts on what was taking place at the London conference. When the American member, Gen. Lucius D. Clay, said that he was not going to discuss the London meetings, Sokolovsky demanded to know what point there was in having an Allied Control Council if such matters could not be discussed at it, whereupon he walked out of the meeting taking all of his aides with him. In fact, Sokolovsky, like Stalin, knew from Soviet intelligence all about the Western allies' plans, including those concerning the establishment of a western defense alliance that would include the U.S—and eventually Canada—and would develop into NATO.

Soviet annoyance at what was transpiring in London began to show in the one place where the Western allies were most vulnerable: Berlin. First it was petty bureaucratic obstacles to goods and people going in and out of West Berlin. Then a bridge was closed "for maintenance," and when the British offered to erect another the offer was declined. Next, all cargo going into West Berlin had to be inspected by Soviet troops. When this was applied to Allied military trains, the Allies refused, resulting in a standoff. The trains went back to where they had come from rather than submit to Soviet inspection. General Clay called for the same supplies to be flown in by air, enough for forty-five days. Soviet Yak fighters then began "buzzing" the flights even though they were confined to the three air corridors across the Soviet zone agreed to by treaty. The inevitable happened on April 5, 1948, when a British Vickers Viking collided with a Soviet Yak that had been harassing it and both planes crashed, killing all ten aboard the British plane as well as the Soviet pilot. The incident was dubbed "an accident" by both sides, but Soviet fighters henceforth kept their distance.

The London Conference, which had recessed in late March, began again in late April and continued through May. Its conclusions were announced on June 7. The Western powers were inviting the presidents of all of the German *Länder* (states) of their zones to draw up a constitution for a federal German state. The *Grundgesetz* (basic law or constitution) that eventually emerged bore heavy markings of input from John J. McCloy, American high commissioner, though this was well shielded from the German public.

The second decision, for an overnight currency reform, entailed all of the new currency for the federal state being printed in the U.S. and shipped secretly into distribution points in all three zones. The Soviets, well aware of what was going to take place, tightened access to West Berlin. On June 18 the Western allies announced the currency reform: forty new Deutschmarks for sixty old Reichsmarks, but as the amount permitted to be exchanged by each individual was strictly limited; millionaires and some middle class savings were wiped out overnight. But so were the millions owned by black marketeers, and so was inflation eliminated in one blow. Everyone was now on a relatively even footing. The Soviet military commander immediately denounced the new currency and declared it illegal in the Soviet zone and in all of Berlin. The frontier between the Soviet and Western zones was sealed off, as was the border around Berlin. New restrictions on road, rail, and canal traffic into Berlin effective at midnight were announced by the Soviet authorities.

Four days later the Soviets announced their own currency reform and began exchanging Ostmarks for the old Reichsmarks in their zone and in Berlin. General Clay, meanwhile, without consulting Washington, had simply had a large letter "B" in a circle (for Berlin) printed on the new Deutschmarks and declared them valid for the three western zones of Berlin. Marshall Sokolovsky furiously announced that this new currency was invalid for Berlin since Berlin was deep in the Soviet zone and totally involved with its economy, which was quite true in that food, electric power, sewage disposal, and many other things were provided to all sectors of Berlin from the Soviet zone. Tension mounted as all waited to see which decree would prevail.

The issue came to a vote in a nighttime meeting of the Berlin Assembly at Berlin's city hall, deep in the Soviet sector. Despite attempts to disrupt the meeting and numerous beatings given Western delegates by communist hoodlums, the assembly finally decided that the Ostmarks would be valid in the Soviet sector and the Deutschmarks with the overprinted "B" in the three Western sectors.

Enraged, Sokolovsky asked Moscow for instructions. Should he move up his tanks? No, came the reply from Molotov; if the West brings up their tanks the only way out may be a military clash. That cannot be risked. Instead it was decided that a full blockade of West Berlin should be undertaken starting at 6 A.M. the next day, June 24, and continuing until the Allies caved in.

Having struck at the Allies' weak point, Stalin decided to strike simultaneously at those he felt to be his internal enemies. Tito, one of two East European leaders who had not come out of Moscow,[*] had proved difficult to manage. Having liberated most of Yugoslavia before the Red Army got there, he had a strong base of support from the Yugoslav people. His refusal to obey or take hints on a number of small matters rankled. This was a bad example for the other East European leaders, so the sooner Stalin eliminated the problem the better. On spurious charges Stalin now had Tito and Yugoslavia expelled from the newly formed Cominform. This was scarcely remarked in the West, as all eyes were focused on Berlin.

The story of the great airlift, which eventually defeated the blockade and reached its peak on Easter Sunday, 1949, of 1,398 flights into West Berlin carrying 13,000 tons of supplies, is well known. During its course the Soviets offered many inducements to the West to lift the blockade. These involved not just Berlin but all of Germany; had they been accepted, they would have totally derailed Western plans for Germany. All were in vain. The Soviets could easily have overrun the Western garrisons in West Berlin, were that the

---

[*] The other was Poland's Gomułka.

only consideration. The Soviet decision not to do so was based on their knowledge that the Americans had the atom bomb and might be provoked into starting World War III, which the Soviets knew they could never win.

In the summer of 1948, as the blockade continued, a fleet of sixty American B-29 "superfortress" bombers—the kind that had dropped the atomic bombs on Japan—was ostentatiously flown from the States to bases in England. No one knew then what we know today: they had no atomic bombs with them.

Another Western move that helped to break the Berlin blockade was the formal establishment of NATO on April 4, 1949. Eventually, Stalin began to realize that by squeezing Berlin in order to achieve certain goals he had achieved totally counterproductive results. The Allies were more unified than ever, West Berliners were heroes, and the Soviets were put in a bad light before the world. Worst of all, the thing he feared most, a military alliance against the Soviet Union—NATO—had become a reality. The blockade needed to be called off before more damage was done to the Soviet cause. Through diplomatic contacts at the United Nations in New York a formula was worked out whereby the Soviets could announce the ending of the blockade and still save some face. This occurred in May. The airlift, however, continued through September in order to build up a surplus that would discourage the Soviets from further "monkey business." In fifteen months the airlift had moved 2,300,000 tons of fuel, food, and machinery into West Berlin from the West.

Euphoria in the West over the blockade's lifting was short-lived. In the summer of 1949 routine military flights of U.S. Air Force planes over the Pacific detected radioactive particles in the stratosphere which could mean only one thing: the Soviets had tested their own nuclear bomb.

When President Truman made the announcement, Americans went into a state of shock. American scientists had assured everyone that the Soviets could not possibly build a bomb before 1952 or 1953. How had they done it so quickly? The answer was not long in coming: they had stolen America's secrets.

America was already becoming aware of Soviet espionage through revelations of such former Soviet spies as Elizabeth Bentley, Louis Budenz, and Whittaker Chambers. The first trial of Alger Hiss—which resulted in a hung jury, eight to four for conviction—had started on June 1, 1949. Soon some of the culprits involved in the theft of atomic secrets—Julius Rosenberg, Harry Gold and David Greenglass—were apprehended by the F.B.I. Klaus Fuchs, the German-born British physicist who had worked at Los Alamos and was part of a different spy ring, was arrested in Britain the following January. In the U.S. spying for the enemy during wartime carried an automatic death penalty. The fact that during the war the Soviet Union was an ally, not an enemy, was entirely overlooked.

On top of the worrisome news of the Soviets acquiring the atomic bomb, Americans now reeled at the news of the victory of the Chinese Communists over their wartime ally, Chiang Kai-shek. Suddenly, 600 million Chinese had been added to the growing communist empire. Though many knew that Chiang's Kuo Ming Tang government was hopelessly corrupt, Chiang, thanks to the "China Lobby" headed by Henry R. Luce, publisher of popular magazines, had become a hero to Americans. Chiang fled with the remnants of his army to the island of Taiwan. Mao proclaimed the People's Republic of China on October 4, 1949.

How had it happened? Who was responsible for the "loss" of China? Americans, unprepared for all this bad news, wanted answers, answers they could understand. They cast about for quick and simple answers, in fact, for scapegoats. In such a situation scapegoats are nearly always found, as are the demagogues to point them out. This time one emerged who ended up putting his name on a whole era: Senator Joseph McCarthy.

Before the U.S. found itself in the grip of McCarthy and his wild accusations, however, one more shocking event that affected the whole society occurred: the war in Korea. Many in America thought it was the beginning of World War III. Stalin had the bomb; he had flexed his muscles in Berlin before he had the bomb. Now, it was believed, he was starting a war in Asia to take U.S. attention off Europe where he would strike next, taking West Berlin in a day and sweeping across Western Europe with his vastly superior forces. This scenario, fortunately, was far from reality. In fact we now know that the North Korean premier, Kim Il Sung, had been after Stalin for more than a year for permission to overrun South Korea and unify the country which he and the Americans had so casually split in the middle. Stalin only gave his permission in January 1950, a few days after U.S. secretary of state Dean Acheson, in a policy speech on January 12, had said that Korea, from which the U.S. had withdrawn its troops, was outside the perimeter of American concern.[11] The timing of the attack actually had more to do with Kim's preparations and Stalin's insistence that there would be no Soviet support until he had gotten Mao's approval as well. This took several months.

The Korean War needs no detailed account here. In brief, North Korea's army invaded South Korea on June 25, 1950, overrunning most of South Korea and almost driving the remnants of the South Korean army and the American expeditionary force into the sea. Because of the Soviets' self-imposed absence from the UN Security Council at the time, the Council was able to pass a "uniting for peace" resolution calling for member nations to send troops to defend South Korea.* General Douglas MacArthur, commander of the United Nations forces, sent an amphibious force up to Inchon, northwest of Seoul, which succeeded in outflanking and thus routing the North Koreans. He then pursued the North Korean army all the way through North Korea until his army had reached the Yalu River, a borderline between Korea and Manchuria, part of China. At this point China sent in hundreds of thousands of "volunteers" (which were, in fact, whole units of Mao's army) who drove the UN forces back, taking many prisoners. At length the two armies found themselves locked in entrenched positions slightly north of the 38th parallel, the original dividing line, and fighting went on until the armistice in 1953. By that time Stalin had died and Eisenhower had been elected president of the United States.

While a nationwide fear of communist spies prevailed in America and liberals and left-wing intellectuals lost or feared losing their jobs due to the excesses of McCarthyism, real terror was sweeping Eastern Europe. Midnight arrests, deportations, torture, fake confessions, show trials, and executions were being orchestrated by Stalin in his campaign to root out all those communist leaders who had shown the slightest independence, a sign to Stalin of potential disloyalty or opposition at some future time.

Billed as a campaign against "Titoism," the net drew in major figures such as Rudolf Slánský, former secretary general of the Czechoslovak Communist Party and László Rajk, foreign minister of Hungary, both of whom, along with a number of their colleagues, were tried, convicted and executed after confessing to the most outlandish activities connected with Tito and with Western intelligence agencies. There was a strong anti-Semitic component to the terror, with the charge of "cosmopolitanism" added if the victims were Jewish.

Simultaneously, with this ruthless purging of communists, there was a massive assault on the Church. In Hungary, Cardinal Mindszenty was arrested, tortured, drugged, tried, and jailed. In Poland, where the Catholic Church was more powerful, the primate, Cardinal Wyszynsky, was put under house arrest but never tried. Meantime, in all countries priests were arrested, tried, convicted, and executed—or sometimes simply murdered. Churches, monasteries, and convents were closed. Many who were not actually arrested were prohibited from functioning as priests. Not a few, particularly among

---

* While the great majority of the UN troops were American, at least a dozen other UN member states sent troops to Korea, the largest units from Britain, Canada, Australia, Turkey, New Zealand, and Brazil.

the Protestant clergy, gave in to threats and agreed to cooperate with the régime, whether by reporting on their flock to the secret police or by furthering the current party line in their sermons.

Terror even reached down into the masses, for in each country the local secret police set up huge networks of informants. A person could lose his job or even go to jail for simply saying something uncomplimentary about a local communist or about Stalin, for being caught listening to a Western radio station, or for simply passing on what someone else had heard.

Western radios were not just BBC, Radio Diffusion Française, and Deutsche Welle, but the VOA (Voice of America) and the two other American radio stations operating from West Germany which had been clandestinely set up by the CIA as private radios: Radio Free Europe, which broadcast to the countries of east-central Europe, and Radio Liberation (later renamed "Radio Liberty"), which broadcast to the nationalities within the Soviet Union. The word "liberation" was taken directly from the Republican presidential campaign of 1952. It was coined by John Foster Dulles—soon to become secretary of state—who claimed that "containment" was not enough, that there should be a policy of "rolling back the Iron Curtain" and "liberation" for the peoples of east-central Europe who were suffering under the communist yoke.

The first major cold war crisis faced by the new Eisenhower administration in 1953 was the death of Stalin on March 5. Having no one left alive to trust in his old age, Stalin had become totally paranoid. Several months before his death he initiated a new terrorist binge against "doctor plotters," · doctors who took care of all of the élite officials of the régime. That a majority of these doctors were Jewish fit in very well with Stalin's basic anti-Semitism. While Stalin's henchmen were devastated at his death, they were happy to put an end to the "doctors' plot" lest it eventually involve one of them. But they were even more fearful of what might occur outside the Soviet Union at Stalin's passing. "In the days leading up to Stalin's death," wrote Khrushchev in his memoirs, "we believed that America would invade the Soviet Union and we would go to war."[12]

With the Eisenhower administration's rhetoric of "rollback" and "liberation," such a fear was not entirely unwarranted. More than one public official in the U.S. had called for a "pre-emptive" attack on the Soviet Union[13] and *Colliers* magazine had devoted an entire illustrated issue to an imagined American attack, invasion, and occupation of the Soviet Union, complete with a map showing dozens of mushroom clouds obliterating Soviet cities.

No wonder that the first actions of Stalin's heirs on the international scene were entirely conciliatory. Malenkov, the new first secretary of the

party, said, "there is no disputed or unsolved question which could not be settled by peaceful means with any foreign country, including the United
States."[14] Offers to renegotiate completely the whole question of Germany
were made. Churchill was all for arranging a summit meeting with Malenkov
as quickly as possible lest he and Eisenhower be "called to account if no
attempt were made to turn over a new leaf,"[15] but Eisenhower, who was furious to discover that despite Dulles's rhetoric there were no contingency plans
at the State Department about what to do in the case of Stalin's death, ruled
out any direct contact with the new Soviet rulers. He was easily persuaded by
Dulles that this complete change of tone on the part of the Soviets was a trick,
a trap to be avoided. Instead of putting the Soviet peace offensive to the test,
Dulles concluded that the best response was to keep up the pressure. Six
weeks later, however, Eisenhower did offer an olive branch of sorts, but only
if the Soviets gave evidence of their good faith by easing up their domination
of Eastern Europe, signing a peace pact in Korea, and negotiating a peace
treaty on Austria, ending the occupation and making that country neutral. The
Soviets over time were to respond positively to each of these issues, but
Dulles's hostile attitude made them so cautious that no answer to Eisenhower
was immediately forthcoming.

Contrary to impressions at the time, Levrenti Beria, the much-feared
head of the MVD (later KGB) was the most liberal and imaginative member
of the new leadership. Malenkov's secretary, Sukhanov, years later recalled:

> that Beria would suddenly raise important questions demonstrating his
> interest in a broad scope of issues. Beria's international initiatives were
> combined with even more far-reaching proposals on domestic changes.
> Among them were the proposals to grant amnesty to one million prisoners
> of the Gulag, approved by the Party on March 27, and the memoranda of
> May 8 and 16 in which Beria proposed canceling Stalin's policies of "russi-
> fication" and "de-nationalization" of the party, Soviet and economic cadres
> in the Baltic Republics and Western Ukraine. They, too, were approved by
> the Party Presidium on May 20.[16]

Beria also linked forces with Malenkov to counter Molotov's conserva-
tism. Molotov regarded Eisenhower's speech as provocative propaganda, but
they took a much more positive view and pressed Molotov to negotiate an
Austrian treaty as a way of countering U.S. moves in Germany. Beria, like
Stalin, was a fiery Georgian who frequently shouted and lost his temper. He
began to lose patience with those mouthing old Stalinist clichés without
knowing the reality of the situation. He told MVD General Pavel Sudoplatov
that "the Kremlin believes the best way to strengthen our position would be
to create a neutral, unified Germany under a coalition government." He was

quite willing to sacrifice the GDR. "We need a peaceful Germany, it does not matter to us whether they will be socialist or not ... What does it amount to, this GDR? It is not even a real state. It is only kept in being by Soviet troops."[17] Beria's words were soon to be verified.

It is still not entirely clear what Beria's role in Soviet policy toward the GDR was, but the fast deteriorating situation there made the GDR number one on the Soviet agenda. A meeting of the presidium of the Council of Ministers held on May 27 was devoted entirely to the political and economic problems that caused it. Beria seems to have proposed drastic changes in the GDR—disbanding the collective farms, canceling policies designed to suppress capitalist elements in industry, trade, and agriculture—that were too extreme for his colleagues. Molotov's more conservative draft stating that they should no longer "carry out a forced policy of constructing socialism" carried the day.

When the East German leaders, Walter Ulbricht and Otto Grotewohl showed up in Moscow to get their marching orders—as well as to request more aid—a few days later, Beria "yelled at them as though they were his lackeys."[18]

"It is clear now that Stalin never wanted a separate East German state," writes John Lewis Gaddis in his recent book, *We Now Know: Rethinking Cold War History.* "He repeatedly sought to restrain the German communists from taking measures within the Soviet zone that might alienate Germans elsewhere, and he appears to have agreed only reluctantly—after it had become obvious that there was to be an independent West Germany—to the establishment of the German Democratic Republic."[19]

Only in July 1952, when it was already obvious that Stalin's goals were impossible to attain, was the decision for "the construction of socialism" in the GDR made. This had the unfortunate effect, however, not only of destabilizing the newly created nation by causing a mass exodus of its citizens to the West, but of speeding up the rearmament of West Germany.

Ulbricht and Grotewohl, when they returned to the GDR on June 5, were not pleased with the new orders to ease up. But they dutifully proclaimed the "New Course," which meant a suspension of all laws harassing private firms and an end to forced collectivization of farms. Oddly enough, their new orders did not include rescinding the recently raised work norms, to which the workers so strongly objected, and about which there had been hints that they would be reduced.

Both the populace and the party faithful regarded these new measures as a sign of weakness on the régime's part. The workers, on the other hand, were enraged to have been left out of the general easing up, which had been as good as promised. Quitting work early on June 16, construction workers in East Berlin held a mass meeting at which they vowed to go out on strike the next day and hold a demonstration for their rights.

Because the uprising started in Berlin and because almost all of the pictures reaching the West came from Western correspondents and photographers in Berlin, many people for years thought of it as the Uprising of East Berlin. In fact, it was not confined to Berlin; it was zone-wide. Huge demonstrations were held in every major East German city and many minor ones. Arrests and fighting took place throughout the zone. One might as well ask how it was possible for a labor disturbance in Berlin to erupt overnight into a nationwide uprising. The answer is RIAS (Radio im Amerikanische Sektor). This German-language American radio, ostensibly just for the American sector of Berlin, had been beefed up to where it could reach every corner of the GDR loud and clear. Coming from the exact center of the Soviet zone, the RIAS broadcasts were difficult for the communists to jam without interfering with their own communications. With thousands of East Germans informing RIAS by letter or courageously by phone, RIAS was able to broadcast accurate information about what was occurring in the entire zone, not just Berlin. It thus had a wide audience. Already on the evening of June 16 people all over the GDR were aware of what the workers in East Berlin were going to do the next day and what their grievances were. All during the uprising RIAS kept up a stream of reports about what was happening where. But never did it call for action or violence. On the contrary, "on the evening of June 17," reported the Soviet Command in Berlin to Moscow some days later, "the broadcasts of the American radio RIAS urged the rebels to obey the orders of Soviet officials and to avoid clashes with Soviet troops."[20]

As a result of RIAS broadcasts, strikes and demonstrations occurred on June 17 in 274 cities and towns with millions of bystanders, including women and children, cheering them on. The Soviets were forced to intervene militarily in more than 150 locations to suppress the uprising. Soviet commanders had at least 26 persons executed on the spot, scores were wounded, and about 50,000 people were detained temporarily.[21] Another 13,000 were arrested in late June and early July in connection with the uprising,[22] yet by the end of 1953 only 177 had been tried and sentenced.

This was the first test[*] of Dulles's "rollback" and "liberation," a policy of which the East Germans were well aware. Many East Germans had liter-

---

[*] Actually, it was the second. Workers in Plzeň, Czechoslovakia, had rioted on June 1 in response to a currency reform that had wiped out their savings. Several workers had been killed by the police. Washington, which could not have been unaware of it, simply ignored it.

ally expected to see liberating American troops within a few days. Unlike its radio in West Berlin, Washington became the soul of caution. The consensus was that the U.S. "should do nothing at this time to incite … further actions."[23] An uprising in East Germany was not on its agenda. It was most inconvenient. It might well upset plans for getting Adenauer elected as the first chancellor of the new West Germany. Any thought of re-unification of Germany would negate plans for integrating West Germany into the Western alliance.

Secretary of State John Foster Dulles, who had recently authored the "rollback, liberation" policy, was forced to acknowledge in a cable sent to overseas posts in July that "the absence of overt Western support … in full view of Western observers, with American, British and French troops close at hand" had provided a dispiriting lesson to the peoples of east-central Europe.[24]

While the Eisenhower government did not counsel helping the Soviets save face and get things back to "normal"—like the British military commander in Berlin, so that his boss, Churchill, might get on with his campaign to get the Americans to agree to hold a summit with Malenkov—the first U.S. reaction to the uprising, nevertheless, was the same as when Stalin had died: "Wait and see." Eventually, the psychological warfare people around Eisenhower persuaded him to mount a food package program for the people of East Germany. Soon every GDR citizen who was able to find transportation to Berlin was going there to pick up an "Eisenhower package" or two in the thirty-five distribution centers in West Berlin. Though they tried everything, nothing the communists could say or do could prevent this and it was most embarrassing for them. As the U.S. high commissioner in Bonn, James B. Conant, cabled to Dulles in mid-summer, as far as he understood it it was Dulles's policy "to keep the pot simmering, but not to let it boil over."[25]

Hundreds of thousands of East German citizens flooded West Berlin that summer "keeping the pot simmering." By the end of July and early August two hundred thousand people a day were coming to the West Berlin distribution centers. By the end of the first phase, 2.6 million citizens of the GDR had collected one or more packages.[26] U.S. officials in Berlin, however, thought that opening negotiations on an all-German Commission as proposed by the Soviets "would be a greater blow to their equilibrium than if we succeeded in getting the entire population of the Soviet zone into West Berlin for a turkey dinner."[27]

The leadership in Moscow was worried. They were appalled at the uprising, during which the SED party appeared to disintegrate. They needed a scapegoat. Beria had been the most outspoken about liberalizing conditions in East Germany as well as cavalier in his treatment of the East German leaders. More important, he was the most dangerous member of the politburo with a vast army of secret police behind him. Most important, he had been showing signs of wanting to grab power. Malenkov and Khrushchev succeeded in persuading a majority of the other politburo members as well as Marshall Zhukov that Beria had to go. Moreover, there was no shortage of Stalinist crimes that could be laid at his feet. On June 26 Beria was caught off guard, in fact without his MVD guard, and Red Army officers under Zhukov arrested him. Beria's many associates were also rounded up and tried with him. While his arrest was announced on July 10, his secret trial and execution did not take place until the following December.

The struggle in the Kremlin for Stalin's mantle continued. Malenkov had already been forced to give up the position of first party secretary to Khrushchev, when it was agreed that never again should all the top posts be held by one man. Malenkov continued to be premier and president of the Council of Ministers. Krushchev had learned from Stalin how crucial it was to be head of the party, but having so different a temperament from Stalin, he was underestimated by most of his colleagues. Over the next few years Krushchev, like the pig "Napoleon" in George Orwell's *Animal Farm*, became "more equal" than the others. He did, however, preside over a genuine "thaw" that included giving his personal permission for the publication of *One Day in the Life of Ivan Denisovich* by Alexander Solzhenitsyn.

The "thaw" extended to the satellite countries of east-central Europe. In Hungary, an explosive situation had built up because of the ultra-Stalinist practices of its party chief and premier, Mátyás Rákosi. The Kremlin decided that Rákosi had to be replaced. The obvious choice was Imre Nagy, a Muscovite who had grown popular in Hungary for having carried out the land reform after the war. Rákosi's ability, however, and his slavish loyalty to the Russians convinced them that he should remain as party chairman. Nagy immediately introduced his own "New Course" which attempted to undo many of the unpopular things Rákosi had done in over-Sovietizing the country.

In January 1954 the Soviets finally managed to get the Western allies to agree to a meeting of foreign ministers in Berlin to discuss the future of Germany, by which they meant the neutralization of the country. But by now the two sides were too locked into the development of their own Germanies for any progress to be made. Austria, which for the first time had been allowed to send delegates to the conference, was dismayed at the outcome.

Nevertheless, in early 1955 the Soviet government, apparently feeling that a neutral Austria might give a big boost to their drive for a neutral Germany, suddenly changed their position on an Austrian peace treaty and agreed to the negotiations they had so long spurned on grounds that a German peace treaty must precede all other settlements. Negotiations got under way in Vienna, and on May 15, 1955, the treaty calling for the withdrawal of all occupation troops and the permanent neutrality of Austria was signed. It included large reparations for Russia, such as ten thousand tons of crude oil per year, but this seemed a small price to pay for its freedom.

Just days before West Germany had formally joined NATO, and in response to this long-expected move, the Kremlin called together the foreign ministers of all of its satellite states to a conference in Warsaw where a defense pact was signed, codifying a situation which had long existed unofficially. While it was strictly for defense, the communist countries now had a counter to NATO—the Warsaw Pact. Two months later it looked as though this new organization had been created just to become a bargaining chip when the Soviets offered to scrap it if the Western powers would scrap NATO and join the Soviets in an all-European security system that would allow the participation of the United States and Canada. The U.S. and its allies did not respond to this offer other than to call it propaganda.

About this time a new phenomenon occurred which caught public attention. Members of the top Kremlin leadership began to travel outside of the Soviet Union. First it was Khrushchev's trip to Belgrade to try to patch things up with Tito. Then Khrushchev and his new premier, Marshall Bulganin, traveled to Indonesia for a meeting of the Third World leaders.

Meanwhile the "thaw," particularly in the press and cultural matters, continued. As might be expected in countries that had come under communist control more recently than Russia, the "thaw" went further and faster in east-central Europe than in the Soviet Union. "Revolts" took place in both the Hungarian and Polish writers' associations, though it was only "liberal" communists versus "Stalinists." People also noticed that there was less police harassment of ordinary citizens. In Hungary, however, Rákosi, who had successfully sabotaged Imre Nagy's "New Course" and thus lessened Nagy's popularity considerably, now succeeded in persuading the Kremlin that Nagy was incompetent and weak and that he, Rákosi, should be reinstated as premier. Being the "little Stalin" he was, Rákosi soon began to tighten the screws again in Hungary without reference to what his masters in the Kremlin wanted and without reference to the considerably changed political atmosphere in Hungary after two years of Nagy. In Poland and Czechoslovakia, meanwhile, the Kremlin-appointed leaders continued to mimic slavishly the Soviet example. Stalinism was not yet dead.

CHAPTER III[1]

Majáles:[2] *The Abortive Student Revolt in Czechoslovakia*

After Khrushchev had delivered his secret speech, it was impossible to conceal the impact of these explosive revelations. The foreign comrades had to be told something, and they were told the truth, in outline if not in detail. Regarding the speech as primarily a Soviet matter, Khrushchev decided that the foreign communists could handle it as they thought best as long as they kept the information strictly within the party and did not challenge the new Soviet line on "collective leadership."

Within weeks, however, the gist of the speech began to leak out to the Western press and attacks on the "cult of personality" began to appear in the satellite press. These articles usually did not refer directly to Stalin, but to the local example of a "personality cult"—for among the many things Stalin had cultivated in the satellites were clones of himself.

Not long before Stalin died there had been a series of show trials in Eastern Europe—remarkably similar to the Moscow show trials of the 1930s—in which the accused confessed to a startlingly similar set of crimes involving "Trotskyism, Titoism, and Zionism." The biggest show trial by far had taken place in Czechoslovakia in late November 1952. There, Rudolf Slánský, the former secretary general of the Czechoslovak party, Vladimir Clementis, the former foreign minister, and twelve other prominent party officials abjectly confessed to the above trinity of "crimes," as well as to being in the pay of Western, particularly American, intelligence services.

It was no accident that Slánský and ten others in the trial were Jewish. A majority of the victims in other East European show trials and the Soviet doctors accused by Stalin two months later of plotting to kill him had also been Jewish. Slánský, Clementis, and nine others were executed by hanging in Pankrac Prison in Prague on December 3, 1952; the three remaining were

55

given life sentences. Only Stalin's death, on March 5, 1953, had saved the doctors from a similar fate.

The first news of Khrushchev's secret speech undoubtedly reached Czechoslovak ears in March 1956 via Western radios: Radio Free Europe, BBC, VOA, Radio Diffusion Française, and others in their Czech and Slovak language broadcasts. These broadcasts, especially RFE's, were heavily jammed. Radio Belgrade, on the other hand, was less often blocked, and the Yugoslavs were particularly eager to spread what they had learned about the speech. Nevertheless, because the text of the speech had not yet reached the West (nor, presumably, the Yugoslav Communist Party), news of it, no matter how sensational, was necessarily vague. And this encouraged the spokesmen for the Czechoslovak régime to brand all references to the speech as "slanderous capitalist lies."

On March 5, 1956, in the more important population centers throughout Czechoslovakia, meetings of leading party cadres were held.[3] Each was addressed by a member of the Communist Party Central Committee. These were a stolid lot, for not only had many of the intellectuals been purged or executed, but the Czechoslovak party had a firm base in the country's highly industrialized proletariat going back to the inter-war years.

Excerpts of the party leaders' speeches were carried in the press the following day, but whether through confusion or design, these accounts were not very enlightening. The speeches echoed the main points of the Soviet Twentieth Party Congress and what was already known of the speech in the West. But most references to Czechoslovakia were to the effect that the revelations only concerned the Soviet Union and did not apply to conditions in the Czechoslovak republic. The speeches were followed by discussions that in some case were unusually frank. Most ordinary party members were taken completely by surprise and many were stunned and bewildered.[4]

Such turmoil was generated at these meetings that the Central Committee decided it had to meet to resolve the problems that had arisen. A two-day meeting was held on March 29-30. Later accounts of this meeting, leaked to the press and the diplomatic community, indicate that the crux of these discussions was what to do about the trial and executions of Rudolf Slánský and his colleagues.[5] Should the trial be reopened, with the possibility of the victims being posthumously rehabilitated, or should a tight lid be kept on the matter? The Czechoslovak party found itself in a bind. The Hungarian first party secretary, Mátyás Rákosi, had just announced that the trial of László Rajk, the Hungarian analogue to Slánský, had been based upon a provocation and that he was being posthumously rehabilitated. In Poland everyone knew that the very-much-alive Władysław Gomułka was in the process of being rehabilitated.

The situation in these three national parties, however, was not the same. The Poles had just lost their first party secretary, Bolesław Bierut, who had died on March 13 during his visit to Moscow. His replacement, Edward Ochab, was known to be more flexible.[6] In Hungary, the Imre Nagy wing of the party was forcing Rákosi into a tactical retreat. No such split existed in the Czechoslovak party. They sensed the need to stick together. Rehabilitating Slánský would be reopening a Pandora's Box none of them was willing to face. But the opprobrium before their people, if and when they announced the decision *not* to reopen the Slánský trial, was something they were equally loathe to confront. Thus, they chose not to mention Slánský at all in the published text of the report by the Czechoslovak Communist Party leader, Antonín Novotný.

The otherwise astute British ambassador, Sir George Pelham, missed the point when he reported to Whitehall a few days later:

> The Central Committee's resolution and Mr. Novotný's report are not necessarily of great interest or significance. They bear the stamp of hesitation and mediocrity by which the present regime in Czechoslovakia has long distinguished itself, and the high principles which have been now restated are so hedged about with qualifications that it is not possible to predict any radical change.[7]

Radical change was exactly what the Czechoslovak party was trying to avoid. And their apparently united determination to quash what Khrushchev had unleashed, a determinantion soon to be bolstered by the upheaval in Poznań, Poland, and later by the revolution in Hungary, turned out to be radical indeed.

The full report was, of course, not for public consumption, but only for the party. It was printed up in a little blue booklet and used as a basis for carefully spreading the Khrushchev speech to the party faithful around the country. However watered-down the Novotný version may have been, it still came as a brutal shock to many communists, particularly the true believers. Scandalous claims about Stalin that had long been labeled "slanders" and "bourgeois capitalist nonsense" were now confirmed from the highest level of the Soviet hierarchy.

One such true believer was Ladislav Němec, a fourth-year chemistry student at Charles University in Prague. He was not a full communist, but a candidate member, which he had been for four years. This was rather longer than the norm; both the party and he had lingering doubts about one another. But he was nonetheless included in a secret party meeting of about three hundred students, faculty and administrative employees of the School of Mathematics and Physics (which included chemistry) in early April. This meeting was held in the school's main lecture hall and was attended by its party members, approximately one-tenth of the school's population. Student party membership in Czechoslovakia at this time was not more than five percent.[8]

Němec had been a marxist for almost as long as he could remember. It had defined him and made it possible for him to stand up to and even oppose his father. There had been many arguments, with the result that, while he was still living at home, there was a definite estrangement between them. Now everything his father had said about Stalin turned out to be true. The party had lied to him. What was worse, the party, or at least the leadership, was now denying its own culpability in the trial and execution of Slánský and his fellow victims as well as avoiding the necessary purging of itself. He felt flushed with shame and anger. Something had to be done.[9]

As a fourth-year student, Němec by now had some close friends among his fellow chemistry students. These included Michael Heyrovský, Stanislav Vavřička, Zdeněk Dolejšek, and Zdeněk Herman. None were party members, though one later joined briefly before quitting in 1968. Němec told them what he had learned at the party meeting and they agreed with him that they could not just sit back and accept it. Revelations and reform were in the air, particularly in the news from Poland. Radio Free Europe's Czech and Slovak language broadcasts could not be heard in Prague because they were so heavily jammed, but many young Czechs had learned Polish or could already understand some, and the Polish broadcasts of RFE, while jammed in Poland, nonetheless came in loud and clear in Prague.[10]

At first Němec, as chairman of the fourth-year chemistry students, called a couple of meetings only within that body. These gatherings were held in the chemistry auditorium and consisted of only a few dozen students. But the word got out and soon the chemistry students from the other classes began showing up as the meetings continued. Someone suggested that the physicists and mathematicians, since they were part of the same school, should also be included. The auditorium began to get crowded and the meetings a bit unwieldy. It was decided that an *ad hoc* steering committee was needed to draft a statement incorporating the most pressing matters which had come up at these meetings. Němec was chosen to head this group, which met several times in a small classroom, where they not only drafted the declaration but planned the plenary meeting at which the resolution would be discussed, amended, and approved.

The only legitimate way the students could accomplish their objective was to proceed under the auspices of the Czechoslovak Youth Union, an all-encompassing organization to which all students automatically belonged.

Unlike the charter of the Soviet Union's Union of Communist Youth, the charter of the Czechoslovak Youth Union (CSM) was thoroughly democratic. Since it was now under the domination of the Communist Party, however, these democratic rules had seldom been observed by the organization's leadership. The steering committee decided from the outset that these democratic rules would be meticulously observed. Everyone at the plenary session was to have his or her say, no one was to be shouted down or harassed in any way. Nor was anyone to be excluded. In addition, Němec was determined *not* to notify any foreign embassies or foreign journalists. All of the students' meetings had been open, and they knew that the secret police were well-informed of them. They did not want to risk the accusation that there had been any influence from abroad.[11]

Just as all previous meetings had been held openly, this plenary meeting was open to all and publicized throughout the academic community. Even the minister of education, František Kahuda, was invited—an invitation he ignored, although it appears he made his decision not to attend at the last minute.

The meeting took place in the main lecture hall of the School of Chemistry at Albertov on the evening of April 26.

⌐

"The hall was crowded to capacity and the air was electrified with a militant spirit," reports one eye-witness informant to the British embassy some days later.[12] "A resolution was passed in which the minister of education, Dr. Kahuda, was criticized for not having accepted an invitation to attend, nor having sent a deputy in his place."

Mladá Frontá, the official Czech communist youth newspaper, cannot, without losing all credibility, ignore the meeting. It sends Ivo Kalvinský, whose report appears only in the April 28 edition, because the meeting lasts well into the early hours of April 27. Hedged as it is, his is the only eyewitness account ever to appear in print. It is worth quoting, therefore, at some length.

Kalvinský begins by chiding his fellow communist journalists as "newsmongers" who feel themselves so much "in the know" that they do not need to cover the meeting. And then he writes: "I hope the newsmongers will not be angry with me—I did not witness any uproars. Just the opposite—I was

struck by the attentiveness with which the students listened to the proposal of
a resolution that had been the result of several preceding discussions.

> I was struck by the real interest with which the participants greeted every
> point of the resolution and, for that matter, every idea and formulation, and
> by the thoroughness and frankness with which they articulated their points
> of view. Ultimately, though, the most eloquent token of their real interest
> was the jammed auditorium and the fact that the meeting, which had been
> called for 7 P.M., ended long after midnight, and those who did not get seats
> ... stood for almost the whole time in the gallery.

Kalvinský concentrates his report on the resolution's criticism of the
Ministry of Education. The resolution attacks compulsory attendance at
courses on Marxism-Leninism, the excessive number of hours spent in the
classroom, and the gross imbalance in each student's "plan of study."
Kalvinský even mentions several of the twelve requests (in effect demands)
made of the ministry, adding that, naturally, these are talked about the most
and the longest. In fact, the "requests" are part of merely one section, number
6, in a resolution covering seven different areas of public life. The reporter so
waters down the other sections that it is best to turn to the actual words of the
resolution.

The student who reads the resolution is Němec's good friend, Michael
Heyrovský. He has been chosen for his strong voice and clear enunciation,
but also for the fact that he has a prominent, respected father. Here are some
of the words he speaks to that jam-packed auditorium:

> We consider it necessary that all important measures in individual areas of
> our national and economic life be discussed in advance with ... workers in
> the areas in question and that they be submitted for public discussion in the
> press.

> Some shortcomings in our political and economic life have been caused by
> failure to observe in practice the principles of socialist democracy ... all
> leading organs and those who work for them bear full responsibility to
> account for their work and be subject to full scrutiny and control from
> below ... All citizens [should] be acquainted ... with the means they will
> have to exercise this scrutiny and control over their representatives at the
> highest echelons and when necessary, exercise the right to recall them ...

> We consider it necessary that all persons be suitably and truthfully informed
> upon request about the contents of their personnel files ...

> We ask that our press, radio and film reporting services inform the public
> much more promptly, more accurately, and with more independence than

heretofore ... We [are] often forced to confront the paradox that we first learn about party matters from bourgeois sources ... The fear of bourgeois views ... is totally unsubstantiated ...

We do not understand the reason for jamming Western radio broadcasts or why this practice is necessary at all.

[By the final version, three weeks later, this passage will become: "We consider the jamming of foreign broadcasts (even in the case of such a station as "Radio Free Europe") to be beneath the dignity of our State ... Regular and timely information about events in this country and the rest of the world would be the best weapon against unfriendly propaganda ..."]

On relations with the Soviet Union, Heyrovský goes on:

Mechanically adopting the Soviet experience has done great harm to our educational system and, in particular, to our economic system ... An end must be made to mere copying of the U.S.S.R. ... Indiscriminate adoption of Soviet works of little value into our cultural life has ... severely damaged the attitude of some of our people toward the Soviet Union ... Further harm has been done by playing the Soviet national anthem at the end of every broadcast day and the displaying of the Soviet flag at all occasions. We ask that the Soviet national anthem and Soviet flag be present only on occasions which directly involve the Soviet Union: e.g., the November 7 and May 9 celebrations.

Next comes the unprecedented frontal challenge to the régime:

We do not consider correct the view of Mr. Novotný [that] "The Central Committee ... decides and must decide the most important questions of the party and state. Its decisions are binding ..." The conclusion reflected in this statement does not express the principle that workers must be governed according to their own convictions and thereby distorts the real content and leading role of the party.

We ask for a public review of the Slánský trial and other political trials. We ask for a guarantee of rightful political punishment for persons who tolerated illegal procedures during interrogations and for those who directly carried out these procedures. We maintain that it is necessary to publish materials ... about what kind of measures will be taken to guarantee control of the legal apparatus so that such cases will not be repeated.

We ask for amnesty for convicted persons similar to the amnesty recently declared in the Polish People's Republic.[13]

Given the oppressive power of the régime, these are courageous words, a kind of student Declaration of Independence.

Hours of debate take place before the above words are agreed upon, as the reporter from *Mladá Frontá* testifies:

> Whoever thought that all views would be united and exactly in the spirit of the proposed resolution would have been severely mistaken. Almost every question drew the comments of students, many standpoints were diametrically opposed and some students were downright wrong in their views. But, ultimately, the important thing was that the students of the Mathematics-Physics Department cared only about eliminating the insufficiencies and mistakes in our life as soon as possible and that is what all honest people today care about ... When I left the Albertov last night, I thought a long time about one remark that got lost in all the things that were said during the discussion: 'This time a lot of functionaries have come to our plenary session, but how many of them have we seen any other time? And how many of them really know about our needs and problems?' This remark ought to lead to some serious thought about how little the organs of the Czechoslovak Youth Movement know about the real life of college students ... No wonder, then, that in the eyes of many students the Youth Movement has no great authority.[14]

Comrade Kalvinský has reason to be impressed with the earnestness, thoroughness and democratic character of that meeting. Forty years later its leaders and main authors of that resolution speak with emotion and pride when they recall that evening.

"We were so excited that the resolution was accepted unanimously by all the students," says Heyrovský.[15] "There were different interests we were trying truly to represent for one of the first times [since 1948]," says Němec.[16] "We knew we were being watched by the secret police. So we were trying to be careful, because we really wanted to keep everything within this theoretically most democratic structure in the world ... I was not given a mandate, but I still felt it was my duty to do something ... I felt morally obligated because [the Slánský trial and execution] was such a horror."

Němec remembers one communist student named Kladec having "great reservations about what we were doing ... You know we listened to him, but the fact was the majority of people did not share his opinions ... it was one of the rare moments under the Communist régime where democracy for a brief, fleeting moment, seemed to take hold. [Some] raised objections, everyone listened to them and then, of course, there was the vote."

The leaders are gratified by the number of their own professors who attend. These, for the most part, are older, distinguished men who might never attend a student-organized meeting had they been in the West. Nor are all the outsiders who attend just Youth Union functionaries or secret police. At least one member of the party Central Committee, Jan Zalenka, is there in his capacity as editor-in-chief of *Večerni Praha* ("Evening Prague"). Zalenka is the son-in-law of Party Secretary Antonín Novotný, and as such has a long career ahead of him. He will eventually head the national TV. He tells the students he feels the resolution should stick to academic matters, but then raises no serious objections to the proceedings. Nor, however, does he print an accurate account of the meeting in his newspaper. But the fact that such a man sits through the whole meeting to the very end and observes near unanimity in the final vote convinces Němec and his group that they are on the right track and that what they are doing is important.

This naive euphoria carries the students through the next few days. Now they bend all of their energies toward getting the resolution published. The favorable report in *Mladá Fronta* is most encouraging. Since reproduction facilities like mimeograph are forbidden them, fellow chemistry student Míla Prusíková and others have to retype the resolution with as many carbons as possible. These are then dispatched by mail to various publications, ministries, and party organizations.[17]

The students are not able to see or talk to any party officials, but they are still riding high when it comes time for their mandatory participation in the May Day parade four days later. As usual, the different schools and individual classes of Charles University march together by year. The route is always the same. The students assemble in a side street near the top of Wenceslas Square, march down the square to the big reviewing stand set up at *Na Příkope* (or *Můstek*); there the marchers split, one group to the left, the next to the right to keep things moving along at a good clip.

"As students we tried to make the best of it," recalls Němec, "so we had some fun.

"As we were marching down the square loudspeakers were blasting all kinds of nonsense like 'With the Soviet Union forever!' or 'Long live the friendship of the workers and the students!' ... So we were chanting—I remember these slogans were quite funny, but completely harmless—things like 'Long live the person in charge of official enthusiasm!'

"Most importantly, we stopped—and that was really unheard of, because the whole procession had to keep moving—in front of the podium and started to chant a slogan which really characterizes the period. I remember it because it was in rhyme. I did not invent it; it just came naturally as young people can do ... the bottom line was: 'We don't want to rebel, we just want discussion,' and of course it rhymes in Czech. We were chanting this in front of President Zapotocký and Party Secretary Novotný. So naively and with good humor we thought it was proper thing because we could not get through to those people ... we were not quite sure why ... we just felt isolated from them.

"Novotný was smiling," recalls Heyrovský.[18] "He thought that we were praising the party." On a scientific mission to China years later Heyrovský will run across his old professor of Marxism-Leninism who marched with the students that day and who soon thereafter disappears from the university. Far from avoiding him, the professor approaches him and says: "Do you remember those glorious days?"

"We did not want to start a revolution," says Heyrovský. "We accepted the fact that the party was in power and would be for a long time. We wanted to improve the régime, not oppose it."

But the régime thinks otherwise. Every paragraph of that resolution contains a direct threat to its monopoly of power. No other mention of the students' meeting appears in the press for eleven days; then *Mladá Frontá* carries a second article, this time unsigned, giving a distorted account of the resolution.

It is not until June 2, long after many other events have occurred, that a long analysis by Antonín Jelínek of the student demands appears in *Literarní Noviný*, a literary journal with a relatively small circulation. At first Jelínek appears to be defending the students from the charge of "ingratitude" toward the "working class," and starts by stating that the students "mistakes in the ideological field" are no proof of "reactionary intentions." But he condescendingly says that a "lack of political experience and youthful zeal" succeed in "introducing into the resolutions, demands which are erroneous, misleading and provocative. It is necessary to pay attention to those demands which are arguable, but which could result in many fruitful solutions ... it is not necessary to refute exaggerated demands merely because Free Europe quotes them." Jelínek is careful not to say what *any* of these demands are, good or bad.[19] In the meantime, not a single ministry, party organ, or mass organization to which the resolution has been sent ever acknowledges receiving it.

When nothing else appears in the press after the single *Mladá Frontá* report, the Němec group decides to publicize the resolution themselves by carrying it personally to other departments of the university and to other institutions of higher learning in Prague.

Heyrovský remembers going in that first week of May with a few colleagues to the medical school and getting a very cool reception. "They were careful about committing themselves to dangerous matters," he comments. "They were thinking [too] much of their careers."[20] But Zdeněk Herman gets a much better reception when he takes it to the Technical University. Němec remembers giving it to his brother in the Academy of Arts and knows "he definitely showed it to others."[21]

Soon derivative resolutions begin to appear. Students living in dormitories on the outskirts of Prague carry these resolutions by motorcycle to other dormitories and even to other cities. One member of the core group at the Mathematics and Physics School, Saša Mangel, is a Slovak who happens to be living in Prague. When he is unable to find anyone to carry the resolution to Bratislava for him, he decides to mail four copies to colleagues at Comenius University, Bratislava, despite his knowledge that the post is controlled.[22] Soon similar meetings and resolutions with parallel demands occur in universities and colleges in such major towns as Brno, Ostrava, Plzeň, Košice, Banská Bystrica, and Nitra.[23]

On May 4, a deputation of students in Prague calls on the minister of education with their resolution. Whether this is the original resolution or a later one is not clear, for Němec is not a member of this delegation. And there is no particular reason why he should be, for the steering committee he has headed has dissolved itself after the successful plenary on the night of April 26. The resolution now belongs to the Youth Union and its appointed officers. According to a later account in *Mladá Fronta*, Dr. Kahuda temporizes with them, promising serious consideration of their demands. Whether or not he also agrees to see that the resolution is published is not clear, but by the time of the Majáles (the student carnival parade) on May 20, most students in Prague believe he has made, and then reneged on, such a promise.

Němec is still attending closed party meetings. At the next, held only a day or so after the May Day parade, he learns that the party is furious at the students' behavior. One top apparatchik calls it "totally unacceptable." It is at this point that Němec realizes that if the party is making such a fuss over such relatively harmless behavior, a crackdown is surely coming. Seeing the handwriting on the wall and knowing how deeply implicated he is, he offers to "back off," so as to "stop all this nonsense." But during an intermission in the meeting he is approached by a young party member who has never been active in these matters. "I don't like what I hear from you," she says. "You cannot back off now. We are into it, and if you continue it, if you pursue it, we will all be behind you." That does it. It is, as Němec later describes it, "the turning point of my life." He decides not to "back off." From then on he redoubles his efforts to put pressure on the party by spreading the resolution and urging public discussion of it. Now there is no turning back.

While the régime continues to suppress the resolutions, it adopts an attitude of ostensible reasonableness which minimizes the extent of the students' revolt. From the few references made in editorials, no one can get the impression that their complaints exceed routine troubles in academia. *Večerní Praha* on May 11 attempts to make up for Minister Kahuda's mistake in not attending the April 26 meeting by blending it, and his reception of the delegation on May 4 into one dateless (and fictional) meeting in which the minister replies to sixty-four speakers in a seven-hour session attended by the rector and dean of Charles University.[24]

From May 11 to 13 the central committee of the Czechoslovak Union of Youth holds a plenary session in Prague during which all of the students' complaints about the organization surface as self-criticism. A resolution is adopted which not only upholds decisions reached at the second congress, held the previous year, but which now attacks the ministries of Manpower, Education, Culture, Foreign Affairs and Finance for shortcomings in handling young people. The resolution then goes on to incorporate many of the demands of the original April 26 resolution.[25]

Meanwhile, on May 12, a second meeting takes place between Minister Kahuda and student representatives, who are from the Youth Union of Prague II. This time university authorities are also present, and a new composite resolution, probably the one just adopted at the School of Pedagogy (see Appendix B) is handed to Kahuda. In the verbal exchange that takes place, the students' pent up feeling breaks out into a hail of shouts. Kahuda tells them that if they had behaved this way under the First Republic, police would have dispersed them with clubs. Then the rector of the Mathematics-Physics School orders the students to disband and go home. Several students are reported to have roughed him up, though this is most unlikely.[26]

Close observers of Czechoslovakia—Western embassy personnel and people in Radio Free Europe in Munich—are aware that there is great ferment among the students at this time, though they lack detailed information. They know, for instance, that the Majáles, forbidden since 1948, is being reinstated.[27]

The idea for reinstating the Majáles comes from the party-controlled Czechoslovak Union of Youth (CSM). Nonetheless, it has to be approved at the highest level of the party. Approval comes just when the full liberating force of Khrushchev's speech is being felt and its consequences not yet foreseen. The CSM's reasoning is twofold. First they know the student discontent is reaching a dangerous level and needs to be vented before an explosion occurs.[28] Second, they hope to recover the respect and control they have lost in recent years by organizing something they know the students will enjoy.[29]

The Slovak students in Bratislava are allowed to hold their Majáles on May 12, closer to the traditional time. The Prague Majáles is to be held a week later on May 19. Rumors of the raucous Majáles in Bratislava bring *The*

New York Times correspondent Sydney Gruson down from his base in Warsaw to observe the Prague Majáles a week later. Gruson's colorful report of five thousand students being applauded on their two-mile route through Prague emphasizes that for all the lampooning, "no effort was made to turn the occasion into a huge anticommunist demonstration as had been rumored in Prague."

The students in Bratislava have not only advertised their Majáles in the student newspaper, *Our University*, in addition, a bizarre student duo—"Mr. Carnivalist," dressed in a bear skin, and Prosecutor "Grand Papulos" (Big Mouth), wearing a mask with a gigantic mouth—has been visiting the outlying dormitories of the university for several weeks drumming up interest.[30]

The Bratislava parade has the full cooperation of the city authorities and police. It follows almost exactly the route of the official May Day parade just twelve days earlier. The dense crowd of spectators lining the streets an hour before the parade begins is even larger.[31] While the 6 P.M. starting time seems dangerously late in the day (torchlight parades being volatile), in fact there is daylight well past 8 P.M. at this time of the year and the weather is fine.

Hundreds of student participants with their costumes and placards assemble in Hodža Square in front of Grassakovič Palace (then the Palace of Young Pioneers, today the palace of the president of the Slovak Republic). Led by "Mr. Carnivalist," the bear, who is surrounded by bodyguards with chain whips, the procession crosses the wide Staromestka, proceeds down Postova Street and into the Square of the Slovak National Rising, on to Štúrova Street, right onto Jesenského past the National Theatre and then left to the Danube River where it ends.

While the signs the students carry are humorous, evoking laughter, gasps, and even applause, the content behind them is not. Most refer to the scandalous conditions in which they live and study, or ridicule the emphasis on Marxism to the detriment of traditional academic disciplines. Several call attention to the party's secret decree of two years' mandatory army service after graduation.[32] A few are downright political—such as one clearly referring to Marxism: "The principle stands firm, but the house tumbles down."[33] At the front of the parade six students carry a black coffin with white lettering on each side reading "Academic Freedom." When their part of the procession reaches the Danube embankment, whether by design or sudden inspiration, the six rush forward and heave the coffin into the Danube amid roars of approval from their fellow students and other onlookers. Some students are costumed as American and Soviet soldiers. The Americans all carry Colt revolvers. The Soviet soldiers carry flasks of Pitralon shaving lotion or Eau-de-Cologne. From time to time the Soviet soldiers hold up their flasks and roar: "Eau-de-Cologne—Vodka! Pitralon—Vodka!" At the rear of the parade is a truck with chemistry students on it producing rose-colored fumes as they cry out: "Finally a little fresh air in Bratislava!"[34] Less than two hours after its start, the carnival parade simply melts into the crowd, and everyone goes off to the pubs to celebrate tweaking the noses of those in power.

Early references to the event in the local press and radio take a tolerant view, saying it was "lots of fun" with "plenty of justified criticism," but these reports disguise the bitterness of the students' complaints. Within a few days, however, the tone of the Slovak press changes radically, and there are complaints that "a few malcontents" have "attempted to provoke students" into opposition to the Youth League, the university administration, the party and the government.[35]

The reason for this change in tone is not so much a reappraisal of the Majáles as something that has occurred afterward and is spreading like wildfire.

Sunday, May 13, the day after the Bratislava Majáles, two Slovak student athletes from the Mladá Garda dormitory of Comenius University return by airplane from Prague, where they have been competing in a national student competition. They bring with them one of the student resolutions, from the School of Mechanical Engineering, which has been circulating in Prague. Unlike the Němec resolution, it concerns only academic matters. But it causes a sensation. The next afternoon, after classes and lectures are over, the students of Mladá Garda gather in their dining room and elect two of their number, Ladislav Kliman and Mrna Volek, as their speakers. These two then conduct a meeting in which it is decided that they should adopt, with only minor changes, the Prague resolution as their own. Once it has been typed up in Slovak, it is posted in the main entrance where all can see.[36]

Though Mladá Garda dormitory is about three kilometers to the south of the city's center, it is on a main street with a tram. It is not long before word reaches Suvorov dormitory in downtown Bratislava.

Jozef Jablonický, who lived there, recalls that he had just finished his evening meal and was upstairs brushing his teeth when a friend called out: "Jozef! Jozef! Come quick! There's something big going on at Mladá Garda!" Jablonický, who has been in his home village on Saturday and thus missed the Majáles everyone is talking about, is not about to miss out on this. With the taste of toothpaste still in his mouth, he runs with his friend to catch a tram to Mladá Garda.

When they arrive they are immediately offered a copy of the resolution. Not stopping to read it there, they jump on a return tram and devour it together on their homeward journey.

As they reach the steps of the main foyer of the Suvorov dormitory, they call out to everyone to see what they have. Within seconds a knot of students gathers around them, Others call to friends and soon the foyer is jammed. "Let's go to the dining hall," someone suggests, and the crowd surges into the dining room, startling the few late diners. Soon the confusion is more than Jablonický can endure. A big lad with a booming voice, he climbs onto a table and yells "Shut up!" As the din subsides, he announces, "Only if we speak one at a time will we get anything accomplished."

"You be the speaker, Jozef," shouts a friend. A chorus of voices calls out, "Yes, Jablonický, you run it."

"The meeting proceeded in an orderly fashion," recalls Jablonický. "We made a few changes to make it to conform to the Faculty of Arts, but otherwise it was the same as the Mladá Garda resolution. And it passed by hand vote unanimously. An hour earlier, as I was brushing my teeth, I could never have dreamed that this would happen. The State Security later said that it was a well-planned conspiracy. But they were wrong. It was completely spontaneous."[37]

By the next day the resolution reaches the women's dormitory way off in Horský Park overlooking the northern sector of the city. There it meets with even more impassioned acclaim and the young women add political sections, including a call for an opposition party.[38] Meanwhile a movement to collect signatures for a petition to force *Smena*, the Slovak counterpart to the Czech *Mladá Frontá*, to print the resolution, has gotten underway.

The party, fully aware of what is going on, has not yet decided how to handle the situation. On May 16, one party member, the manager of Mladá Garda dormitory, decides to take things into his own hands; he tears the student resolution off the bulletin board where it had been affixed two days earlier. This precipitates an uproar among the students, some of whom take to the streets.[39]

No students are more eager to take to the streets than the young women of Horský Park, isolated as they are from the rest of the city. Jablonický, who has gone there to collect signatures, remembers being present at a meeting there in which the issue of taking to the streets is seriously debated. The party, now concerned enough to ring both of these dormitories with motorized police, sends a delegation of "workers" to address this meeting. They accuse the students of wanting to "liquidate socialism." "But they aren't workers," Jablonický recalls, "They are policemen dressed in workers' clothes."[40]

The party is terrified of street demonstrations. Karol Bacílek, first secretary of the Slovak party's central committee, is prepared to call in the army.

Novotný in Prague is said to be eager to close down the universities. The situation is saved by three students from the Philosophical School in Bratislava: R. Olinský, F. Vilsvader, and M. Vrbican. Accompanied by two senior lecturers from the school, they insist that only by direct negotiations with Bacílek can bloodshed be avoided. Bacílek agrees to receive them and spends much of May 16 negotiating with them. In the end Bacílek promises that all of their demands will be met and even agrees to the publication of the student resolution in *Smena* the very next day. In exchange, the student spokesmen agree to keep the students from taking to the streets. Only this news, delivered breathlessly by the delegation itself, persuades the young women of Horský Park not to go into the streets.[41]

The next day the full text of the resolution *does* appear on an inside page of *Smena* next to the text of the party's politburo resolution calling for similar liberalizing measures, which had been passed a month before on April 16, but not made public until today. Only weeks later, when they return to their homes in other parts of Slovakia for their summer holiday will the students learn that they have been tricked; only the Bratislava edition of *Smena* had carried their resolution—all the other editions carried only the party resolution.

The Slovak paper *Pravda* complains on May 19 of the students' "ultimatum." The party organ claims that when the students read the party's April 16 resolution they found it "broader than their own." This statement is utterly untrue, but the readers of *Pravda* have no way of knowing this since the student text is not included. The article continues:

> In the beginning [these elements] ... were able to win the confidence of others by proclaiming justified demands. [However, the real aim was] to set the student resolutions against the document of the Central Committee ... to misuse ... the student movement for obscure purposes. This is proved by their attempt to recruit female students at the Horský Park dormitory for demonstrations under the pretext of having them sign the resolution of the Mladá Garda dormitory ... A definite end must be put to the signing of resolutions with declarative solutions of problems. Discussions by students, teachers and university workers must be based on party documents on higher education.

On May 22, *Smena* complains that at many meetings organized by the Youth Union in Slovakia the students, instead of discussing the party resolution as they are supposed to, discuss instead the resolution prepared by the students of Mladá Garda dormitory.[42] The communists do everything they can to convey the impression that the students are not speaking for all citizens, but are ungratefully agitating against the working class. "Compare, friends of Mladá Garda," intones the publication *Lud* on May 19, "your own housing conditions with those of the workers ... Be more modest, students, when voicing your demands ..."

Only one account in the Slovak press deviates from the tone of condescension and recognizes the legitimacy of the students' complaints even as it generally hews to the party line. The young writer Milan Ferko, in an article published in *Kulturný Život* ("Cultural Life") on May 26 writes:

> Why wasn't a thorough and open discussion on universities ... developed in connection with the preparation of the [party] resolution? ... And ... why was the publication of the resolution delayed a whole month? Would "democracy" have broken out among Youth Union members if they had known about the document and participated in the making of it?... [The student demonstration] is a clear example of how such a thing can be misused. Furthermore if the Union and party organizations constituted a [true] clearing ground for the exchange of views ... would the students have resorted to an imported and forged Prague resolution? We must condemn the fact that certain people sent instructions by means of airplane between Bratislava and Prague [and] that motorcycle groups went from one dormitory to another ... [But] it is necessary to condemn tendencies such as giving false information to Bratislava factory workers [about the student demands] ... or the practice of pitting the workers against university students ... instead of taking the [students' resolutions and meetings] into consideration as a fact, instead of considering them an objective reality ... and meeting the suggestions half way ... we began to seek saboteurs, provocateurs and evil doers.

Back in Prague, the pressure that Němec and his friends have tried to exert on the party is beginning to turn back on them.[43] Through an informant with access to the police, they learn that the secret police are watching them closely. They begin to weigh carefully what they should and should not do to avoid entrapment. Though by tradition it is the arts and humanities students who put on the Majáles, Němec and his friends can participate if they want to. They choose not to.

But it is not just Němec and his friends the party is watching. At an emergency meeting of the party's Central Committee on May 14, brought on by the Bratislava Majáles just two days earlier, the minister of the interior, Rudolf Barák, gives an oral report on what he calls "provocations" being prepared by the students for the Prague Majáles. The resolution following his report calls on party secretary Novotný and interior minister Barák to follow the developing situation and, if need be, call another emergency meeting of the politburo "to introduce the necessary measures."[44]

A few days later, as things appear to be getting out of hand in Bratislava, Novotný sends a delegation to the universities warning the students not to

Young pioneers march down Wenceslas Square in a demonstration similar to the annual
May Day parade in communist Czechoslovakia. *East Europe* magazine, 1959.
Photo from *Svet v Obrazech* (Prague), July 4, 1959.

start anything. Minister of Education Kahuda even notifies the universities that they may soon be shut down.[45]

Like the one in Bratislava, the Prague Majáles has been scheduled for Saturday afternoon.[46] Fearful of what may happen if student protests mix with proletarian drinking on Saturday night, the authorities prudently insist it take place instead on Sunday at 1 P.M., when there will be fewer people in the streets. The original date and time is carried in one of the daily newspapers, but not the last minute postponement. Only by word of mouth do people learn of this change of date and time.

Sunday, May 20, begins as a typical spring day in Prague: cool and cloudless blue sky that does not start to gray over until noon, after which fragmented clouds let bursts of warm sunshine through to those on the right side of the street. It is still overcoat weather.

By one o'clock, hundreds of people have gathered along Národní Boulevard near the street called Perštýně, for that, rather than the traditional Wenceslas Square, is where the authorities have given permission for the parade to start. This crowd, however, has not gotten wind of a still more recent change

Jiří Skopec, dressed as a monk, carries a sign saying, "Let's hear it for the new educational reform." Purchased by the author from Jiří Pešek, private photographer.

Law students carry many signs. One reads: "Long live demagoguery. Hurrah!"
Purchased by the author from Jiří Pešek.

The banner reads: "Poor wandering students, mischievous baccalaureates."
Purchased by the author from Jiří Pešek.

The banner reads: "Youth Front [the main youth newspaper] where are your resolutions?"
Purchased by the author from Jiří Pešek.

Students carry a whole library of books with the sign "ON INDEX" across the front.
Purchased by the author from Jiří Pešek.

Students dressed as Neanderthal men accompany the dragon/dinosaur.
Purchased by the author from Jiří Pešek.

Skits and floats contrasting wealth and poverty pass along Paris Street.
Purchased by the author from Jiří Pešek.

Students lampoon the communist educational system.
Purchased by the author from Jiří Pešek.

The dragon/dinosaur with different posters on each side, makes a slow turn.
Purchased by the author from Jiří Pešek.

of mind on the part of the régime. Within a few minutes there is a roar of motorcycles in the trafficless streets. Student riders shout over their idling motors that the parade's starting point has been shifted to Old Town Square, about seven minutes away by foot.

Jiří Skopec and his colleagues, all dressed as monks, are among those who get word of the change only at the last minute. As they hurry through the narrow streets to Old Town Square they are joined by a contingent of thirty to forty students they don't know. Skopec is a geology student at Charles University. He has not been to any meeting where resolutions have been discussed, but knowing that his department's professors have no objection to the Majáles, he has joined in the fun. He has his monk's cowl up, is wearing a false gray beard, and is carrying a sign, burned around the edges to depict age, which exhorts: "Let's go for the new educational reforms!"

"You have to realize," says Skopec, "that we had had about four serious reforms in less than eight years and people were bored with it."[47]

For a Sunday afternoon, the streets and sidewalks of Prague are packed. Crowds gather along the route of the march which follows the Paris Street, past the law school on the Vltava Embankment, across the bridge under the shadow of the giant Stalin statue, then to the right along the river to Fučik Park. Police are out in force to keep the route clear at intersections, but the crowds on the sidewalks are self-disciplined and in no need of police control.

"But most important," says Michael Heyrovský, who watches the Majáles from in front of the law school, "are the non-uniformed policemen who were in great numbers everywhere around. Many of them you could not identify because they were dressed like students." Some of the signs are just too offensive for these plainclothes policemen to stomach. "I remember several times they jumped out of the crowd from the pavement and took the signs from the students," recalls Skopec. "But they did not take anybody with them," he adds.[48] What Skopec does not know is that many of these placards are quickly replaced by a brigade of students who have brought sheets of blank cardboard and paint in anticipation of such confiscation.[49]

The parade is led by a King and Queen.[50] The King is "Marxism," which is masculine in Czech, and the Queen is "Russian Language," which is feminine in Czech: two things pervading Czech life at this time people are heartily sick of.

The five thousand marchers do not flow along like the May Day parade, but come in groups, occasionally stopping and performing or showing their signs to particular parts of the crowd before moving on. Laughter and applause accompany each group, more for some than others. One group near Skopec and his fellow monks is made up of a dozen scantily clothed Neanderthal men with clubs and sticks with which they perform various tricks. They surround a dinosaur or dragon that walks on the legs of four students struggling to hold it up. The apparatus is so heavy, in fact, that two platoons of spare legs (students) follow along to spell them. Two signs are pinned to the beast, one on each side, and it laboriously turns around so all can see what they say. One reads "This is for the student mensa." The other reads "I have leathery skin as thick as the Minister of Education's." ("Minister," however, is abbreviated so that it can be taken for "Ministry" as well.)

Instead of just a sign on the theory and practice of Marxism, as in Bratislava, there are two signs leading two groups. The sign "The theory" is followed by students dressed to the hilt in top hats, cutaways, and fine silks; "The practice" is followed by a motley group in rags and tatters. A dozen blindfolded and gagged young men and women represent reporters and editors of the newspaper *Mladá Frontá*. Another group carries a sign saying "We want world literature," followed by a group carrying a large bookshelf with fake bookfronts all marked "on the index." The party's current line of making the "cult of the individual" a scapegoat for all ills is lampooned by three students walking in file. The first tall one carries a sign saying "Small cult," the next somewhat shorter student carries a sign saying "Smaller cult," and the third and smallest student carries a sign saying "Tiny cult."[51] Resentment of the government's coddling of North Korean students at the Czech students' expense comes out in a placard reading "Long live the Korean students!—but on their own money!"[52]

There are hundreds of signs and slogans, but only the most memorable are later recalled by the thousands of onlookers. There has been some form of self-censorship so that nothing is too blatant. And, of course, there are many "in" jokes meant only for their fellow students or citizens of Prague. One such is ""Have no fear, Citizens of Prague, the students are still here!" Josef Holler, writing in *Mladá Frontá* six days later asks, "What should the people of Prague be afraid of?"—missing the point. The point is that the exact same sign had been carried in the last Majáles Prague had seen in May 1948, shortly after the takeover of the country by the communists. It underlines another slogan that reads, "We students are young, but we remember a lot."

A few slogans jotted down by an observer from the U.S. embassy are: "Long live the first and last Majáles!" (Under communism, being understood.) "Long live Minister Kahuda! April fool!" "What Comenius [a seventeenth century Czech educator] designed, Kahuda bartered away!" "Tomorrow buy *Mladá Frontá*, there will be nothing in it."[53] (Indeed, there *is* no mention of the Majáles in the next day's edition.)

Michael Heyrovský remembers one placard that is ecologically before its time. "Save our forests! You can keep all of your bureaucratic forms!" Perhaps the most daring sign refers, indirectly, but unmistakably, to the Slánský trials. It comes in the form of four signs carried one after the other. The first sign is simply a question mark. The second reads, "Which is better?" The third says, "To execute the little criminals and let the big ones go free?" and the last sign reads, "Or execute the big criminals and let the little ones take their places?"[54] It would take four alert secret policemen to pull that one out of the parade.

Not all the signs mock the authorities. Placards carried by the law students are loyal to the régime. The youth union officers are only too aware of what the students are up to and they try to counteract it wherever they can. But when the law students' main sign, which reads, "We thank the working class for having an opportunity to attend the university," goes by, most people think it is meant ironically and laugh and cheer lustily.[55]

And there are a few lone mavericks. Heyrovský remembers one brave, possibly crazy, Bulgarian student carrying a sign in Czech that reads, "Zhivkov, the murderer of our nation!" (Todor Zhivkov, the Bulgarian first party secretary, is to remain in power until 1989.)

The goal of the procession, Fučik Park, with its open-air theater, is supposed to be the scene of some additional dramatic skits prepared by the students. In fact, the CSM has managed to turn it into a separate event by dubbing it the "Students' Carnival," to which entry can be gained only by written invitation. This is not at all what the students had intended. Moreover, many of the invitations intended for students have been sent to party activists and secret police intent on sabotaging the event. As a result, many students who should have received invitations do not, and others lacking them are turned away by the police.[56] The American embassy reports extra police in unusually large numbers on duty at principal intersections well into the evening and speaks of the students being "compelled to break up into groups" on their way to the park.[57]

After dark there is a ruckus followed by some arrests in the park in connection with a jazz band, but Skopec suspects that this is a police provocation designed so that something might appear in the papers the next day saying that hooligans had participated in the Majáles.[58]

Rumors of arrests circulate among Western correspondents and Western embassies. A dispatch from the first secretary of the American embassy, Albert S. Sherer, Jr., reports to Washington on June 6:

It is ... believed that the students planned to distribute abbreviated versions of the enclosed draft resolution among the crowds who witnessed the Majáles parade on May 20. It has been reliably reported that the students hoped to turn that parade into a demonstration in which factory youth would also participate ... Although a few placards carried that day reflected the demands in the enclosed draft resolution, it was, on the whole, a mild affair. The prime minister made a flat statement in his press conference on May 24 that no students had been arrested as a result of the Majáles demonstration. The embassy is inclined to believe ... either that the prime minister is misinformed ... or that he did not speak the truth. It is believed that several students were picked up prior to the May 20 parade and immediately thereafter. These, however, were merely enthusiastic demonstrators and not the real organizers of what some students had hoped would turn out to be a mass protest meeting. It is believed that these latter were expelled from the university on May 20 and arrested on May 21-22. Since they were expelled prior to their arrest, Široký may be technically correct ... There are persistent rumors that the ringleaders were found for the most part in the Faculties [Schools] of Law, Medicine and Mathematics at Charles University, and that approximately 30 of these are still under arrest.

The students hoped that the draft resolution would receive widespread publicity within the country, and it is said that they sent it to several diplomatic missions as well as to the newspapers in the hope that their demands would be widely known. If a copy of the draft resolution was in fact sent to the embassy, it was intercepted, as we have received the enclosed copy from another source.[59]

By the fall of 1956, United Press will be referring to three hundred students across all of Czechoslovakia as having been arrested after the Majáles.[60] Only when the police records of the Ministry of the Interior for the period are made public will the full truth be known.

But Ladislav Němec, who is certainly the ringleader at the School of Mathematics and Physics, does not believe that *any* students are arrested. *He is never arrested nor does he ever hear of any student who is.* He believes that the party and secret police deliberately spread these rumors to induce fear in the populace as well as to mislead the West.

Certainly there is punishment; but it comes in stages. For example, Němec and his fellow chemistry students are scheduled to take part next autumn in a first-ever exchange which they themselves have arranged with East German chemistry students at the Technical University at Dresden. Němec's and Heyrovský's names simply disappear from the list with no explanation given or needed. Minister Kahuda eventually calls Němec's dean and orders him to expel Němec permanently from all institutions of higher learning.

But the dean, like most faculty members of the time, fights to protect his student. After a protracted debate, the dean manages to reduce the punishment to one year's suspension from the university with the possibility of completing his studies and getting his degree later. The party takes care of the rest of his punishment: work in a factory to get him closer to the masses. This turns out to be not so bad. He manages to get a job related to his chemistry background and within a year has joined the management as an expert, while finishing his studies by attending night classes at the university.

In the fall Němec is expelled from the party, but here again he is saved from arrest by a party member, Líza Pačesová, who argues that the only thing Němec did wrong was to break the party's rule of secrecy in revealing to non-party people something which had been said in a closed party meeting.[61] This deserves expulsion, but hardly arrest and imprisonment. The party has built up a detailed case against Němec, but the unexpected remarks of this comrade take the wind out of its sails. Rather than go through with a controversial exercise, the comrades agree to expel him on the strength of her extemporaneous motion.[62]

Though he suffers minor privations, Michael Heyrovský is probably saved from real punishment by being the son of a famous man. Indeed, his father will be awarded the Nobel Prize for chemistry just three years later. Němec, during the time he still has access to party information, finds out that the older Heyrovský has been accused, at a hearing of the Central Committee, of having started the whole affair and using his son and his son's student friends to spread his ideas. The older Heyrovský dismisses the accusations as "poppycock." He is interested in his science "period," but he secretly approves of his son's activities.[63]

As to reports of leaflets, or shorter versions of the resolution being given out by the students to the crowds at the Majáles, the students themselves dismiss this as ludicrous. They may be naive, but not so naive as to do something that would provoke immediate arrest with all those secret policemen around. No, they speculate, if any resolutions were handed out, it was surely the work of the secret police's agent provocateurs.

And this fits neatly with the charges brought against the persons who *are* arrested and accused of having put the students up to their activities: Jaroslav Hajček, a fifty-seven-year-old former colonel, Božena Plchová, and three others, all in their forties and fifties. Their arrest is announced in the Prague press on June 14. At their trial in September, one of the charges of the prosecution is that they distributed brief versions of the resolution during the Majáles. They are also accused of taking their lead from Radio Free Europe.

But the most telling evidence of a régime-orchestrated plot are the light sentences meted out. These range from six months to three years.[64]

By mid-June the students are thoroughly discouraged. Their resolution, particularly the composite resolution handed to Minister Kahuda on May 12, has been completely ignored, then distorted, and finally quashed. Soon they will be off doing their military service away from the cities.

Before that happens, however, the party strikes back at the Prague II (Charles University) section of the CSM, where it had all started. It is less a question of revenge than fear that these students might infect the international as well as Czechoslovak student movement with their ideas of freedom and democracy. The International Union of Students, the world communist student organization with its headquarters in Prague, is due to hold its Fourth World Congress in Prague from August 26 to September 3.[65] The absence of delegates from the host city's Charles University would be difficult to explain unless, of course, no vehicle for such representation exists. Thus the temporary liquidation of the Prague II section due to "administrative reorganization" is decreed.

A meeting of the section is called at the main lecture hall of the Natural Sciences School in the first week of June. The dean of this faculty, Miloslav Valouch, a loyal Communist, is given the task of explaining to a bitter, sullen crowd of students just why it is necessary to disband their particular section for technical, reorganizational reasons. He wants to make it very clear that this has nothing whatsoever to do with the students' behavior in April and May. Before Dean Valouch has gotten far into his prepared remarks, a young female student, Vera Čáslavská, stands up and conspicuously turns her back on him. Once the gesture has been noted by all, she makes her way out of the row, her back still to the stage and face to the people she is passing—European style—until she can stalk loudly out of the hall. Before the sound of her footsteps has faded, several other students follow her example. Soon it is scores. Not a word is spoken, only the sound of shuffling feet and Valouch's voice droning on through his tortuous text. By the time he finishes and looks up, not a student is left in the room.[66]

Now only the last nail remains to be driven in.

This is accomplished by the Communist Party conference from June 11 to 15. There Novotný makes it unmistakably clear that the party line of the Tenth Party Congress in 1954 is correct and needs no revision; that attacks on the party as a result of the Soviet Twentieth Party Congress are wrong and should stop; that students must not alienate themselves from the people or misuse the universities; that student manifestations are taken seriously by the régime as a direct threat and control measures are consequently being imposed; that "intrigues and aggressive plans of imperialist circles" in the form of hostile foreign radio broadcasts and leaflet activities, the introduction of agents into Czechoslovakia for acts of sabotage and diversion, hardly less apparent now than in Stalin's time, will continue to be opposed; that there will be *no* rehabilitation for Slánský, now accused of still further crimes so as to disassociate him from the connection with Tito; and that, while the campaign to remove the worst police excesses will continue, in fact, "at present there are no cases of the violation of socialist legality in investigation."[67]

Deputy Prime Minister Václav Kopecký complains of "certain particularly tendentious demands contained in the resolutions passed by university students ... Those university students who have allowed themselves to be led astray into resistance to lectures on Marxism-Leninism should understand that they have not fully understood their duty ..." He then leans on the old saw about the working class providing all the sums to maintain the universities and that students must realize that "conditions in this country have undergone a fundamental change ..."

> The bourgeoisie could admit of various interpretations of "academic liberties" ... But we want our universities ... to be a starting point for the diffusion of a maximum of learning to serve the requirements of the building of socialism ... For this very reason the universities must be tied to our life and our [communist] system as closely as possible.[68]

Later in the month, Minister Kahuda puts in a final word. He complains that the students who had demonstrated belong to a "classless" ideology (i.e., people who do not recognize the need for class struggle). He writes: "If we were to analyze the composition of the students who played a prominent part in the provocations, especially in the Majáles celebrations, we find that ... the most aggressive and incorrect expressions came from students in the third year, who came to the universities at a time when we had relaxed requirements of class selection.[69] ... It is our sincere desire to understand the errors which could have been committed in relation to misguided youth, and we shall be satisfied if we are not forced to use administrative solutions [i.e., firings and arrests] in individual cases. However, in ideological questions we shall take ... an uncompromising stand ..."[70]

Those beholden to the discipline of the Communist Party are incapable of seeing—or unwilling to see—reality as these bright, idealistic, naive students see it. "We didn't intend to make any sort of organized resistance against the Communist régime," recalls Heyrovský. "We just thought we should be ... trying to improve conditions in this country. We wanted to say how we would like to do it ... We were naive at that time. That is how the

Communists easily suppressed our ambitions."[71] Indeed, with all of the power of a police state and total control of the media, the régime has little difficulty in snuffing out this student rebellion and making it seem as though it has never happened.

And yet, those resolutions do not just vanish into thin air. True, except for the instance in Bratislava, they are never published. But they are read in dormitories, in party headquarters, and in police stations all over the country and then filed away in secret files where some of them may remain to this day. The party studies them, not just to see where and how the students may be turned and exploited, but to see where the party *has* to give way if it is to maintain power and a semblance of credibility. "The Soviet flag has been withdrawn since last week from its special place of honor alongside the Czechoslovak flag over public buildings in this capital for the first time since the Communists assumed power in 1948," reports Sidney Gruson to *The New York Times* on June 4. As late as September, a student magazine from May with a two-page supplement containing the main student demands, plus many privately taken pictures of the Majáles, are still being clandestinely circulated around Bohemia.[72] And there are surely tens of thousands of readers who secretly agree with much of what these young people have dared to say.

CHAPTER IV

Uprising in Poznań

Historical differences between the countries of east-central Europe are more numerous than their similarities. Poland, for example, ceased to exist on the European map for over a century and did not emerge again until 1918. During this time, despite the tri-part occupation of the Russian, Prussian, and Austrian empires, the Roman Catholic Church kept the standard of Polish language, culture and nationhood effectively flying. As a result, when the nation did reappear, the Poles had a high regard for the Roman Catholic Church unmatched by any other East European country.

Simularly, the Polish Communist Party's history differs from all others. Poles fought against Nazi Germany, both inside Poland and on many fronts in Europe, for longer than the citizens of any other country in Europe. They paid a fearful price in casualties: far higher per capita than that of Nazi Germany or Soviet Russia. One out of every six Poles was killed. And the ratio for Polish communists was even more drastic. Some died in the fighting, others by execution, and still others in the death camps.

Stalin had already wiped out much of the Polish party leadership in the Moscow show trials of the late 1930s. Thus, when the Second World War erupted only a small number remained. A few of these managed to flee the Nazi invasion and, in many cases, took on the insurance of Soviet citizenship. The result was that by the war's end in 1945 the Polish party was particularly depleted, and those leaders who had spent the war safely in Moscow were badly out of touch with those who had survived the devastation of six years in the underground fighting the Germans. It was inevitable that those in Poland preferred their underground leaders to the imports from Moscow. Władysław Gomułka, who had escaped Stalin's purges by being in a Polish jail at the time, thereby emerged as the party leader. Stalin, who doubtless would have preferred one of his own choosing, had to accept Gomułka—at least for the time being.

Under Gomułka the Polish Communist Party was neither so indecisive nor so unpopular as it later became. In the years just after the war it attracted a number of idealists, young and old, who saw in communism the hope of the future. Many of these were Poles who had survived the Nazi death camps. In the case of those few Polish Jews who had survived, it was not just the camps but postwar pogroms (for, shockingly, there had been a few of these) that had persuaded them to opt for communism. Many found jobs and dignity in the Communist Party, and a few found revenge in the communist terror that was to come. By early 1948 the communists, with the full backing of the Soviet occupation forces, had forced the left-wing branch of the much larger Socialist Party to merge into a new party totally dominated by them. The party had reached the height of its prestige. It was then that Józef Cyrankiewicz, who had helped to arrange the subversion of his own Socialist Party, became premier of the country and Władysław Gomułka became party first secretary.

As soon as he could, however, Stalin got rid of Gomułka. The ostensible reason was Tito's expulsion from the newly created Cominform for trying to lead Yugoslavia on its own road to socialism instead of following the Soviet model. Stalin took advantage of this to accuse all East European party leaders who had shown any signs of independence or nationalism of the new heresy of "Titoism" and all of the unspeakable crimes, like spying for the CIA, that went with it. Once purged from their posts, these nationalists were quickly arrested and frequently tried and executed. But in Poland the party was already so weak and Gomułka himself so strong-willed, that although he was accused and arrested, he was never actually brought to trial. Instead he was imprisoned and tortured.

Gomułka's replacement was Bolesław Bierut, a man totally subservient to Moscow, who simply carried out Stalin's orders to make everything in Poland follow the Soviet model. It was a program that impoverished the country even as it built up heavy industry and transformed peasants into industrial workers.

All did not go as smoothly as it appeared. In 1951, unknown to the outside world and to most of the people in Poland, the coal miners of the Dąbrowa mining district in Silesia refused to work when saddled with greatly increased production norms. This brought worried government and party officials running to the scene. Only after three days of turmoil was the strike quashed and all the leaders arrested.[1] Then, a year after Stalin's death the Polish party received a blow from which it never recovered.[2] In March 1954 a former lieutenant colonel in the Polish secret police, Józef Światło, began a series of broadcasts to Poland over Radio Free Europe in Munich, West Germany. He had quietly defected while in West Berlin the previous December.

There was nothing that Światło did not know about the scandalous behavior, not just of high police officials, but of high party officials. He had been in on the interrogation of Gomułka, and he told his Polish listeners that the accusations against Gomułka were totally false. In addition he told how well Gomułka had stood up to the torture; he had refused to admit anything.

Secrecy was the key to the party's domination of Poland, just as secrecy was the key to the party élite's control over the rest of the party. When Światło revealed not only how the system of terror worked, but also who had what on whom and cited the juicy details in broadcast after broadcast, the party's hold on the country and on its own unity was severely weakened.

The broadcasts set off an explosive chain reaction in the security apparatus culminating, at the January 1955 Third Party Plenum, in the firing of Światło's old boss, Minister Stanisław Radkiewicz. Radkiewicz was first sent to be minister of state farms and then, as the revelations became more widely known around the country, was expelled from one post after another. The reorganized ministry became the Committee on Public Security. One report, printed long after the plenum, in referring to this reorganization, admitted that "many innocent people [had been] held in prison without justification" and "there [had been] cases of using shameful and infamous methods of investigation."

By 1956 living standards all over Poland were still well below the 1939 level. The real value of wages had reached 67% of the 1939 level only the previous year. The lowest 30% of Polish workers lived on the margin of survival. Nearly every working family in Poznań had at least one relative close to starvation. Prices of food and other essentials regularly increased faster than wages—it was planned that way so that the government could gain more money. Agricultural output was always "below plan," food shortages were pervasive, and the average number of years a worker had to wait for decent housing had reached, by 1956, eight years. The workers had no recourse through their trade unions because the trade unions—as in the Soviet Union—had become completely subverted by the Communist Party and now were nothing but one-way transmission belts from management to the factory floor.

But times had actually been worse than in June 1956. During the last years of Stalin—1950 to 1953—the country had been ruthlessly exploited by the Soviets. The head of the party, Władysław Gomułka, and the head of the Church, Cardinal Wyszyński, were both under arrest and terror had ruled the land. Under the pressure generated by the system of terror, people in all walks of life had cracked. These individuals had finally compromised and agreed to work with the obsequious secret police (UB), agreeing to spy on their neighbors in return for some favor which gave them some extra sustenance or promise of security. And the Russians, never popular in Poland, had, by their cruel overlordship, come to be hated as much as the Nazis had been. Stalin and his Polish henchmen so feared and hated the West that for a Pole just to have been a member of the Home Army (A.K.) during the War or fought with Anders's Polish Army Corps in the west was to be treated like a common criminal and to have things like education, jobs, or any privileges denied him. The Church was savagely persecuted, with many priests falsely arrested and put to death.

Since Stalin's death, however, things had gradually gotten a bit better. By 1955 the hated "yellow curtain shops"—special shops all over Poland where party members, government officials, and secret police collaborators could buy food and luxury items not available to the general public—had disappeared, at least from public view, and some of these items were now available on the general market, though at prices most people could not afford. In the past year there had been a slight increase in the standard of living and a general relaxation from the previous strident tone of the government. Some of the press had become quite readable and interesting. There was a lot of party talk about a "Polish road to socialism" and "fresh beginnings." But to the average bitter Pole, who was staunchly anticommunist, all of this talk in the press and government was still a lot of hot air. The party, the Russians, and the secret police were all still there. So were the shortages and the everyday lies.

Now, in the wake of Khrushchev's secret speech, the party was undergoing even greater turmoil. It turned out that much of what they had been trying to build in Poland had been based upon Soviet lies; the great Soviet leader of the world's communists turned out to have been a monster. And even before these revelations had reached Poland, news arrived that First Party Secretary Bierut, who had stayed on in Moscow after the Twentieth Party Congress ended, had suddenly and mysteriously died there on March 12. Bierut had not been all that popular in Poland, but this news unleashed a wave of national suspicion among Poles, and there had been cries of "Down with his Soviet murderers!" at his funeral in Warsaw four days later.

The hastily called plenum of the Polish Central Committee had revealed a deep split between conservatives backing Zenon Nowak and liberals backing Roman Zambrowski, a prewar communist. Against all protocol, Khrushchev had insisted on attending the meeting and pushing the candidacy of Moscow-oriented and anti-Semitic Nowak, unaware that even Polish communists do not relish being lectured to on their own territory by a Russian.[*] The result was a compromise candidate, Edward Ochab, a colorless apparatchik.

Because he kept changing his mind, few knew where Ochab stood. He had inherited a party whose leadership was split down the middle and whose vast membership was demoralized both by Khrushchev's revelations about Stalin and by the dismal economic state of the country. And one did not have to be a party member to be demoralized about the state of the country. Nearly everyone outside the party blamed the government (read "party") for the dismal conditions that prevailed. But it was the secret police (UB) for which people reserved their real hatred. It was a hatred based upon personal experience, theirs or that of close friends or relatives, just as hatred of the Russians was based on living memory and not just on the long history of animosity between the Polish and Russian peoples. In the case of the Russians, there were many Poles still alive who had fought, or remembered the fighting,

---

[*] It was recently discovered (see *Cold War International History Project Bulletin*, issue 10, March 1998, pp. 44-49) that Khrushchev gave a second "secret speech" at this Polish plenum, just a month after his famous secret speech before the Twentieth Party Congress in Moscow. This, too, was devoted entirely to Stalin and why Khrushchev had felt it necessary to denounce him. Speaking probably from notes rather than from a prepared text as he had in Moscow, his remarks were an almost incoherent mishmash of revelations and excuses including such things as the current leadership's belief that the war would have ended much sooner with much less loss of life had Stalin been deposed after the Nazi invasion and that had Stalin lived a few more months he might well have started World War III. But it also indicates Khrushchev's suspicion that he himself may have gone too far and that it was already time to put on the brakes.

Speaking of the de-Stalinization process now under way, Khruschev says: "We ourselves aren't guaranteeing that mistakes won't be made ... We also arrested people and will probably make arrests in the future. I think that you'll also have to do this. But, if you now become liberals, and look at everybody and pat everybody on the back, then these enemies will bite your hands off. We have such enemies and you have them. You probably have more enemies, because you're younger than we are, and we destroyed more, and you're closer to them. So I think even in the future mistakes are possible ... When I worked in the Ukraine we destroyed not one, but many of our enemies using the hands of our enemies ... We forged some documents. We would place them surreptitiously everywhere ... [We] arrested them, tortured them, and hung them. But, you'll say, this is cruel. But comrades, we're fighting with the enemy. Is this method with enemies allowed? I think it allowable. Will we give it up now? I, for example, won't refuse to use it, if it's used to destroy the enemy ... If we are going to be cowardly, it means we are cowards."

against the invading Red Army on Polish territory in the 1920s. Still more remembered the backstabbing invasion and occupation by the Soviet army on September 17, 1939, while Poles were in the midst of desperately fighting the invading Germans. Shortly after the 1939 "partition," over a million Polish families from all walks of life were deported to Siberia, many of whom died there and some of whom were not able to return to Poland until the mid-1950s. Still more remembered how in the summer of 1944 the Soviet army, now pursuing the Wehrmacht and having reached the east bank of the Vistula and liberated that part of Warsaw known as Praga, sat there and watched for sixty-three days while the Nazis on the other side of the Vistula slowly crushed the Warsaw Uprising of the Polish Home Army. This uprising, in fact, had been encouraged by the Soviets, who then did nothing to support it and even prevented Allied air support. When the Nazis finally succeeded in forcing the remnants of the starving insurgents to surrender, the Russians still did nothing to prevent the German army's savage dynamiting, on Hitler's orders, of the Polish capital, block by block, until it was totally destroyed. The peoples's hatred of Russians in general, however, bore little resemblance to their hatred of the secret police, whose midnight arrests and torturings were still fresh in people's minds.

The Światło revelations over Radio Free Europe had confirmed people's experiences and suspicions of the régime and its secret police, but they had not emboldened any action from below, for nothing much had changed and fear still permeated the country. It took the physical presence of people from the West to trigger the first real action against the régime. This occurred when the World Youth Festival was held in Warsaw in the summer of 1955. Not all the young people from the West were communists, and even those who were, were somehow different. Most were there to have a good time and they were open and candid about it. Moreover, the things they revealed about their respective countries went directly counter to what the régime propaganda had been saying. Within a week of their departure from Poland and before the spell of those days had worn off, a communist poet, Adam Ważyk, published his "Poem for Adults," in the party's weekly cultural magazine, *Nowa Kultura*. This poem, which raised many subjects that had hitherto been taboo, caused a sensation and led, later that year, to a flowering of literature critical of the régime as well as a revolt in the party-controlled Writers' Union. This, in turn, had helped to give birth to an extraordinarily outspoken student magazine, *Po Prostu*, which carried article after article exposing waste, corruption, and hypocrisy in every imaginable field and yet, since the writers were young—in fact, idealistic, believing communists—they always suggested that there was a "socialist" solution to each of these ills. The workers of Poznań neither read nor had heard of *Po Prostu;* nevertheless, the latter helped to develop a climate in which people who had long been fed up finally spoke out.

Worker unrest and brief work stoppages occurred all over Poland in the spring of 1956, but there were sound historical reasons why an eruption should occur in Poznań.

Poznań is one of the oldest cities in Poland, indeed its cathedral, founded in A.D. 968, is the oldest in the country. Once at the heart of the city, the cathedral sits on an island of the Warta River, which splits the city south to north, on an open green space that almost suggests countryside. Many centuries ago, as Pożnań grew from a provincial market town to a medieval city, its center shifted west, leaving the cathedral to itself. The city lies on the Polish plain halfway between the Sudeten Mountains to the south and the Baltic Sea to the north and, on an east-west axis, half way between Warsaw and Berlin. It is connected by rail, road, and air with all other major Polish cities. Though largely destroyed by the Swedish wars of the mid-seventeenth century, Poznań managed to rebuild and even flourish during the 123 years of Prussian occupation, particularly after German unification in 1871. Though the Germans did their best to colonize it and make it into a Germany city, Poznań (Posen) remained fiercely Polish throughout the century of Poland's disappearance from the map of Europe, as well as when Nazi Germany tried to absorb it into the Greater Reich during nearly six years of occupation in World War II. The most Western Polish city in style as well as geography, Poznań became the center not only for heavy industry in the nineteenth century but for international trade in the twentieth century, beginning its famous international trade fairs in 1921, just three years after Poland's newly acquired independence. Partially destroyed in World War II, the city had been completely rebuilt by 1956, though sloppy masonry betrayed which buildings had been rebuilt or added to, and which predated the war. The city retained its many open spaces and no building was higher than five or six stories. The monotonous dark red brick of its industrial suburbs gave way to lighter stuccoed buildings near the center. And the center holds Poznań's four distinctive features. First, there is an old town square, not unlike Cracow's; next is a massive Prussian stone palace on the central square, then known as Stalin Square and today once again as Freedom Square. The central railroad station, resembling a square box atop a long box, is sunk below the level of the city, and rising just above it to the west is the sharply contrasting white, modernistic buildings of the International Trade Fair grounds, dominated by the round central hall with its continuous row of glass windows and conical tower giving the effect of an enormous superstructure of some futuristic ocean liner. In 1956, Poznań, with its disciplined, largely working class population of about 350,000, was considered to be the vanguard city of communist Poland.

But precisely because of its disciplined and proud workers, the population of Poznań felt the injustices of the communist system that much more deeply. This was particularly so in the largest industrial enterprise in Poznań, the Hipolit Cegielski Machine Industry Works—renamed Joseph Stalin Factory of Poznań in 1949 and thus known in 1956 by its Polish acronym: ZISPO. Every type of ship engine, locomotive, and railroad car was (and still is) manufactured here as well as a variety of machine tools and metal products. The quality of its products was known throughout Europe. While discontent was rife throughout the 15,000-worker plant, those in one section of about 3,000 workers, known as W-3, which produced railroad cars, felt particularly aggrieved.

The first collective protest at W-3 had been a silent demonstration in the traverser hall back in September 1954. Since that time the workers grievances had snowballed.[3] The response from management, government, and the Communist Party, however, had been consistently evasive and minimal. The previous November the workers had discovered that management had improperly overtaxed 5,074 workers a total of 11 million zlotys, which worked out to approximately two months' wages annually for each worker involved. Complaints of shockingly bad working conditions, foul air, cramped space, unsafe equipment were rampant. Worst of all, the workers of W-3 paid a terrible price in accidents because of what was known as "storming." Because they had a monthly quota and were paid in accordance with how well they met that quota, and because for the first twenty days of every month there was virtually no material, due to late shipments and no inventory to work with, they found themselves working frantically twelve to sixteen hours a day for the last ten days of every month to meet the quota. In order to keep up the frantic pace, protective shields, which got in the way of fast production, had to be removed. If they were not, the pay packet would be even less than the previous month. There had been more serious accidents in the first five months of 1956 than in the whole of the previous year. Monthly earnings in this period had fallen 6.7 percent. By February more than 4,700 petitions had been submitted to management—all of them unanswered. And that is what rankled most: no one listened; no one ever answered.

Throughout May and June representatives of the workers had met with one layer after another of trade union and party functionaries in the sections, the plant, and the city of Poznań until it became clear that no action would be taken until the word was given in Warsaw—hence this last desperate delega-

94

tion. It was, in fact, the fourth delegation from ZISPO to Warsaw in the space of eight months and everyone felt it had to be the last.

The delegation, which consisted of seventeen workers and a dozen officials from top management, had left Poznań for Warsaw by train on the night of June 24. The next morning the secretary of the Board of Metal Workers Trade Unions fed them a hearty breakfast at the union's headquarters before taking them to the Ministry of Machine Industry where talks with Minister Roman Fidelski went on from 11 A.M. to 7 P.M. There was an initial attempt to intimidate the workers and interspersed among them were "some strangers who never spoke" but had ominous bulges in their pockets. Party officials threatened, "If you strike you will get tanks."

But the workers stood their ground. Seeing they were not in the slightest subdued, Fidelski heard them out and finally ended the heated discussion by giving in to most of their demands. In his summary, Fidelski agreed that all workers owed improperly collected taxes over the past three years would get them repaid within three months; all those who had been denied their rightful bonuses would get them; the ministry would eliminate late shipments of materials, and workers demands on the calculation of contract work pay would be met. "Fine," said the delegation, in effect, "now to prove you are serious; come to Poznań and spell this out clearly to the work force at a mass meeting." Consternation broke out among the party officials at such a bold reply, but Fidelski was determined to avoid a strike, so he agreed, as a gesture to restoring peace at ZISPO, that he would address the workers and that the meeting would continue in Poznań the next day. The worker section of the delegation then boarded the night train for Poznań convinced that they had won a significant victory.

The next day the meeting continued in Poznań, but Fidelski's summary of what had been agreed upon was less than the delegation remembered, and all sorts of bureaucratic excuses for not revising the wage system were put forward. Fidelski himself had gone to W-3 to confront the workers. After he had presented his "corrected" version of what had been agreed upon, a number of disappointed, irritated workers had taken the floor, accusing Fidelski of belittling their statements and insulting them. They accused him of not believing in their threat of a strike and of just stalling to push the confrontation past the date of June 30 when the Twenty-Fifth International Poznań Trade Fair would close. To take some of the sting out of his tough new position, Fidelski promised that he would call upon their delegation when it came to revising the wage calculations later that day, but he had ended his speech by yelling: "Things are not so bad—just get back to work!"

But when Fidelski met with the ZISPO management and party and trade union leaders over hors d'oeuvres and cognac that night to discuss the new wages calculations, the workers' delegation was refused entry. By 8 P.M., having waited in vain to be included in the talks, the last workers dispersed. They were now in a mood to strike.

A mile away at the Poznań Rolling Stock Repair Factory (ZNTK), Poznań's second largest factory, the mood was every bit as militant. Indeed, there had been several brief strikes there this spring, and only the previous day the first shift had struck and called a mass meeting demanding the appearance of the minister of transportation. The ministry was more worried about an explosion there than at Cegielski.

⌒

Thursday, June 26, 1956

Dawn is slowly coming over Poznań; though cool just now, it promises to be another warm day. Streetlights are still burning for it is only 5 A.M. and the traffic is light. Only occasional buses and streetcars rattle through the empty streets taking workers to the industrial parts of the city where most factories have been operating through the night. Over at the century-old Hipolit Cegielski Machine Industry Works—renamed Joseph Stalin Factory of Poznań in 1949 and now called by its Polish acronym, ZISPO—the third (that is, night) shift workers are breaking their routine.[4] Rather than head for the locker rooms to change their clothes, they remain at their machines waiting for their comrades of the first shift to arrive. The same phenomenon occurs in other units of the gigantic ZISPO complex which straddles Wilda Gorna Street, recently renamed Dzierżyński Street, after the first head of the Soviet secret police, a Pole by birth.

At 5:50 A.M. the first shift (day) workers, already in their overalls, are filtering through the idle night workers to their machines; but no one begins to work. In W-3, where railway cars are produced and one of the largest factories of the complex, the workers from both shifts, amidst low mutterings, pour into the traverser hall. A familiar voice calls out to them; it is bespectacled Edmund Taszer, chairman of W-3's Communist Party plant committee, in effect the chief watchdog of the section-level party watchdogs, a man with clout, but also sympathetic to the workers' plight.

"I cannot tell you the exact results of yesterday's meeting," he confesses, "but I can assure you that the talks are supposed to continue."

"Talks, talks talks!" someone shouts back. "We're sick of talks. They are just trying to pull the wool over our eyes."

Taszer, his spectacles steaming up, tries to answer but is drowned out by angry shouts. There is a stir at the other end of the room. Stanisław Matyja has arrived and a cheer goes up as he is noticed. Taszer tries to quiet the crowd, but they are no longer listening to him and turn their backs on him.

Matyja, a short man, who is a carpenter, is the workers' hero—and rightly so. For four months he had been quietly agitating within W-3 to get the authorities to listen to their innumerable grievances. He had fed so many specific grievances to Taszer that the latter had become a compiler of these grievances as well as a conduit to those higher up in the party and government. Matyja's persistence had resulted in delegations being sent several times to the Ministry of Machine Industry in Warsaw. The first of these had been in October 1955, and the latest had included both him and Taszer, a trip from which they had just returned. He is one of several non-party workers who had been elected to the delegation, but he is the real leader insofar as the rank and file are concerned.

Precisely at 6 A.M. the great siren signaling the beginning of the first work shift goes off. The several thousand workers in the traverser hall begin to leave. As the crowd exits into the open air it divides into groups headed for other divisions of Cegielski, where the majority of workers have been waiting to join them. First they pass by W-2, where diesel engines are made and W-8, the presswork factory, both across the street from W-3, then W-4 and W-5 where mechanical equipment is manufactured, and finally W-9 further along Dzierżyński Street. Each unit greatly swells their numbers as they march through the factory streets.

It is now fully daylight and, despite all the caps and berets, individual faces can now be made out. Bogdan Matyjas sets off the siren at a side gate, the actual signal for the strike to begin. But seeing what is going on and not wishing to cooperate, the man on duty at the electric works has locked himself inside his control booth. Twenty-eight-year-old locksmith Bogdan Marianowski climbs into the booth through an open window. He, too, is a party member and even a correspondent for the factory gazette, *On Stalinist Guard*, but he is in favor of the strike. He sets off the main siren, the signal to all workers inside the complex and workers in nearby factories that ZISPO, which everyone still calls Cegielski, is now on strike.

At 6:35 A.M. the main gate of the complex on the west side swings open and the crowd pushes out into Dzierżyński Street, turning right and north towards the center of the city, some two miles away. There is no plan, no obvious leaders, but already some workers are breaking out banners they have secreted for just such an occasion. Others are already busy working to remove the sign "Joseph Stalin Factory of Poznań" beside the main entrance. Before the last contingent of workers pour through the brick gates the sign is down.

By the factory hospital a car attempts to block the way. It is Jan Krabik, the generally respected technical director of the factory. The workers allow him to enter the management building and then flow on around his car. By the time they reach Traugutta Street at 6:45 A.M. the vanguard of the demonstrators is confronted by another car blocking the way. It is the first secretary of the regional Communist Party committee, Leon Stasiak, who, thanks to secret police informers within the factory, has known for days everything that has been going on among the workers of ZISPO. He harangues the crowd but gets only catcalls in return. It takes more than one man to stop twelve thousdand workers on the march. He is cursed and roughly thrown aside.

Someone begins to sing. It is a good place for it, for the street has become a manmade canyon with five-storey apartment houses on either side with no gaps between them. Others join in. The songs are religious and patriotic, long forbidden by the party, and everyone knows them and sings along. Interspersed between the songs sporadic slogans and shouts are heard. Some of these are picked up by the crowd until entire sections of several thousand people are chanting them. Banners and flags are now raised in all parts of the procession. Women watch and wave from apartment windows, and men standing on the sidewalks remove their hats in respect.

It is now 7:00 A.M. and the demonstration has turned down into Wildecki Square. By prior agreement one part splits off to the left and goes along Przemysłowa Street to Robocza Street. The other proceeds along Gwardia Ludowa Street. Robocza Street is the address of the Poznań Rolling Stock Repair Factory (ZNTK) where the workers have long been in communication with their colleagues at Cegielski. They too have frequently threatened to strike and only minutes before were being addressed in a mass meeting in Room 8 by the vice minister of transportation, Józef Popielas, who was desperately trying to prevent them from joining the demonstration. But the noise of the demonstration outside can be heard by the ZNTK workers, and at 7:20 the main gates to the factory complex are opened from within. Some Cegielski workers rush in and are greeted with shouts of welcome; within seconds the traffic is reversed and five thousand Rolling Stock Repair workers stream out of the gate, augmenting the demonstration.

In Warsaw, first secretary of the Communist Party, Edward Ochab, on hearing by phone that the ZISPO workers have taken to the streets, calls a meeting of the Central Committee for 10:00 A.M.[5] Now the workers march-

98

ing along Robocza Street are beginning to merge again with the other branch as they enter Marchlewski Street. New groups of workers are joining the parade at every intersection, particularly from the factories in the Łazarz and Górczyn sections west of the main rail line. Slogans no one would have dared to shout out yesterday are taken up and chanted by the crowd or hastily scrawled on signs and held up for citizens gathering on the sidewalks to see.

The head of the column now reaches a "T" and turns abruptly left onto Towarowa Street. Now the white pointed tower of the Great Hall of the Trade Fair rises before them. Like a flow of lava the crowd flows into several streets. One curves right along Towarowa Street until the great clock tower of the palace at Stalin (formerly "Freedom") Square comes into sight; the other pushes straight on as it crosses over the wide train station bridge to the main entrance of fair grounds of the international trade fair. A group of young people enters the fairgrounds shouting excitedly about the citywide demonstration. Several single out the Soviet flag flying in a row with dozens of other national flags, shinny up the pole, and remove it to the cheers of their comrades. But the fair is not the demonstrators' goal, and the leaders quickly call them back and head the demonstration along Roosevelt Street so that it can turn back across University Bridge toward Stalin Square in the city's center.

Across the Warta River, workers who heard the Cegielski siren and who have meanwhile received emissaries leave their plants and head in large groups toward the city's center. The main stream of demonstrators, meanwhile, again splits into two branches. One crosses Roosevelt Street and reaches the chief streetcar depot at Zwierzyniecka Street. The other keeps on toward Stalin Square. The City Transportation Enterprise workers have already beaten and doused their director with oil for opposing their walkout. Now some twelve hundred of them (a majority of them party members) stream out to join the demonstration. Across the city their colleagues already manning the streetcars (mostly women) are stopping them by prearrangement, asking their passengers to disembark, then locking and abandoning them and heading home or for Stalin Square. Streetcar traffic in the city is soon at a standstill. It is about eight o'clock and the sun, now well up in the sky, glows copper colored through the humid haze.

From the windows of the Paris Commune Clothing Industry Enterprise in Kraszewski Street women workers, who have been locked into their rooms by the management, call out their predicament to the passing demonstrators. Within a few minutes the main gates are broken open by the workers who then force the management to unlock all the rooms. The women, many in kerchiefs and jackets despite the warmth, joyfully join the hitherto largely male crowd. Now other workers arrive from the Kapszak Graphic Design

Enterprise, the Mechanical Equipment Production Enterprise, the Mechanical Equipment Factory, the State Cigarette Factory, the meatpacking plant, the brewery, and other small factories and workshops, stores and offices. Like a river taking in tributaries, the demonstration flows on.

In the painting shop on Szamarzewski Street four banners are hurriedly finished: "We want to eat!" "We demand bread!" "Down with the bloodsuckers!" "We demand more pay and lower prices!" These are not the specific demands of the Cegielski workers; no one has ordered these particular slogans; but they are typical of what is going through the people's minds.

Throughout the city Polish national flags are appearing; for once, no red flags are in evidence.

By 8:40 A.M. another column of demonstrators who have marched up Ratajczaka Street begins to pour into Stalin Square. They are mainly rubber and granary workers from the right bank of the Warta River whose route to the city center has been shorter. There are now over twenty thousand workers in the square and people are flowing in from all directions, not just factory workers now, but office workers, shopkeepers, teachers, students from the university and high schools and even some children from grade schools. These groups are easily distinguished from the workers, who are mostly in dark blue overalls, by their overcoats, neckties and occasional fedoras. A few foreign businessmen, having returned from the fairgrounds to fetch their cameras from their hotel rooms, are taking photographs. Even without cameras, their well-fitting, quality clothes make them stand out in the crowd. Rows of stalled trams line one side of the square. They are empty, but people are climbing up on them to get a better view.[6]

Some men and women who have been designated to keep order reveal Poznań's Prussian heritage with cries of "Don't walk on the grass!" But these commands are overwhelmed by growing shouts of "We want bread!" We demand freedom!" "Down with Bolshevism!" "Down with the red bourgeoisie!" "We demand lower prices!" and, of particular interest to the foreign businessmen, "We demand free elections under United Nations supervision!"

Once more the crowd takes up the old hymn "God, You Who have saved Poland ..." and the national anthem, "Poland is not yet lost," but now thousands, not hundreds, are singing. Except for those whose families take them to church, the students are hearing these hymns for the first time, for it is the first time in nine years they have been sung in public. A feeling of joy and tremendous solidarity runs through the crowd. Everywhere people are smiling and tears are streaming. Across the square a newly arrived group begins to chant "We want Cyrankiewicz!" (the country's premier). Another answers "Let's go to Frąckowiak" (Poznań's mayor). Nobody moves; people are streaming into the square from all directions. The crowd has now reached fifty thousand. Some of the new arrivals are passers-by or Poles from other parts of the country who have come to Poznań for the fair, but the majority continue to be workers.

One group of about a thousand coming from the northeast pass in front of the prison on Młyńska Street … A chant goes up: "Release innocent prisoners!" People bang various objects against the iron gates, but these are locked and there seems to be no way of forcing them. Inside, the prison director, Jan Lewandowski, unable to get a direct phone line to Warsaw, has to go through the county police headquarters. His instructions from Warsaw are clear: "Do not shoot. There are no dangerous criminals among your prisoners." Outside the group decides to move on to the main demonstration in Stalin Square.

All rail activity has now come to a halt and workers in the main station cease working. Those manning newspaper kiosks close, lock them, and leave. Throughout the city, Communist Party membership cards are being thrown away, torn up, or burned. Non-party citizens have a different reaction: they line up in front of grocery stores; whatever the outcome, they know there will be food shortages.

As he drives from the Wielkopolski Hotel to the fairgrounds, Knut Breda, director of the Norwegian Import-Export Company A/S IMKO, marvels at the orderliness of the marchers and the complete absence of police.[7]

Back in the square the black iron hands of the huge clock on the palace's tower shows ten minutes after nine. The palace, a massive building of rough-hewn brown stone, is a legacy of Poznań's Prussian past. Built just before the turn of the century to be a palace for the kaiser, it never actually served that purpose. Today it serves as Poznań's town hall and holds the city administration. Mayor Franciszek Frąckowiak now comes out of the building and the crowd suddenly presses around him. Frąckowiak realizes he cannot hold a conversation with so many people, so he asks that a delegation be sent in to see him.

Unfortunately, none of the demonstration's organizers are within shouting distance. A few natural leaders step out of the crowd, one of them a lively polytechnic student named Tadeusz Bieniek. Soon a delegation of about fifteen persons goes with Frąckowiak to his office. On the way they decide to make a single demand: either Prime Minister Józef Cyrankiewicz or First Party Secretary Edward Ochab must fly to Poznań immediately. They have learned the uselessness of trying to deal with anyone but the top authorities.

Frackowkiak does not call Warsaw. He calls the party county committee in its new building only thirty meters away. First Secretary Leon Stasiak is not there, but Wincenty Krasko, secretary for propaganda, and a few others

Five pictures taken by a German businessman from his hotel window. The first is taken about 8:30 A.M., the second about 9:15, the third about 10:00, the fourth about 2:00 P.M., and the fifth about 3:30 to 4:00 P.M. The first picture, 8:30 A.M.

The second picture, 9:15 A.M.

The third picture, about 10:00 A.M.

The fourth picture, about 2:00 P.M. Note the smoke at the far end of the street.

The fifth picture, about 4:00 P.M.

are. Everyone else has been sent out onto the square to speak up for the party. The delegation demands of Krasko that he bring either Premier Cyrankiewicz or Party Secretary Ochab to Poznań within half an hour. Meanwhile, part of the crowd has already entered the palace and is raging through it. City council employees leave their offices, and the demonstrators put out a white flag from one of the palace's windows to indicate that the authorities have surrendered to the people. Others clamber out onto the conical roof of the tower and raise the national flag on the flagpole jutting out of its center. A cheer rises from the square as the flag reaches the top of the long pole.

The sun, now breaking through the haze, casts sharp shadows on the cobblestones of the square.

Young Tadeusz Bieniek is a party member and a leader of the Polish Youth Association, but he doesn't trust Mayor Frąckowiak. He insists on leading the delegation to party headquarters one block away so that they can have a direct conversation with Wincenty Krasko. They find him without difficulty in the nearly deserted modern glass and steel structure and once again demand that Cyrankiewicz make an immediate appearance in Poznań. The crowd, says Bieniek, is getting restless. They need to be addressed by someone in authority. Krasko is finally persuaded to go outside to speak to the demonstrators, at least those who are outside of the party headquarters. Bieniek then climbs up on a nearby truck and announces to the crowd that the del-

104

Demonstrators raise the Polish flag over the castle (town hall) early in the day.
Wide World Photos.

egation's talks with Mayor Frąckowiak have been fruitless, but that Wincenty Krasko, the highest party official they can find, has agreed to address them.

Krasko begins his address, but without amplification his voice doesn't carry and people soon give up trying to hear him. After a while he gives up and goes back into the party building.

Meanwhile, three trucks arrive but are stopped in the middle of the square by the crowd. Under the tarpaulin of each are armed militiamen who have been called by Krasko to come and defend the party building. As the crowd peers in, a cry goes up "It's the militia! The militia are with us!" They insist the militia get out of the stalled trucks, but the atmosphere is friendly. Nobody attempts to disarm them and, after their initial fear, they make their way to the party building and disappear into it. Young workers in the crowd, however, take a precaution; they let the air out of the truck tires.

All morning long the vice minister of internal affairs, Ryszard Dobieszak, has been making calls from his office in Warsaw to various militia contingents in the Poznań area prohibiting the use of arms.

Now the head of the civic militia in Poznań, Major Tadeusz Pietrzak, arrives on the scene accompanied by high officers of the civic militia. He has a booming voice and has no trouble being heard, but the people do not care for what he is saying. Two workers from the Butchery Company, still in their bloodied leather aprons, jump up on the platform from which he is speaking; one of them punches him in the face. At that his fellow officers desert him and disperse as quickly as they can into the crowd, removing their conspicuous military caps as they do.

A large group now enters the party headquarters, disarming the newly arrived militia as they come in. Not far away in the square a very unhappy Major Popeda, leader of the three truckloads of militia, is being tossed high into the air amid shouts of "The militia are with us! The militia are with us!"

While this is going on, a group of demonstrators some blocks away at 77 Kościuszki Street take possession of a radio car in front of the County Communications Bureau. This car, with a loudspeaker on top, is driven to the square and parked at the base of the palace's massive stone clock tower. Members of the crowd are invited to say a few words to their fellow citizens, and soon the speaker is in full use with teachers addressing fellow teachers, students addressing students, but most of those who speak do so in slogans and not very clearly.

Tadeusz Bieniek has not given up on getting his man to speak. He leads Wincenty Krasko to the radio car so that Krasko can address the crowd, which has now grown to nearly one hundred thousand. Unfortunately Krasko is incapable to speaking straight Polish. He speaks in bureaucratic party lingo and tries to use this opportunity to make propaganda. He says that the governmental delegation is "already on its way," but among other things he denies that a worker named Rutkowski has been arrested yesterday at ZNTK. Unfortunately for him, there are ZNTK workers right there who witnessed the arrest, so boos and whistles put an end to his harangue.

News of Rutkowski's arrest spreads like wildfire through the crowd. By the time it has reached the periphery, however, it is no longer Rutkowski but the Cegielski delegation to Warsaw that has been allegedly arrested. When they hear this rumor, individual members of that delegation try to assure people near them that no one has been arrested, but to no avail. The crowd is getting angry. Krasko finds himself being pulled out of the radio car and roughed up. He is saved from further humiliation by some workers from the Stomil Rubber Works and Cegielski who pull off those who are molesting him and escort him through the crowd to safety.

Stanisław Matyja, the Cegielski worker who has done more than anyone to bring about this demonstration, has the radio car moved to a spot near the university auditorium. He then speaks to the crowd over its loudspeaker asking them to choose representatives for the talks that are to be held with the government delegation which Krasko had claimed is on its way.

At the far end of the square an even larger group invades the party headquarters building. Stefania Gocwińska, a nurse, has brought some hand-painted signs into the building. They read "Freedom" and "Bread." These she places in windows on the third floor and roof facing out on the square. Foreign businessmen soon are taking pictures of them. On the outside wall, somebody writes in large letters: "House for rent." Inside, some demonstrators turn a bust of Lenin to the wall. Desk drawers are pulled open and papers are thrown about, but little damage is done to the office equipment.

The crowd, still growing, has been standing in the square now for well over an hour without anyone in authority making a real attempt to address their complaints.

The authorities have known for days that such a demonstration was a distinct possibility. As early as June 23, Col. Antoni Filipowicz, commanding officer of the Officers School of Army Armored and Mechanized Forces in Poznań, had told his assembled officer candidates that worker street demonstrations were to be expected. Even First Party Secretary Edward Ochab off in Warsaw had been monitoring the situation. Only the previous night he had assured a high-ranking delegation of Committee on Public Security officials on the eve of their departure that they should go ahead to their meeting in

Hand-painted signs in the windows of the Communist Party building read "*Chleba*" (Bread) and "*Wolnosc*" (Freedom). Purchased by the author from a German businessman.

Student and worker demonstrators carry the bloodied Polish flag past the main building of
the Poznań International Fair. Purchased by the author from a German businessman.

Moscow, "because there are no signs that the situation in Poznań is getting
complicated."

In Warsaw, Marshal Konstanty Rokossowsky, Polish minister of
defense, who is also a Soviet citizen, first phones and then visits First Secretary Ochab some minutes before the Central Committee is to meet. "The situation in Poznań," he says, "is not good. The militia and the army may not be
enough to handle it." He requests freedom of action to contain the situation,
including the use of armed force. Ochab agrees and gives it to him, but says
he will have to get the politburo to approve this action ... retroactively.[8]

It is now ten o'clock and the crowd in Stalin Square is becoming more
and more impatient. No one can confirm whether or not Premier Cyrankiewicz has arrived and more and more people are convinced that the worker
delegation which had gone to Warsaw two days before had been arrested on
their return to Poznań. People speaking from the radio car become more and
more impassioned. Some call for freeing the "imprisoned delegates," others
condemn the jamming of radio broadcasts from the West, and soon there are
cries of "Let's go to Młyńska Prison to free our brothers!" "Let's go to the

Spider's Web!" (their name for the secret police headquarters), "Let's go to Kochanowski Street to free the prisoners!"

Within minutes the pent up frustration of the crowd is dissipated as large sections of it break off to accomplish these spontaneously articulated goals. One group of several thousand led by the radio car heads northeast to Młyńska Prison, another northwest to secret police headquarters at Kochanowski Street, and a third breaks off at the insurance building at the intersection of Dąbrowski and Mickiewicz streets where the radio jammer is known to be housed. A fourth group carrying black banners heads southwest in the direction of the international fair grounds.

The remains of radio jamming equipment of the sidewalk of Dąbrowski Street at the intersection of Mickiewicz Street. Purchased by the author from a German businessman.

In Warsaw the hastily called meeting of the Central Committee's politburo is just getting under way.

The demonstrators led by the radio car stop in front of the Bazar Hotel where many foreign businessmen are staying. They call attention to their presence by singing in unison "God, who saved Poland," then, after expressing their demands, the radio car announces: "We are going to Młyńska Street to free our fathers and brothers ..."

Meanwhile, those who had headed for the Insurance building, having already penetrated the premises, are happily heaving great sections of jamming equipment from the seventh-floor windows. Cheers go up from the crowd as each piece smashes into the pavement below. The last to come hurtling down is the antenna torn from the roof.

Not far away the first group of about five hundred people turn from Dąbrowski Street down Kochanowski Street and arrive in front of the UB (secret police) building about 10:15 A.M. Occupying the middle section of the west side of the street, this four-storey, stucco building with many evenly spaced, white-framed windows is well known to all Poznań citizens.

The former UB building on Kochanowski Street, as it exists today (2001).
Taken by the author.

One section of the demonstrators is led by women streetcar drivers carrying banners. Another consists of schoolchildren led by their teachers. The latter group had been marching to Poznańska Street when they turned around to join those headed toward Kochanowski Street. The officer in command of the UB building, Lt. Col. Feliks Dwojak, has already given the order to barricade the main door. (Permanent cross-guard barriers have long stood at either end of the sidewalk in front of the building.) Some minutes before the crowd arrived, a platoon from the Tenth Regiment of the Army Security Corps had come to reinforce the building, taking over the second floor. Since young employees of the security forces had arrived still earlier to defend the building, this makes for quite a crowd, and two or three faces can be seen staring warily out of each of the building's many windows.

The crowd is convinced that members of the worker delegation are being held prisoner in the UB building. Many in the crowd are familiar with the interior of the UB building, particularly its cellars. They had been arrested for trivial or possibly never explained reasons and then tortured and interrogated for days and nights without end to get them to sign totally bogus confessions. Few had been able to withstand it.

Now a delegation emerges from the crowd and approaches the door of the building. But the latter is barricaded, and they cannot open it. Angry shouts burst out: "Let our delegates in!" "Down with the servants of Bolshevism!"

Suddenly several windows on the ground floor of the UB building screech open and fire hoses point out at the crowd. An explosion of water streams out soaking the first ranks of the crowd and causing people to fall back in confusion. Even before the hoses are turned off rocks begin to fly from the crowd at the UB building. There is a more than ample supply of these because the sidewalks on both sides of the street are paved with small basalt stones easily pried out with a knife. In the first salvo of rocks one of the guards by the main entrance is hit in the eye. His cry of anguish cannot be heard above the roar of the crowd, but the spurt of blood and his collapse can be seen.

The firehoses are withdrawn from the ground-floor windows, but quickly appear out of the windows on the second floor. The streams of water do not reach quite as far due to reduced water pressure, but fewer rocks reach the second-floor windows. Orders from Warsaw still forbid any use of firearms. It is now 10:40 A.M.

Over at the Młyńska Street Prison the guards in the outside booths behave passively; they too have orders not to shoot. The prison director, Lewandowski, appears in a window and conducts talks with a "committee" of demonstrators, but they are not allowed into the building. After this conversation Lewandowski goes back to his now open phone line to the Ministry of the Interior in Warsaw to await orders. He is told not to resist, even if the demonstrators break into the prison. Many demonstrators, meanwhile, are searching through nearby buildings for hammers and crowbars with which to break down the main prison gate. The guards open several fire hydrants to

The corner of the UB building on Kochanowski Street the day after it was attacked. Associated Press.

spray the crowd, attempting to keep them at bay. Heedless of this, the crowd storms the gate—in vain. The heavy doors do not budge. Unseen by the guards, several youths have managed to scale the wall, however, and within minutes the gates are opened from within and the crowd surges forward. Led by former inmates who know the interior layout all too well, the crowd quickly disarms the guards, locates keys and frees all 257 prisoners. All but five, who stubbornly refuse to leave their cells, rush out into the courtyard and thence into Młyńska Street. Some demonstrators take over part of the weapons, a few of which are freely handed over by the guards. Others take delight in toppling and burning the prison van popularly known as "the Bitch." As one of the freed prisoners reaches the street, he recognizes a young woman in the crowd who had nursed him in the hospital not long before. "Thank you, sister," he says running to her side, "for saving us," and gives her a big hug. Nurse Aleksandra Banasiak is embarrassed. She had done nothing but observe what was going on from the sidewalk. Though it is her day off, she decides to return to her hospital.[9]

Just as the main body of prisoners is pouring out into the street to mingle with the crowd, there is a burst of machine-gun fire. No one knows where it comes from, but Stefania Owsianna, a twenty-year-old milk bar cashier, falls to the ground, her thigh and shin bleeding profusely. Two young people carry her into the vestibule of the courthouse. Worried at her great loss of blood, they call for an ambulance. None arrives, but after quite a while a car from one of the Poznań fair exhibitors appears and takes her off to the hospital on Szkolna Street. Miss Owsianna has by this time lost consciousness.

Word of the shooting has reached the radio car parked in front of the hotel "Bazar." In no time the news is being blared to the crowd outside the hotel and everyone is urged to go to the prison to avenge this outrage.

Now the crowd re-enters the prison and begins to plunder it. The court-house next door is also invaded, and judges and prosecutors flee as their robes as well as innumerable court files and police records are heaved out of the windows onto the street. The dossiers are not only of prisoners but of many innocent people who had been spied on. Bonfires are started to the chants of "Freedom from police spies!" and "Freedom from the party!" The court usher is able to prevent the crowd from destroying the real estate regis-ters, but it is too late to save anything else. The acrid smoke quickly drifts to other parts of the city; the blackened piles will smolder for hours.

As the crowd moves off to return to Stalin Square, forty soldiers from the Army Security Corps arrive on the scene, but they are too late. The last "looter" has left the buildings as the soldiers take up positions in the adminis-trative part of the prison.

Back at Kochanowski Street the insurgents around the UB building are growing increasingly tense. Despite the cascades of water, there are several attempts to storm the main door with crowbars—none successful. In its frus-tration the crowd gets more and more volatile. Sections take up different impromptu slogans: "Down with the communists!" "Down with the Rus-sians!" "Down with the executioners of our nation!" and "Your time is come, today we will be rid of you!" Each is followed by a rain of stones. Most of the building's occupants are transfixed with fear; a few lose control of their blad-ders. But the order not to open fire still stands. And there is another reason not to fire: quite a few of their own people, that is undercover UB agents, are known to be mixed in among the demonstrators.

It is now about 10:30 A.M. and some three hundred young people of high school age led by three grown men enter the fair through the main gate. They carry signs reading "We want bread!" and are singing the national anthem. Chinese in the nearby communist Chinese pavilion ignore them, as do most of the employees of the other communist countries. Many Western exhibitors

114

The remains of police and court files still burning in Młyńska Street hours after they had been removed from the courthouse. Associated Press.

have already fled the fairgrounds in their cars. But those who remain attempt to talk to the demonstrators and take pictures of them. One Danish business-man who knows Polish gives a brief speech. The group does not penetrate far into the fairgrounds for word has reached the authorities that the party head-quarters in the center of town has been occupied by the mob, and the decision has been made to close down the fair. Ten minutes later a smaller group of young people, less organized than the first, enters the fairgrounds from the gate on Grundwaldzka Street. They are shouting slogans and carry a tattered Polish flag. A few youths, who by their dress appear to be workers, strike with their fists those fair visitors and several Polish soldiers who do not remove their caps before the raised flag. Despite some scuffling, no real fights break out. One young leader, however, is arrested by the police and taken away.

About this time in Kochanowski Street a shot rings out. It comes from a window on the second floor of the UB building and is followed by several more. A woman streetcar driver who had been leading a group of youths in the direction of the UB building falls to the ground, her flag falling on top of her. The crowd, suddenly stunned into silence, retreats into a semicircle. New shots and then a burst of machine-gun fire. In a window above the main entrance of the UB building, a woman can clearly be seen shooting. The crowd panics and appears to evaporate, but soon regroups behind the corners of buildings. Half a dozen people, mostly woman streetcar drivers and several children, have been hit. Thirteen-year-old music student Romek Strzałkowski runs up to the fallen streetcar drivers. He has discarded his smaller banner calling for the teaching of religion in schools and takes up a Polish flag which he holds high above where the drivers had fallen standing his ground as the women are carried off. He is a handsome lad with a serious demeanor; only his short pants betray his age.

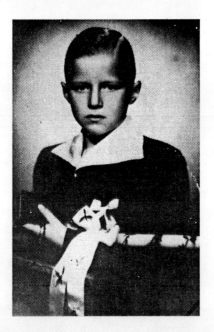

Thirteen-year-old music student Romek Strzałkowski from his first communion picture.
Taken from *Poznański Czerwiec 1956*.

There is a brief lull. People call for an ambulance to be summoned. Moments later, Franciszek Figler, driving his ambulance along Dąbrowski Street, is stopped by the crowd and directed to Kochanowski Street to pick up the wounded. Six of them are carried or helped into the ambulance, all of them workers. Figler drives them to Pawłowa Hospital, the one designated as "on duty" for emergencies. It is his first delivery. For the remainder of the day until 7:00 P.M. he is kept busy picking up wounded and taking them to different hospitals according to the nature of their wounds, but most often to Raszeja Hospital on Mickiewicz Street, considered the front line hospital as it is only one block from Kochanowski Street. It is from this hospital, in fact, that patrols of nurses with gurneys pick up the first victims even before Figler arrives with his ambulance. The ages of the first five victims range from twenty-seven to nine years old.

The sound of shooting has attracted more of the crowd from Stalin Square, but also some people returning from Młyńska Prison with their newly acquired guns. People are incensed that unarmed women and children demonstrators should be shot down in cold blood. Someone takes a Polish flag and dips it into the blood of one of the fallen teenagers. It is at once taken back to the square as testimony as to what has happened. A surge of moral outrage sweeps through the crowd, and many run off to Kochanowski Street shouting that they must avenge this atrocity.

Shots are fired on the UB building and a security soldier on the ground floor, Jakub Czekaj, is hit and quickly dies from his wound. The siege of the UB building is beginning.

Now the radio car can be heard driving along Poznańska Street. The speaker's voice reverberating off the buildings is urging people to take over the UB headquarters. He says that insurrections like this are taking place all over Poland; that the UB headquarters is the last bastion which has not fallen. There is no one to dispute these totally false and provocative claims, but the young people now laying siege to the UB building are quite oblivious to such urgings. They have motive enough for what they are doing. Without apparent leadership, they take up positions across the street, on rooftops and behind an overturned streetcar at one end of Kochanowski Street. Some take over the UB garage catty-corner to the headquarters across Kochanowski Street, using the courtyard as a staging area. A nearby beer bottling plant is transformed into a makeshift Molotov cocktail factory, and soon Molotov cocktails smash against and into the UB building through several of the downstairs windows. Flames from these instant fires flicker through the broken windows, blackening the outside walls above them; but each is quickly extinguished by the building's desperate occupants, who move filing cabinets against the lower windows to prevent more Molotov cocktails from penetrating the building.

Young Romek Strzałkowski has not retreated. He walks back and forth in full view of the UB building waving his flag. Suddenly two people—one a civilian, the other in uniform—jump him. They rip the flag out of his hands and threaten him. They want no more provocations, no more martyrs, and they succeed in scaring him away. But on his way to Dąbrowski Street, Romek meets his school friend Lechosław Stasik. They decide on the spur of the moment to exit the scene via the UB garage. They slip into the garage courtyard through the stairs between the building at 16 Kochanowski Street and the building adjacent to it. But once inside, they find the garage doors locked and the window they thought they could get through inaccessible. As they wander around the courtyard a UB employee suddenly emerges from the dispatcher's office they had thought was deserted. He seizes Romek while a terrified Stasik runs away through the way they had entered. Romek is taken upstairs to the drivers' quarters. Some hours later his body is found there in a chair, bullet holes through his neck and chest. Within twenty-four hours all of Poznań will know of his murder.

It is now noon. Clouds have covered the sun and the air has grown more humid. The army's Nineteenth Armored Division is pulling out of its permanent quarters and heading for Poznań on orders from Premier Cyrankiewicz. They travel with live ammunition.

At the Poznań radio station on Berwiński Street, about a mile and a half southwest of Stalin Square, Andrzej Górny and some fellow university students persuade the person who answers the door to let them in. They have written an announcement about the demonstration, which they feel the radio should broadcast to its listeners. Embarrassed, the radio officials agree that an announcement should be made, but they insist on altering the text, removing all emotional words and simply stating the fact that a large demonstration is taking place.[10]

In Schleissheim, West Germany, twenty kilometers north of Munich, Radio Free Europe's powerful monitors pick up this announcement. It will be several hours before it is noticed and relayed to RFE's headquarters in Munich's Englischer Garten. By that time the first West German businessmen driving back from Poznań have begun to reach West Berlin.

Many in the crowd at Stalin Square have grown restless. Others are frustrated. They feel humiliated that the authorities have not seen fit to meet with them and disgusted that things are getting out of control. They can hear the gunfire from Kochanowski Street. This is not at all what they intended. They declare their disgust out loud to their fellow workers and slowly begin to disperse, some going back to their work places, others heading home. Among these is Stanisław Matyja. He walks back to ZISPO, changes his clothes and goes home. But frustration drives others to action. Trucks and cars are commandeered by ZISPO workers who know where the small arms produced by their factory are stored and off they go to collect them and distribute them to those who ask for them. They never succeed in this, however, for those who have the keys to these storage rooms are opposed to the strike and throw the keys away before their colleagues get there.

118

As the demonstration gathers in Stalin (Freedom) Square, demonstrators climb onto stalled streetcars for a better view. Purchased by the author from a German businessman.

Not far from the conflict on Kochanowski Street, three tanks driven by officer cadets from the Officers School of Army Armored and Mechanized Forces turn onto Dąbrowski Street, followed by officer cadets with rifles marching in close order. The tanks are actually manned by reserve officers recently called up. The cannons in them have no ammunition; only the machine guns on top are loaded. The cadets with rifles are forbidden to shoot. While they are pleased to hear bystanders shout, "Long live the Polish Army!" and "The Army is with us!" they resist attempts by members of the crowd to disarm them and soon return to their barracks. The tanks, however, are surrounded by the crowd and momentarily immobilized. Some demonstrators pour cement mix powder from a nearby building site over the tank hatchways, making it totally dark inside. One by one the hatchways open, and the terrified occupants of the tanks emerge to see the "enemy" they have been called out to fight. People cheer them, but also tell them to take off their helmets and earphones and go back to their barracks. Relieved to find there is no "enemy" and flattered at the cheering, two of the crews do as they are bidden. The third crew turns its tank around and drives off. A few members of

119

the crowd who know how to operate the vehicles disappear down the hatches of the other two, and after some backing and filling, the two tanks rumble off in the direction of Kochanowski Street.

A familiar smell now envelops Kochanowski Street: spilled gasoline from metal barrels being rolled down the slight incline of the cobblestone street at the UB headquarters. The insurgents try to set the spilled gasoline ablaze, but gunfire from the UB building is too strong. The gasoline quickly evaporates.[11] Now the first insurgent-controlled tank turns into Kochanowski Street and heads toward the UB building at the far end. Under its cover a group of civilians advance shooting while others enter 16 Kochanowski Street, which houses UB members and their families. Meanwhile, a large group of armed youths take up firing positions on the far side of the UB building, along Poznańska Street.

In other parts of the city, tanks, still with no live ammunition, take up positions in front of public buildings, such as the Polish National Bank.

As the crowds thin, those who have occupied the radio car decide to abandon it. The driver, A. Tylski, returns it to the courtyard in front of the Communications Bureau from which it had been taken.

On Kochanowski Street the first civilian-operated tank fires several bursts of machine-gun fire as it passes the UB building, then swivels around on Poznański Street and backs into a small courtyard. Elsewhere, the ad hoc crew of the second tank, having inadvertently backed it into a building, cannot make it go forward and reluctantly abandon it.

Along Mickiewicz Street, not far from Dąbrowski Street, forty soldiers walk in single file with their rifles at the ready. From time to time they shoot single shots into clots of demonstrators. The commander orders windows in the nearby Raszeja Hospital closed; no one from inside is to approach them. Seeing a group of pre-teenage children, he yells at them, "Break it up or I'll shoot. Those are my orders; shoot any group of people." That is too much for nurse Aleksandra Banasiak, now in uniform, who has been watching from the hospital entrance. She runs into the street screaming: "You son-of-a-bitch! What are you doing?" "Following my orders," the officer yells back impassively. "How could you shoot at children?" she screams derisively and then, noticing no hint of shame or change in his face, she suddenly realizes that this crazy man means what he says and that she herself is in danger. She runs over to the children and herds them, half-running, down to a quiet part of Poznańska Street and out of harm's way. Then she returns to Raszaja Hospital, from which she has been making forays to Kochanowski Street to tend those wounded from the shooting.[12] Though it is her day off, she has been working ever since she returned from observing the liberation of prisoners at the Młyńska Street prison. When she returned to the hospital, she had unthinkingly fulfilled the urgent request of one of the young insurgents for bottles of benzine. She had found and handed over half a dozen bottles before the hospital director caught her and forbade her to continue. Later, during a truce in the shooting, while she was bandaging a stomach wound of a young man who had fallen in front of the UB Headquarters, she hears shouts from within that building calling "Sister, why don't you come to us too? There are wounded who need you." As she helps the young man away, she calls back over her shoulder, "I'll be back!"

At the hospital Sister Banasiak learns that the UB had already phoned for help. Now she is one of a team of two other nurses and Drs. Karon and Śli-wiński who head for the UB building on foot. Insurgents block their way. A shouting match ensues. At length, they are reluctantly allowed through and are able to enter the UB building. Inside the scene is utter chaos, for not only are the extra soldiers there, all of the UB personnel's wives and children have taken refuge in the building as well and are jammed into the windowless cor-ridors and stairwells. It is not only the wounded who must be seen to; nearly everyone has to be given some sort of sedative to prevent hysteria. While the nurses are bandaging and giving out sedatives, the doctors certify those who are already dead: three men. Nurse Banasiak, while bandaging a victim in a hallway, overhears a conversation—one which is to prove crucial four months later in the trials. "How did the shooting start?" asks the head doctor of the commanding UB officer. "It was obvious that we had to open fire," replied the UB commander. "Rocks were coming in the windows, and they had Molotov cocktails. We had to defend ourselves."[13]

An argument soon develops between the officers and the hospital team over what is to be done with the wounded. The UB officers want them imme-diately taken to the hospital. The team from the hospital says this cannot be done. They feel guilty about refusing this, but they know the wounded have a better chance of surviving if they remain in the UB building. Trying to trans-port them through that bitter, irate mob would mean their certain death. The team leaves the building and returns to the hospital. The minute their white coats are out of sight, firing resumes.

But Nurse Banasiak, confident that her ankle-length white uniform and broad, white cap with its distinctive black ribbon across its middle will pro-tect her from the bullets, is soon back out on the streets. Her exhausting day will not end until 9:30 P.M. Later she will recall the most gruesome scene she was to witness that day: the bayoneting of the eighteen-year-old polytechnic student, Marian Kubiak, as he emerged with a white flag from the captured tank on Poznański street. After the soldier who had performed the grisly act had left the young man for dead, Miss Banasiak, small but strong, had clambered up on the tank and managed to pull him off and half-carry, half-drag him, oozing blood from every part of his lower body but still breathing, a city block to the hospital. He died shortly after the operation to save him.[14]

On Dąbrowski Street Stanisław Porodzyński is hurrying home. Purposefully not dressed in his UB police uniform, he hopes no one will recognize him. Suddenly someone in the crowd does, and calls the alarm. Within seconds he is seized, thrown upon the pavement, kicked and beaten. Cooler heads prevent his murder and stand guard until an ambulance can be fetched from the hospital of the Ministry of the Interior. He is to remain there until August 18.

A group of demonstrators not far away on Roosevelt Street near the "Bałtyk" cinema are marching toward the international fairgrounds. The group is led by a teacher carrying a briefcase and a young man with a Polish flag, its white top recently soaked in blood. It is the one taken from Kochanowski Street. The marching crowd, which is made up of young students and young workers with many school children tagging along, head for the Grunwaldzka Street entrance to the fair. After a short walk through the fair grounds they emerge through the main entrance. It is there that several foreign exhibitors take their picture. Over the next week these pictures, with the bloodstained flag, will be seen by millions of people all over the noncommunist world as they unfold their morning newspapers.

It is now about 1:00 P.M. The main square is almost empty as tanks begin to roar through the city and take up positions in front of public buildings. A light mist is falling and tanks and other vehicles leave telltale tracks behind them on the cobblestone streets.

Near the fighting, at the corner of Dąbrowski and Kochanowski Streets, the "Konsum" store is being looted. Further along Kochanowski Street the UB apartments are also being looted and vandalized. One unfortunate occupant, Henryk Halbowski, is discovered hiding there and is severely beaten. The UB orderly who comes to his rescue and tries to get him away is also seized and beaten. Only ariving help from Raszeja Hospital prevents the situation from getting out of hand.

Now some of the workers and students with guns take over the UB office at number 3 Kochanowski Street from which they can get a better shot at the UB headquarters' southern wall across the street. Firing is sporadic and comes in bursts. There are no more truces for removing the wounded. Except for an occasional insurgent running from one bit of cover to another, the nearby streets are now deserted.

The bloodied Polish flag, taken from Kochanowski Street, is displayed by a crowd of students at the Poznań International Fair in front of a sample Polish railroad car. Note teacher with briefcase. Purchased by the author from a German businessman.

At the prison on Młyńska Street more firearms are discovered; altogether 76 guns, 43 hand grenades and more than 20,000 rounds of ammunition are taken from the prison armory. Other guns are collected from district police stations where they are either taken at gunpoint or surrendered willingly.

Another UB employee in civilian clothes, Zygmunt Izdebny, is on the run. Someone has identified him as a UB corporal and people try to seize him, but he breaks free and escapes several times. His running, however, attracts attention. Someone yells out that he is a UB who has just killed a woman and her child. No one doubts this accusation and he is pursued to the railway station where he is cornered on the fourth platform and beaten mercilessly while over one hundred people look on. As he is kicked and has his head struck against the platform, people shriek, "He killed a woman and a baby." Someone presses burning cigarettes against his face and he cries out in agony. While people continue to kick and stomp on his prostrate form, others in the crowd phone for an ambulance. When this arrives the crowd blocks the way. The ambulance makes two futile attempts. Finally, on the third try, they manage to convince the people to give way. But they are too late. Izdebny dies on the way to the hospital. Only at the trial, months later, will people learn that while he was UB, he was innocent of the accusation—a case of mistaken identity.

Jan Witkiewicz is also the victim of delay and suspicion. Cut down by a UB bullet in the courtyard of the UB garage, but only badly wounded, he is pulled into the nearest car by Zdzisław Imieliński, who does not know him but saw him go down and wants to take him to the hospital. Insurgents refuse to let the car go through because it has UB plates. Imieliński finally convinces the gunmen that neither of them are UB. He drives to the hospital, but is too late; Witkiewicz soon dies. Imieliński decides on the spot that saving lives is what he should be doing. With the help of various nurses he will, with his "borrowed" car, take no less than thirty-seven people to various hospitals around the city until around 11 P.M., when himself is struck by a bullet. After a night of misery, he will be admitted at 8:20 Friday morning to J. Struś Hospital.

It is now 2:00 P.M. At the army firing range at Biedrusko, not far from Poznań, a proclamation is distributed and read out loud to the subunits of army unit 1606. Although these soldiers do belong to the regular army, these are not regular army soldiers. They are especially selected for their political reliability to the régime and are trained for riot control and suppression of the civilian populace. "Soldiers!" reads the proclamation, "The enemies of our country—the foreign imperialist forces and their supporters in this country, in an attempt to compromise Poland in the eyes of foreigners, have provoked serious disturbances in the city of Poznań during the International Poznań Fair …"

The proclamation goes on to claim that pamphlets printed in German "by fascists" have stirred up these "acts against their own nation," which includes "destroying state property" and that as soldiers they are at the "forefront of People's Poland" and must "fulfill the honorable task" of putting down these disturbances. Since many ethnic Germans live in the Poznań area, it is not unreasonable for this claim to be believed, yet no pamphlets in German are ever found.

In Raszeja Hospital there are no more beds. Wounded people are being put on mattresses on the floor of the conference room. The shooting has spread from the Kochanowski Street area to other parts of the city. There are now about fifty sites from which single gunmen or groups of gunmen are firing. Some of the officer cadets have gone over to the side of the people and are instructing them in the use of firearms and directing the assault on the UB Headquarters.

A special plane from Warsaw with General Stanisław Popławski and his staff is landing at Ławica Airport at the western edge of the city. As soon as they disembark, they set up a temporary headquarters in the barracks near the runway. Within a few minutes the general is receiving reports of heavy exchanges of fire in much of the central part of the city.

Back in the city a second group from the Officers School of Army Armored and Mechanized Forces is making a concerted effort to lift the siege of the UB building. A column of their tanks moving down Dąbrowski Street is making a terrible racket, which can be heard many blocks away. It meets with a sudden ambush of Molotov cocktails near the bottling plant and several tanks are set ablaze and put out of commission. After a pause the others move on to Kochanowski Street. Other tanks from the Nineteenth Armored Division, with units of cars from the Fourth Army Corps, are entering the city at the far end of Dąbrowski Street. They, too, receive a hail of Molotov cocktails when they reach the vicinity of the bottling plant, and several tanks catch fire and burn fiercely. Rather than push on, the column backs up and goes over to Wielkopolska Avenue via Kościelna Street. From there they fan out to assigned positions in front of all army barracks, the Młyńska Prison, the electrical works, the main and west railroad stations and the radio station. Tear gas bombs are fired wherever clusters of people have gathered, and the stench soon drifts through many streets.

On Dąbrowski Street the tanks headed for the UB headquarters spot crowds of people attempting to flee. One of the tanks opens fire, and Roman Jankowski, a forty-two-year-old electrician from ZNTK, falls mortally wounded. His eighteen-year-old daughter, Janina, leaps to catch him and holds him in her arms throughout the long ambulance ride to St. Joseph's Hospital. He is already dead when they carry him into the operating room.

The same round that kills Roman Jankowski caught Paweł Wasylik, a baker from Szczecin, in the head. Not knowing he is dead, his sixteen-year-old daughter, Lucyna, tries to hold him up. Next to them stands his nine-year-old son, Piotruś.

Outside the hospital Janina Jankowska, tears streaming, shouts to anyone who can hear: "They killed my father!" People on a truck going by call to her. Without a second thought she climbs into the truck. It is on its way to collect weapons.

Seven tanks and several armored cars are now parked around the UB building, protecting it, but the insurgents have since managed to barricade both ends of Kochanowski Street with overturned streetcars and parked trucks. The régime now has vastly superior firepower, but the firing from the insurgents goes on as though nothing had changed. The tanks are not yet using their cannons, but the heavy slugs from their machine-guns are devastatingly effective. One of these catches Andrzej Górny, the young Polish literature student from Adam Mickiewicz University, in the head. Fortunately, the slug has caromed off a wall in the courtyard of the UB garage from which he and friends have been shooting at the UB Headquarters; otherwise it would have killed him outright. Blinded and seared in pain, he slumps to the ground. He is not one of those whom nurse Aleksandra Banasiak will treat and evacuate to Raszeja Hospital, but is taken to another hospital where they will operate several hours later in an attempt to save his sight in at least one eye. The doctors will hide him from the subsequent visits of the UB, so that unlike most of those taken to Raszeja Hospital, he will never be arrested. It will be weeks before the bandages can be removed and he will not emerge from the hospital, able to see from one eye, until late August.[15]

It is now about 2:30 P.M. Airplanes are circling low over the city. Someone identifies a Soviet-made YAK fighter, which actually dives and lets go a blast of machine-gun fire at a group of people standing on Walki Młodych Street in front of Struś Hospital. Miraculously, no one is hit.

At Ławica Airport Leon Stasiak, the regional party first secretary who had failed to stop the workers seven hours before and has not been seen in public since, is waiting for Prime Minister Cyrankiewicz and other high officials to arrive from Warsaw. Central Committee secretary Edward Gierek arrived by car early in the morning, but neither he nor Stasiak had felt it necessary to address the demonstrators when they were still peacefully assembled in Stalin Square. As soon as the plane arrives, all of these party officials join General Popławski in temporary headquarters in the nearby barracks.

By three o'clock it seems that all of Poznań is enveloped in the sounds and smoke of battle. Tanks not in fixed positions are rushing around firing bursts at what they believe to be places where the insurgents are entrenched; but more often than not the firing comes from rooftops, and those doing the shooting quickly change positions and hide behind chimneys.

On Świerczewski Street near the "Bałtyk" cinema a group of boys are hiding under a truck. A tank, aware of their presence, drives into it, crushing it. Fifteen-year-old Leon Kluj does not manage to get away in time. Friday, his father, on learning his son had been in that vicinity, will go there and find one of his shoes. Later he and his wife will find their son's crushed body in the mortuary.

In Warsaw an unscheduled flight prepares to land. It is the delegation of officials of the Committee on Public Security, which had left early this morning for Moscow with Ochab's assurance that things in Poznań were under control. On their landing in Moscow, Ivan Serov, Soviet state security head, had briefed them on events in Poznań and they decided to return at once to Warsaw. Once on the ground they rush off to the meeting of the politburo of the Central Committee, which is still in session.

Not all the trucks rushing around Poznań belong to the army. A number are manned by insurgents who are still raiding police stations for more guns. Around 3:30 the Fifth Civic Militia (police) station on Krzyżowa Street in the Wilda district surrenders 29 guns and 200 rounds of ammunition to one such truckload. At the Sixth Civic Militia Station on Dębiec Street two truckloads of insurgents are not so lucky. There the police refuse to hand over anything. After an exchange of curses the two trucks drive off empty-handed.

By 4:00 P.M. the shooting is getting more sporadic. In those sections of the city where the shooting has died down, army and UB plainclothesmen are stopping at random people they suspect, demanding and then confiscating identity cards and advising all such persons to go home.

But around the UB building the firing has not diminished and has even grown more intense. A youth behind an overturned streetcar on Dąbrowski Street is struggling to master the gun he has just acquired. A young officer walks up to him, takes the gun and fires at the UB building himself. Now they take turns. Around 4:00 P.M., however, a round of machine-gun fire cuts down the officer and young Roman Nowak who has been shooting next to him. Others behind the streetcar run into the ZUS building where they take up positions on the sixth floor.

At Wedra near Sulęcin, some few kilometers from Poznań, units of the Second Corps are pulling out of their training grounds and heading toward Poznań. More and more planes are circling low over the city. On the streets the UB plainclothesmen, who had earlier mingled in the crowds, surreptitiously taking hundreds of pictures with cameras hidden in their clothing, now show their pistols and accost everyone they can, confiscating identity cards from all persons they manage to catch.

A group of soldiers entering the UB garages find someone wounded. They call to two nurses, Aleksandra Kozłowska and Joanna Janke, to come tend the wounded man. When the nurses come they find not a wounded man, but Romek Strzałkowski, tied to a chair, dead, and already stiff.

From the roof of the international fair's Market Hall on Roosevelt Street machine guns spray bullets at people walking toward the railroad station. Within seconds the street is clear, all pedestrians having scrambled down the embankment to walk along the tracks where the embankment protects them from the line of fire. No trains are moving, but soon they will start up again after sitting locked and motionless all day, victims of the general strike.

The air is filled with the smell of burnt gunpowder and diesel exhaust.

127

Behind bursts of machine-gun fire and the sharp cracks of single rifle shots a steady roar of tank and truck traffic coming from all portions of the city is punctured by the eerie "oo-ah, oo-ah" of ambulances operating from a half a dozen hospitals. At least forty-eight firing positions are still in the hands of the insurgents, but most are quite isolated. There is no particular rationale to the situation, and both sides are confused as to what is happening. Gradually, with the help of the airplanes, the army figures out where most of the pockets of resistance are located, and deploys its forces accordingly. But the "enemy" proves elusive, and these pockets of resistance sometimes simply disappear and are replaced by new ones.

It is 5:00 P.M. and still the UB headquarters is under heavy fire. The tanks in front of it move down Kochanowski Street to try to break the barrier of overturned trucks and streetcars on the south side. Relentlessly they smash into this ad hoc barricade, finally succeeding, but not without a price. (Weeks later secret army tallies show the full military price of the uprising; 14 tanks set afire, 15 tanks and 8 army vehicles destroyed by other means. The true number of human casualties among the army and police is never to be revealed; the official figure will be ridiculously low. Civilian casualties will total 58 dead and about 300 wounded.)

As darkness begins to descend, the city remains a city under siege. The circling planes continue to fly low, the roar of their engines striking terror into the hearts of people now cowering in their apartments, reminding them of the pervasive power of the régime and the certainty of coming revenge. Andrzej Górny, lying blind on his hospital bed, is to remember the sound of those planes through his long sleepless night for the rest of his life.

Before darkness takes over, several skirmishes occur in parts of the city where there has been no previous fighting. But they are rather one-sided. At Fedry a whole platoon of civic militia attack a group of young people on their way home, killing several and wounding many. In the Old Market a patrol of ten militiamen march through, shooting at anyone they can spot. They manage to wound several unarmed people.

In faraway Washington, D.C., where it is only 1:55 in the afternoon, the secretary of state, John Foster Dulles, returns a call from his brother, Allen W. Dulles, director of the Central Intelligence Agency. "Have you heard the news, Foster? There's been some sort of riot in Posen. [German for Poznań— ed.] I don't know what it's all about, but it has been coming out on the ticker." Allen Dulles reads him the first couple of sentences. "When they begin to crack," comments the secretary, "they can crack fast. We have to keep the pressure on."[16]

In Poznań, sporadic gunfire continues through the night and throughout much of the next day punctuated by occasional booms of cannon fire. Indeed many people will recall hearing gunfire on Saturday morning as well. But by nightfall on Thursday the mood of the entire city has swung from the ecstatic and unified elation of the morning demonstration to deep and lonely depression as they listen to the régime broadcasting its lies and threats of repression. Most memorable is the speech of Cyrankiewicz himself and his closing threat that "every provocateur or madman who dares to lift his hand against the power of People's Poland will have that hand chopped off." Even the remarkably accurate, if sketchy, account of the day's events broadcast by Radio Free Europe—which they can now hear clear as a bell with the local jammer destroyed—does not dispel their gloom and sense of foreboding.

On Friday morning twenty-seven-year-old Włodzimierz Kaczmarek hears on Radio Warsaw that order has been restored in Poznań, trams are running and shops open. When he leaves his Grunwald district apartment to test the veracity of this report he finds the center of the city dead, no shops open and nothing but tanks and heavily armed patrols in the streets.[17]

Others remain indoors; their radios tuned to the now unimpeded broadcasts of Radio Free Europe. They hear the familiar voice of Jan Nowak, chief of the Polish desk, as he assures them that "the world saw yesterday ... the infinite precipice between [the régime's] propaganda ... and the antisocial, antihuman and antidemocratic reality ... Hunger and poverty have been the true enemy of Polish people throughout the eleven years of communist and Soviet rule ... They are the only instigators of yesterday's bloody riots ... The protesters marching through the city were calling to foreigners: 'Tell the whole world ... that we are on strike so that something may change ... so that one may live in a human way in Poland."[18]

Nowak ends his broadcast by warning that riots and protests will only be used by "the Soviet servants against the Polish people. Remember that no government ... can remain in power if tanks, bayonets and police terror are its only supports ... the spirit of freedom, that manifested itself in the streets of Poznań, will win ... We summon you to remain calm, hold in check acts of despair, and uphold the powerful spirit that has always accompanied the Polish nation through the darkest nights of captivity."

Stirring words, but they do not hold back the worst as it unfolds in Poznań.

In a few households the worst is not long in coming, for the UB waste no time in making use of the identity cards they have confiscated during the latter part of the day. Thousands of photos developed in UB laboratories are passed around. Whenever a person shouting or someone carrying a gun is recognized and can be matched to a confiscated ID card, a posse of a dozen or more police set out in a lorry to the indicated address to make the arrest. This process continues all day Friday and gets into high gear by the night of June 29-30.

Jan Wieczorek, an eighteen-year-old ZISPO worker, is arrested and taken off the street on the 29th. He has been easy to spot in the photos because he and some other workers were not in their working clothes, but—having been given the day off and tickets to the International Trade Fair for that day—in their Sunday suits. He is taken to the UB headquarters on Kochanowski Street where the fighting has ceased, held for five hours, beaten like a dog, and then released. Unknown to him he is denounced later on that day by a fellow worker from W-4, his shop, the 19-year-old Miss Krause, a secret UB informer. That night, at 1:30 A.M. the Wieczorek family is awakened by a group of UB policemen come to take young Jan away. His parents cannot believe they are seeing so many policemen. During the hour and a half the police take to tear up the apartment and then the building's cellar looking for a gun they never find. His parents carefully count them: there are twenty-two![19]

Jan is made to lie face down in the truck while the men pick up several more arrestees. At UB headquarters they are kept for an hour in a hallway with their hands above their heads. Jan is so thirsty he licks the damp wall. They are placed in a big room and forbidden to speak to one another. Their terror is heightened when they notice all the fresh blood on the walls and floor of the room they are moved to. Jan is then put in a small cell with six other persons. All night long they are interrogated with bright lights shining in their eyes. In between questionings they are beaten. Soon they cannot tell whether it is night or day. The cruel and repetitious interrogations and brutal beatings are to go on for two weeks. Finally the interrogations are taken over by the Warsaw prosecutor and they are taken to the main Młyńska Street prison. The beatings stop but the conditions are not much better. There is a simple bucket in the corner for all bodily wastes and no toilet paper. Only at the end of August is Jan released from jail and the charges against him dropped.

Stanisław Matyja, though he had nothing to do with the uprising, is one of the earliest ones arrested. Interrogated for long hours and badly beaten, he is released only after sixteen days of this relentless routine and has to be hospitalized for the next six weeks and put in a convalescence home for another six weeks after that. He will never fully recover physically and eventually will even lose his job at Cegielski.

On Saturday morning as the city comes back to life, traffic resumes, and people go off to work, they notice that during the night small crosses and flowers have appeared in every spot where civilians died in the fighting.

On Radio Free Europe a rebroadcast from yesterday of the popular writer, Tadeusz Nowakowski, is reminding the populace of "the revolution of 1848 when Słowacki cried out: 'Long live the people of Poznań!' These shots aimed at the Poznań workers' hearts," he says, "killed not only a few despaired patriots ... they also inflicted deadly wounds on communism ... Because you can kill a man, but you cannot kill the ideas of freedom and social justice."[20]

Sporadic shooting, if not killing, nonetheless goes on in scattered parts of the subdued city.

Sister Aleksandra Banasiak is not arrested until Sunday, July 1. The UB had traced her to her father's house in her home village to which she had fled. Dressed in a simple skirt and blouse, her raven-black hair now covered by a kerchief, she seems to be the simple peasant girl she once was. No less than three jeeps full of policemen come to pick her up and take her back to the Kochanowski headquarters where she is questioned on and off until 11 P.M., when she is let go. They want to know what she has overheard while in the UB headquarters bandaging the wounded, and she steadfastly maintains that she heard nothing. The questioning occurs in an upstairs room, and at one point her interrogator is called away. Through the open window she cannot avoid seeing a man in the courtyard with his hands tied behind his back being hit with a truncheon by a UB policeman. She cannot only see the beating, but can hear each vicious blow. For the first time she feels sickened and begins to cry. Later, she is convinced that her inability to answer, due to this uncontrollable crying, is what persuades them to let her go.[21]

During the first three days following the outbreak of the uprising, nearly six hundred people are arrested in Poznań. But it is not just in Poznań that arrests are made. With Radio Warsaw as well as Radio Free Europe giving virtually hourly reports on the events, there is scarcely a person in Poland who has not heard something by Saturday morning. By 7:30 A.M. on that day (June 30), 232 persons have been arrested in Warsaw alone for indicating in public some approval of the workers uprising in Poznań.[22] The workers of a prefabrication plant in Jelonki greet each other with "Long live the workers of Poznań!" All over Poland workers meet to draft letters and telegrams of congratulations and encouragement to the workers at ZISPO and the other striking enterprises in Poznań. Almost none of these messages get through, for where the UB agents embedded in the postal system do not catch them, the plant managers at ZISPO and other plants succeed in intercepting them.

In the weeks to come scores of similar communications are sent to individual factories in Poznań, not only from around Poland but from labor unions in France and other West European countries.

Eloquent statements of support are also sent from American labor unions and from the International Confederation of Free Trade Unions in Brussels. These latter messages do get through after a fashion for they are carried verbatim by Western radio stations broadcasting to Poland. Wherever the authors of such messages from within Poland can be identified, however, arrests are made.

Graffiti referring to Poznań begin to appear on walls and bridges all over Poland as early as 5 A.M. Saturday morning. "Poznań summons you to Solidarity! Down with Red Russia!" reads a leaflet found by a prison guard near the Sielski railroad station at that hour. Similar leaflets are found inside the railroad car factory in Swidnica near Wrocław. High over the nearby town of Inowrocław an inscription has appeared on the water tower during the night. "Away with Moscow," it reads, "Hail to Poznań." Twenty-eight leaflets found in Nowy Tomyśl read: "Hail to the heroes of Poznań, down with communism!" Two signs nailed to a wooden door in the town of Kościan read: "Poznań, June 28, 1956. Long live the revolution. We want freedom. Away with the occupiers—The Committee for Freedom" and "Comrade Ochab, you have sold yourself to Russia. If you want to be on our side, you must respect the Poles—Polish Liberation Committee."

On July 2 the citizens of Krosno read on the wall of their bus station: "Hey Polish brothers! We live in the hope that our people live, feel and see what communism is doing. The best example of that is Poznań. Its people are the first to fight for us all." In Grudziądz near Bydgoszcz on the same day this hand-written message can be read: "Citizens! May the Communist Party and the People's authorities in Poznań rot. The general strike was put down with tanks and guns, about 200 people were killed, 600 wounded and 6,000 arrested. Down with the régime, give bread to the workers of Poznań."

In Washington, amid much fanfare, it is announced that the United States is offering Poland one hundred million dollars worth of free food.

On July 3 inside the Szczecin Synthetic Fibers Plant graffiti appears reading: "Hail to the workers of Poznań! Down with Communism and the Soviet Union!" On a railroad car transporting ore to the Lenin Steels Works, someone writes in chalk, "Long live the Poznań strike!" Inside the Seventh Military Communication Regiment a soldier has scribbled on the wall: "We soldiers want a free Poland, one no longer subject to the red bandits."

In its issue of July 4 the Polish youth newspaper, *Sztandar Młodych*, admits that "it is possible to understand the reasons for the dissatisfaction of the Poznań workers," and calls for improved living standards.

Three days later on the door of the Fourteenth Anti-Aircraft Artillery Regiment, someone writes, "Soldier, fire at the communists!"

Printed leaflets appear in Tarnów on July 7 with the following slogans: "Down with the Bolshevik occupation. Workers, let's follow the example set by Poznań. We want religion in schools. Down with communism!"

In almost every case the graffiti are quickly erased by local authorities and leaflets confiscated. But more keep appearing. And the true test of how the people feel comes in the private letters that the régime's censorship is reading and keeping careful score on. These are overwhelmingly in favor of the workers' action and blame the Communist Party. Many letters are written directly to the authorities, and while they are never published, they have their effect. A metal worker from Warsaw, for instance, writes to Radio Warsaw:

> I cannot agree with the statements made on this station in reference to the Poznań riots ... I blame the party itself and the government of the People's Republic of Poland for this state of affairs ... A nation that is faring badly, that is living in poverty, whose children are hungry and poorly clad, a nation in which families argue over money and curse the government—that nation is prone to take up any possible course of action ... Ninety-five percent of the people do not support this system of government. The Poznań events tarnished Poland's reputation in the international arena.

Aleksander K. writes another station:

> On behalf of all the residents of Poznań, I want to remind the Communists that despite 11 years of Communist rule, you were unable to squelch the spirit of the Polish nation. Realize that this nation is against you and that it will never defend the People's Democracy. It is not true that the Poznań events were a provocation ... no one will believe that. This was a general armed strike. The people of Poznań demanded what they rightly deserved, that is, a raise. They did not go to the streets because they live well, but because they live in poverty. The Polish nation wants freedom from Soviet rule and from the theft of its resources by Russia. You glorified so loudly the strikes in the West, and condemned the police for shooting at workers; but you weren't justified in doing that because, despite the magnitude of those strikes, not as many people were wounded and killed there as were in Poznań ... our brothers' deaths will be avenged.

Many of the letters are not just angry but threatening. An anonymous letter from the Zielona Góra region concludes:

You who sit up there at the top under the emblem of a hammer and sickle, remember that a storm is brewing and that the people's wrath is growing because they are losing their patience. This is why there was an unexpected, volcanic eruption in Poznań. Remember that the whole world is watching this event ...

Deciding it must tighten its screws on the press, the party fires Jerzy Morawski, editor of the party's main daily, *Trybuna Ludu*, for allowing his paper to contradict *Pravda*. It also sacks Eligiusz Lasota, the crusading editor of the student magazine, *Po Prostu*, and also fires Irena Tarnowska, the equally courageous editor of the youth daily newspaper, *Sztandar Młodych.*

Four days later *Trybuna Ludu* announces a series of ministerial shifts in the economic and industrial areas, most of them demotions.

The UB has never been busier. While it is removed by the government from the interrogations of those arrested in Poznań after the first two weeks, it has its hands full trying to snuff out all signs of dissent in the country, while at the same time trying to report accurately to the party, and particularly to the leadership, the full nature and extent of that dissent. It is no wonder that the government changes its line rather quickly. Despite the Soviet Communist Party's statement of July 2 laying down the Soviet line that the uprising was all caused by "provocateurs and diversionists paid by foreign agents," in Poland there is no more talk of foreign instigators having provoked the uprising. Indeed, an admission of "mistakes" having been made comes more and more into the régime's continuing commentary.

In Katowice (recently renamed Stalinogrod by the communists), party authorities abandon plans for organizing a mass worker's meeting to "protest" against "the machinations of foreign agents in Poznań," as they realize the likelihood of such a meeting turning against the régime.

Many high party members consider Cyrankiewicz's outburst about "chopping off hands" ill-considered. A number of students mock this outburst of Cyrankiewicz's by going around in public with their right hand tucked into their shirts, Napoleon fashion, implying, of course, that it had been cut off. The UB takes this gesture not as a joke, however, but as blatant opposition to the régime, and scores of students are arrested simply for doing this within sight of a UB informer.[23]

Cyrankiewicz's hard line did not hold for long. Indeed, so urgent was it that the party develop a unified line on the uprising, that an emergency plenum of the Central Committee was called on July 18, just twenty days after the events.

The Soviets, noting that their Polish colleagues were not following Moscow's policy line, sent the prime minister of the U.S.S.R., Marshall Nikolai Bulganin, to see that the Polish Central Committee got into line. The ostensi-

ble reason for Bulganin's visit was the anniversary of the Red Army's liberation of Poland celebrated on July 22, a national holiday with military parades
and receptions. But the Polish politburo steadfastly refused to let Bulganin
attend their sessions. He retaliated in his official liberation day speech by
declaring that not only was the uprising "proof that international reaction has
not abandoned its attempts to restore capitalism in the socialist countries,"
but that

> elements hostile to our cause utilize the press organs [in Poland] in order to
> sow their poisonous seeds. Certain managers of these press organs have
> yielded to hostile influence, forgetting that the party press should be above
> all a faithful and consistent herald of the Marxist-Leninist idea, and a mili-
> tant propagator in the struggle for building socialism.

This crude attempt to dictate publicly what the Polish party line should
be followed four days of no-holds-barred secret debates in the Polish Central
Committee, in which sixty-five speeches had been made. There were many
hard-line supporters of the Soviet position on gagging the press, but even
more who took a liberal stand. Jerzy Albrecht, the young committee secretary
who had been assigned to investigate the causes of the Poznań Uprising, said
he had been unable to find any evidence of foreign instigators and he was not
going to manufacture any just to fit some comrades' preconceptions. In fact,
he had found no original intention to revolt when the demonstration began,
for the very workers who led the demonstration (from the Cegielski plant)
had access in their own plant to numerous Kalashnikov automatic rifles that
were made there under license for the Soviet Union. They would not have
passed up such an opportunity to help themselves to these weapons had the
uprising been planned. No, the riots had been spontaneous.[24]

The final resolution isssued by the Central Committee was neither a
compromise nor a clear turn to either side, but an attempt to gloss over the
main issues, saying on the one hand that the party would "guarantee conditions for a frank exchange of opinions among party members," and on the
other that "the party will not agree with ... opinions which are against the
Marxist-Leninist ideology and not in accordance with the general party
line."* The trouble, of course, was that no party line had been established.

---

* U.S. Ambassador Jacobs's comment was that the resolution "reflects hasty
drafting by many persons with frequent references to the need for higher living standards in the light of the Poznań riots, but no significant new steps." The better
informed British ambassador, Sir A. Noble, learned from an eyewitness that Premier
Cyrankiewicz had pushed the majority liberal line, while Nowak with a small
minority towed the Soviet line and Ochab sat in the middle.[26]

Bulganin was told in no uncertain terms, however, that "your speech does not correspond with present conditions in Poland."[25]

About the only thing on which agreement was reached during the plenum was that Gomułka, still under house arrest, needed to be brought back into the picture. A delegation was duly sent to sound him out. Gomułka, having smarted all these years while his enemies were driving the country to ruin, was not about to haggle. He insisted on full rehabilitation and reinstatement not just to party membership but to full membership on the Central Committee. Ochab and others were not prepared to go this far, but when word of the negotiations leaked out the party felt it could not deny them and on August 4 the announcement of Gomułka's readmittance into the party was made. While the party lost all respect in the countryside and some collectives were even broken up, hard-liners, strongly backed by their Soviet colleagues, had managed an early purge in the press. *Po Prostu* editor Eligiusz Lasota and *Sztandar Młodych* editor Irena Tarnowska refused to take their dismissals lying down. They had the affront to protest and were allowed to take their case before the Central Committee. In the ensuing debate in a special meeting of the politburo, the liberals succeeded in having both of them reinstated. Both went off to write even more critical editorials on the failures of the government and the party.

It was only a matter of time before the first party secretaries of the Poznań region and ZISPO were fired. The announcement was made on August 7.

The next day, *Trybuna Opolska*, the main party organ in the Silesian city of Opole, told its readers that a recent six-member worker delegation sent off to Warsaw to complain of the appalling food situation in that city had resulted in the immediate dispatch of trucks loaded with food imported from abroad, plus a promise for preparations for constructing additional bakeries and slaughterhouses in Opole.

On August 14 *The New York Times* correspondent in Poland revealed what someone high within the party had told him, namely, that Poles in the coming December elections would be given a choice; no more ballots with a single list of names. Moreover, some of these "choices" might not even be party members. Some weeks later the Polish press confirmed this as fact.

Then on August 16, *Nowa Kultura*, the party's cultural weekly, gave its readers an inside view of why the workers of Poznań had revolted. Shortly before the eruption in Poznań, it revealed, a small industrial plant, the United Plumbing Industries of Poznań, had been given wage increases to alleviate some of their misery. Only 45% of the money allotted went to the two hundred workers. This increased their miserable pay packets by 4.4%. Another

45% of the money went to the fifty "supervisory personnel." This increased their salaries by 10.5 % The remaining 10% of the money was divided among the three directors, increasing their pay by 25%.[27]

All through the summer and early fall of 1956 reports were filed by Western correspondents concerning rumors of diminishing numbers of those still held in prison in Poznań, and unofficial announcements about the dates of the trial, or trials, of those remaining. But, while the coming trials held the attention of people in the West, in Poland and in neighboring East European countries, it was the changes—or paranoid reaction against changes—taking place in the ruling communist parties that fascinated these long suppressed populations. Many changes had already been triggered by the Soviet Twentieth Party Congress and Khrushchev's secret speech denouncing Stalin. But the unexpected explosion of proletarian fury at Poznań sent shock waves throughout the communist world (and not just the Soviet empire, for the Chinese Communists were to make much of Poznań in their dealings with Moscow). Without Poznań, few of these new changes would have occurred so quickly and the later upheavals—the "Polish October" and the Hungarian Revolution—might never have taken place.

CHAPTER V

The Petőfi Circle:
Party Ferment in Hungary

Unlike the other countries of Eastern Europe, Hungary experienced a communist régime not long after the Bolsheviks seized power in Russia. The collapse of the Austro-Hungarian Monarchy at the close of World War I brought more turmoil to Hungary than Austria, for, while Austria was bereft of its Slavic holdings as well as the Hungarian half of the monarchy, and thus became almost totally Germanic, Hungary had fewer Hungarians than Slavs and Romanians within its borders, all of them clamoring for freedom. When the Treaty of Trianon was signed in June 1920, Hungary was deprived of 71.4 percent of its pre-war territory and 63.5 percent of her population.[1] Hungary's pre-war population of over 20 million was reduced to about 7.5 million, leaving approximately 3.2 million Hungarian-speakers outside its new borders. These now became citizens of Romanian Transylvania, Czechoslovakian Ruthenia, the Slovak portion of Czechoslovakia, the Croatian, Serbian and Slovenian portions of Yugoslavia and part of Burgenland in Austria. In the immediate confusion after the collapse of the Monarchy, a small group of communists, under the leadership of Béla Kun, seized power and established, for four turbulent and bloody months from March 21 to August 1, 1919, a Soviet Hungarian republic or commune. Only the invasion and occupation by Romanian troops brought the experiment to an abrupt end.

There followed a period of fierce persecution of the communists, which quickly became known as the "White Terror," as opposed to the "Red Terror" which had taken place under Béla Kun's régime. A strong streak of anti-Semitism emerged in the midst of this persecution. While anti-Semitism in Hungary had been on the increase since the turn of the century, it achieved particular virulence at this time for the simple reason that Jews had been in the majority of the Béla Kun government leaders. This phenomenon was the natural result of the position of Jews in Hungary, which differed markedly from other countries in east-central Europe. Unlike Jews in the surrounding countries, Jews in Hungary had found a high degree of integration into Hungarian society and many of the country's leading citizens in the arts, business, banking, and even government were Jews.[2] By 1910, for instance, half of Budapest's lawyers and half of its physicians and 70 percent of its journalists were Jewish.[3] While Jews were found all across the political spectrum, it was only natural that those who had not done so well tended toward the left.

The summary "justice" of the Hungarian communists had been every bit as brutal as that which had emerged in the new Union of Soviet Socialist Republics; but the "White Terror" that followed under the regent, Admiral Miklós Horthy, was even more brutal, for it went on far longer and was thus more thorough. Those communists who did not slip out to Vienna, and later move on to Moscow, faced execution or long jail terms.

Under the authoritarian régime of Admiral Horthy—admiral in a nonexistent navy and regent to a nonexistent king—the communists were outlawed and thus had no seats in the parliament and no influence in the country. They were not to reappear on the Hungarian political scene until late 1944 when they arrived with the Red Army.

Three weeks before the establishment of the provisional assembly in Debrecen on December 21, 1944, a national front had been proclaimed in Szeged with participation of Communists, Smallholders, Social Democrats, the National Peasant Party, the Civic Democratic Party—all of which, with the exception of the Communists, had all been part of the nonfascist politics of interbellum Hungary—and the free trade unions. The front's program was heavily influenced by the Communist Party's program, which had been issued just a few days before. This called for a clear break with the Arrow Cross (fascist) régime, which the Nazis had helped to bring to power in October 1944, seven months after they had occupied Hungary and forced Horthy to appoint a pro-German government. The program included land reform, nationalization of mines, the oil and electrical generating industries, and state supervision of large industries and banking. The program was careful, however, not to outlaw private industry.

It was not until the provisional assembly met three weeks after this in newly liberated Debrecen that the communists reemerged as a major political entity. Even then their numbers in the entire country were no more than five thousand. That figure was to grow quickly. The reasons for the growth were no different from the reasons for the sudden expansion of Communist Party membership in nearby countries: idealism, the experience of Nazi barbarism (particularly against the Jews), the belief that communism was the wave of the future, the need for a sharp break with the past and, in a few cases, the fact that free food was handed out at Communist Party headquarters. But, in its effort to expand rapidly, the party soon began to attract opportunists, even small fry who had recently served the fascist Arrow Cross Party or the Horthy government. Nearly all were welcome.

Under the influence of the Soviet army of occupation, party membership was to grow to 150,000 in just five months, to 500,000 by October 1945, and to nearly 900,000 by mid-1948.[4]

In the government that emerged from the Debrecen national assembly meeting in December 1944, communists gained only three portfolios out of a possible twelve. But in November 1945 they were to gain two portfolios that were key to their strategy: agriculture and interior. Everyone but the fleeing nobility was in favor of land reform—though not necessarily the communist version—and those who controlled the Interior Ministry controlled the police.

Land reform was universally popular because Hungary, insofar as land ownership was concerned, and unlike all other countries of east-central Europe, was still a feudal country in 1945. It was a country of vast estates, several million landed peasants and an equal number of landless peasants. The communist leader who carried out the land reform was Imre Nagy, and it was this national exposure in carrying out what people felt was so necessary and good that gained Nagy—a Muscovite who also happened not to be Jewish—the fame and popularity which brought him to power in 1953, and back to power in 1956.

By November 1945 the communists thought they were ready for an open, nation-wide election. It turned out to be a crushing disappointment. The Smallholders Party received a clear majority of 57 percent, while the communists, despite much help from the Russian occupation authorities, received only 17 percent, the same as the Social Democrats.

The leadership of the Hungarian Communist Party was in the hands of four men: Mátyás Rákosi, Ernő Gerő, Mihály Farkas, and József Révai. All were Muscovites and all were Jewish. The leader whom Stalin had hand-picked was Mátyás Rákosi, who was well aware of Stalin's anti-Semitism. In intellect and willpower Rákosi was vastly superior to the other three. Clever, decisive, fluent in many foreign languages, Rákosi, despite his short, stocky build and bald, bullet-shaped head, could be smooth and charming when he needed to be. Seeing that the party had a long way to go before it could take over the country, he introduced what he later boasted were "salami tactics." He worked at subverting the other parties, dividing, neutralizing, slandering, and arresting on false charges when it could be done—and always with the

Official portrait of Imre Nagy, former premier, who, albeit in official disgrace in the summer of 1956, was actually the most popular man in Hungary. Wide World.

full backing of the occupying Soviet authorities. By stages he subverted the regular police and established a secret police (ÁVO) on the Soviet model.

By 1947, when communists were forced out of the French and Italian governments, the reverse was happening in Eastern Europe. The noncommunist prime minister, Ferenc Nagy, was aware of Rákosi's "salami tactics" but felt increasingly powerless to resist them. When Nagy was invited to confer with noncommunist politicians from Western Europe at a gathering in Switzerland, the temptation was too much for him and he gladly seized the opportunity for some respite from the communist pressure he was under. Rákosi, by then a deputy prime minister and the source of a slanderous campaign recently launched by the Interior Ministry against Nagy, informed him secretly that should he ever return to Hungary his life would be in danger. When the thoroughly demoralized and intimidated Nagy decided to heed Rákosi's threat by remaining in Switzerland, Rákosi used his failure to return to Hungary as proof of the truth of the trumped-up charges.

A paramount reason why Ferenc Nagy and other noncommunist politicians felt that the situation was so hopeless in Hungary was the dashing of their expectations after the signing of the peace treaty in February 1947. This treaty, signed in Trianon, France, ended the state of war between the Allies and all those countries, save Austria, which had fought on the German side.

The Hungarians had been counting on this settlement to remove the excuse for further occupation by the Soviet army. When the Soviets announced that in order to secure the links to their troops in Austria, Soviet troops were going to continue to remain in Hungary, their hopes were dashed.

On May 30, 1947, after the Soviet-dominated Allied Control Commission had renewed the charges against him, Ferenc Nagy, still in Switzerland, announced his resignation.

Now Rákosi's salami tactics moved into high gear. Content to remain only a deputy prime minister (he did not assume the position of prime minister until early in 1952), Rákosi prepared for new elections at the end of August 1947. This time the elections, thoroughly rigged and with maximum help from the Soviet high command, garnered the Communists only 22 percent of the vote. Rákosi, however, was not disappointed; the leftist bloc led by the party had gotten 60.8 percent. The Communists, in fact, were now in charge. But Rákosi kept up the pretense that the country was still ruled by a coalition. As late as October 1948 as many as ten ministerial posts were still held by noncommunist politicians. But, since all were fellow-travelers, this was just window-dressing. The country was in the total grip of the communists from September 1947 on.

The Sovietization of Hungary proceeded apace. This included the establishment of steel mills where neither iron ore nor coal was readily available, ruthless forced collectivization of farms that had only recently been doled out to landless peasants and nationalization of all businesses with more than five nonfamily employees.

Rákosi, aware of Stalin's prejudice against Jews, determined to gain his favor by outdoing him in ruthlessness and brutality. Jewish intellectuals, businessmen, and bankers suffered these injustices just as much as non-Jews. The infamous prison camp, Recsk, was established where brutality approached that of the Nazi death camps. Abusive forced collectivization soured what had been a successful land reform.

With Stalin's campaign against Tito, whose Yugoslavia was expelled from the Cominform in 1948, Rákosi had a tool for not only pleasing Stalin, but also for removing high party officials whom he distrusted or disliked. Interior Minister László Rajk, who had just been made foreign minister, headed the list. Rajk and a number of other high officials were arrested on May 30, 1949, and tortured and drugged so that at their trial in September they confessed to unbelievable crimes against the Hungarian People's Republic. He and seven others were found guilty and he and two of these sentenced to death. Others later tried by military courts were also found guilty and executed. Only his popularity as the man who had carried out the land reform (plus some possible protection from Beria, who favored him) kept Imre Nagy from Rajk's fate.

Meanwhile, the persecution of the Church culminated in the arrest of Cardinal Mindszenty in December 1948 and his bogus show trial and sentencing to life imprisonment in February 1949. A general reign of terror imposed by the party but enforced by the greatly expanded secret police (ÁVO) gripped the country as thousands were arrested in the dead of night and thousands of others were deported from the cities to the countryside.

For the next four years Rákosi, aping Stalin more closely than any other East European communist leader, applied the screws to the communist lid on Hungary to the point where, after Stalin's death in March 1953, the Soviet collective leadership was afraid that if they did not do something soon, they would have an explosion on their hands in Hungary. They decided to remove Rákosi from the premiership and give the job to someone recommended by certain "liberals"* in the Soviet politburo: Imre Nagy. Since Rákosi was still the most dependable and trusted member of the Hungarian leadership, however, they decided to keep him as the party secretary. Nagy, whom Rákosi despised, immediately began to undo some of the worst things Rákosi had imposed and declared a "New Course," based on his program first revealed in June 1953. This entailed curbing the secret police; closing the infamous Recsk camp; declaring a general amnesty; allowing peasants to leave the collective farms if they so wished, and generally improving the outlook, if not the immediate economic condition, of the country. Since Rákosi had ground the country down, this miserable condition would take considerable time to improve.

Rákosi had no desire to see Nagy's New Course succeed. He immediately set out to slow things down and to sabotage Nagy's plans and was soon speaking openly against the New Course and contemptuously of Nagy.

As people began to see that Nagy's fine words and good intentions were coming to naught, his popularity began to slip. Noting the extreme economic difficulties that continued to plague Hungary and feeling that Nagy—a true believer with blinders—could not be trusted to do their bidding, the Kremlin leadership succumbed to the arguments of Rákosi—who visited Moscow frequently during this period.[5] In April 1955 Rákosi had his man András Hegedűs installed as premier, simultaneously removing Nagy.

Once again Rákosi began to apply the screws. Nagy was expelled from the party but again his popularity saved him from actual arrest, trial and imprisonment or execution. The nearly two years of the New Course had

---

* Probably Malenkov, Beria, and Mikoyan.

considerably changed the internal structure of the Hungarian party, though the real power still lay in the hands of the original four leaders. There was clearly a split between those who still felt that Nagy and the New Course were the way to go and those who felt primary loyalty to Rákosi and Moscow. The intellectuals and writers tended toward Nagy, as did most people who were not party members, and in November 1955 a significant writers' revolt took place at the party-dominated Writers' Congress, which brought on a sharp condemnation from the Central Committee.

As Rákosi had proudly worn the title of "Hungary's Stalin," it seemed inconceivable that he could remain in office once Khrushchev had denounced Stalin and the "cult of personality" so ringingly. Inconceivable, that is, to everyone but Rákosi. He promptly had his dead rival Rajk posthumously "rehabilitated," blaming the whole thing on already-purged Gábor Péter, the ex-chief of the secret police, and began mouthing the latest slogans emanating from Moscow. Rákosi, in fact, had to use all his wiles to stay in place. Aware that the Soviet leadership had many larger things to worry about than the party leadership of little Hungary, he took full advantage of their lack of concerted attention, reminding them at every opportunity that he was still their most trusted man in Hungary and that any extreme alternative—like bringing back Nagy—would be unthinkably dangerous.[6]

Rákosi's tactic worked for a time, but it could not cover the widening split in the party—or the growing restlessness in the country as the consequences of Khrushchev's denunciation of Stalin reverberated through the entire Eastern bloc.

Many party intellectuals saw that some sort of safety valve would have to be found to let out the growing frustration within party ranks. They also felt the need to win back those intellectuals who had once supported, though never joined, the party, and who were now leading the swelling intellectual ferment. At length these party leaders found their vehicle in a group newly formed by the Association of Working Youth (DISZ), which was the main communist youth organization. The new group was meant to be a discussion group for young communists seeking routes to renewal. It called itself the "Petőfi Circle," after the great nationalist poet of the revolution of 1848.

The Petőfi Circle had its beginnings in 1954 when a small number of young staff members at the Hungarian National Museum utilized the more liberal atmosphere under Imre Nagy to debate the social, literary, and political problems that the relaxed attitude of the New Course had brought to the surface. One of their friends, a non-party member and poet, István Lakatos, had been asked to set up a program of debates. Basing his approach on that of György Bessenyei, the prominent Hungarian poet of the eighteenth century

Officers' Club in Budapest, where most of the Petőfi Circle discussions were held.

Enlightenment and author of *A Humble Request for a Hungarian Society*, Lakatos decided to call the group the "Bessenyei Circle."

Lakatos's liberalism, however, irritated the party functionaries, and the DISZ leadership disliked the circle being named for a nonmarxist poet. Considering themselves successors to the Hungarian revolutionaries of 1848, they changed the name to the Petőfi Circle, in honor of Sándor Petőfi, the main poet of that Revolution, and co-opted Lakatos into agreeing to this change. Then, on March 25, 1955, the new leadership, consisting largely of Communist Party members, was elected and Lakatos was soon thrown out for failing "to fulfill his share of the circle's activities."

Among the new leadership of the circle, however, there were still adherents of Imre Nagy's 1953 "June way" and Gábor Tánczos, who had unfairly been dismissed from DISZ at the time of the Rajk trial, now became the new secretary. Tánczos, whose family were assimilated Jews with a strong sense of Hungarian nationality, had been influenced by populist writers ever since he had attended Catholic secondary school, even though he later joined the communist youth movement.[7]

Under the leadership of Gábor Tánczos a new series of meetings of the circle began in March 1956. The first few were not much more than reunions of "veteran" youth activists, but as the group came to the attention of higher party officials looking for a means to engage those intellectuals whom they felt they were losing and whose ideas and energy they wished to channel into the party, it was decided that the meetings should concern specific areas so as to attract the best minds of young professionals in any given field. The evening devoted to Yugoslav literature, for instance, attracted a larger-than-usual audience and ended with the drafting of a declaration of sympathy for Hungarian-Yugoslav friendship.

In May and June the discussions were expanded to publicly advertised (by word of mouth) open sessions and each, in turn, had to be held in a different, progressively larger meeting place to accommodate the audience. These discussions, which usually entailed a panel with a chair and then open discussion and questions from the audience, were held on the following topics: economics, history, ideology, philosophy, antifascist resistance, and finally, the role of the press.

By June 5, when the circle discussed history, audience participation had become not just lively, but quite unpredictable. For example, when Erzsébet Andics, a professor of history at Budapest University, began solemnly intoning: "In the last ten years we have made a lot of mistakes concerning Hungarian history ..." somebody from the audience yelled "Haven't we!" before she could finish her sentence. Turning crimson in embarrassment, Andics, who was known as a fire-breathing communist, continued: "In fact, we made some very serious mistakes."

A shower of catcalls arose from the audience through which one voice called clearly, "Why not tell us exactly what they were!"[8]

The meetings became the talk of Budapest. At the one on philosophy on June 14, the world-famous marxist philosopher, György Lukács, disparagingly complained about the government's "assembly-line production of philosophers unable to do anything but spout the marxist line."

Many of the party members, even ÁVH (secret police)[*] men sent to monitor the meetings, found themselves agreeing with what the rebels were saying. Some even signed a memorandum to ÁVH headquarters to that effect.[9]

On the evening of June 19 some two thousand former partisans met to hear the discussion of "The Old Illegal Communist and the Young Intellectuals of Today."

Party veterans who had fought in the Spanish Civil War and/or endured long jail terms were the first to speak; mostly they shared reminiscences. At length someone from the audience challenged them by pointing out that in five years under Rákosi from 1948 to 1953 more communists were arrested,

---

[*] During the New Course the ÁVO had changed its name from Division of State Security (Hungarians acronym ÁVO) to Office of State Security (acronym ÁVH). But neither the personnel nor practices changed one iota, so people went on calling it the ÁVO.

tortured, and murdered than during the entire twenty-five years of Horthy's right-wing régime. One of the voices from the audience belonged to Júlia Rajk, widow of László Rajk. As people recognized who she was, a hush fell over the crowd. When she was given permission to speak from the rostrum, swelling applause accompanied her dignified walk to the stage. Turning to the older men on the rostrum, this tall, gaunt woman, who had been imprisoned at the same time as her husband, said: "Comrades, after five years of prison and humiliation I stand before you shaking with emotion … Not only did you kill my husband; you took my baby boy away from me. Not only did you criminals murder László Rajk, you killed all decency in our country." Then, turning to the audience, she shouted: "Where were the members of the party when these things were happening? How could they allow such degeneration to take place without rising in holy anger against the guilty?"

Mrs. Rajk went on to describe her experiences in prison, saying that the prisons in Hungary were a "disgrace" to any people's democracy and that prison conditions under the Horthy régime were much better. During the whole time she was in jail she had been permitted neither visitors nor mail nor packages that had been sent her. She had been completely isolated from her newborn child. Mrs. Rajk finally ended her remarks with this ringing affirmation: "I will not rest until every one of them—the men who have ruined this country, corrupted the party, liquidated thousands and driven millions to desperation—have received their just deserts. Comrades, stand by me in this struggle!"

Thunderous applause erupted in the hall, and as she made her way back to her seat, calls of "Down with Rákosi!" "Down with the guilty men!" and "Long live Hungary!" could be heard through the din.[10]

Word of Mrs. Rajk's speaking her mind in front of those two thousand party members spread like wildfire around Budapest. It was the strongest attack that anyone of any prominence had yet made on the régime.

Until then, the main newspapers had ignored the existence of the Petőfi Circle, feeling it was too new and too dangerous to comment upon. But on June 24 the main party paper, *Szabad Nép* ("Free People") finally came out in favor of the circle, calling it "a shaft of sunlight" and recommending that more government employees and party members get involved in its discussions. Whether this official stamp of approval or simply the subject of the next meeting—"The Role of the Press"—was responsible for the size of the turn-out on the evening of June 27 is debatable, but estimates agree that some seven thousand people attended that meeting.

This meeting took place in the Central Officers' Club of the Hungarian People's Army off Váci Street, Budapest's most fashionable shopping street.

It was the most famous of the great public meetings and also the last, because its length and raucous nature went far beyond what the authorities had intended.

⌒

Budapest, June 27, 1956

The day begins without sharp shadows, for the cloud cover over the city is complete. The unseasonable heat, even for June, of the previous day continues; the humidity is even greater. Electricity permeates the atmosphere and it is not all due to the gathering clouds, which scatter showers on both halves of the city around midday. Many people are aware that over in Pest along Váci Street, something of great importance is going to take place. The Central Officers' Club, which was the site of the Petőfi Circle meeting addressed by Júlia Rajk just last week, is about to host another meeting of the circle this evening—this one on the role of the press. The theater has eight hundred seats, but of course with people sitting and standing on stairs and aisles, it can hold more than twice that number.

The club is a massive turn-of-the-century freestanding building, which, in effect, takes up a city block on the east side of Váci Street not far from the famous Mátyás Pince restaurant and just south of the Erzsébet Bridge. In front of the building, Váci Street is twice as wide as anywhere else, almost making it a plaza rather than a street. Wrought-iron lanterns flank the main entrance over which the inevitable small balcony juts out a few feet. Across the top of the four-storey building a slogan is deeply carved into the stone: "A haza minden előtt!" ("The homeland before all else!") denoting the extreme patriotism of the day, and it is fitting that a rebirth of Hungarian nationalism should take place in such a setting.

Although the meeting is not scheduled to begin until 7:00 P.M., already at 4:30 a crowd is beginning to bulge out into Váci Street in front of the building's main entrance, causing stares and comments from passersby. The theater inside the club is, in fact, already full. The persons in charge are not letting any more people in. Not yet, at least.

But when it appears the crowd will push in the iron gates, they relent. The bulge is sucked into the building and all possible spaces in and around the theater that can accommodate people, sitting or standing—including the inner courtyard—begin to fill up.

But still they come, some of them important people with written invitations who insist on being allowed to squeeze in. Márton Horváth, editor of

Szabad Nép, who had authorized (and written) the favorable editorial on the Petőfi Circle, is one of the late arrivals. He has the devil of a time pushing his way through the packed auditorium and up to the podium.

Horváth is one of the designated discussion leaders of the evening, the others being Géza Losonczy, a journalist who was imprisoned without trial under Rákosi and then joined Imre Nagy's government in 1953, and György Máté, a one-time editor of *Szabad Nép* and party secretary of the Writers' Association. They are seated on the dais along with those who are to chair the discussion: Ervin Hollós, Tibor Huszár (main chairman) János Kéri, Imre Komor, Sándor Nógrádi, and Gábor Tánczos.

Because of the extreme heat, many in the crowd remove ties and jackets as do one or two on the dais. It is understood by all that there is to be no smoking in the theatre, nor for that matter any drinking or eating, for it will be difficult for anyone to leave for calls of nature.

Though it is only 6:30—half an hour before the scheduled start of the meeting—the room has long since been full and there is no point in further waiting. Chairman Tibor Huszár calls the gathering to order and announces that the first speaker will be Imre Csatár, editor of the youth newspaper, *Szabad Ifjúság*.[11]

Csatár begins by referring to earlier meetings of the Petőfi Circle in this room and in the Kossuth Club in the nearby Karl Marx University of Economics and states that this evening devoted to problems of the press will be no different from the other meetings. The faults of the press, he is quick to point out, are not entirely its responsibility: "The majority of its mistakes reflect the mistakes the party has made."

There is some stirring on the dais. A direct attack on the party has not been expected in the very first speech.

Csatár continues with a fairly long recitation of the party's mistakes, during which he is frequently interrupted by applause. At length Chairman Huszár interrupts: "We have another sixty speakers. We would like to remind Comrade Csatár to be brief."

Csatár repeats his last point and adds, "If the false reality of a bourgeois society is able to cultivate such talent as the Alsops and Whitman,* then our real and total social justice will be suitable soil for talented and feisty journalists." The room explodes in applause, which is punctuated with others yelling, "Time! Time!" "If my comrades will allow me," says Csatár, "I would

---

* Csatár probably means, or may actually have said, "Lippmann," meaning Walter Lippmann, who, like the Alsops, was a leading American syndicated columnist of the time.

like to address three other issues." Shouts of "No!" drown him out. The comrades feel he has already gone on too long.

At this point Chairman Huszár cuts in. "Just a brief announcement. We managed to mount loudspeakers in the courtyard as well, considering that a lot of people are worried about their families outside." (The street outside, in fact, is no longer a thoroughfare. The crowd is now packed in tight across its twenty-five-meter width. Estimates run to five thousand people.)

Before Csatár can resume speaking, Huszár announces the next speaker, Péter Nagy.

Nagy is somehat briefer, as is the next speaker, András Tábori.

Then comes Tibor Tardos, a journalist noted and liked for his forthright attitude.

He is greeted with applause even before he can speak. His main attack is on "dogmatic thinking" in the government and the party. "We didn't gather here tonight to hide it, but to remedy it," he says to cries of "Yes! Yes!" He mocks the typical newspaper article, which does not deal with facts, but with party goals in the future. "Our scientific clairvoyance works weeks, months, even yearly quarters ahead." (Laughter breaks out in the hall and down in Váci Street.) Then he turns serious and says that such dogmatism led directly to forced collectivization, show trials, and deportations. Getting rid of dogmatism must not be "done over a period of time, but immediately!" This brings another burst of applause and shouts of "Well said!"

Tardos speaks of a time when young journalists at *Szabad Nép*, complaining about not being allowed enough sources of information, were told by the deputy chief editor, Oszkár Betlen, to "read *Szabad Nép* as the only important source of information." "In other words, do and write what we tell you." But Tardos says it in a way that makes the room erupt with laughter.

The party, says Tardos frankly, is now split, and the non-Stalinist faction is growing. The accusation that this faction does not criticize from the inside is true, he says, because it is impossible to get inside the dogmatic inner circle. He ends his speech with a ringing affirmation that everything and everyone—ancient culture, modern technical research, Lenin, "who predicted the people's revolution" and "even Petőfi is with us."

Long, rhythmic applause shakes the hall through which clear shouts can be heard: "Publish this speech. Publish it in *Szabad Ifjúság*!"

Lajos Jánossy, an eminent physicist and foster son of the world-famous marxist philosopher, György Lukács, is now called on to speak. Jánossy used to be at Trinity College, Dublin, doing research in atomic physics. When he returned to Budapest in 1949 to visit his mother, his passport had been lifted and he was unable to return to Ireland.

Tibor Méray (left) and Tibor Déry (right) addressing the assembly with prepared remarks.
Photos by Erik Lessing. Used by permission.

Tibor Tardos answers back from the floor. Tibor Déry addressing the assembly with
prepared remarks. Photo by Erik Lessing. Used by permission.

The Hungarian press's main problem, Jánossy says, is its lack of respect: lack of respect for its readers, whom it patronizes as incapable of understanding anything the slightest bit complex, and lack of respect for scientists and, indeed, for science itself, which it woefully oversimplifies. He tells of being sent with a delegation of scientists to Moscow without any of them being told why, until they arrived and learned the reason from their Soviet hosts. He also tells of the nonsensical articles printed about things that are scientifically quite impossible—articles that are quite obviously copied verbatim from the Soviet press.

Then there is important scientific news, which gets suppressed until the authorities decide to print it. A colleague had complained of not being informed that uranium had been found in Hungary and having to read about it only in the newspaper. "Well," says Jánossy, "I am one of the presidents of the Hungarian Nuclear Energy Committee. How come I have not received any notification of the fact either?"

Newspaper reporters, he says, are so lacking in scientific education these days that they get many things totally wrong. Shouts of approval come from so many in the audience that Chairman Huszár interjects: "Please, comrades, don't bother the speaker with interruptions."

"It's not the speaker we are bothering!" someone shouts back, cupping his hands to be heard over the din.

Jánossy soon brings his talk to a conclusion to loud applause.

Fewer interruptions punctuate Gábor Mocsár's talk—even though he mentions Imre Nagy in passing. Mocsár is not one of the persons people have come to hear. But when Huszár announces that it is the Kossuth Prize-winning writer Tibor Déry's turn to speak, the applause swells and goes on for several minutes. Déry is a popular writer and long-time communist who spent many years in Horthy jails. His frail figure and hollow cheeks are a familiar sight. His voice is thin, but with the help of the public address system, all seven thousand present can hear him easily.

"Comrades," says Déry, "I just want to let you know that interruptions don't bother me." (The hall erupts with long and loud applause.) With such encouragement, in fact, the crowd now applauds, laughs, or comments at the end of nearly every paragraph or long sentence Déry utters. The men on the dais are clearly uncomfortable; fearing things may soon get out of hand.

Indeed, Déry proceeds to criticize previous speakers and many in the audience for not realizing that they are doing all of this fine talking because we have "been given permission by the authorities to do so. We are only characters in a play we didn't write."

"Not any more," yells someone, "The play has surpassed the playwright!"

"Fifteen hundred to two thousand of the same people go from discussion to discussion—it's only a different group of professionals who air their grievances. We keep blowing on horns like kids at a fair and don't seem to notice; the words remain words and the facts are unchanged. I can't help suspecting that this is part of a psychological maneuver … It's approved and supported because they know that steam is dangerous ... and they need to open the valves. We enjoy listening to our words. But everything continues the same."

Déry then electrifies the audience with the announcement that he will examine some specific examples, namely three prominent men in his field, one of whom, Márton Horváth, is sitting on the dais; the others are comrades József Révai, one of the four most powerful men in Hungary and the party's theoretician, and József Darvas, an old "populist" writer and former member of the Peasant Party, who is now a loyal communist and minister of education.

"Comrade Horváth," Déry begins "has frequently changed his position ... I have said 'position,' since I don't know his opinion. At times he spoke about my works with great appreciation. Other times ... he attacked me so viciously that it ... crossed the line of basic decency and endangered my personal security."

"When was that?" interrupts a voice from the audience. Déry pauses, looks up from his text and seeks the face of his questioner. "I refer to the well-known party decree issued in December. It was meant to prepare the soil for a literary trial in the nature of Rajk's. Why is it still in effect? Fortunately, the events in the Soviet Union [i.e., the Twentieth Party Congress] put a stop to these fine plans."

Déry goes on to explain that Horváth changed his position at the April meeting of the Writers' Association, which he, Déry, had been prevented by the decree from attending, on the grounds the party's position had changed and Central Committee members had to follow the party line even more strictly than regular party members, regardless of what their own opinion was. "What does that lead to?" he asks. "My answer is that I don't have confidence in Comrade Horváth now, or in the future."

As to Comrade Révai, Déry doesn't trust him for the opposite reason. "He is way too true to himself and never changes." This statement is too much for Ervin Hollós on the dais. "We trust Comrade Révai and the party!" he calls out. Then glaring at Déry, he admonishes, "Don't badmouth the party!" The crowd erupts with whistles and some applause, toward the end of which a voice calls out, "Let's hear the speaker!"

"Please, comrades," pleads chairman Huszár.

"We can't let him ruin the reputation of the party's leaders," cuts in Hollós as the din increases.

"Please, comrades," pleads Huszár again, "listen to Comrade Déry." (Applause.)

"Interruptions don't bother me," says Déry.

"But such talk bothers us!" interrupts Hollós.

Once more the hall erupts. "What do you know about journalism?" someone shouts at Hollós triggering a barrage of catcalls and expletives. Through the general uproar individual shouts of "Long live Déry!" "Out with Hollós!" and "Let's hear Déry!" can be distinguished.

At this point Gábor Tánczos, secretary of the Petőfi Circle, intervenes on behalf of the circle leadership. "I would ask all comrades present" (more noise) "to please allow Comrade Déry to speak." Révai's supporters now try to drown out Tánczos. "I have only one question," Tánczos tries to shout over the din, "Do six thousand comrades who are present[*] want to continue tonight's discussion?" "Yes!" comes the booming reply. "Then I will ask all of you to let Comrade Déry speak. Everyone has the right to reject his criticism, but in literary and intellectual questions, everyone in Hungary is entitled to criticize anyone." (Loud applause follows these remarks.)

Déry points out that while he is being blunt, he is also respectful. This unleashes another shouting match between Révai's supporters and the majority. "We can criticize Stalin, but not Révai?" someone asks mockingly. Hollós, spotting the provocateur, tries to shout an explanation in his direction, but he is quickly drowned out by cries of "Out with Hollós!"

Déry repeats why he cannot trust Révai and adds sarcastically that despite Révai's undeniable generosity and forceful charm," his political career lacks both.

"I assure you," he continues, "that it is Comrade Révai's fault that Hungarian literature and art declined gradually from the year 1948 ... up until recent days." (Cries of "Yes!" and "True!" come from the floor.) "It is high time that we got rid of the true-sounding statement used by dogmatic thinkers that actually murder truth. They keep referring to 'achievements of our young literature.' In my opinion our literature is not young; it is about 800 years old."

Révai, says Déry, had made it impossible for him, Déry, to publish for years, yet one of Révai's reviews of an unpublished Déry book was published in China in the form of a book! "Révai cannot be trusted. He does not learn from his mistakes."

Darvas, on the other hand, does not have the excuse of being mainly a politician, like Horváth and Révai.

"And just what are *your* faults?" calls out a voice near Déry."

"If you interrupt like that again," shouts Gábor Tánczos, "we'll have you bodily removed from the room!"

---

[*] Tánczos is aware of how many more people there are standing in the street and courtyard.

Huszár agrees with Tánczos and pleads that everyone will be given a chance to speak. Several voices, nonetheless, call out "Time's up! Time's up!"

Déry appeals to the crowd. Yes, they want him to go on.

Darvas is mostly a writer, regardless of how much time he's spent with politics, says Déry, but of "all our ministers in charge of public education, Darvas has been the biggest disappointment." In trying to serve both literature and politics, Darvas always went with politics because that is where the power is.

But criticizing these three men, says Déry, is no substitute for global and analytical criticism, which we need to have "if we are ever to find our way out of this swamp."

"When I look at our country and how much it has suffered," says Déry, "when I look at where we are and where we could be, and when I see how hurt our people are and still strong, then it becomes obvious to me that the present miserable situation is only partly due to the wrongdoers ... We must find the mistakes in our socialist system which made not only the leaders abuse their power, but made us, the people, incompetent in dealing with each other ...

"In this country of ours ... something terrible is happening. We forget what is the foundation of socialism and leave it out of our political system: trust in the individual." (Applause.) "Probably the most terrible mistake of the present leadership is that they don't trust the individual ... They base their entire thinking, methods and practices on the lack of trust. They underestimate the intellectual capabilities of the people ... They underestimate their decency and their sense of justice ... They expected the worst from us, and they got the worst of us. It was a normal human response. You think I am a thief, I will be a thief ... Our task is nothing less than to create conditions whereby our suppressed aspiration for life and work will be restored ... We are standing on the foundations of socialism ... We are entitled to free speech and free thinking. Let's make an effort to protect both even if there are new attempts to take those away from us ... Comrades, please don't forget that it is easier to hold onto freedom once it is achieved than to regain it once it has been lost. We should insist with all of our strength that our legal socialist right be respected ...

"We were invited here by this youth organization. I am sincere when I say that I trust our youth. I am asking these young people, these young Hungarians, to keep in mind the deeds of the young people of 1848." (Loud applause.) "As people today refer to the young people of 1848, so I wish that history will remember the young people of 1956 who will help our nation in creating a better future!" (Long rhythmic applause.)

Déry is followed by János Fürjes and Sándor Nógrádi, both of whom defend Horváth. Fürjes is hooted away from the microphone after only two minutes. Nógrádi lasts somewhat longer, but when he shouts, "I want to protect the party!" and a voice from the audience yells: "From whom?" the ensuing noise from the crowd forces him to break off.

György Máté, less passionate than some of his predecessors, nevertheless manages to get in a number of trenchant digs at the contemporary Hungarian press by comparing it extremely unfavorably to a single issue of a bourgeois newspaper, the July 7, 1929 issue of *Pesti Napló*, a popular newspaper which had flourished under Horthy. He ends by saying it is past time the people of Hungary were given freedom of speech.

Only polite applause greets the next speaker, Márton Horváth, who, as a "discussion leader," had not anticipated such a barrage of complaints. He begins by admitting that Déry's criticism of him was "mostly appropriate and fair," (brief applause) but then claims he will not hide behind the guidelines he has been obliged to follow and that, in fact, each of his many shifts has been of his own volition. He objects less to Déry's sarcasm than that Déry had made him look "like some kind of timeserver." Déry was wrong about these meetings being "some sort of propaganda maneuver. On the contrary, the Central Committee facilitates these discussions ..." (he has to pause while he lets a roar from the crowd subside) "because it trusts communists ... it is a sign of trust in the people ..." (Shouts of disbelief come from the audience.) "Articles in *Szabad Nép* are not the Bible," he goes on. "True," shouts Péter Kuczka, "only the really good articles should be considered the Bible, like the one written in *Szabad Nép* about the Petőfi Circle."[*]

"Please, listen to Comrade Horváth patiently," says chairman Huszár. "Comrade Kuczka will get his time too."

Horváth begins a long defense of *Szabad Nép*, ending up with his assurance that "all communists want to have *Szabad Nép* paint a realistic picture of the domestic and international affairs and economy of Hungary." ("When will it be able to?" shouts someone from the audience. "Who's preventing it?" shouts someone else.) "Comrades," Horváth replies, "that depends upon a lot of things." (The crowd erupts once again with jeers and one voice yell-

---

[*] For many months in the spring of 1956, as the meetings of the Petőfi Circle became more and more notorious, *Szabad Nép* completely ignored the circle's existence. Then on June 24, practically the eve of the session on the press, it came out with a very favorable article calling the Petőfi Circle "a shaft of sunlight."

ing, "Don't beat around the bush!") "Number one, we have not completed the application of the 20th Party Congress to Hungary. This ... task requires a lot of struggle." ("Who are you struggling with?" yells someone. "Why didn't you publish Togliatti's speech?" yells another.[*] "Why is Togliatti censored?") Horváth plows on through the hubbub. "To complete our task we must be able to rid ourselves of our mistakes." ("That would be good," yells someone sarcastically.) "We must join the mighty progressive flow of the international labor movement." (More noise. "You don't give us anything concrete," shouts someone in the front.) Horváth loses his place in his text and asks people on the dais why people are yelling at him. "Comrades," he tries to sum up, "I made many mistakes, like other comrades." The crowd has had it, and says so in so many words. "They were not mistakes," yells someone, "they were crimes. Draw your own conclusions."

"I accept criticism," Horváth shouts back at the crowd, "but I cannot accept reprimanding from the likes of you." (Roars from the crowd.) "The uncertainties and questions must be answered by actions from all communists." "Let's see that!" exclaims someone from the audience, and applause rings out as much for that remark as for Horváth who is pocketing his speech and retreating to his seat on the dais.

György Nemes, a forty-six-year-old journalist who writes largely for economic journals, follows Horváth. He complains that the party's entire cadre policy of training journalists is a failure. "Bourgeois journalists are much better trained than ours are now. As for selection, it is absurd to deny ourselves the best candidates merely because they do not have workers or peasants for parents. People must no longer be judged entirely on their social background."

Nemes now traces the sorry history of personnel at *Szabad Nép,* almost putting his audience to sleep as he drones off in roll-call fashion the names of fifty journalists who had worked for *Szabad Nép* in 1951. After most of the names he says in a raised monotone: "imprisoned," or "restricted," and follows this with the date of that action. "Well," he shouts as nodding heads pop up, "Do you know how many of those are working for *Szabad Nép* today?" and he pauses for emphasis ... "Exactly nine!"

---

* Togliatti, the first secretary of the Italian Communist Party, had given a speech in Italy about Khrushchev's secret speech at the Twentieth Party Congress, the full text of which had been carried in the Italian communist newspaper *L'Unita.* Many days after Togliatti's speech there had been some criticism of it in *Szabad Nép,* but never any report of the speech itself nor any undoctored portion of the text.

Nemes is followed by Zoltán Vas, former communist mayor of Budapest and long-time member of the régime's inner circle. Vas, short in stature and slow of speech, admits this is his first appearance at a meeting of the Petőfi Circle and he tends to agree with much that has been said. He does not agree with Déry and Tardos, whom he calls "extremists." This annoys the majority, who then interrupt him more and more frequently until Vas loses himself in the web of communist generalities and jargon. He asks to be permitted to fin-
· ish his speech, which then he does to scattered applause.

In sharp contrast to Vas, the next speaker, Tibor Méray, is explicit in his criticism. He has been a true believer and even became Hungary's expert on American "germ warfare" when he covered the Korean War for *Szabad Nép*, but he is contrite when proven wrong and his language is as clear and precise as his pencil moustache. He pokes fun at *Szabad Nép* for not daring to carry the weather forecast for May Day whenever there is the slightest chance of rain. But he also speaks of the "terrifying events" of 1949, such as the show trial of Rajk, and the imprisonment and execution of innocent party members, and he admits that he is one of those who had been "totally brainwashed." At the mention of Rajk, someone from the back of the room booms out, "Why don't we dig up Rajk's corpse from the ditch it was buried in and give it a proper, solemn funeral!" (Cheers greet this proposal, and similar suggestions are shouted back and forth across the theater.) Méray smiles faintly, but makes no comment and goes on with his prepared text. He speaks of Hungary needing a "purifying storm of history," a cleansing from top to bottom which will not be rationed into "a gentle breeze." These poetic words bring silence to that steaming, humid hall. He then brings up the case of Imre Nagy; before he can finish, voices begin to chant "Long live Imre Nagy," and some even begin to chant "Down with the régime!" As the room calms down, Méray says passionately: "I don't want freedom for the enemies of the people. But I want freedom for the people!" He then ends his speech with a ringing quote from Petőfi, which brings down the house.

Sándor Fekete, a correspondent for *Szabad Nép*, is not one of those orig- inally scheduled to speak, but he has been included at the last minute. "Dear Comrades," he says, "I have just arrived from Moscow … and came straight to the meeting." (Loud applause.) "First, the month and a half I spent there convinced me that there is a definite reform movement there … These reforms are impossible to stop by any force. Secondly, during my conversa- tions with Yugoslav Communists I found they approve of our fight against domination imposed on us by the enemy of the people [i.e., Rákosi]." (Long, loud applause.) "Thirdly, our fight for the truths revealed by the Twentieth

Party Congress will not be fought in Belgrade, or Moscow, but right here in Budapest." (Long, loud rhythmic applause.)

It is now well past midnight. Géza Losonczy, the last of the major discussion leaders on the dais and the last formally scheduled speaker—though he is by no means last on the list—begins his speech. He is an outstanding member of the communist intelligentsia, but almost everything, he says, that he wanted to say has already been said. But he does not let that fact curtail him. He assures everyone that there is now no going back to positions held prior to the Twentieth Party Congress and that such a thing as another Rajk trial is impossible. He is powerful in his language and accurate in his accusations. "When the Central Committee decided to expel Imre Nagy from the party," he says, "why wasn't this decision published in the party's central newspaper [i.e., *Szabad Nép*]? Why was it published only in the magazine *Pártépítés?*" ("They had a bad conscience," yells somebody.)

Losonczy reviews the whole totally inadequate and false handling of the Togliatti speech by all of the Hungarian press, not just *Szabad Nép*, and brings up the subject of the mysterious knowledge that a visiting delegation of the British Socialist Party have about the release of Hungarian socialists from prison when no one in Hungary knew about their release, since there had been no mention of it in the press.

"If they stop considering people as minors," he concludes, "and start providing information to the people, if editors will be able to work independently, free from central control, the independent voice of the press will be heard, information will not be falsified, and the public will be better informed."

There are still nine more speakers on the schedule who have not yet spoken, but so many persons from the audience have demanded to be allowed to speak or pressed for the right of reply that the chairpeople on the dais can no longer hold them back. The meeting is thrown open to those from the floor who have requested, via written notes, to speak. Many attack Horváth.

Three times Horváth gets up to protest and defend himself, and each time he is shouted down. Grown furious, he finally screams into the microphone "How dare you insult the party!"

"The party?" yells a voice from the crowd. "We are the party!" (Pandemonium breaks out at this exchange.)[12]

Through the hubbub groups begin to chant slogans, and one in particular begins to take over as its chanters rise to their feet shouting rhythmically: "Down with the government! Long live Imre Nagy!"

Someone at the microphone asks, "How come we call this the 'Sándor Petőfi Club'? Petőfi fought for freedom of the press!" "Which we don't have!" shouts somebody jumping to his feet. Then Horváth, who is also on his feet on the podium, shouts "That's right!" Someone else jumps up and shouts, "You're telling us that? You're the editor of *Szabad Nép!*" Horváth shrugs his shoulders in reply and shuffles back to his seat.

The meeting continues its chaotic course. Most persons who came intending to speak have spoken, in many cases more than once, and now many who came with no intention of speaking are getting up to add their opinion to the cauldron. Everyone is soaked with sweat and hoarse with shouting; yet no one makes any attempt to leave. Sheer exhaustion finally overtakes the assemblage, but it is after 3 A.M. that the meeting is officially ended with the announcement by Chairman Huszár that it is *not* being ended, but merely suspended. He promises that the meeting will be reconvened in a few days. They have been at it for nine hours!

While most who were at the meeting sleep it off, word races around Budapest. The city is electrified, and people can talk of nothing else. Surely something big is now going to happen. Many people speak of a second Hungarian Revolution (the first being that of March 1848), saying this is the way things are going to be from now on. Others are more cautious, saying, "At least no one was arrested on the spot."

By late afternoon people in government offices and news organizations become aware of something ominous happening in Poznań, Poland, but it is some days before the general populace have any idea of just what has taken place.

The party, however, is suddenly galvanized. Stung by all it had been accused of, it calls a meeting of the Central Committee for June 30. The resolution Rákosi and his henchmen ram through is a blistering attack on the Petőfi Circle calling it "counterrevolutionary ... full of fascists, imperialists, and paid agents of the Americans" and charging that "this open opposition to the party and to the People's Democracy was organized mainly by a certain group around Imre Nagy."

The full text is carried in *Szabad Nép*, which had praised the Petőfi Circle just five days earlier. To no one's surprise Tibor Déry and Tibor Tardos are expelled from the party.

While no one is arrested, the circle itself pulls in its horns and beats a full retreat. The next scheduled debate, on education, is postponed "for technical reasons" (summer vacations). While the circle's activities do spread to the provinces and there are actually six meetings held in September and October, these are narrowly defined and attended only by invitation. The circle ceases to exist in the public's mind. Ironically, its last meeting, one on the medical profession, is scheduled for the night of October 23. (When fighting breaks out on that night at the nearby radio headquarters and one of the armed insurgents breaks into their meeting to announce that the revolution has begun, the circle members shoo him out, despite the sound of nearby gunfire, so that they can go on with their important discussions. History is passing the circle by.)[13]

The meeting of June 27, however, has had its effect. Support for Nagy and things articulated at the meeting grow daily among the populace. At a mass workers meeting called by the government to condemn the Petőfi Circle the workers show their feelings by staying away in droves. Encouraged by this show of mass support, the Writers' Association refuses to recognize the expulsion of Déry and Tardos from the party. This, too, is unheard of.[14]

For the first time Western journalists hear party and government officials say that Rákosi has to go.[15]

Rákosi has no intention of going. He draws up a secret list of four hundred high, or once high, party officials who are to be arrested in one fell swoop. Naturally Imre Nagy, and such recently rehabilitated persons as János Kádár and people who were on the dais of that Petőfi Circle meeting, such as Géza Losonczy, are at the top of the list.

The leaders in the Kremlin are alarmed by all the reports coming from Hungary. They dispatch Mikhail Suslov, the politburo's ideological watchdog, to Budapest for a first-hand reading of the situation. On his return Suslov recommends that Rákosi be retained. Khrushchev explains to the surprised Yugoslav ambassador: "We Russians haven't any choice in the matter." But he is not wholly convinced that this is the case, so he decides to send Mikoyan to Budapest for a more sophisticated reading. Mikoyan, who has been reading many good things about the Petőfi Circle and may not have yet read of the meeting on the 27th, is being sent ostensibly to attend the July 17th meeting of the party's Central Committee. Much to his horror, he hears Rákosi unveil his plan for the immediate arrest of four hundred leading party members. Allowing Rákosi to finish, he asks him his opinion of the Petőfi Circle. "Organized by enemies of the party," replies Rákosi. At this point Rákosi's right-hand man of eleven years, Ernő Gerő, rises to say, "Might I suggest to our beloved and wise father of the people that mass arrests are not reconciliable with our new brand of socialist legality."[16]

Ultimately the vote goes against Rákosi. Ashen white, he rushes into a room next door where he can be heard speaking Russian to Khrushchev: "But the party needs me. If I go it will just cave in."

In fact, it is Rákosi who is ready to cave in—physically—for the events of the past several months have raised his blood pressure alarmingly.

In the early evening of July 17 all newspapers in Budapest are told over a special phone line to hold their pages open; there will be a special announcement at nine o'clock. People brace themselves for the news that Imre Nagy and his friends have been arrested. Instead, when the message finally comes it is that the secretary general of the party is retiring "for reasons of health" and will be replaced by Ernő Gerő. Mihály Farkas, the former minister of the interior, who has already been fired from the government, is now expelled from the party.

On July 21 Rákosi is secretly flown to Moscow, whence he will never return, and two days later the Central Committee begins to rehabilitate many of Rákosi's party victims. Júlia Rajk, however, declines the 200,000 forints offered her as compensation. She is holding out for justice and a proper burial for her husband. Within months she will get it.

CHAPTER VI

A Chronology of Events from Khrushchev's Speech to the Poznań Trials

We have witnessed the seminal event of 1956—Khrushchev's secret speech—and the first major consequences of that event as they occurred in the three east-central European countries most affected by it. It is now time to change our focus, to step back, as it were, and view what we have experienced in the larger context of what was going on throughout the area as these events unfolded. What follows in this chapter is a time-line, a chronology of events large and small as reported by journalists, diplomats, and policy makers of the time. Each item is incomplete, with only the bare bones of the event or policy being recorded. Taken together it is like a large daily newspaper, disjointed, incomplete, and far too much to absorb. The intent, however, is not so much to impart factual information—though some of this is bound to stick—but to give the reader the impression of what that time was like, both in the complexity and the speed with which changes were taking place.

Of course, there was a great deal else that was going on—the run-up to the U.S. national election and trouble in the Middle East centering on Egypt, to name just two—but our focus is on east-central Europe and the policies of the two major cold war rivals toward this area as well as their actual activities in it. A great deal has had to be omitted,[*] yet the reader will probably find it more than enough.

Before we begin, there are some constants that need to be mentioned here so that the reader may keep them in the back of his mind as he reads.

---

[*] For instance, nearly all of the "spy" and "sabotage" trials that took place in Czechoslovakia at this time were only reported, if at all, in the provincial press.

One constant is the incessant Communist Party line that permeated everything citizens of these countries read or heard from their controlled media. Since most people were not communists or even sympathizers, they learned to ignore or at least compensate for it. Nevertheless, it affected their thinking if only for all the information it excluded.

This—the information excluded—is another constant to bear in mind. This excluded or missing information had to be gleaned, for the most part, from foreign radio broadcasts; and this was difficult. People living in large cities found it almost impossible to hear foreign radios because jamming stations surrounding all cities emitted an irritating, high-pitched wa-oo-wa-oo— so fast that it sounded like rapid bubbles—on the same wavelengths of these foreign broadcasts so as to completely obliterate them. Only in the countryside could the radios be heard without too much interference. The favorite of the educated classes, of course, was the BBC, which had gained great credibility during the Second World War. Now the BBC continued in its dispassionate, objective-sounding style. The VOA was listened to because it was the authoritative voice of the free world's most powerful country. The favorite of the common people, however, was Radio Free Europe—for two reasons. First of all, it purported to be a home radio—Radio Free Hungary, Radio Free Poland, Radio Free Czechoslovakia—and its programs were designed as if they were being broadcast from within these countries, though everyone knew they were coming from Munich. Second, they broadcast from between eighteen to twenty hours each day, whereas the other radios were seldom on the air for more than three or four hours per day. Added to RFE's radios were the balloon-borne leaflets* of Free Europe Press, sister organization to RFE. Starting tentatively with leaflets to Czechoslovakia in April 1954, the operations expanded to Hungary and Poland in 1955, and were in full swing until November 1956. These leaflets, while tangible evidence of Western concern, were far more hit-or-miss, with accent on the latter. The vast majority fell over forests, lakes and rivers from which they were never recovered. But there were so many—over 500 million launched between April 1954 and November 1956[1]—that tens of thousands did get into the hands of the populace and were doubtless passed on to friends. The average leaflet was an eight-page, accordion folded miniature illustrated newspaper

---

* Leaflet delivery was possible on a continuous basis because at 18,000 to 20,000 feet prevailing winds are east to west all around the globe. Not all Free Europe balloons made it to that level before encountering surface winds that blew them badly off course. In the summer of 1956 the citizens of Helsinki, Stockholm, and even Edinburgh were treated to the sight of Polish and Hungarian language leaflets fluttering down upon them.

covering all manner of events in the free world over the past fortnight (Czechoslovakia) or month (Hungary), and even less frequently for Poland, because its distance and direction from Bavaria required special weather conditions for the balloons to reach their destinations. Interspersed with these regularly appearing leaflets were special booklet leaflets such as Orwell's *Animal Farm* or Świątło's revelations or the full text of Khrushchev's secret speech with commentary. Parts of western Bohemia were so littered with these leaflets that the Czechoslovak army was turned out to collect and destroy them.

So, while the régimes were telling the populace one thing, the Western radios—and particularly Free Europe, with its leaflet-augmented broadcasts—was telling them quite another.

A third constant which the reader should try to keep in mind, but which cannot be so easily defined because it was *not* consistent, was the policy being pursued by each of the two world antagonists toward the area. After Poznań the Soviets did an about face in their policy toward their East European satellites and spent the rest of 1956 trying to get matters back under their control. The United States, on the other hand, had two mutually opposing policies, one reflected by Secretary Dulles of "keeping the pot simmering" in the Soviets' backyard, and the other by President Eisenhower, of seeking *genuine* accommodation with them through reciprocal peaceful exchanges designed to break down hostility.

Nor was the U.S. policy of "keeping the pressure on" shared by America's allies, Britain and France. The British dislike of both U.S. ends *and* means in Eastern Europe cannot be discerned from the few dispatches quoted below. What can be seen, perhaps, is the more realistic, as well as more accurate, observations of Her Majesty's representatives due to their longer familiarity with the area and superior contacts in high places. The U.S. embassies seem more dependent upon the local press and diplomatic corps for their information than on long-cultivated informants in the local populace.

Here, then, is an arbitrary, but representative, selection of current events as a backdrop to the more focused events treated earlier.

☞

Sat., Feb 24	Khrushchev delivers his secret speech denouncing Stalin.
Tue., Feb. 27	Secretary of State John Foster Dulles, at a meeting of the National Security Council discussing aid to underdeveloped countries, suggests a scheme of offering a number of items, including food, to Czechoslovakia, which they really need.

Such a proposal, he says, "would simply raise hell" in the satellite countries because the Soviets would never allow them to accept it. This was just an "off-the-cuff suggestion," of the kind of flexibility the U.S. president may need in the future. President Eisenhower replies that the trouble is that Congress believes that any and all trade with the Soviet bloc is wrong and bad. (Even in this brief exchange it is clear that the president is talking about real trade and the secretary about mere "offers" of trade which he believes will never have to be followed through on.)[2]

Wed., Feb. 28   In Washington the Operations Coordinating Board submits its second progress report on NSC-174, first issued in 1953, stating that it sees no likelihood of Titoism emerging elsewhere, but recommends that "attention should be given to determining what courses of action to induce the Soviet and satellite leadership to be more receptive to negotiated settlements and what degree of stress should be placed on encouragement of Titoist tendencies of 'national communist movements.'" The same progress report states that "any movement toward relaxation of tension between East and West is bound to be widely interpreted in the Satellites as a weakening of Western determination to achieve their liberation ... (The dilemma U.S. policy faces of whether to use a carrot or a stick, or rather, how much carrot and how much stick, is clear from this committee-authored report.)[3]

Mon., March 5   Students riot in T'bilisi, the capital of Soviet Georgia, over the denigration of Georgia's native son, Stalin, and order is not restored until March 9.[4]

Wed., March 14   The Hungarian party Central Committee, after hearing a report from First Secretary Mátyás Rákosi on the new Soviet line against the "cult of the individual" and the importance of "collective leadership," adopts his report wholeheartedly but adds somewhat enigmatically that this gives "new emphasis" to the "correct policies of the Third Hungarian Party Congress resolution of 1955," which, in fact, ran quite counter to it.[5]

Thu., March 15   The International Court in the Hague drops U.S. applications against the U.S.S.R. and Czechoslovakia for shooting down U.S. planes on March 7, 1952, and March 10, 1953, respectively, due to these countries' refusal to recognize the jurisdiction of the International Court in these cases.[6]

Wed., March 21   The United States Air Force's Strategic Air Command (SAC) begins a series of secret overflights of the entire Soviet Union's northern coastal area from the Bering Sea to Murmansk, flying from Thule Airbase in northern Greenland. The flights, which are refueled over the North Pole, are to continue sporadically until May 10. (No admission of these overflights is ever made by the U.S. government, nor will any information about them be published until 1997.)[7]

Thu., March 22   Allen Dulles, director of the Central Intelligence Agency (CIA) tells the U.S. National Security Council the "dramatic" news that Khrushchev, in a secret speech at the Twentieth Party Congress appears to have "deliberately sought to destroy Stalin, and that this "afforded the U.S. a great opportunity, both overtly and covertly, to exploit the situation to its advantage." Dulles also states that the student "uprising" in T'bilisi went so far that the Soviet government was obliged to relax some of its major anti-Stalinist measures in Georgia.[8]

Sat., March 24   In Munich, Germany, a special "guidance" referring to reports of Khrushchev's secret speech is circulated around the offices of Radio Free Europe (RFE) and its sister organization Free Europe Press (FEP), which sends leaflets via balloons into Czechoslovakia, Poland and Hungary, stating that "not in a long time [have we] had a topic so rich in substance, so favorable to our purposes ..."[9]

Sun., March 25   The dismissal of the Polish minister of culture, Sokorski, is announced at a meeting of the Council of Culture and Art in Warsaw.[10]

An entire work force of 2,000 women in a textile factory near Białystok, Poland, goes on strike for a day protesting not only their miserable working conditions, but the facts that they are housed ten and twelve to a room, are given food unfit to eat, and have no recreational facilities whatsoever.[11]

Radio Warsaw tells the Polish people that Stalin's "false theory about the alleged continuous increase of the enemy's forces has done a great deal of harm. It has barred the road back to Poland to many ... for instance to the former soldiers of the A.K. [Home Army] who believed that they were fighting for a free and democratic Poland and shed their blood for the cause." The Home Army, an underground military organization which fought the Nazis during the entire occupation, was under the direct command of the Polish government in exile in London, and thus an anathema to Stalin.[12]

Reviewing Polish-American relations, the Department of State in Washington tells its Warsaw embassy that "even making allowances for the many reservations and qualifications with which the British ambassador has supported his analysis of present Soviet-Polish relations, the department cannot agree with his basic thesis that a definite Polish policy independent of Moscow is now emerging." This statement is based largely upon facts and analysis supplied by the embassy in Warsaw and thus is more loyal backup than independent analysis.[13]

Thu., March 29   In Bucharest, First Party Secretary Gheorghe Gheorghiu-Dej in his first report to the Romanian Central Committee on the Twentieth Party Congress spends five times as much time on praising Stalin's importance, virtues, and popularity than he does on negative aspects of the "cult of personality." Like Rákosi in Hungary, Gheorghiu-Dej has emulated Stalin closely.[14]

Radio Warsaw, calling Stalin "monstrously and pathologically suspicious," tells its listeners: "To keep people obedient, terror was required. Stalin put forth the theory that the more socialism develops, the more acute become the activities of the enemy. Thus the security organization was expanded and the use of terror began, first against ideological opponents ... and then against everyone who expressed different opinions."[15]

Fri., March 30   The Hungarian Writers' Association holds a tumultuous session which becomes so raucous that outside help in the form of Márton Horváth, editor of *Szabad Nép,* has to be called in. He promptly suspends the meeting for two weeks. The régime finds itself attacked not only for its policies on literature, but for promoting heavy industry, and agricultural collectivization, and for the undemocratic way that the central leadership, expecting only rubberstamped approval, dictates its view to the party.[16]

Mon., April 2   Czechoslovak authorities will neither confirm nor deny that three men tried with Rudolf Slánský, but not condemned to die, have been released. They have been reported seen in Prague in the last few days.[17]

The Bulgarian Communist Party's Central Committee launches an attack upon "the cult of personality surrounding the person of Comrade Vulko Chervenkov," first party secretary.[18]

Wed., April 4   Great publicity is given in the Budapest press this morning to Khrushchev and Bulganin's message of "warm greetings" to Rákosi, which readers take to be Soviet support for his remaining in power.[19]

Fri., April 6   In Warsaw, First Party Secretary Edward Ochab tries to put the brakes on the spreading ferment when he says in a speech that "some comrades seem to be losing their sense of balance ... There are people who in public ... and in the press come out against the party. This shows ... a confusion of ideas ... The words themselves speak of concern for the party, but in fact they attack the party." Ochab is not just reacting to Soviet complaints, he really thinks things are going too far for comfort.[20]

Sat., April 7   Georgi Malenkov, Soviet minister for electric power ever since his demotion from premier in 1955, completes a three-week goodwill tour of the United Kingdom which is preparatory to a visit by Khrushchev and Bulganin later this month. Soviet politburo member Ivan Serov is being discouraged from accompanying them by the British foreign office due to his great unpopularity in Britain.[21]

In Budapest Rákosi is again attacked at the resumed Writers' Association Congress, which culminates in the poet Gyula Hay proposing that a memo be sent to the party Central Committee demanding Rákosi's immediate removal. The resulting ruckus continues beyond the official ending of the meeting. Many critical views expressed at the congress begin to be repeated at meetings of the Petőfi Circle.[22]

Tue., April 10   A fully armed Czech border guard crosses the Iron Curtain near Fassmannsreuth, West Germany, after apparently shooting his companion guard. The lethal shot is heard on both sides of the border, but the dead man is only discovered many hours later, since shots on the Czechoslovak side are such a common occurrence.[23]

Wed., April 11   Under Secretary of State Robert D. Murphy decides that "any action leading to the re-establishment of relations with Bulgaria should be deferred for at least a few months ..." Diplomatic relations with Bulgaria were severed in 1950 after the régime accused the American minister of being a subversive influence and declaring him persona non grata. Murphy's comment comes in the wake of Bulgaria's recent admission into the

United Nations (along with Hungary, Romania, and Albania), and indicates their eagerness to gain what all of the other satellites but Albania have: diplomatic relations with the U.S.[24]

Thu., April 12   The U.S. legation in Budapest cables the Department of State that "Rákosi's Stalinist background, his unsavory record and his current political acrobatics make him an extremely vulnerable target. A carefully prepared diplomatic offensive with coordinated propaganda exploitation could not only provide his opponents with valuable ammunition, but possibly even render his position untenable in the eyes of Moscow." The Budapest legation is the only U.S. outpost in Eastern Europe at this time that recognizes the importance of America's propaganda radios, VOA and RFE, and tries to give them guidance.[25]

Fri., April 13   Allen Dulles tells the World Affairs Council in Los Angeles that "the men in the Kremlin ... admit that the past adulation of Stalin was based on fear, not on fact. The man they themselves used to call 'glorious Stalin, genius of mankind' is now publicly accused of 'grave errors' and privately described as a 'malicious monster.'" The clue to this present policy, Dulles continues, "lies more to the internal Soviet situation than in ... foreign policy ... They hope to preserve many of the essentials of the Stalinist system, now labeling it 'Leninist.' The degradation of Stalin ... was to be under strict party discipline. But it seems to have gotten out of hand."[26]

Workers at the Pafaweg Works in Wrocław, finding their work norm raised by 11 percent without any corresponding compensation, are refusing to work. A few days later, lest the situation deteriorate further, the management gives in to the workers' demands. No mention of this appears in the Polish press.[27]

The British embassy in Prague points out to the foreign office that the confusion Novotný's recent Central Committee speech is causing the Czechoslovak press can be seen in a number of contradictory interpretations.[28]

Sat., April 14   The Bulgarian government announces today that the December 1949 trial and execution of Traicho Kostov, former deputy premier, was totally fake and that Kostow and "all the defendants at the trial are [posthumously] rehabilitated." Kostov, leader of the national (vs. Soviet) faction of the Bulgarian Communist Party, was tried and convicted with others in December 1949. Only he was put to death, courageously maintaining his innocence to the end.[29]

Khrushchev and Bulganin board a train for Kaliningrad on the first leg of their trip to Great Britain. This is not their first time outside of the communist world—they attended the meeting of nonaligned nations in Indonesia in 1955—but it will be their first time in the West.[30]

. Sun., April 15   Khrushchev and Bulganin board the Soviet cruiser *Ordzhomikdze*, which sails out into the Baltic Sea.[31]

Mon., April 16   In Sofia, Bulgarian premier Vulko Chervenkov resigns his position admitting his "violation of collective leadership" and "encouraging the cult of the individual." He is replaced by Anton Yugov, a former deputy premier and member of the nationalist faction.[32]

Tue., April 17   The Soviet Union announces the dissolution of the Cominform, the organization designed to coordinate the foreign operations of all communist parties around the world. Stalin ejected Yugoslavia from the organization in 1948 just a year after it was founded with headquarters in Belgrade. The headquarters had to be quickly shifted to Bucharest. Its only publication has been a weekly newspaper printed in many languages with the cumbersome title: *For a Lasting Peace, For a People's Democracy.* But like its forerunner, the Comintern, it has been heavily engaged in secret, underground activities.[33]

Wed. April 18   Khrushchev and Bulganin, having landed five hours earlier in Portsmouth, receive a cool reception in London from the reserved British public and angry exiles groups from the Soviet Union and Eastern Europe. Official talks begin.[34]

The Department of State, in a review of escapees from the communist-dominated portion of Europe, acknowledges that "Soviet bloc countries have launched a far-reaching program against escapees" involving "radio broadcasts, publications, personal appeals, chain letters, formal proclamations of amnesty, and isolated examples of violence against important individual escapees. The results have been a lowering of morale among the escapees, the actual return and subsequent exploitation of some, and a decrease in willingness to cooperate with U.S. ... programs."[35]

In an analysis of the situation in Czechoslovakia, the British ambassador in Prague tells the foreign office in London that "it might have been expected that the rehabilitation ... of Gomułka in Poland, Mr. Kostov in Bulgaria and the late László Rajk in Hungary, would evoke a similar rehabilitation of

Slánský. Despite the fact that the Czechoslovak party leaders have in the past shown themselves more eager than most to keep in step with their comrades in other satellite states, they have not done so on this occasion. Slánský, far from being rehabilitated, has been branded as the initiator of the cult of personality in Czechoslovakia and the arch-violator of socialist legality."[36]

Workers at the Warsaw "September 22" chocolate factory go out on strike for higher wages. The Central Committee gives in to their demands after they refuse to negotiate with the factory management or the government. This is just one of many reports of works stoppages reaching the U.S. embassy in Warsaw.[37]

Sat., April 21   The Polish prosecutor general, Stefan Kalinowski, and the minister of justice are fired. Marian Rybicki is the new prosecutor general and the new minister of justice will be a woman, Zofia Wasilkowska. Also fired from his position as minister of state farms is Stanisław Radkiewicz, the former minister of security, who had been removed from his position in 1954 following the revelations of Światło over Radio Free Europe.[38]

Thu., April 26   A Czech informant tells the U.S. embassy that the Czech minister of culture, Ladislav Stoll, is on the way out and that he may be replaced by a man named Kokecký. He adds that the recent dismissal of Defense Minister Alexej Čepička has lifted the spirits of the Czechoslovak people. The same informant, accompanying an American troop performing "Porgy and Bess" to several Czechoslovak cities, points out the many radio towers in towns they drive through saying they are "RFE jammers." He adds that most people try to listen to RFE on short wave sets and that there was great interest in the programs as well as those of the Voice of America.[39]

Fri., April 27   The Soviet leaders depart London after more than a week of official talks and touring in Great Britain. Eden is issued an invitation to visit the Soviet Union. During the visit the headless body of British "frogman" Commander Crabbe is retrieved from Plymouth harbor. He had been attempting to inspect the undersides of the Soviet cruiser that brought them.[40]

The U.S. legation in Budapest reports to Washington that "the dominoes in Eastern Europe [have] begun to fall. Whatever course may have been intended for Hungary, it is certainly true that the situation here has deteriorated very rapidly ... faster

174

and further than originally intended. The very sudden decision to postpone the transfer of Soviet ambassador Andropov is probably an indication of Soviet concern. We ... are inclined to believe that there are good chances for Rákosi's eventual removal."[41]

Sat., April 28 Radio Warsaw announces the resignation of Foreign Minister Stanisław Skrzeszewski and the appointment of Adam Rapacki to replace him. Rapacki is a liberal and known to be a friend of the former first party secretary, Gomułka. His name will become well known in the West during the 1960s as the author of the "Rapacki Plan"—a scheme for détente and disengagement in central Europe which, while never realized, is taken by many in the West to be genuine, and not just Soviet propaganda.[42]

Mladá Frontá, the Czech party's youth newspaper, reports that a lively meeting of the youth union took place at Charles University last Thursday evening, April 26, with a resulting resolution calling for many liberal changes in Czechoslovak society and revisions in the university curriculum.[43]

Soviet ambassador to Budapest Yuri Andropov telegraphs Moscow that the Hungarian politburo "still believes that the right-wing opportunists ... continue to undermine the party's reputation through their demagogy and provocations." By "right-wing opportunists" he means the liberal, Imre Nagy wing of the party that has been attacking Rákosi.[44]

Sun., April 29 The Hungarian government announces price reductions on a number of consumer items, mainly clothes. This is the first price reduction since March 1954. Some 6,500 items are affected, mostly clothing but many food items as well. The average price of menus in restaurants is predicted to drop by 10 percent. The population, says the party daily *Szabad Nép,* will save 900 million forints yearly.[45]

Mon., April 30 The U.S. secretary of state, John Foster Dulles, in a letter to Ambassador Henry Cabot Lodge at the UN, tells him that this is not the time to push for the "Volunteer Freedom Corps"—a military unit to be made up entirely of East European exiles for possible use in case of war—which Lodge had been promoting. The idea of forming military units consisting wholly of East European exiles has been around since before the Republicans came in in 1952. It did not originate with Lodge, but he has become one of its most ardent advocates.[46]

Wed., May 2	The Czech literary paper, *Literarní Noviný* today carries many of the texts of the speeches at the recent, explosive meeting of the Czech Writers' Congress. The U.S. and British embassies note the extraordinary frankness of the criticism of the government and attacks on the minister of culture. These attacks had only been hinted at in press accounts. Considerable controversy must have preceded the decision to publish them.[47]
	In Moscow, *Pravda* prints an article by Mátyás Rákosi on Leninist principles. Having such a controversial figure write this feature article in *Pravda* is an unmistakable sign of full Soviet approval.
Thu., May 3,	*Szabad Nép* reprints the full text of Rákosi's *Pravda* article. By Soviet dictated practice, all such *Pravda* articles must be printed the next day in the party dailies of the satellite countries.
Sun., May 6	Jakub Berman, deputy premier and hardline member of the Polish politburo, suddenly resigns his post. He had been close to Bierut.[48]
	Sir Andrew Noble, British ambassador to Warsaw, attributes Berman's firing to the fact that he was in charge of the show trials now exposed as fraudulent; also that he and M. Minc, now fatally ill in Moscow, had both been protected by Bierut.[49]
Mon., May 7	A formation of six U.S. RB-47E's (reconnaissance bombers) based in Thule, Greenland, overflies eastern Siberia and lands in Alaska. Since the flight is in daylight and clearly observable from the ground, a diplomatic protest can be expected.[50]
	A Polish economic periodical, *Chłopska Droga,* prints a letter from a Lublin farmer which states: "If Stalin made so many mistakes, the establishment of kolkhozes [collective farms] in the U.S.S.R. and Poland was a mistake. What's the idea of urging me to join a collective? The possibility exists that the collectives will be dissolved eventually."[51]
Tue., May 8	The American ambassador to Czechoslovakia, finding this year's invitation to the Czechoslovak Liberation Day reception containing "no objectionable language," attends the reception and finds no attempt, as in former years, to segregate Western diplomats. He is greeted in friendly fashion by Premier Široký, who takes the initiative in opening a conversation. Such changes, though seemingly slight, are felt to be extremely significant and thus are noted in all diplomatic reporting from Western embassies.[52]

Thu., May 10   It is announced in Budapest that mines and barbed wire on the Austrian border are to be removed in the near future. This is being done in accordance with the new slogan of Leninist principle of each country's right to find its "own way to socialism." Nothing is said about the Yugoslav border. Hungary is the only nation in the bloc ever to make such an announcement. Its example will not be followed.[53]

Fri., May 11   In Hungary, Archbishop Grősz is freed from prison and resumes his archbishopric at Kalocsa. He had been sentenced in June 1951 to fifteen years in prison. In October 1955 his sentence was "interrupted" because of ill health and he was allowed to go live in a monastery. He will also resume his duties as president of the Hungarian Council of Bishops. No mention is made of Cardinal Mindszenty, still in prison.[54]

Szabad Nép prints a statement by Soviet president Kliment Voroshilov, in which he addresses Rákosi as "dear friend." (To Hungarians, this salutation means "Watch out! We Soviets still support Rákosi. Stop criticising him.")[55]

Sat. May 12   In Bratislava, Slovak students hold their first Majáles parade since 1948.[56]

Sun., May 13   The central board of the Association of Polish Lawyers says that in addition to restoring confidence in the legal profession the association needs to set up broader legal foundations "to compensate the rehabilitated citizens for material losses." The April issue of the party's theoretical journal *Nowe Drogi* has already stated that "violation of legality, no matter in what field it takes place … immediately creates a tendency to violate legality in general." The association also passes a resolution insisting that the "complete independence" of judges is a "prerequisite for the rule of law."[57]

Mon., May 14   The Soviet government delivers to the U.S. embassy in Moscow a note of strong protest against the U.S. overflights of Soviet territory.[58]

The American embassy in Prague notes that the official Czechoslovak telegraph agency, CETEKA, failed to carry the passage in Široký's recent Bratislava address in which he confesses that the "security organs, prosecutors offices and courts of law in the past thought that their principle aim was to make [the accused] confess his guilt at any cost … thus determining to a great extent the outcome of the trials."[59]

177

The British ambassador to Moscow, Sir William Hayter, reports that Khrushchev recently told a delegation of visiting French socialists that the Soviet government would be making a major disarmament announcement at the next meeting of the Supreme Soviet, and that this may be the same as the rumors which Sir Andrew Noble in Warsaw had heard about the withdrawal of Soviet troops from satellite territory.[60]

Tue., May 15   The Soviet government announces that it is preparing to reduce its military forces outside its territory and that this will be "discussed" at the forthcoming meeting of the Supreme Soviet. The British embassy notes that "there is no indication of force levels before and after the projected reduction of Soviet forces in the satellites, other than East Germany, where a reduction of 30,000 is planned."[61]

Radio Warsaw announces that under the new amnesty law some 30,000 persons convicted of "crimes" before April 1956 have already been released.[62]

Wed., May 16   Writing in the Hungarian publication *Béke és Szabadság*, Tamás Aczél complains that the government's shortening of the Christmas and Easter holidays to one day each has had an adverse effect: "It strengthens religious feelings." Like all Europeans, East and West, Hungarians traditionally take at least two days off for Christmas and Easter.[63]

Thu., May 17   CIA Director Allen Dulles tells the National Security Council in Washington that "Poland has been the most seriously affected by the development of the de-Stalinization campaign," and that the U.S. should take pains to "exploit developments in Poland." He says that he hopes to present the council next week with a full text of Khrushchev's secret speech. In answer to his brother's comment that the speech, as he understood it, was extemporaneous, he replies that Khrushchev spoke from a prepared text *and* extemporaneously."[64]

Fri., May 18   Hungarian first party secretary Mátyás Rákosi, while conceding some guilt in cultivating and tolerating "the cult of personality" delivers a harsh, uncompromising speech ending all speculation that he might show a real change of attitude.[65]

Polish premier Józef Cyrankiewicz is the object of many rumors in Warsaw. British ambassador Sir Andrew Noble notes in a message to the foreign office that his "star [is] still in the ascendant. He is credited with being the shrewdest politician of the lot and I should have thought that his past record as

178

a socialist would have made him a useful personality to have in the middle of the stage at present."[66]

Sun., May 20   Czech students celebrate the Majáles with a large parade through Prague for the first time since 1948.

Tue., May 22   The Hungarian workers' newspaper *Népszava* announces that the workweek is to be shortened to 42, 40, and in some cases 36 hours per week. Most workers will continue to work half a day on Saturdays; only the hours per day will be shortened.[67]

Thu., May 24   The U.S. legation in Budapest reports that the tone of Rákosi's May 18 speech seems "almost a throwback to old Stalinist times ... particularly noticeable ... on foreign affairs where he ranted against U.S. imperialism and spoke openly about American support of spies and saboteurs in Hungary."[68]

Tue., May 29   The Department of State presents the Soviet embassy in Washington with a note explaining that "navigational difficulties in the Arctic region may have caused unintentional violations of Soviet air space, which, if in fact they occurred, the department regrets." Both the Soviets and the department know that this is a lie, used in diplomacy to wriggle out of tight spots. A majority of the American public, however—including some journalists—take the department's statement at face value.[69]

Joseph Jacobs, the American ambassador to Poland, reports to the Department of State that the Western (including American) press has given more importance to the changes in Poland than is "warranted." "There is no reason ... to consider the changes as more than surface in nature." Taken collectively, however, they "may engender in independence-loving Poles' feelings that the regime may find it expedient to grant further concessions."[70]

Sat. June 2   Tito arrives in the U.S.S.R. for an extended state visit just as it is announced that Molotov has been replaced as foreign minister by Dmitri Shepilov. (Molotov had been foreign minister at the time Tito's Yugoslavia was kicked out of the Cominform, so keeping him in place would have signalled no change in policy and would have been considered an insult to Tito.)[71]

Writing in the Hungarian literary periodical *Irodalmi Újság,* Sándor Fekete demands broader exchanges with the West and wider circulation in Hungary of Western books and motion pictures. (Cultural exchanges, books, and movies will come, but not before the signing of a cultural agreement between the U.S.S.R. and the U.S. in 1958.) In the same issue of *Irodalmi*

Ujsag, Tibor Tardos demands freedom to travel. He quotes from the Polish poet Adam Ważyk's "Poem for Adults," published in September 1955, agreeing with his pain at the distortion of truth. Tardos adds: "All young people have a desire to travel and learn new things ... If there is anything our present-day youth consistently reiterates it is: to travel, to see, to compare ... to think clearly and courageously like an adult."[72]

Mon., June 4   The full text of the Khrushchev secret speech, as released by the Department of State, is printed in *The New York Times* this morning, while large extracts are carried in other American newspapers. (The department has actually obtained the text from the CIA which obtained it through the Israeli intelligence agency from a member of the Polish Central Committee.)[73]

The American embassy in Moscow tells the State Department that it is their belief that Tito's current visit to the Soviet Union may presage his full return to the Soviet fold. This view is not shared by the British and French embassies that have followed Soviet-Yugoslav relations more closely.[74]

Tue., June 5   A secret information memorandum circulating in the Department of State states that the replacement of Molotov by Shepilov as foreign minister "does not in itself forecast change in current Soviet foreign policy since he will have no independent or determinate voice in its formation." But it "appears to confirm ... that the Soviet government does not plan serious negotiations ... with the Western powers ... in the immediate future ... Shepilov is a complete party man with no real experience in foreign affairs." The communication goes on to note the British ambassador's assessment of Shepilov: "unoriginal in thought and perhaps more ambitious than able."[75]

In London, a confidential memorandum circulating in the foreign office speaks of repeated rumors reported by their embassies in Moscow, Warsaw, and Budapest that the Soviets are preparing a major announcement about the satellites, possibly involving troop withdrawal, and comments that troop withdrawals would "be quite possible, since Soviet control can be maintained by economic and administrative means without the presence of the Red Army."[76]

Wed., June 6   American ambassador to Prague, U. Alexis Johnson, reports that the Yugoslav ambassador is deluged with requests for information about Yugoslavia by Czech party officials, some of whom seem to know more about Yugoslavia than he does.

However, the ambassador had told Johnson, "there were many Czech party members whose thinking was still so rigidly in the Stalinist mold that they found it impossible to understand or accept Yugoslav experience."[77]

Sun., June 10   In Austria, Hungarians living in Burgenland, which was once part of Hungary, celebrate the 500th anniversary of the Hungarian victory over the Turks at Nándorfehérvár, today's Belgrade in Serbia. Radio Free Europe broadcasts the ceremonies live to Hungarians in the homeland who cannot cross the Iron Curtain to take part.[78]

Mon., June 11   Hungary's deputy minister of the interior, Tibor Pőcze, admits in *Szabad Nép* that police often take people into custody unnecessarily and treat them brutally. "All police who break the law," he writes, "will be called to account." Thus, Pőcze continues, "former police sergeant Mulicz was court martialled for assaulting a citizen." High police chiefs have been fired or demoted in the past, but this is the first instance of a lower grade policeman being convicted for a specific incident.[79]

In Washington, Secretary of State John Foster Dulles is asked at a press conference about the apparent contradiction between his recent statement about neutrality being "immoral" and President Eisenhower's almost simultaneous statement that he would not be at all surprised if some "nations preferred" to be neutral, in view of the risks involved in becoming a member of an alliance. The secretary responds that he has been quoted out of context and that in any case there is "no difference between [his] and the president's views." Their consistently different approaches to many foreign policy problems, however, seems to indicate otherwise.[80]

Fri., June 15   As the national Communist Party conference in Czechoslovakia comes to an end the U.S. embassy gives its initial assessment: the new "collective leadership" is Party Secretary Novotný, President Zapotocký and Premier Široký, there are no "radical departures," no rehabilitation of Slánský, and there are "no police excesses" being investigated. The student manifestations, on the other hand, are "taken very seriously as a threat," and means of control are being imposed.[81] A few days later the embassy adds "The party conference ... presents a picture of little men of the old guard who showed abject fright at the first sign of freedom of expression and the continued existence of liberal elements in the population and who ran for cover of the old party line."[82]

Sun., June 17　Quoting from recent press interviews with the new Polish prosecutor general, Marian Rybicki, and the new chairman of the Security Committee, Edmund Pszczolkowski, the British embassy reports that people are being rehabilitated as inquiries into past trials proceeds. The former chief interrogator, who had been tried and sentenced to five years, has now been charged with more serious crimes. Two directors under Rybicki have been fired, security officials in several Polish cities, including Poznań, have secretly been brought to trial for using illegal methods of investigation; and the security apparatus has been reduced by 22 percent since the end of 1954.[83]

Mon., June 18　At a conference of party activists in Stalinograd, Poland, First Secretary Ochab states that coal production is lagging seriously behind schedule and that there will be in 1956 a 2,500,000 ton deficit. After making this admission, Ochab urged the miners to help make up this deficit by selling to the state part of the coal alowances they receive in the form of wages. He further admitted that coal reserves in industry and transportation are "low," threatening a dangerous situation for the coming winter. Coal is Poland's main export.[84]

Fri., June 22　The political indoctrination of Romanian students has "serious shortcomings" according to the Romanian party Central Committee. As a result, "students will cease to be members of trade unions and other mass organizations ... There will be no meetings of students ... except within the framework of the party and the Union of Working Youth." The Central Committee justifies its decree by saying that university students, whose number has trebled since 1938, have developed "unhealthy attitudes," antisocial behavior, and "manifestations of moral decay" due to the communist student organization's failure to carry on "a sustained ... propagation of Marxist-Leninist ideology." The decree also proposes that food allowances for scholarship students be raised by 27.3 percent.[85]

Sat., June 23　Marshall Tito completes his visit to the U.S.S.R. and returns to Belgrade via Bucharest. While in Bucharest, after a flurry of speeches and receptions, Tito and his Romanian host, Gheorghiu-Dej, announced that major trade and other agreements will soon be negotiated between the two countries. This is

Tito's first visit to Romania since Stalin expelled Yugoslavia from the Cominform in 1948.[86]

Tue., June 26   In Prague, U.S. ambassador U. Alexis Johnson begins a long dispatch to Washington with these words: "During the past months a number of indications have appeared that the Czechoslovak government desires to improve and extend its relations with the United States."[87]

Secretary of State John Foster Dulles tells the Senate Foreign Relations Committee that he believes that "Khrushchev is on the ropes, and, if we can keep the pressure up ... there is going to be a very great disintegration within ... the international communist organization ... While I do not want to predict what form it will take or how soon it will occur, certainly there are developments here ... which are not superficial ... If we can hold to the unity and vigor which we have had over the past years ... I believe things are going to crack.

"As the threat seems to diminish, there is a tendency on the part of the free nations to fall apart. Fear has been the cement which has largely bound [us] together, and as that fear disappears, there is a natural tendency to fall apart.

"And the question is: who is going to fall apart first, the Communists or we?... We have to stay strong and united so that they are the ones who fall apart first ..."[88]

Wed., June 27   Rákosi and the Hungarian government come under very strong attack at a nine-hour meeting of the Petőfi Circle attended by thousands of party members.

Thu., June 28   In Poznań, Poland, a massive workers' strike and peaceful demonstration turns into a virtual uprising against the régime which is only suppressed by tanks.

On being informed on the phone by his brother Allen, director of the CIA, that some sort of "riot" is going on in "Posen" (German for Poznań), Secretary of State John Foster Dulles comments, "When they begin to crack they can crack fast. We have to keep the pressure on."[89]

Fri., June 29   In Washington, the secretary of state phones his brother Allen to ask what he thinks of the U.S. offering food to Poland on condition that the Soviet Union "would agree not to exploit Poland further." Allen replies he would not put conditions on the offer. To that the secretary responds: "If there's no hooker, we'll be in trouble." (Presumably he means with Congress, which is bound to demand a quid pro quo.)[90]

Later in the day Allen Dulles phones his brother to tell him that "it is pretty important to set it up so that it does not look like propaganda." (Ironically, it is the younger brother, with the propaganda agencies of RFE and RL under him, who is sensitive to the phony aspects of U.S. foreign policy and not his diplomat, older brother.)[91]

In Prague the Central Committee issues a directive, signed by Novotný, instructing lower party organs on precautions to be taken in view of the Poznań riots.[92]

In Washington, President Eisenhower, in a major policy move, approves the National Security Council's recommendation that "the United States should seek exchanges between the U.S. and the countries of Eastern Europe, including the U.S.S.R., along the lines ... put forward at Geneva in October 1955 ... Such a program, if carried out in good faith and with true reciprocity, may now contribute to the better understanding of the peoples of the world that must be the foundation of peace." (Such a program will indeed get under way in earnest in two years' time.)[93]

Sun., July 1   Hungarian peasants who fulfill their grain delivery obligations to the state from now on may sell their surplus on the free market and may transport as much as they desire, according to an announcement from the Hungarian Ministry of Produce Collection. While this is good news for Hungarian peasants, who will now make much more money on the free market, it is also good for the state in that more bread, at lower prices, will become available in Budapest and other Hungarian cities.[94]

The U.S. House of Representatives passes a resolution urging the president to bring the "situation in Poland before the United Nations." (While it is the Senate which is supposed to be concerned with foreign policy, the House is much more sensitive to the moods and opinions of its constituents and some districts, particularly in the Middle West, are heavily Polish-American.)[95]

Also in Washington, the National Security Council's Staff Study on U.S. Policy toward the Soviet Satellites notes that "the many changes in the U.S.S.R. ... are being reflected in current Satellite developments ... in each ... but common to them all are a reduction in the role of the secret police embodied in the … need for 'socialist legality' and admission of past errors attributed to the 'cult of the personality.'" On the subject of 'Titoism' the study notes that "since the combination of basic factors which made the successful Yugoslav break with Moscow is lacking in the Satellites, it is unlikely that the Yugoslav experience will be repeated in any of them." Nonetheless, the study feels that the "fluid situation in the Satellites has increased the previously limited U.S. capabilities to influence a basic change in Soviet domination of the Satellites."[96]

Wed., July 4   In Bucharest, at the U.S. legation's July Fourth reception, First Secretary Gheorghe Gheorghiu-Dej berates U.S. minister Charles Thayer over VOA and RFE broadcasts. When Thayer gives his standard reply that he is unaware of the content of these broadcasts due to Romania's heavy jamming of them, Gheorghiu-Dej smiles and says that Thayer knows very well that the jamming is "completely ineffective" and that the vast majority of the Romanian people are listening to these broadcasts.[97]

Fri., July 6   In Belgrade, British ambassador Sir Frank Roberts reports to the foreign office something he believes to be reliable, namely that the Soviets are putting the brakes on in Eastern Europe in light of the Poznań riots. He also reports that the barriers on the Yugoslav-Hungarian border are being removed.[98]

Sat., July 7   In Washington, in an annex to the National Security Staff Study, it is noted that "Soviet domination of the Satellites remains a basic fact," and that "any unforeseen local challenge to that control would precipitate swift Soviet intervention … To all intents and purposes the Satellites are as much at Moscow's disposal economically, politically and militarily as if they were formally member republics of the U.S.S.R." In assessing the ferment, the study says "the recent Writers' Congresses in Poland, Czechoslovakia and Hungary offer striking examples of the phenomenon (i.e., criticism of the regimes); the May demonstrations of Czechoslovak students and the resolutions adopted at the Czech student meetings are other examples. This has led the regimes to seek to impose definite limits on criticism … However, it may be expected that East European intelligentsia … will exert pressure on the regimes for more freedom." In its country-by-country assessments the study says under 'Hungary': "Open popular revolt is not possible and, if attempted under present conditions, could only be abortive and result in useless bloodshed."[99]

Sun., July 8   Hungarian minister of justice, Erik Molnár declares that since a rehabilitation commission was established several months ago, a total of 11, 398 Hungarian citizens have been amnestied. Twelve days earlier Molnár announced that 22,000 workers had been released from prison or exempted from court sentences since 1953. He admitted that the security organs and the police had made many "mistakes" and carried out "illegal actions" prior to 1953. Today he makes the claim that the minister of justice had been unable to control the activities of law courts in "certain groups of political trials," which is his way of admitting to the Hungarian people that these trials were perpetrated and controlled by Moscow.[100]

Tue., July 10   A former RFE employee, Karel Kasal, who redefected to Czechoslovakia a few days ago, is featured on the front pages of today's Czechoslovak press making denigrating remarks about his former colleagues in Munich. This is neither the first nor the last such "redefection" since the Czechoslovak secret police are determined to penetrate the Czech section of RFE and, from time to time, manage to succeed.[101]

M. Morawski, editor of Poland's Communist Party daily, *Trybuna Ludu,* is fired for criticizing *Pravda* and allowing his paper to become too liberal.[102]

Henry Cabot Lodge, U.S. ambassador to the UN, phones Secretary of State John Foster Dulles to get him to authorize his calling for a UN Peace Observation Commission to be sent to Poland to investigate the Poznań riots, which Lodge feels would be most popular with Polish-Americans and Polish exiles. The secretary replies that he has "been trying to think of some way of usefully bringing it up and which won't backfire." He will have to answer questions on it tomorrow and has been wondering what position to take. "We don't want to be too negative," he says, "in denying that we had anything to do with it because, while it is true that we never instigated anything at all and no money has been spent, nevertheless we do try to keep alive the spirit of liberty in these people." (By "no money being spent" he means no specific action by the CIA was taken to cause the revolt.)[103]

Wed., July 11   The East Germans announce that they are going to try a number of agents of U.S. intelligence on charges of having helped to foment the Poznań riots, according to a dispatch in today's *International Herald Tribune.*

Thu., July 12

Romania is cutting its armed forces by twenty thousand, says the party daily *Scinteia.* Last year Romanian forces were cut by forty thousand. Like other troop cutting announcements from the Eastern bloc, no mention is made of the actual size of the armed forces following the cut.[104]

The U.S. National Security Council meets and adopts, with minor amendments, the Staff Study and Annex on U.S. Policy toward the East European Satellites (NSC-174). The sole controversy is between the secretary of the treasury, George Humphrey, and the secretary of state over the efficacy of asking Congress to authorize food shipments to Eastern Europe. Humphrey says it is simply impossible to get such a concession through Congress. Secretary Dulles, who agrees to drop the matter, explains that the intention is not to raise the living standards of the satellites, but "simply to put the U.S. Government in a position to be able to make offers of surplus materials ... which these governments could not reject without simultaneously putting pressure on the U.S.S.R. to match the U.S. offer ..." (Without spelling it out in so many words, Dulles is telling the council that the possibility of having to make good on the offer is remote.)[105]

Fri., July 13

A joint Polish-Czechoslovak communiqué, following talks between the two governments, stresses similar views on the international situation, calling attention to the "initiative of the U.S.S.R. and other countries including Poland and Czechoslovakia for reducing armed forces." The communiqué also states that both of the two Germanies' nonparticipation in either of the two blocs is the best way to advance German reunification. (Detaching the two Germanies from their respective blocs continues to be Soviet—and satellite—policy. A neutral, unified Germany would be much easier prey for the communists.)[106]

As of October 1, 1956, custom duties on goods and gifts coming into Poland from abroad will be greatly reduced or eliminated, Radio Warsaw announces today.[107]

A Czechoslovak secret police agent, Václav Pavlašek, fails in his attempt to kidnap a Czech refugee, František Polešek, in Linz, Austria. Then, after wounding Polešek in the arm, Pavlašek manages to escape back across the Czech border. Polešek is taken to the hospital. Austria, and particularly

Vienna, which have been free of Soviet and Allied occupation for only a year, continue to be the site of much cold war activity and intrigue.[108]

Sat., July 14   U.S. ambassador in Prague, U. Alexis Johnson, in conversation with the Soviet charge d'affaires, Sytenko, expresses disappointment that developments in Czechoslovakia are not keeping pace with those in the U.S.S.R. Sytenko responds that conditions are different in each country and each must decide for itself.[109]

Mon., July 16   In Washington the Polish ambassador to the U.S. officially protests to the Department of State over the invasion of Polish air space by Free Europe balloons.[110]

Wed., July 18   Rákosi resigns during a stormy meeting of the Hungarian Central Committee attended by Soviet politburo member Anastas Mikoyan. Ernő Gerő is made first party secretary, which according to the U.S. legation's analysis, "makes Rákosi's sacrifice more symbol than substance," as Gerő is known to be a hardliner.[111]

Thu., July 19   Regarding the Czechoslovak request that the escaped Czech border guard be extradited from West Germany back to Czechoslovakia, the federal government in Bonn says "it does not consider itself in a position at the present time to enter into an examination of the Czechoslovak request" and asks the U.S. government to pass this response on to the Czechoslovak government. The West Germans are able to use this ruse because, under their "Halstein Doctrine," they have no diplomatic relations with Czechoslovakia. The doctrine states that Bonn will have no diplomatic relations with any country which recognizes the German Democratic Republic.[112]

In Paris, American diplomats learn from the Quai d'Orsay that Yugoslav diplomats in both Paris and Warsaw "consider it necessary to be very prudent concerning statements related to Poland in order not to stop the trend toward liberalization." The Yugoslavs consider that liberalization has gone furthest in Poland and that "to welcome Poznań riots would provide an opportunity for the Stalinist element in Poland to regain ascendancy."[113]

The U.S. legation in Budapest, in a long analysis of the political situation in Hungary, concludes that an "unstable compromise" has been reached between the party liberals and the conservatives and that "efforts to reinstate tighter controls might in fact work to speed a new outburst."[114]

Fri., July 20   In the railroad station in the town of Usti n. Laben, Czechoslovakia, a railroad tankcar filled with gasoline mysteriously catches fire and explodes, causing thirty other railroad cars loaded with goods bound for East Germany to catch fire and be destroyed. Sabotage is suspected, but no mention of the incident is ever carried in the Czechoslovak press.[115]

Sat., July 21   The Hungarian Central Committee meeting ends. Rákosi is secretly flown to Moscow whence he will never return and Mikoyan leaves for Brioni, Yugoslavia, where he is joined by the Hungarian minister to Belgrade for talks with Tito.[116]

At a reception at the Palace of Science and Culture in Warsaw, Marshal Nikolai Bulganin, Soviet premier, warns that "foreign imperialists" and "reactionary elements" inside Poland are planning to bring back capitalism and he points to the Poznań uprising as evidence of this. Bulganin and Marshal Zhukov are in Poland to celebrate its national day on July 22, but they also hope to attend the Polish party's Central Committee meeting.[117]

Sun., July 22   In Budapest, *Szabad Nép* reveals that Gen. Mihály Farkas has been expelled from the Central Committee and soon will be stripped of his military rank. Farkas had earlier been removed from his role as head of the dreaded secret police (ÁVO).[118]

In Moscow, all Soviet newspapers carry articles on Poland's national day and feature Bulganin's remarks of yesterday evening.

Mon., July 23   The Hungarian party's Central Committee is recommending that Hungary cut its army by an additional 15,000 men. Last year the army was cut by twenty thousand men. Once again, no mention is made of the actual size of the army.[119]

In Washington the U.S. Congress passes a joint resolution stating that "the cause of a just and lasting peace would be served best through the presence in Poland of official observers for the free world during all such trials of persons involved in the Poznań uprising in order that a complete and factual report of the circumstances surrounding the trial, the validity of the charges, the trial proceedings and the justice of the verdicts may be known to the entire world."[120]

Tue., July 24   Radio Bucharest says that the Romanian labor code is being altered so that no worker can be transferred against his volition. No other nation in the bloc, save Albania, has had such a draconian labor law, making Romanian workers virtual slave laborers.[121]

In analyzing the speeches of Bulganin and the Polish hardliner Zenon Nowak, the U.S. embassy in Warsaw notes that while Bulganin did not mention the U.S. by name, Nowak made a direct attack on the U.S., accusing it of financing espionage and of violations of Polish air space (a reference to Free Europe's balloon-borne leaflets).[122]

Fri., July 27   The Operations Coordinating Board of the U.S. National Security Council circulates a memorandum on the subject of its working groups, listing those that have not met for at least two months. From this it can be seen that the working group on Eastern Europe and the U.S.S.R. has not met since March 26, 1956.[123]

Sun., July 29   Polish readers note another advance in information as *Trybuna Ludu* gives a short biography of each new government appointee listed in today's edition. While this has never been done before, it appears this time there may have been a special reason: readers can clearly see from the backgrounds of all of these men that none have training in the Soviet Union in their background.[124]

Mon., July 30   Czechoslovak premier Široký, in an address before the country's national assembly, characterizes "recent declarations of United States officials, among them Mr. Dulles," as gross interference in our domestic affairs," and he castigates the U.S. not only for its hostile propaganda but for "trying to expand the network of their agents in Czechoslovakia." Indeed, there has been a recent spate of arrests of U.S. "agents" all over Czechoslovakia, but the trials are mentioned only in the local press, if at all.[125]

Tue., July 31   Ceremonies are held throughout Warsaw commemorating the twelfth anniversary of the Warsaw Uprising. Radio Warsaw stresses that participants of the A.K. (Home Army) are well represented. This is the first official celebration of the uprising, which the communists have hitherto ignored. Until now, all veterans of the Home Army have been treated like second-class citizens.[126]

Wed., Aug. 1   President Eisenhower, in discussing the Republican Party platform with the chairman of the Platform Committee, Senator
Prescott Bush of Connecticut, refers to several of his "statements on the liberation of the peoples behind the Iron Curtain"
and states that "this particular plank should make it clear that
we advocate liberation by all peaceful means, but not to give
any indication that we advocate going to the point of war to
accomplish this liberation."[127]

Hungarian prosecutor general György Non says that three hundred political prisoners "groundlessly condemned, have been
freed." The overwhelming majority of these are party members. Non adds that: "Disciplinary action has been started
against fifty-four members of the state security forces while
thirteen persons charged with more serious violations ... have
been brought before the military courts."[128]

Sat., Aug. 4   Władysław Gomułka, former first secretary of the Polish Communist Party, who was rehabilitated four months ago, is readmitted to the party. British ambassador Noble notes that this is
being done without Gomułka recanting any of his "false ideological conceptions," which had prevented him from regaining
his party membership four months ago.[129]

Mon., Aug. 6   In Poznań, a military court begins the trial of four persons
accused of being in the employ of an "imperialist intelligence
service." There is no mention of any connection with the
Poznań uprising.[130]

Thu., Aug. 9   The U.S. embassy in Warsaw tells Washington that even if
Gomułka is "subsequently given an important party and/or
government post ... this could be merely window dressing ...
The embassy is inclined to doubt 'democratization of the party
line' and that any 'rehabilitated' communist will be allowed
freedom of action in party circles."[131]

In the Polish city Opole, worker unrest causes the government
to rush truckloads of food to the city and to begin immediately
the promised construction of bakeries and slaughterhouses. On
August 1 a delegation of six party and labor union officials had
journeyed to Warsaw where they pleaded with the authorities
to take immediate action lest another explosion like Poznań
occur.[132]

Sun., Aug. 12   CIA director Allen W. Dulles begins a world tour of CIA posts
accompanied by an entourage of five (including his wife) on a
luxurious, VIP configured DC-6 aircraft provided by the air

force. One of the participants, Ray Cline, will later refer to it as "one of the most highly publicized clandestine expeditions ever made."[133]

Mon. Aug. 13   In Paris, the CIA welcoming party is 15 minutes late. Following the director's lecture on the importance of punctuality, warning cables go out to the remaining 22 posts on the itinerary.[134]

Tue., Aug. 14   The Polish prosecutor general Rybicki announces that investigations of the Poznań events will be completed by the end of August and the trials will be held in September.[135]

The Polish people will have some choice when their next elections are held in December, according to *The New York Times* correspondent Sydney Gruson. There will be alternative candidates listed in most cases and these will not necessarily all be Communist Party members.

Wed., Aug. 15   All of the "technical barriers" on the border with Yugoslavia have been removed, says Hungarian premier András Hegedűs, "with the exception of one short section which is under water."[136]

The Hungarian Communist Party's ideological journal, *Társadalmi Szemle* concedes that the party's policy toward intellectuals (i.e., professional people), has been unjust. "In numerous offices of the party apparatus," for instance, "the number of college and university graduates is small. In the [regional] Council apparatus only 4.3% have a college or secondary school diploma and of the Secretaries of Municipal Party Committees only 1.7% have college degrees."[137]

Sat., Aug. 18   Radio Warsaw announces that Polish armed forces are to be reduced by 50,000 men. As in other announcements of force reductions in the bloc, the actual size of the forces after the reduction is not given.[138]

Allen Dulles and entourage check in at Claridges Hotel, London, before attending a reception at the American embassy.[139]

Fri., Aug. 24   More power is to be given to the Polish trade unions according to the Polish Central Council of Trade Unions. "All decisions which stifle the independence and democracy of the trade unions must be reviewed and abolished."[140]

Sat., Aug. 25   Romania and Greece are resuming diplomatic relations, interrupted since 1939. An economic agreement provides compensation for war damages suffered by Greek citizens as well as payment for ships seized by the communists after the war. Romania was aligned with the Nazis for most of the war, while Greece was with the Allies.[141]

A nine-person Polish Communist Party delegation led by polit-buro member Franciszek Mazur departs for Belgrade for party-to-party talks with their Yugoslavian colleagues. The high rank of its leader, comments U.S. ambassador Jacobs in a cable to Washington, "indicates the Poles attach considerable impor-tance to the visit."[142]

General Wacław Komar, a one-time victim of the "generals" trial in the late 1940s, is being put in charge of Poland's Inter-nal Forces, replacing General Julian Hibner. General Komar was rehabilitated in April along with Gomułka. Hibner has faithfully executed Soviet orders in Poland.[143]

Mon., Aug. 27 In Paris, *Le Monde* announces that busloads of Polish tourists to France are expected on September 4 and September 18. Tourist trade from Poland has increased considerably in the past twelve months with over 100 Poles arriving in France each month. Nearly all are party members being rewarded for faith-ful service.

Tue., Aug. 28 The annual pilgrimage of Polish Catholics to the Black Madonna icon of Częstochowa culminates in an open air mass of several hundred thousand pilgrims (described later by Polish American priests who attended as at least one million). Among the many clergy delegations from abroad are bishops from Holland and Hungary as well as the United States. The "mira-cle" of Poland's being saved from an invading Swedish army exactly 300 years ago is attributed to the Black Madonna in the monastery there.[144]

· Thu., Aug. 30 American charge d'affaires at the U.S. legation in Budapest, Tracy Barnes, lists eight characteristics of the new "era" in Hungary since Rákosi's fall. Among these: the growing influ-ence of János Kádár, the change for the better in the govern-ment's attitude toward intellectuals, a number of modest concessions to the populace, and the fact that "the régime has adorned itself with a new halo of democracy, progressiveness and freedom."[145]

Mon., Sept. 3 The Soviet Union's Central Committee sends a secret letter to all East European satellite central committees denying that Tito's status is that of a bone fide communist, warning that they should not follow the Yugoslav example too closely, and attacking Yugoslavia's foreign policy as "pro-Western." The contents of this letter will be leaked by a Polish comrade to the Yugoslavs within the week.[146]

Tue., Sept. 4 In Stockholm, six Poles who defected from Poland on July 28 hold a press conference describing the situation in Poland today, including a number of strikes not reported in the Polish press. Recently, for instance, there was a three-day strike of printers in Warsaw during which all of the Warsaw newspapers had to be printed in Łódź and flown to Warsaw.[147]

Wed., Sept 5 In Warsaw, the ninth session of the Sejm (Polish parliament) opens with an extraordinarily conciliatory speech by Premier Cyrankiewicz, admitting the widespread discontent in the country and saying that the solution lay in solving economic problems. In this connection he announces that as of September 1 the real wages of 3,259,000 manual and office workers has been raised and that 600,000 more workers will get raises as soon as possible. Cyrankiewicz says he realized that in appraising the results of economic policy, the average citizen uses "his own pocket and his own stomach as guides." Toward the end of his speech Cyrankiewicz reveals that new talks have recently been held with the Soviet Union concerning the further repatriation of hundreds of thousands of Poles still being held against their will in the Soviet Union, a sore subject to which Free Europe Press had recently devoted an entire ballooned leaflet.[148]

John Foster Dulles, in a letter to President Eisenhower, assures his boss that there is no "liberation" pledge in the Republican platform as the Democrats are claiming. Instead, writes Dulles, quoting the platform: "United States policy ... looks happily forward to the genuine independence of those captive peoples." At another point the platform says, "The policies we espouse ... will inevitably set up strains and stresses within the captive world which will make the rulers impotent to continue their monstrous ways and mark the beginning of the end."[149]

The Soviet Union is granting Poland a loan of 100 million rubles, which will enable the country to purchase consumer goods and food from abroad, Cyrankiewicz reveals to the Sejm. Additional consumer goods will be coming from Czechoslovakia. On the subject of the upcoming Poznań trials, Cyrankiewicz assures the Sejm that the "court proceedings are and will be in keeping with the strictest requirements of the rule of law and legality. The trials, of course will be public ... We have nothing to conceal here but we don't intend to turn a normal court trial in Poland into an international spectacle."[150]

In Warsaw, the appropriate committee of the Sejm votes to abolish the "socialist worker discipline" law instituted in 1950. This means that Polish workers who arrive late on the job or who are absent without leave no longer will face court orders to work three months at lower pay or face six months in jail.[151]

Mon., Sept. 10   The Central Council of Trade Unions in Warsaw renews its April invitation to the United Auto Workers of the U.S. to send a delegation to Poland. The UAW had turned down the offer and then, after the explosion in Poznań, had reopened the issue. The Polish labor organization's renewed invitation says the delegation may visit a number of Polish cities, "not excluding Poznań."[152]

Tue., Sept. 11   In an effort to increase workers' confidence in Hungarian trade unions, the Hungarian government appoints the recently pardoned noncommunist Zoltán Horváth as a member of the trade union council. He is also made editor of the trade union organ, *Népszava*. Horváth, formerly a leader of the Social Democratic Party, was recently released after six years' imprisonment.[153]

Wed., Sept. 12   The American legation in Budapest quotes a recent article in *Irodalmi Újság* as the clearest evidence of how far "liberalization is desired by an important segment of the Hungarian élite." In the article the poet Gyula Hay demands the right of complete freedom of expression in the upcoming meeting of the Hungarian Writers' Association on September 17. This demand recognizes no restrictions other than those set up by society to prevent slander, incitement to crime, treason or immorality. "Until all kinds of censorship are abolished," writes Hay, "we cannot speak of literary freedom. At most we can speak of a relative liberalism, which can be cancelled at any moment."[154]

Thu., Sept. 13   Leon Stasiak, the first secretary of the Poznań provincial party committee, is released from his post and reassigned to the party Central Committee in Warsaw.[155]

Fri., Sept. 14   Average Poles are still wary of the changes in Poland, writes *The New York Times* correspondent Sidney Gruson today. They are fearful that "a window has been opened not to let fresh air in, but to see who sticks his neck out." Gruson quotes one Pole as saying: "The same people who made the mistakes, with the exception of Berman (who recently resigned) are in the same positions. The people want not only changes in tactics, but changes in personnel before they will believe what the Communists say. We want new men to take over—young men whose past is blank or men who have records as good organizers. We want the leaders to take the consequences of their mistakes. If they cannot produce economically, we will not believe them politically."

Allen Dulles and party arrive in Teheran where they are met by the Shah and a full military review.[156]

Sun. Sept. 16   Zoltán Tildy, former president of Hungary from 1946 to 1948, reappears in public after years of house arrest. "For eight years," says Tildy over Radio Budapest, "the only connection I had with public life was reading newspapers and listening to news broadcasts."[157]

Mon., Sept. 17   In Budapest, at the opening of the Writers' Association Congress, Hungarian authors, irritated by two recent attacks upon them in the party newspaper *Szabad Nép*, indulge in one defiant outburst after another. In the course of the first day's twelve-hour session the entire Stalinist leadership of the union is swept aside and a new leadership of liberals elected. References to Imre Nagy result in rhythmic clapping in probably the stormiest applause of the meeting.[158]

The Hungarian youth newspaper *Szabad Ifjúság* prints a firsthand account of youths who recently managed to cross the border into Austria, only to be arrested by Austrian police and returned to Hungarian border guards.[159]

Wed., Sept. 19   The Bulgarian Central Committee approves "the findings and conclusions" of the commission studying the December 1949 trial of Traicho Kostov. All but two of the defendants are being restored to party membership and will be legally rehabilitated. This clears up speculation from earlier reports which had made it seem that Kostov, like Slánský in Czechoslovakia, might be forgiven his Titoist crimes, but left with other charges justifying his execution.[160]

Thu., Sept. 20   Radio Warsaw, in a Yiddish-language broadcast, reports the Soviets are planning to establish a Yiddish-language theater in Moscow to replace the one destroyed in Stalin's anti-Semitic purges.[161]

Fri., Sept. 21   In Paris the United States informs the North Atlantic Council confidentially that "in accordance with President Eisenhower's program of increased contacts between peoples, the U.S. government is extending an invitation to the governments of the U.S.S.R., Poland, Czechoslovakia, Hungary and Romania to send 2 or 3 representatives to the U.S. for a fortnight late in October to familiarize themselves with the two-party electoral process in our national elections." These visits, if they take place, are being offered only on a reciprocal basis. (Here the duality of American policy—the communists would say "duplicity"—can clearly be seen with the magnanimity of Eisenhower being qualified by Dulles to the point where the offer is made unacceptable to the other side.)[162]

Sat., Sept. 22   In Moscow, TASS announces that the Soviet government has agreed to grant Poland a loan of 100 million rubles at 2% interest to be paid in gold and in needed commodities in an agreement signed four days ago.[163]

In Copenhagen, a twenty-two-year-old Czech music student, Ivan Vince, defects from the visiting Czechoslovak dance troop "Lunica" and asks the local police for political asylum.[164]

Sun., Sept. 23   In London the British-Soviet Friendship Society cables both Prime Minister Eden and Premier Bulganin in an effort to get shoplifting charges against Soviet discus thrower Nina Pomanorova withdrawn so that the Bolshoi Ballet can visit Britain as scheduled. Ponomarova is charged with stealing five hats.[165]

A Czechoslovak air force lieutenant with a friend in a training plane flies over the Iron Curtain, lands in a Bavarian meadow, and asks for political asylum.[166]

Some 300 boarding schools—the first ever for the Soviet Union—are just opening according to *Pravda* and *Izvestia.* By 1960 more than a million students are expected to be enrolled in state boarding schools.[167]

In Vienna it is learned that a major Soviet naval base in the Mediterranean, which has been under construction in Albania since 1948, has just become operational.[168]

Mon., Sept. 24   In a report from Washington today's *The New York Times* says that the Soviet Union is unwilling to agree to a U.S. request for safeguards against diversions to military programs in the two countries' atoms-for-peace programs, saying it infringes on the sovereignty of the recipient nation. The American proposal insists on on-site inspection by the other side and this to the

Soviet Union, with its totally closed society, is tantamount to espionage.

The Polish Council of State announces that the next elections of the Sejm will be held on December 16. A commission of forty experts is working on a new election law to be submitted for approval next month.[169]

Hungary's minister for foreign trade, József Bognár, says Hungary will benefit greatly from the recently signed trade agreement with Yugoslavia. The Hungarians will help the Yugoslavs construct electric power plants in Yugoslavia which will feed power to Hungary's industrial center in the Dunántúl. It will also "enormously increase" the flow of goods from Hungary to the West through Yugoslavia's Adriatic port of Rijeka.[170]

Officials of the German Federal Republic in Bonn report that 6,095 East Germans fled to West Berlin last week. Since the registration of refugees began in January 1949, approximately one million have fled to West Berlin. More than 2.6 million have fled from the Soviet zone to the West since 1945.[171]

In Moscow the Soviet Ministry of Culture says it has asked the British Council to use its authority to "make possible" the planned visit of the Bolshoi Ballet to London. Unless charges of shoplifting against Nina Pomanorova are dropped, the Bolshoi will be unable to come.[172]

Tue., Sept. 25   Polish authorities announce that the Poznań trials will begin on September 27. One hundred and fifty-four men are charged with various crimes committed during the Poznań uprising and will be tried in groups, with several trials taking place at the same time.[173]

The Hungarian government is ordering the suspension of 600 passenger trains in the country "because of a serious coal shortage." Long distance bus lines were suspended several days ago due to a shortage of gasoline.[174]

A Polish air force pilot lands his MIG-15 jet fighter plane on the Danish island of Bornholm and asks for political asylum. This is the first time this has happened since two Polish pilots, in separate flights, flew their MIGs to Bornholm in the Spring of 1953.[175]

Two young Hungarians, László Kancis and Gyula Spanyol, are caught in barbed wire on the Hungarian-Austrian border and are gunned down by Hungarian border guards with their machine pistols. A third youth, Gyula Szilágyi, makes it safely to Austrian soil and is not turned back by the Austrian police.[176]

Five East Germans are found guilty of spying for the United States in Erfurt, East Germany, and are given from four to twelve years imprisonment.[177]

In New York, high officials of the Soviet Red Cross are shown around the New York Stock Exchange by exchange president Keith Funston in the company of the American Red Cross president, Ellsworth Bunker.[178]

In Stockholm, the prosecution demands a sentence of life at hard labor for Anatole Ericsson, a forty-six-year-old Swedish instrument maker, charged with passing radar secrets to Soviet embassy officials.[179]

Workers of a foundry and casting works near Cracow, Poland, roar applause at a mass meeting here when it is announced that the newly appointed factory director has been told to clear up the bad conditions and injustices by the end of the month.[180]

Propaganda balloons launched from West Germany have caused "another accident" says *Szabad Nép*. A few days ago a 14-year-old daughter of a peasant in a village near Nyárlőrinc, found a balloon with a load of leaflets in the garden. When she took it inside to dry it off on the stove, the balloon exploded causing grave burns to her and to members of her family and rendering the house inhabitable.[181]

In Prague, Czech dailies carry reports of a trial, just opening before a Prague regional court, of five adults charged with producing "forged student resolutions" which they distributed during the Majáles parade last May. The leader, a former army colonel, is said to have been a British intelligence agent during the Second World War.[182]

Reacting to the news of the Poznań trials about to be held, President Eisenhower, through his press secretary, James Hagerty, says he hopes for a "fair and genuinely open trial with bona fide legal counsel to defend them" as this "would provide tangible evidence that some so-called Stalinists' methods will be abandoned in practice as well as theory." He concludes that the basic problem in Poland is a lack of freedom. Poles "should be given the opportunity ... to decide for themselves ... in free and unfettered elections."[183]

Poland's largest Lutheran church, used since 1950 as a youth center and concert hall, is being returned by the Polish government to the Lutheran Church authorities.[184]

CHAPTER VII

Rajk Reburied:
Massive Demonstration in
Budapest, October 6

It is late September and, while the weather is still warm, leaves edged brown already lie on the streets and sidewalks of Budapest. A Yugoslav journalist, Đorđe Zelmanović, is walking through the Ninth District searching for the "Ervin Szabó" public library. His paper, *Vjesnik*, of Zagreb, has asked him to find and interview the widow of László Rajk, the former foreign minister and minister of the interior, who had been tried, convicted, and executed in September 1949.[1]

The official government portrait of László Rajk when he was minister of the interior, 1948. Purchased from Associated Press Wide World Photos in 2002.

Júlia Rajk has already become something of a celebrity this year, speaking out courageously at several meetings of the Petőfi Circle. After the fall of Rákosi and his departure for Moscow, the Hungarian Ministry of Justice had issued her the sum of 200,000 forints. Only a few days ago Zelmanović had learned of her contemptuous rejection of this "guilt money" when he read a short statement she had sent to the party newspaper, *Szabad Nép*, which the paper had printed in full. "The years of terror may not be compensated for," she had told them flatly. "Let this money be used for those who shall correct the mistakes." As a librarian with a salary, who had also begun to receive social security payments in August; she said she was financially secure. On the other hand, she had written, the money would "cover the clothing and furnishing necessities for several of the previously persecuted families, and also would help pay back the debt to those who were left without income for many years."[2]

Zelmanović knows the library is housed in an exquisite rococo palace built not far from Calvin Square two centuries ago for the counts of Wenckheim. Shortly after leaving the noisy square for a cool side street, he notices several small rococo fountains spouting small trickles of water. A broken statue of an antique goddess of justice tilts over one basin, one arm extended over her head. Her hand holds only a handle; the two scales are missing.

Zelmanović mounts the stone steps, enters through the tall wooden doors and, after climbing a broad staircase, enters a dark, quiet room permeated by the dry odor which fills all libraries: the smell of decaying paper. He spots a strikingly erect, dark-haired woman whose figure is partially hidden by the brown library smock she wears over her street clothes. Her bright blue polyvinyl shoes contrast sharply with the smock. She is sitting next to a pile of periodicals skimming through a copy of *Nyugat* ("West"), the organ of choice for "modern" Hungarian writers. She looks up and greets the stranger, whom she is obviously expecting. As he approaches, he notes strands of gray in her dark hair. This is not her first such interview since she reappeared in public—a correspondent from *L'Humanité* had visited her several weeks earlier. But his report, when it had finally appeared, had been vague and far from satisfying. After a brief exchange with Zelmanović she senses his report will be much friendlier.

Her visitor has done his homework. He knows that this proud, sober person, one of five children born to a working-class family, was once an émigré in Paris, that she endured the hardships of the underground opposition during the German occupation, was arrested in 1944 by the Nazis, placed in prisons of Budapest and Sopronkőhida, and finally sent to a concentration camp in Germany. Upon her return to Hungary in 1945, she began to play an active role at her husband's side. In 1947 she was appointed chairman of the communist-dominated Democratic Association of Hungarian Women and, from May 1949 until two years ago, had languished in a Budapest maximum-security prison.

But it is not about herself that she wants to talk but about her husband.

László Rajk, the son of a shoeshop owner, was born on March 8, 1909, in the Transylvanian town of Székelyudvarhely. An early member of the Hungarian Communist Party, he was organizing communist cells in various student organizations by 1930. In 1935 he was a key organizer in the great strike of construction workers in Budapest. Two years later he was in Spain fighting on the loyalist side of the Spanish civil war, where he was wounded by a landmine. In 1939, after the long, bitter retreat across the Pyrenees, he was interned by the French in a concentration camp along with all of the other foreign volunteers who had survived. After the fall of France, the Vichy government sent him back to Hungary, where he quickly became secretary of the illegal Communist Party in Hungary. Soon thereafter he became head of the underground and a leader in the military resistance as well. In late 1944 he was arrested by the Gestapo. Under normal circumsances he would have been sent to a death camp, but the intervention of his brother András, who was a high-ranking Arrow Cross official, saved him and he was sent to Germany as a slave laborer. He survived this experience and returned to Budapest in April 1945. Thus, unlike Rákosi's other rival, Imre Nagy, who was a member of the Moscow clique which had returned to Hungary on the coattails of the Red Army, Rajk had no special protectors in the Kremlin, and thus felt less duty-bound to Stalin's discipline than did the other Hungarian Communist leaders. As minister of the interior he resisted Rákosi's desire that the ÁVO answer directly to the party's politburo (i.e., Rákosi) and, when he was suddenly shifted from minister of the interior to foreign minister, he was put into a position particularly vulnerable to the charge of being a "Titoist"—the charge leveled at him after his surprise arrest on May 30, 1949.

"It is terrible what they did to a man like László!" exclaims Mrs. Rajk, her emotional voice suddenly filling that semidark room after a moment of silence. "From the day they arrested us we were not allowed to see one another. They even took my four-month-old baby from me! I was sick with worry for they never answered any of my questions about either one of them."

Mrs. Rajk goes on to tell of her husband's trial—that is, what she had been able to learn of it from friends after her release from prison—how that tall, gaunt figure with the high, wide cheekbones of a true Magyar had "stood like a stick and recited the most appalling rubbish with a singsong voice of a schoolboy reciting a poem he had learned by heart but didn't understand.

"Only after the trial was over did they tell me that he had been sentenced to death and that I would also be tried and sentenced.

"But the worst was discovering that he had been executed right under my cell. It was a pre-dawn morning in early October ... To my dying day I will remember that voice calling out 'Géza ... the execution can be carried out.' And then I heard the sound of the chair being kicked. Only during the great morning silence did I learn that it had been Laci they had killed and that a physician had confirmed that he was dead.

"Laci was the first. But during those terrible months I counted fifty-one executions in that courtyard.

"Only after they had killed him did they begin my own interrogation and tortures.

"Part of my husband's sentence read: 'For active participation in destroying the People's Republic of Hungary: High Treason.' What were they going to accuse me of? Well, there was a great deal, but the only thing that was true, of course, was that I shared my husband's views. But all the things we were accused of were sheer nonsense.

"During the preparation of my trial I was given a copy of the 'Blue Book' which the government had printed, not just in Hungarian, but in French, English and Russian, listing all of my husband's 'crimes' and giving their version of the trial as well as his so-called 'confession.' I was asked to express my opinion of it, in fact, the judge ordered me to do it in writing.

"What I wrote was 'I think that the whole trial can be characterized by the first sentence of the accusation: everything is a big lie!'

"You see in the first sentence of the indictment it is written that László Rajk was born on May 8, 1909. But that is not correct. Laci must have fooled them. He was born on *March* 8, 1909 and only someone like me who knew him intimately would have known this.

"Those months after his execution were the worst. I was mourning him and the loss of my baby and every day; I was tortured to confess to things I hadn't done and knew nothing about.

"It lasted until March 1950. Then, and it was by then 10 months after my arrest, I was given my indictment. And the only truth in the entire indictment is that I agreed with my husband's ideas. The sentence was five years of penal servitude.

"I was not sent to prison camp. I spent those years wholly in prison. I was aware, of course, that some camps were closed and many prison doors opened during Imre Nagy's New Course, but my sentence was not shortened and I did not get out until 1954.

"When I was discharged I was totally alone. No husband, no child, no job. I was not even allowed to be myself! My papers said that I was Mrs. László Györki. If I made any reference to myself as 'Mrs. Rajk' it would be right back into prison for me. The régime was scared to have the name Rajk appear in public again. I petitioned them in vain to let me use my own name, but only in October 1955, less than a year ago, was the permission granted.

"I *did* recover my son—sort of. I was forced to pose as his aunt and even he had been given a new name. Though I had named him for his father he was now officially István Kovács. Believe me, it was hard.

"My sister had gotten custody of him, but not until they kept him for over two years. Then one day this official from the police arrives in her apartment and asks 'Would you like to take care of Mrs. Rajk's baby?' 'Of course, where can I pick him up … or will you bring him here?' It turned out to be neither. She was given written instructions to go to a certain address on Váci Street at a certain time of day and wait. This she did and eventually a large black car with curtained windows drives up, the door opens and a little boy is just put out onto the sidewalk. The car door shuts and the car drives off.

"Only last October was I able to tell him the truth, that I was not his aunt but his mother and he began to call me 'Mummy'.

"Here," says the widow Rajk smiling, and she hands Zelmanović a photo of a fair-haired boy of seven in his white shirt and pioneer neckerchief. "He certainly looks like his father," comments Zelmanović.

"The first year out of prison was the hardest. Only with the greatest difficulty was I finally able to get a job in a delicatessen. People did not know what to do with me. When they finally gave me my name back, and also my party book, they also gave me an apartment where I now live with my mother and young Laci. People who recognized me in the street were surprised. There had been nothing in the papers about my release. But people completely unknown to me would come up and say hello and ask how they might help.

"Only old comrades, old co-fighters did not come. They were ashamed to look me in the eyes and even to say 'Don't be angry with us.' Those rare comrades who did dare to come see me tried rather lamely to argue that there was no other way, that we must be patient and that I would have acted as they did had I been in their shoes …

"Maybe they are right," she adds, her voice trailing off.

Then, regaining her composure, Júlia Rajk begins to talk of the present.

After the Twentieth Party Congress in the Soviet Union Mrs. Rajk had found she was not alone in demanding the rehabilitation of her husband. At meeting after meeting party members had brought it up. And she herself had spoken out frequently.

"One day this past July," she says, "a car stopped outside our house on József Katona Street and the supreme prosecutor of the Ministry of Justice entered our house. He handed me two official decisions of the ministry. One was that the sentence against László Rajk had been annulled and the other that my sentence had been annulled and that everything that had taken place in the two trials was now proclaimed to be officially lies … But this cannot be the epilogue," says Júlia Rajk peering into her interviewer's face. "It is the whole Hungarian nation that should be rehabilitated!"

Outside the streetlights are coming on in the dusk. Mrs. Rajk's fellow librarians have long since departed for home. But she takes no notice. She is lost in thought.

Then, out of the silence she speaks, more to herself than to her visitor: "Not even today do I know where my husband is buried; I do not know where his grave is. Today we must move forward. Nothing must be done to prevent this honest man from having his funeral, from having his grave properly marked and from announcing his funeral to all of Budapest, which has been forced for so long now to hear only of his 'crimes.' This," she adds, her voice now quavering with emotion, "is the *least* that can be done!"

As he stands to take his leave of this modern-day Antigone, and she rises with him, he is impressed by her height and the firmness of her handshake. He promises to tell his Yugoslav readers all she has told him. "Do it better than the man from *L'Humanité*," she calls after him. "He failed to mention what I told him about party discipline, that it doesn't mean just head-nodding and blind devotion, but also party democracy and the right for free criticism and control in the whole party."

⸰

It is now several days later, Saturday October 6, to be precise. Júlia Rajk and her friends have prevailed. Her husband is to be reburied.

At first the government had been completely against the idea of a public reburial. Aware of the mood in the country, they were terrified of what might occur at a large public funeral. Even Júlia Rajk's friends had cautioned her not to press the régime on this, lest they retaliate later. It had already been a great victory to get them to agree to reburial. But Mrs. Rajk was adamant. It has to be a public reburial, she insisted, it was a public trial. Only a public funeral will "equalize" the situation. At last she tells them simply: "If it's not a public funeral, then I'm not participating." Eventually all arguments disintegrated upon her simple, rock-like logic. She got her way.

She had chosen a Saturday so that workers, in fact, "all of Budapest" can attend. But this is no ordinary Saturday; it also happens to be an important date in Hungarian history. October 6 is the date in 1849 when thirteen Hungarian generals who had fought under Kossuth in the revolution of 1848 were executed by the Austrians after the defeat of the revolution with the help of czarist Russia. It is a date every Hungarian knows well. The government, in fact, has allowed many shops and factories to close early so that their employees and workers can attend.[3]

All of Budapest is abuzz over the sea change in the government's position. Not only is László Rajk to be reburied today, but also three of his colleagues who were tried and executed with him: Major General György Pálffy, Dr. Tibor Szőnyi, and András Szalai. Yesterday the bodies were exhumed from their secret, unmarked graves and placed in heavy, ornate metal coffins. Now, with appropriate wreaths and ribbons of black they stand on high biers on the east side of the Kossuth Mausoleum deep inside Kerepes Cemetery, Budapest's main burial grounds.[4]

While there is no rain, the day is wet and chilly. With a strong wind gusting, it seems, at times, bitterly cold. People from all over Budapest, singly, or more often in small groups, are beginning to make their way to the cemetery. Along the way, and particularly at the entrance to the cemetery, some stop to buy flowers, often only a single carnation.

The official ceremony is set for 4 P.M., but the four biers with their tall black and gold candelabras smoking in front of them are in place by noon. Júlia Rajk, knowing that many people will be early, sets off for the cemetery with László Jr. around noon. She is determined that not a single person who comes will miss seeing them.

It has been a hectic week for Júlia Rajk. Just getting her black mourning outfit together was a struggle: finding a black dress large enough for her frame, then black stockings, black gloves, and black handbag. It had taken dozens of phone calls and inquiries among family and friends. And young Laci had to have a dark suit made for him—there were no ready-made suits in the stores.

Then there was the business about getting Laci's family into the country to attend the funeral. All three of his sisters and most of his six surviving brothers still live in Transylvania. The authorities could not deny her having his family there since travel to and from Romania had become officially "permissible" in the spring of this year. And just as she had been adamant about public reburial, so she was adamant that all the private traditions of funerals be strictly observed. The post-funeral supper, for instance, which she and friends had long labored to prepare, will be for the family alone. Even her best friends will not be attending it.[5]

At the cemetery Mrs. Rajk and her son take up their position at the left corner of the first bier.

A dais has been constructed in front of the four biers, but this is for the official speakers, and Mrs. Rajk is not one of them. Having no control over what she might say, the government has seen to it that she is not on the program.

A few curious citizens are already there. Those who recognize Mrs. Rajk, even if they do not know her, go up to speak to her. Soon others arrive to pay homage, and those already there give way to the newcomers. Within an hour the arrivals have become a steady stream of people, four to five abreast, passing slowly in review from left to right past the Rajks and the four biers.[6] It is still several hours before the other families and government dignitaries will arrive, but Mrs. Rajk stands bareheaded and erect so that all may see her. Wearing his dark beret, László Jr. stands just in front of her; since he has no overcoat, from time to time she enfolds her shiny raincoat around him when the wind gusts strongly.

Near the philosophical faculty of the university, students have been gathering since early afternoon. Now they move off together in one mass, which the narrow streets soon extrude into a long column. Like many of the workers who march from their factories, they will file past the biers and Mrs. Rajk as distinct units, but then meld into the growing crowd spilling out onto the great open space surrounding the mausoleum on three sides. Many are surprised at the size of the turnout.

Former Premier Imre Nagy and his circle of friends—many, like Miklós Vásárhelyi, journalists—arrive before the start of the ceremonies. He goes up to Mrs. Rajk and kisses her on both cheeks, then wraps his arms around her. Words are exchanged, but the wind is blowing too strongly for them to be overheard. Younger friends of Nagy and Mrs. Rajk, including such Petőfi Circle members as Gábor Tánczos and György Litván, also arrive to pay their respects. Tánczos is secretary of the circle, Litván a young high school teacher.[7]

Although large groups of students and whole factories of workers pass slowly in review, there is no organization, no one giving instructions. Most noteworthy of all, this crowd is not talking. Aside from the shuffling of feet and tramp of boots on pavement and gravel, an eerie silence prevails. It is like the end of a football match at People's Stadium that the other side has

A dense crowd passed by four biers. Note the inscription "Rajk László 1909-1949" on the coffin. From *Nők Lapja*, Oct. 11, 1956.

won. Voices are worn out, and no one feels like talking as the crowd disperses, only in this case the crowd is gathering.

And what a crowd it is. Budapest has not seen anything like it for years, not since the Communists took over nine years ago. Estimates agree that when fully assembled the crowd numbers at least two hundred thousand. People are there for a purpose, else few would have braved this miserable weather. László Rajk had friends, but not 200,000. From the elections of 1947 on, he had, in the view of many, acted abominably; as interior minister he was more feared than liked. People have come to demonstrate their agreement that grave injustice has been done and must be rectified. They know this is no ordinary reburial. Earlier this year they had read to their astonishment that all the victims of the 1949 trials were innocent and were being posthumously rehabilitated. Now, at last, they have an opportunity to demonstrate their approval of this reversal without having to stick their necks out. Some, of course, despise the Communist government and are there to witness the humiliation of the régime which had destroyed its own. Others have come simply to demonstrate their opposition to the old ways and their approval of the changes.

Today, in fact, is only the first day of the reburials; others are scheduled to follow over the next two weeks. It is rumored, for instance, that next week six generals, two colonels, and other victims of the 1950 army purge are to be reburied.[8] But these four because of their importance, and, Mrs. Rajk's insistence, have been selected for reburial on this traditional day of mourning. Both General Pálffy and Dr. Szőnyi had been members of the party's Central Committee, and András Szalai was a leading party organizer.

On the dais many high government officials, including President István Dobi and Premier András Hegedűs, now appear. They are accompanied by many top party officials as well. Conspicuously absent are the party's first secretary, Ernő Gerő, who happens to be in the Crimea conferring with Nikita Khrushchev and Marshal Tito, and János Kádár and others directly involved in the prosecution of Rajk and his fellow victims, who are known to be in the country. It is well known that Tito favors the complete rehabilitation of Imre Nagy and even his reinstatement as head of the government. Nagy, however, is still outside the party, despite a large number of leading party liberals who are gathering around him.

Now police also appear. They try to hold the crowd back from the four metal coffins, from the family members gathered around them and from the dais, but they are unobtrusive and scarcely noticed by the throng pressing around them.

Throughout the three-plus hours that the masses of people have been passing in front of them, László Jr. has stood as somber-faced as his mother just in front of her. Now he finds himself fascinated by all the cameras pointing at him, the whirring of the movie cameras, and the blinding flashes of all the flash bulbs. He has never experienced anything like it and it will remain his most lasting impression of that day.[9]

The main speech of the day is given by Deputy Premier Antal Apró. He claims to speak for both the government and the party when he says:

> Never was there a more tragic duty than ours, rehabilitating our dead comrades whom we cannot resurrect.
>
> We deeply regret that we believed in the malicious slandering that led to their martyrdom.
>
> We have called to account and will call to account those who were responsible for their fate.* [10]

---

* This is a reference to the arrest yesterday, October 5, of Vladimir Farkas, once deputy chief of the security service (ÁVO) under the infamous Gábor Péter, arrested in 1955, and to Ervin Faludy, György Szendi and György Szántó, high ÁVO officers, as well as the future arrest of Farkas's father, Mihály Farkas, who had been a member of Rákosi's politburo, who will be arrested just two days from now.

Apro goes on to attack "the personality cult" (i.e., Rákosi) though even with Rákosi off in disgrace in Moscow he dares not mention his name. And he attacks, of course, all the Stalinist blunders that had accrued under Rákosi's "personality cult."

Communist euphemisms are nothing new to this audience. They know he is talking about a sea change in the régime's direction, a point from which there can be no return—and it is good news for everyone.

A more striking speech is given by Ferenc Münnich, former Hungarian ambassador to Moscow. Those responsible for the executions, he says, are "sadistic criminals, whom, however, we do not want to try on this day of funerals."

It is Béla Szász, however, recently released from eight years in prison, who makes the biggest impression on the crowd. His tone is modest and his language quite different from the others. But he speaks from the heart and is utterly sincere. It is not just a question of giving our comrades a decent burial, he says; it is time once and for all "to bury the law of force" which brought about this tragedy. Heads are nodding, and were it not for the setting, there would be cries of "Yes! Yes!"

The speeches over, the four coffins are removed from their biers by pall-bearer soldiers 'and carried in a quarter arc, not more than fifty feet, to the four graves awaiting them.

An army unit fires three volleys into the air. Then, as the military band begins to play the "Internationale," the coffins are lowered slowly into their new graves. Once they are filled in, people press forward to place their flowers onto the fresh earth so that what remains as the cemetery clears of people are four large mounds of flowers.

(As György Litván will say forty-four years later, "I am not sure whether it would not have been better for the revolution to have started that day.")

But the weather is against such an upheaval. Exhilarated as they are by this massive demonstration, most people are now chilled to the bone and eager to return to the warmth of their homes. The crowd, no longer silent, disperses, feeling confident that what they have seen and heard today means that many more changes will soon be coming in their lives.

Not all go directly home, however. A group of students and professors, most of them former communists or noncommunists, and therefore somewhat to the right of the Petőfi Circle, march off to the Batthyány Memorial Lamp on Báthory Street near the Parliament, which marks the spot where Prime Minister Batthyány was executed 150 years ago. Here the impromptu speeches are far more daring and revolutionary than anything heard in the cemetery.[11] No sparks ignite the small crowd, however, for they are preaching to the already converted. After vowing further action, they too, break up and go home.

Hungarians have to wait until Monday to read about the event so many of them had witnessed, for the presses do not operate on Saturday. When they do get their papers, they are treated to a storm of violent accusations in the commentaries which the speeches at the funeral have unleashed. *Szabad Ifjúság* ("Free Youth") states,

> our consciousness and condemnation of guilt cannot wipe out the responsi-
> bility of the chief criminal [i.e., Rákosi, whom they still do not care to
> name]. How can we be satisfied with our initial results when we want to
> cover the whole field? Don't we have to keep an eye on those who are
> unable to walk over their own shadows and jump out of their sectarian
> skins?[12]

A *Népszava* ("People's Word") editorial warns that

> those who misled the people have a reason to be afraid … Many of the
> funeral orations are sentences. The most avenging, most accusing sentence
> hangs over the perpetrators of the horrors created by the "personality cult."

Magyar Nemzet ("Hungarian Nation") writes,

> the speakers passionately denounced every kind of violation of law and
> demanded these violators answer for their deeds in the courts.

But it is the non-party newspaper *Esti Hírlap* ("Evening Journal") which sums up the event most clearly. It writes:

> The projection of Stalinism in Hungary, the régime of Rákosi's personality
> cult, put into this terrible machinery, as an important part, the Rajk trial.
> This is the reason that October 6, the date of national mourning, was also
> the date of a silent revolution. [On Saturday] we irrevocably buried an
> era …

Off in Belgrade, the official Yugoslav party daily, *Borba*, takes optimistic stock of what is happening to the north. "Everyone understood," says *Borba*, that when one speaker at the Rajk reburial said that "all guilty persons should be put on the pillory of shame," that Rákosi heads the list. The paper points out that Árpád Szakasits, the former leader of the Social Democratic Party, and later a leader of the Communist Party, has been readmitted to the party. Moreover, the former president of the Hungarian Republic and leader of the Smallholders Party, Zoltán Tildy, has recently been allowed to publish.

"All this leads us to the conclusion that the crisis, which had been created by the régime's reluctance to democratize the country, particularly intensified between the Twentieth Party Congress of the CPSU and Rákosi's dismissal, has now been overcome."[13]

CHAPTER VIII

The Poznań Trials

Prelude

Close to a thousand people throughout Poland had been arrested as a result of the Poznań uprising, over six hundred of them in Poznań itself. Within the first two weeks, nearly half this number was released following intensive "interrogation." The severity of the interrogations of those still being held—in sharp contradiction to the new rules publicly proclaimed earlier in the year—gave rise to such popular protest that the UB (secret police) were called out of the process and were replaced by the regular civil police, or militia, as they were known in People's Poland.

Western embassies and journalists heard (and reported) a steady stream of rumors about how many of the arrested were still being held for trial, a number that kept diminishing as time went on. Likewise, the unknown date of the trials, which the régime kept saying would be held "soon," continued to remain unannounced. Rumors continued to circulate, meanwhile, that the trials had already been held in secret, or that they had been put off indefinitely.

In truth, the régime had decided by mid-July that trials *would* be held as soon as possible and that they would not be held in secret, but open to public scrutiny. In theory, all trials in People's Poland were open to the public, but that had seldom been the practice. Now, while the authorities had no intention of staging an international "event," pressure to allow foreign observers was so relentless and the prospect of relieving this pressure and simultaneously taking the wind out of its critics' sails so tempting, that denying foreign observers' access was no longer considered an option. Nonetheless, as the full implications of open trials began to dawn on them, the authorities kept making new, precautionary adjustments, each of which further delayed the date of the trials' opening.

It was not until Premier Cyrankiewicz's opening speech before the Sejm on September 5 that the régime's decision to make the trials "open" to the public was officially confirmed. In making the announcement the premier was careful to add that the Polish government had "no intention of allowing them (the trials) to turn into an international spectacle."[1] And it was not until September 22 that the Polish general state prosecutor, M. Rybicki, revealed that the trials would begin at the end of September, that is, in a matter of a few days. He stated that 323 persons had been arrested (about half the actual number), but that the number held for trial had been whittled down to 154 and that 58 of these would be tried in the immediate future. The rest would follow at a later date. "The scope of investigation concerning the incidents in Poznań," the prosecutor added, "has been limited to the prosecution of concrete crimes committed during these incidents."[2]

While pressure from the U.S. and British embassies on the régime for Western observers to be allowed at the trials was equally great, the methods used were as different as the two embassies' assessment as to how to deal with People's Poland. The Americans sent formal emissaries and notes demanding representation; the British eschewed such a frontal approach for more informal exchanges at the highest possible level. Sir Andrew Noble was much better informed (and probably better liked) than his American counterpart, Joseph E. Jacobs, so it was not surprising that he was the first to receive assurances—long before the official announcement—that correspondents of certain British newspapers and embassy observers would be permitted to attend.

In Washington, American policy toward Poland was seriously split between those who genuinely wanted improved relations through engagement,[*] and those who were content to make matters for the régime as difficult as possible through harassment.[†]

---

[*] Eisenhower and others in his administration had finally gotten Secretary Dulles to agree to a long-planned campaign of friendly cultural exchanges with the Soviet bloc. This major undertaking, first announced within hours of the Poznań uprising, and totally unrelated to it, had as its first step the rather naive invitation for the U.S.S.R. and its satellites to send "observers" to witness the U.S. elections in the fall of 1956. By sheer coincidence the announcement of these invitations was made the day after the first Poznań trials got under way.[3]

[†] Principally John Foster Dulles, whose none-too-subtle offer of $100 million worth of food right after the Poznań riots was ignored by the régime for the propaganda ploy it clearly was. A secret feeler from the Polish government in midsummer asking the US for a loan of $50 million was turned down flat by Dulles.[4]

Ever since the Poznań riots all manner of statements calling the régime to task had been issued by various government bodies and exiles organizations in the United States. As the trials loomed larger and larger on the summer horizon, the feeling grew in Washington that something had to be done to prevent the trials from being the sort of Stalinist show trials so commonly held in the past.

On July 30 British ambassador Sir Andrew Noble received a confidential cable from the foreign secretary, Sir Selwyn Lloyd, stating that

> Her Majesty's government are under increasing pressure, from the United States government as well as from interests in the United Kingdom, to issue a public statement calling on the Polish government to treat the prisoners humanely and give them a fair and public trial ... The matter has also been raised in NATO ...
>
> I am disinclined to interfere in what is quite clearly a Polish internal matter ...

Lloyd went on to urge, however, that Polish-speaking members of the embassy attend the trials.[5]

The next day Noble cabled back:

> The danger of any statement is that, if it angers the Poles, they may take it out on those on trial. A statement by the Americans or Germans will be ill received. It would be less dangerous if we or the French were to make a statement, provided it took the form that the Poles had already declared the trials would be held before the ordinary court under the ordinary law ... On the whole I share your view that it would be better to say nothing ...
>
> The Polish government have publicly confessed that they themselves were much to blame for what happened and they know the workers are still in an angry mood.* The Poles, if left to themselves, will be anxious to demonstrate that the newly established 'rule of law' means something in practice.[6]

British opinion prevailed. No such joint statement was ever made and the Americans sat on their own prepared statement until it was too late for it to have any effect. When finally released as a statement by President Eisen-

---

* A confidential telegram from the U.S. embassy on September 6 stated: "Labor situation Poznań also rumored still unsatisfactory with ZISPO and railway repair shop workers threatening general walkout last week unless economic conditions drastically improved."[7]

hower on the eve of the trials, it was out of date and thus was ignored even by the U.S. press.[8]

A stream of individual voices urging clemency and threatening dire consequences if the trials were not open, however, filled the Polish airwaves via RFE and VOA and other Western radios. And even as late as the trials themselves, Eisenhower's Democratic Party opponent, Adlai Stevenson, was calling for "the restoration of the rights and privileges of the Polish people."[9]

Meanwhile, two totally unrelated events—one public, one hidden from public view—had a profound effect on the conduct of the trials and on how they were received by the Polish people.

The first was a murder trial in Cracow of one Władysław Mazurkiewicz, which the régime was pleased to have the now-much-freer press and radio report extensively, as it helped to draw attention away from Poznań. Mazurkiewicz was an old-fashioned villain who had murdered six people and attempted to kill two others—all to enrich himself. With its sensational daily revelations and tabloid overtones, the coverage of this trial helped to convince the Polish people that much greater press freedom had, in fact, returned to their country and such detailed reporting of trials was to be expected in the future.[10]

The other event was hidden from the populace and only leaked out months later, but it had an equally monumental effect on the trials. This was First Party Secretary Ochab's experience in attending the Chinese party congress in early September. During several private meetings with Chinese first secretary Mao, Ochab was given to understand that China, too, had its own Gomułka, though Mao never mentioned his name. This man had never been expelled from the party and, in fact, was even retained on the Central Committee, though without any assigned power. He was even asked to give his advice from time to time.

Mao also told Ochab, "It seems that China and Poland have been keeping company for some time already without even knowing it. It is good company, and we are glad of it." Proof of Mao's sincerity came a few days later, when Ochab was asked to give his honest opinion of the Poznań events. Ochab's answer so offended the Soviet Union's official representative to the congress, Anastas Mikoyan, that he exploded with a stream of invectives, finishing his outburst with "People who voice such anti-Soviet ideas can only be regarded as enemies and treated accordingly. The same goes," he added, looking at Mao, "to those who listen to them."

Ochab, a heavyset man who towered above both men, was visibly shaken. Without replying to Mikoyan, he shook hands with Mao and left the room. Mao, ignoring Mikoyan, turned and followed Ochab out of the room.

This rebuff was more than Mikoyan could take. Within hours, and without making official farewells with any Chinese official, he departed by plane for Moscow.

The news that the Chinese government accepted the Polish version of the Poznań events rather than the Soviet version galvanized the Cyrankiewicz faction. Ochab now wholeheartedly threw his full weight to the liberals, abandoning his neutral position between them and the Polish Stalinists.[11] The Poznań trials would be genuine, not Stalinist show trials.

Thus, in late September, the Poznań defendants were suddenly told they would be allowed to have defense lawyers of their own choosing, rather than the usual court-appointed party hacks. And, since the trials would be observing the letter of the Polish penal code, there was nothing to fear from foreign observers being present. One thing the government tried to make abundantly clear from the outset, however, was that the 154 being held for trial were not to be tried for having caused the Poznań events, but only for having committed specific crimes during those events. Crimes, clear breakings of the law, were not going to be allowed to go unpunished in People's Poland.

~

The Trials

Today is Thursday, September 27, three months to the day from the Poznań rising. The citizens of Poznań are in a somber mood. Later today the trials of the 154 of their fellow citizens who have been in jail all summer will get underway. At 10:00 A.M. two trials—one of three young men, another of nine—are to begin in the brand new main Voivodship courthouse on Solna Wolnica Avenue, adjacent to Młyńska Street. In a sense, the trials will not be of just those arrested, but of the Communist régime itself, and there is great apprehension that the conduct and results of these trials will be all too like previous trials in People's Poland.

Last June the hotels and fairgrounds were full of foreigners, many from the West. Today there are very few, not more than twenty Westerners among them: three learned jurists from France, Belgium and Britain, a handful of journalists and another handful of observers from Western embassies. What they see is ominous.

While most people are going about their business, more than a few are milling along the sidewalks as close to the main courthouse as the militia will allow them to come. On the square outside the Orbis Hotel, where most of the Westerners are staying, only one block is available to these strollers. The other two blocks are cordoned off by a solid line of sullen, armed militia standing motionless in their gray-blue uniforms. Other militiamen remain sitting in their canvas-covered jeeps and trucks parked in various strategic points around the city. Out-of-town license plates reveal that they are from every part of Poland *but* Poznań.

For the past several evenings trios of machine-gun-toting militia have been combing the city for drunks. Who knows when some inebriate might lose control and blurt out some obvious but painful truth that could enflame similar thoughts in his compatriots, drunk or sober, and lead to some dangerous, inflammatory behavior.[12]

Only persons with tickets are allowed through the militia lines. While some twenty thousand workers are said to have applied for tickets, very few have been granted them.[13] In addition to those given to Western observers and journalists, the bulk of the seats have been allotted to relations of the defendants, government officials, secret police, and members of the Polish press corps.

As the few Westerners slip through the tight cordon of grim-faced, nervous militia, they can feel the resentful eyes of the small crowd that has gathered. "Just who are they to be admitted and not us?" their eyes seem to convey.

Inside two very different-sized courtrooms are filling up, a small one near the front where three youths will be tried for the murder of Corporal Zygmunt Izdebny, the secret policeman who had been stomped to death at the railroad station, and a much larger one where nine young men accused of assaulting the UB headquarters on Kochanowski Street are being tried together. Some are also accused of breaking into the nearby jail, seizing arms, and destroying files.

Despite their disparity in size, the two rooms are similar in layout. There is no jury as there would be in a British or American court. Instead, as in most European courts, there is a panel of three judges. The chief judge is a professional, and the other two are selected from "the people," which, in the case of People's Poland, means staunch members of the Communist Party, who can thus outvote the professional judge to make sure "people's justice" is done in every instance. They are seated behind a table on a raised dais dressed in black robes. Facing each other on either side of the court are the prosecutors and defense counselors, also in black robes, sitting at their tables.

In the smaller court the defendants sit behind the defense counselors in a sort of jury box, each wedged between two armed militiamen. These, in full dress uniforms, wear their caps with the shiny black leather visors with gold braid, making each prisoner between them look small. The remaining space of the small courtroom is packed with spectators, who are almost close enough to the prisoners to touch them.

The arrangement in the larger room is somewhat different. Here the judges dais is ranged along the long concave wall of the basically rectangular room with space for clerks at the ends of their long table. Light streams in over their heads from a bank of high windows that run the length of the slightly curved wall. The prisoners, similarly sandwiched between militiamen in full regalia, fill the whole right side of the room. Half a dozen rows of seats filled with spectators run the length of the long wall facing the judges with an even more spacious gallery jammed with spectators directly above them. At the left side of the room are the prosecutors and their aides. Directly in front of the judges in the middle is the witness stand.

The rooms have been stripped of all adornment. Gone are the symbols of the régime—even the symbols of Poland. Conspicuously absent are the usual oversized portraits of government and party officials. At precisely 10 o'clock the judges enter the courtrooms, all rise and the courts are called into session.

First come the indictments, which are long and read in a bureaucratic monotone. As each prisoner's name is read out, he must stand and walk with his guards to the bar, remaining motionless during the reading. He is then allowed a brief statement to say whether or not he pleads guilty to the charges. He is then marched back to his seat.

The most notable fact about all of the defendants is their extreme youth. Some are nervous; all are casually, some garishly, dressed. They are children of the street. Most are in their early twenties, but many are literally in their teens. There is, in fact, a very clear separation of generations among the main participants of these trials. The accused are all young—all of their formative years have been spent under communism. The judges and prosecutors, who are government officials, and thus party members all, are in their thirties and early forties. But the defense attorneys are all men in their fifties or even early sixties, men who received all their training before the Second World War.

Most of the morning is taken up with the indictments and exchanges between the prosecutors and judges, with occasional interjections from the defense lawyers. What strikes observers of both trials who have witnessed earlier trials in People's Poland is the boldness of the defense counselors, who are not usually permitted to speak until the prosecutor's case is completed—and the exceedingly polite and formal tone which is maintained between the opposing lawyers and the bench throughout the proceedings.

During the noon break Western journalists return to the Orbis Hotel to file their initial stories on how correct and fair the trials appear to be thus far.

A week later, before the close of this first trial, known as the trial of the three, Radio Warsaw broadcasts an interview with two American journalists, Sidney Gruson of *The New York Times* and Daniel Shorr of CBS, and the internationally-known British barrister and judge, Elwyn Jones, who is also a Labour member of Parliament and former prosecutor at the Nuremberg Trials. All three have attended the trial of three. "I was greatly impressed," says Jones,[14] "that the trial was conducted with dignity ... that the court treated the accused and the defense counsels with attention and objectivity."*

"We have all been struck by the fairness," says Gruson, "but there are also certain reservations that our backgrounds ... are bound to raise in our minds ... Some of the defense counsels have told me that they only entered the case seven days before the trials started. I would have thought [they] ... would have been brought in just as quickly as possible after the investigations began ... It will be very interesting to see how the defense conducts this case ...

"Another thing we do not quite understand. Why these particular young men had to be the first ones brought to trial? It is hard to see that they are the main ones responsible for the Poznań riots ... Will the ringleaders be brought to trial as well?"

Daniel Schorr says he agrees with another foreign observer that "this may be one of the most significant trials of the twentieth century because ... in a sense all of Polish justice and communist justice seems to be on trial."

These words are broadcast in Polish to Radio Warsaw's vast domestic audience that has grown far more attentive to its programs since the trials began. But in the areas beyond Poland's main cities where jamming of Western radios is heaviest, far more extensive and accurate reports of the trials are reaching the populace over Radio Free Europe, VOA, and BBC, for they have access to all of the reports of Western correspondents at the trials, correspondents such as Sidney Gruson of *The New York Times* and Philippe Ben

---

* In the British foreign office A. E. Davidson of the Northern Department had already warned the British ambassador that Mr. Jones had been involved in a number of communist front organizations and had recently declared on a visit to Communist China (May 1956) that "the law in China is fair, its enforcement just and the courts humane."[15]

of *Le Monde*, a Polish-speaking Israeli citizen, who grew up with many of the high party officials now running Poland.

The trial of nine, eight youths and a man of thirty-three, understandably progresses more slowly than the trial of three. The alleged crimes of these nine individuals are quite disparate, and even Radio Warsaw agonizes over the great differences not only in the crimes, but in social background and previous record, or lack of it, of those in the dock.[16]

Because at least three of the defendants had nothing in their records to indicate the slightest tendency to wrongdoing, the defense attorneys manage to persuade the court to allow the testimony of expert sociologists on crowd psychology.

After two days of arguments and testimony, both trials adjourn for the weekend while reports of their unprecedented openness and fairness percolate around the world.

By Wednesday, October 3, the trial of three is drawing to a close. The judges reject the defense counsel's request that workers from the ZISPO and railroad car works in Poznań be allowed to testify on the grounds that the influence of the strike and the popular demonstration is well known. Defense attorney M. Kujanek, amid applause from the spectators, gives an impassioned plea for clemency for his twenty-year-old client, Józef Fołtynowicz. He weaves in a few quotations from Party Secretary Ochab in an attempt to give his remarks a veil of respectability in the eyes of the judges.[17]

"There have been numerous riots in history carrying different names," says Kujanek. "What will history give to the Poznań events?…

"The victims … can be divided up into two groups. One was composed of those who were interred at the cemetery with the honor given to heroes and saluted by high officials of the state. The other group is composed of those who were secretly buried without speeches and without mention of their tragedy …

"Your honors: Before signing the sentences, remember that in years to come you may be ashamed of having signed them. As the Poznań events go into history, so will your verdict go into history!"[18]

Le Monde's Philippe Ben notes that one of Poznań's two daily newspapers promises to publish the text of Kujanek's summation speech "according to the Polish Press Agency's version … This means," writes Ben, "that there is at the moment enough freedom in Poland for a lawyer to say all he believes necessary in the interest of this client, but not enough for the counsel's address to be published without previous censorship."[19] Kujanek is followed by his colleague Stanisław Hejmowski, untidy in dress but exuberant in speech, who begins by pointing out that this trial deals with two eighteen-year-olds and one twenty-year-old. He strenuously objects to the prosecutor's insistence in dividing the young people of Poznań into workers and "hooligans." "Hooligans do not exist as a class," he observes. There are only hooligan acts. And what had the judges—or for that matter Hejmowski's own generation—done to prevent these young people from sitting here? The accused had spent their childhood among "murder, atrocities and massacres of innocent people. This is where we should look for the roots of hooliganism. If, today, these young people do not recognize any authority—neither state, nor parents, nor school nor the church—who is responsible?" The fault," he says, "is not theirs alone. Had they been properly brought up by their elders? Had moral principles been inculcated? Was not the whole of society to blame for their crime? Hooliganism, after all, is a totally postwar phenomenon, the word itself having been borrowed from the Russian penal code.[20] During their testimony, moreover, the accused had revealed that they had been beaten up after having been arrested. Was not this a further act of hooliganism?"

Hejmowski points out that the accused had joined a crowd that was already attacking Izdebny. But the people who had begun the attack were not before the court. The accused were only part of a much larger crowd. Moreover they were wrongly charged under Article 1 of the penal code, since this had been written for conditions then existing in 1945, they should instead be charged under Article 240. The minimum sentence under Article 1 is ten years and the maximum death. Article 240, on the other hand, provides for a fight in a crowd from which death results. The penalty is from six months to five years.

Hejmowski's speech is followed by "a short recess," which expands to over a full hour while the prosecution decides how they are going to answer these unexpected arguments of the defense. When they return, the prosecutors admit that Hejmowski is correct on some points but that the three accused must still be charged under Article 1 because they attacked a uniformed official of the state.

Hejmowski boisterously refutes this contention by pointing out that in their testimony all three of the accused said they had attacked Izdebny because they believed he had murdered a woman and child. It had nothing to do with the status of his employment. As for Article 1, it was drawn up when abnormal conditions prevailed throughout Poland right after the war. But that was over twelve years ago. The country has been rebuilt, he says, his words dripping with sarcasm. Under Article 1, there were twelve charges for which the punishment was death, but it is peacetime now, and Article 1 simply does not apply.[21]

The hearing ends with the two eighteen-year-olds, Kazimierz Żurek and Jerzy Sroka, expressing their regrets and asking for leniency, while the twenty-year-old Foltynowicz says, "I admit hitting the corporal, but I do not admit kicking while he was lying on the ground."

"Your sentences," Hejmowski warns the three judges, "will also be a sentence against all of us, because the accused are the product of the situation in our country today."[22] The head judge then adjourns the court until Monday, October 8, when the sentences will be handed down.

Hejmowski is also involved in the trial of nine, which, because of the greater number of defendants, has only reached its half way mark. He is clearly the most outspoken of the defense lawyers, and he soon explains to Western observers, with whom he freely talks, just why: he defended many communists in prewar Poland and even defended Greizer, the Nazi Gauleiter of Poznań, when he was tried by the Poles after the war. The other defense lawyers, with less pro-communist records, are actually risking more than he.[23]

When they are called before the judges to hear their indictment, one after the other of the prisoners withdraw their signed confessions, claiming that these were extorted from them by the police. In response, the representative of the prosecutor general rises to read a statement admitting that "at the very beginning" there had been police misconduct, but that all coerced testimony had already been stricken from the record. He then proceeds to reveal to a startled courtroom what has never before been acknowledged in the state's official media, namely that four UB men had been arrested, six more suspended, and that the Poznań police commander and three other officials under him had been fired for employing such brutality.

Such truth-telling by the authorities unleashes a flood of unexpected testimony.

"I was taken to the commandant of the police," says Stanisław Kaufman, a skinny twenty-year-old, "who put me through my second christening. I was beaten with rods on my face and knocked over with a blow from behind. An officer dragged me up by the hair," he continues in a toneless voice, "down to the second floor where he beat and kicked me. I was stood up with my face against the wall while he pummeled the back of my head, knocking my face into the wall."[24]

Neither the prosecutor nor any of the judges make any attempt to stifle Kaufman's or any of the others' testimony. Though the death of Romek Strzałkowski, the thirteen-year-old boy whose body was found in the UB garage shot through the heart, has no direct bearing on any of the accused, the defense is nevertheless allowed to introduce his father as a witness.

"The boy was helping to give first aid to people when he was shot," says Mr. Strzałkowski, adding that he had learned this story from witnesses and from an official who had come to their apartment to inform him of his son's death. The boy's mother, dressed in black, does not testify, but during a recess she tells reporters, "we were looking for our son all night. He was a good boy. As a piano student he was entered in the local Chopin competition. Now we have had to sell his piano."[25]

The most sensational moment in this trial of nine, however, comes when Janusz Suwart, the twenty-two-year-old son of a long-time communist, tells the story of his torture at the hands of the secret police. He is rudely interrupted by one of the prosecutors who try to paint him as one of the scum of society who already has a previous conviction for theft.

"Yes, I stole! I'll tell you why I did it," screams Suwart. "Poverty made me steal!" Trembling with fury, the boy shouts out his story. Between his bursts only the sobs of his grizzled, sixty-seven-year-old father from the back of the public seats can be heard in the hushed courtroom. "My father was a communist before the war. He spent many years in prison for it then. After the war he went to work for the UB. In January 1952 he was expelled from the party, arrested and accused of having worked for the pre-war police. I have known my father all my life. He raised me as a socialist. He worked hard for the government and he was falsely accused. When my father was arrested it drove my mother insane. My brother also worked for the UB, but he was discharged because of my father and he ended up committing suicide. I was sick: I had a chronic skin disease and couldn't work. But my mother couldn't do anything for herself and my two sisters were too young to work. The Communist Party turned against us. The neighbors never liked us because they knew we were communists and my father worked for the UB. They would not help us. My mother finally went to the Church and begged for soup. Can you imagine how I felt? Did my family deserve this?"[26]

The explosion of murmuring which this outburst evokes does not bring on a command for 'order in the court;' even the judges sit spellbound.

Later, another defendant, Marian Joachimiak, accused of stealing a watch, admits he is guilty of this, but points out that he had not taken any stolen clothes of which he had been charged. His monthly wage, he explains, is only 900 zlotys, enough to buy two pairs of shoes. Then, drawing himself up with dignity, he explains: "I didn't take the clothes because I come from a worker's family that has always earned what it got. But," he adds as his gaze drops to the floor, "all my life I have wanted a watch. I knew I would never be able to afford one. I felt an awful struggle in myself ... but in the end I couldn't resist."[27]

While the verdict in the trial of three is awaited and the trial of nine continues, a third trial involving ten defendants gets under way in a third courtroom of the court building. These young men are also accused of attacking the UB headquarters. The only difference between this group and the two seems to be their source of arms: militia stations around Poznań instead of the prison. But there is a notable change in the prosecution.

Upset at the way the first two trials have been going, the authorities decided to replace the young prosecutor scheduled for this trial with someone from the prosecutor general's office in Warsaw. This man, Joachim Markowicz, is in his mid-fifties. Far more experienced and sure of himself, he is nonetheless a dedicated communist, "a thoroughly nasty piece of work," in the words of one British observer. Markowicz makes himself master of the proceedings almost as soon as the chief judge opens the trial. In a long opening speech he denigrates the various "expert" witnesses the defense has lined up—sociologists, psychologists and medical doctors—and objects to their presence in the courtroom. They may be allowed occasionally to clear up a point or two, but should not be allowed to "make speeches." This is hotly contested by the defense counsels, who have scheduled no fewer than ninety-nine witnesses. Thoroughly bad relations between the prosecution and defense are thus established at the outset.[28]

At the end of the reading of the thirty-three-page indictment the courtroom comes to life when the very first of the accused, a big blond twenty-year-old named Janusz Kulas, who likes to be known and addressed by his street name, "Eddie Polo, the Italian Bandit," takes the stand. He vehemently denies all the charges, repudiates his deposition, which he says was extorted from him by "S.S. methods," and keeps complaining to the chief judge that the prosecutor's questions to him are "unfair." He is a tough customer, and neither the prosecutors nor the judges appear to intimidate him one bit.

The attitude of two of the other nine defendants is dramatically different. They are exceedingly deferential to the court, admit the charges, and go out of their way to say that they have been well treated by the police authorities. It occurs to many observers that they have turned state's evidence in return for lighter sentences.[29]

The extraordinarily selective choices the authorities have made in choosing crimes to be prosecuted emerges from the testimony of several witnesses who describe the destruction of the jamming station prior to the attack on the UB building. This, they say, was carried out entirely by workers. But none of these workers are charged and the destruction of the jamming station is not even mentioned in any of the indictments thus far. "Clearly," writes *Le*

Monde's Philippe Ben, "it was preferable to leave this crime unpunished rather than admit the extensive existence of similar installations in Poland."[30]

One of the more dramatic moments in this trial of ten comes on the ninth day during the testimony of Władysław Kaczkowski, an innocent-looking lad of nineteen with neatly combed, dark hair. As he tells of his exploits on June 28 and how, despite the fact that he had turned himself in voluntarily the next day, he had been beaten. Tears begin to roll down his round cheeks. At last the memory of that horrible time is too much for him and he breaks down into uncontrollable sobs. His story peals the scabs off raw memories of such brutality in every Pole in the courtroom. In the back of the prisoners' dock another defendant jumps up from between his startled guards and shouts a stream of abuse at the secret police. This sets off a tired-faced woman who jumps to her feet in the back of the public gallery and starts screaming hysterically. She is Kaczkowski's older sister. "My father died for Poland in 1939!" she screams. "My mother died in 1942. And now we are more oppressed than ever!"

"It's true," a Polish journalist in the press box says through clenched teeth. "And it's not news. We've known it for a long time."[31]

"The court will now take a short recess!" announces the chief judge from the bench in an effort to defuse the charged atmosphere. Tears can be seen in many eyes besides Kaczkowski's.

Later it is learned that during the hubbub another defendant, Klimecki, with a heart condition, has had a seizure. Doctors had ruled that he was able to stand trial, but his having to be taken out of the courtroom frequently has belied this decision. The chief judge now rules that he be removed from this trial and tried separately. Since another prisoner, Luczak, has been successfully removed from these proceedings by his defense counsel on the grounds that the person to whom he gave aid is not involved with this particular trial, the number of accused now drops to eight.[32]

On Saturday, October 6, one Poznań newspaper tells of a hitherto unnoticed trial that has taken place in the local (Powiat) court, as opposed to the Voivodship court where the public trials are taking place. Three of the men were convicts freed from the Młyńska Street prison during the rising. All had been arrested for looting. The three former convicts had drawn four years of imprisonment and the fourth defendant two years.[33]

On Monday, October 8, following the weekend recess, sentences in the first trial of the three young men accused of murdering the secret policeman are announced. To everyone's astonishment and joy they are exceedingly light: four and a half years apiece for each of the twenty-year-olds and four years for the eighteen-year-old. Judge Witsław Celiński explains that the defense counsel is correct in saying that Article 1 of the penal code should not be applied. Moreover, he says, the prosecution has not proved that any of the three actually caused the death of the victim.

News of these lenient sentences is carried on the front page of newspapers throughout the noncommunist world, and every Polish newspaper carries the story, whether or not on the front page.

A fourth trial of six young men, also accused of stealing arms from a source other than those mentioned in the earlier trials, was to have begun today, October 8, but for some unannounced reason has been postponed.

On the far side of the globe, America's CIA director, Allen Dulles, who has been reading with growing alarm reports of the turmoil in Poland and Hungary, decides to cut short his world tour. Originally scheduled not to return to Washington until around November 20, he hurries back, arriving on October 8. He has been out of the country for fifty-seven days.[34]

Meanwhile, the trial of nine comes to a close the next day, October 9 and the chief judge announces that sentencing will follow on Friday, October 12. When these sentences are rendered, they too are extraordinarily lenient, most of them two years or less, with one outright acquittal.

Despite Prosecutor Markowicz's disdain for them, the "expert" witnesses in the trial of ten (now down to eight) continue to make inroads on his case.

Józef Chałasiński, a professor of sociology at the University of Łódź, is particularly effective. "This trial," he says, "as well as the other trials …

> have shown incontrovertibly that the impact of the crowd began at once, from the first phase of the demonstration in front of the Castle. The crowd … had in its character a great psychological force over its participants … It was perhaps a demonstration of wrongs … The power of the mood was increased by the fact that this was the first demonstration of this type, an illegal demonstration in People's Poland. And for many thousands the first in their life … News that agents of the Security Bureau were firing on children … undoubtedly activated the memory, still fresh, of the lawless and cruel investigative practices of the Security Bureau … The sense of injustice was transformed into moral outrage … The shot which hit a female streetcar conductor across from the UB building, as well as the boy who took the standard from her hands, raised the moral outrage to its highest level and led to further shooting … Under the influence of a strong feeling of moral outrage an individual may completely lose awareness of the illegal or antistate character of his actions … In explaining why he took up arms, the accused worker said that at the sight of dead and wounded people it was as if he became a different person over whom he had no control … The activity of the crowd against agents of the UB was a reaction of moral outrage to cruelty, not an attack on the UB as a government agency … In such

circumstances ... it is not possible to draw conclusions through an analogy to similar action in normal situations of social life or on the basis of conclusion and guesses as to the motives ... [based on a] biography of the accused ...

From the testimony of the prison director we hear that the attackers enabled him to escape so that he would not become a victim of the crowd.

Nothing is as threatening to society as these collective situations in which positive moral and social feelings like compassion and mercy, or a sense of duty or patriotism, are mixed with cruelty and crime in a way difficult to disentangle. That is why so much effort is always put into not allowing that first shot to be fired ...[35]

✑

On October 16, defense counsel Stanisław Hejmowski delivers his summation. "The defense stands," he begins,

on the position that everything that took place on the 28 of June ... is part of a single, undivided whole.

And the prosecution? From that amazing social action which includes tens of thousands of people, they have ... plucked out a dozen or so people, presented these people to the court, and demanded of the court a conviction ... for the crimes committed by them ...

What criterion of selection was used?... One of the most eminent members of the prosecution said "Some of them broke the law, others did not ... We do not pass judgement on participation in the strike and the demonstration, but we will pass judgement on those who were committing crimes ... This is required by the idea of law and order."

Thousands of people on that day broke almost all the laws in the lesser penal code ... Hundreds of people abandoned their jobs in the public services and transportation services, streetcars, buses, railroads, in bakeries and food services. Hundreds of people entered the city council ... forcing the members of the council to leave their offices and interrupt their work ...

False information was spread ...

The national emblems and the flag, ours and those of our allies, were desecrated ...

Hundreds of people held up trains at the Poznań Railway station ...

There was public exhortation to the committing of crimes …

And these hundreds of people, these thousands of perpetrators of criminal acts, all are known. So where is the line of separation between thousands of perpetrators … and this handful of people?

Perhaps only those people who fired shots in front of the UB headquarters? Nothing of the sort. Bulczyński didn't fire a shot. Bulczyński has a clean record … A whole series of people are imprisoned who for the first time found themselves in conflict with the law that day …

There one criterion of division … this criterion is no other than age. Please check the personal data of the accused: seventeen, eighteen, nineteen, twenty, twenty-two, maximum twenty-three years of age …

After being called by the presiding judge, Bulczyński hurried to the table … bowed low, quickly delivered his prepared speech, that he wishes to offer thanks to the authorities for the fact that he was treated decently in the interrogation … In the twentieth century a free man, citizen of a free state, has to thank the authorities that he was not beaten?

This is the same man who in Junikowo calmed the police officer and said to him: "We won't hurt you, don't be afraid of us" and who held back the friends he ran into in the "Fair Restaurant" [saying] "Don't go into the city. Don't get mixed up in all that, it's not safe there, you could get killed …"

He could have freely used a weapon against the representatives of authority, but not one shot was fired …

The feeling of wrong that has been growing in the space of the last ten years caused the crowd to feel great tension, which was only released with the firsts shot fired on June 28 on Kochanowski Street. And it is immaterial whether the shot was aimed into the air or at people. The shot brought an awareness to the masses that now the time of singing and peaceful demonstration had come to an end … And that's why police throughout the world are specially trained to deal with crowds, and that is why the first shot can always be a magical shot … Under no circumstances is it permitted to shoot because that awakens a response of outrage, the desire to shoot back, the desire to answer violence with violence …

It was a tragic day. Thousands of people mourn that day: death, crippling, loss of one's closest, wounds, loss of family inheritance—a tragic, painful day. And who is to take responsibility before the court? Eddie Polo, Bulczyński and the 'Biliczek' group? I assure the High Court that is not what the Polish nation is waiting for. The bureaucrats who are to blame for the June events, who separated themselves from the masses are still waiting for their prosecutors …"[36]

Hejmowski ends with a plea for a humane sentence for his main client, Bulczyński.

A fourth trial, of six persons, which was to have taken place today, October 9, has been canceled. Defense attorneys Kujanek and Hejmowski tell British embassy observers that their briefs for all of the remaining trials have been withdrawn without explanation.[37]

The régime's plan to hold trials, but only for those who committed obvious and ordinary crimes, to try them with scrupulous fairness before the eyes of the world—and especially their fellow Poles—has backfired badly. As one Western correspondent will later observe: "The very decision to let the prisoners speak freely and to let their lawyers defend them honestly wrecked the government's careful scheme."[38]

On the evening of October 16, the day of Hejmowski's summation at the trial of ten (now eight), Radio Warsaw announces that the prosecutor general's office has ordered a review of all indictments and all prisoners among the remaining 134 not yet brought to trial. If they are not accused of murder or robbery, they are to be released from custody.[39]

No further announcements are made. Only six weeks later does the counselor of the British embassy, in private conversation with the public prosecutor general, M. Rybicki, learn that the trials have, in fact, been abandoned and that all sentences, save of the first three youths—those involved in the death of the UB corporal, have been annulled.[40]

So much truth-saying in the Poznań courts has stirred the Polish people to a new level of pride in their nation. Despite the few convictions, it is the régime itself that stands convicted. The middleaged defense attorneys have become heroes overnight and their words are glowingly repeated in shops and restaurants all over the land.[41]

Cyrankiewicz and the Communist liberals, now joined by First Party Secretary Ochab, have been propelled too far by the trials ever to return to any hint of Stalinism. The group of Stalinists in their midst, still strongly backed by Moscow, is their only obstacle.

The two party factions are headed for a showdown—both agree that immediate and drastic action is essential.

Appendix to Chapter VIII

Excerpts from the eighth and last letter of Jacek Wachowiak written from prison to his mother and family before his unexpected release some weeks later and the full text of an open letter written to the authorities of People's Poland sometime in the summer of 1956 and clandestinely distributed in manuscript form around Poland that year. The texts are taken from Poznański Czerwiec 1956, *pp. 387-391, translated for the author by Katarzyna Hagemajer.*

Poznań, Oct. 21, 1956

Dear Mama, Auntie, Mariolka and Jędruś!

I don't know how many of my letters I've written to you now without a response.[*] It doesn't worry me too much, because we saw each other last week, but nevertheless I expected a few words from you, but nothing! Send me those pictures Janek took at home. We really didn't tell each other much when you were here. That's how it is. At the last moment you forget everything you wanted to say. But the most important thing was that after three months we could finally embrace each other, because somehow I didn't feel the letters' embraces. The blanket was perfect, because it's already cold here, and now I don't feel it so much.

... I am waiting for Dr. Hejmowski's visit. I hope I will see him soon. Today I don't have the inspiration to write and I don't really know what I should write to you anyway. Maybe when I get a letter from you some subject will arise. It's a shame to see an unwritten piece of paper, so I write, even if it's like pulling teeth, but I want to fill the quota, i.e., I have to fill the other side ...

---

[*] All the responses to his letters were confiscated by the authorities. But his mother, Emilia Wachowiak, did manage to write her letter to the authorities; it follows this excerpt.

Open Letter from Emilia Wachowiak to the Polish Governmental Authorities

I am no journalist, and it's too bad, because I address myself to the authorities of People's Poland in the name of all the youths arrested, and in the name of their unhappy mothers. You probably know quite well that it was not the youths who are guilty for what happened on the 28th of June, despite the fact that they were armed. It is the MO [Civic Militia] and the UB [Security Bureau] who like fools gave up their arms, without resistance, to fourteen-, sixteen-, eighteen-year-old children. I protest in the name of the entire Poznań society against the torture and coercion of youth being pressured to confess things they didn't do.

I am the mother of an eighteen-year-old son whom the MO [Civic Militia] dragged, wounded and with a fever, out of our house, mistreating him and calling him a criminal. Painfully I must confess that the German Gestapo arresting my husband for state treason acted with more culture and humanity than these representatives of the people. From 1940 I was left alone, without means of subsistence, with three young children. No one came to my aid. On the contrary the authorities of People's Poland took away from my children even what they had rightfully inherited from their father, because the organization to which he belonged was merged, already after his death, with the Armia Krajowa [Home Army]. I am not going to write about past wrongs. There were too many of them. But one thing I will state, that the majority of children of the activists for independence were raised in People's Poland in hunger, cold and poverty. Because with 528 zlotys in monthly earnings and 240 zlotys in family allowance it's not possible to work miracles.

That passed, the children grew up, but something worse has happened, because these same children are sitting in Poznań prisons, tortured by the MO [Civic Militia] and the UB [Security Bureau]. Who is responsible for the bloody riots in Poznań? First of all the government, which couldn't manage to pay the workers of ZISPO 11 million zlotys. But on propaganda they spend millions. Next, our party authorities, who ignored the rightful stance of the workers demanding the freeing of the delegation, and who haven't managed to live up to their task. Did these gentlemen, so ideologically aware, not know that a crowd is menacing and unpredictable? Who fired the first shots? All Poznań knows what can't be hidden, because thousands of people were looking on. The UB began firing on women and children. Only then did the youths allow themselves to be drawn into the action. Anyhow, in any war, revolution and riot the youths are in the front. Don't try to tell us that bands of hooligans came out onto the street. That's a lie! All Poznań came out onto the street and today that same Poznań has a threatening appearance, you know this well, that's why all of Poznań is filled up with your soldiers. The prisons are filled. Arrests continue. And you bring in probably those same executioners who were at Katyń, with one difference, that there adults were murdered, and here children are being tortured.

For such freedom did our husbands, brothers and sisters die in the death camps, blood spilled all over the earth? Who split the nations into two camps? Who taught hatred? Who destroyed everything that existed before? Who depraved our youths with books and films? You did. Who tore out from the souls of the Polish child and youth both God and all principles? Who ridiculed parents and teachers? Organizations and the party, that is, you. And today you reproach that youth which you have raised in a Stalinist spirit, for wanting to bring down the political system and take power. Don't ridicule yourselves in front of the nation and the entire world—fourteen-, sixteen- and eighteen-year-olds bring down the government? Is that government so fragile?

Two days after the arrest of my son a boy came up to me, sixteen to eighteen years old, no more. He didn't give his name because he was afraid, but he showed me his back black with bruises. Enough. He had heard how the torturers were speaking to my son: "We will tear off your leg." Where are we to find justice?

Gentlemen: this is not propaganda from Radio Free Europe. This is the voice of the unhappy children of Poland! This is not the way to the hearts of youth who saw with their own eyes fratricidal murder. One must surround youth with tender care and love, they are the sanctity and future of the nation. Get your filthy executioner's hands and torturer's hands off the children of the best sons of our fatherland. You build peace with a white dove in one hand while the other is armed with a knout. On such foundations there is no genuine peace. Genuine peace grows only out of love. Bring the Ten Commandments into life and imbue them in the hearts of children and youth … Teach how to honor our national heroes and take them as examples. Don't falsify history. Speak the truth to our youth and they will be on your side. Then you won't need all those well-paid employees of the MO and the UB. And those enormous sums of money you will be able to put to use increasing the standard of living of the workers, and then never and nowhere will the 28th of June be repeated.

One of many mothers

CHAPTER IX

The Polish October

Government contact with Gomułka, first initiated back in April, had developed into continuous talks after the Poznań rising.[1] But it was not until the mood of the common people burst into public view at those extraordinary trials in early October that Gomułka dismissed the emissaries of the Natolin group* who had been wooing him, and openly threw his lot with the liberal wing of the party. It was clear that, even though he had not yet been invited back into the leadership of the party, he held the balance of power. Like him, many of the party liberals—people who had been imprisoned, but now were free and active again—had not yet achieved any official status in the party or government. Yet they were capable of wielding significant influence.

Unfortunately, the American embassy seemed unaware of Gomułka's talks with the government and still could not believe that anything much was happening. As late as September 21 in a long cable Ambassador Jacobs informed Washington that:

> Gomułka's reinstatement in the party has as yet revealed no active participation ...

> The authoritative manner and conduct of Bulganin on July 22nd, the continued presence of large numbers of Soviet troops [in] Poland, and the fact that Moscow stooges remain powerful in the régime, the fact that the UB [secret police], though regimented, is still potent, the fact that the Polish armed forces are controlled by Russsophile Rokossovsky, plus numerous other factors, indicate clearly that Poland's politics and economy is still at the mercy of the U.S.S.R.

---

* So called because, as former members of the U.S.S.R.'s puppet government for Poland, established in 1944, they used to meet regularly at the Natolin Château near Warsaw.

Władysław Gomułka. *Swiat* (Warsaw), October 28, 1956.

Significant criticism by the press is now rare, the legislative process in the September Sejm [parliament] meeting was not even as bold as the April session ...

While the embassy feels there is no evidence that the liberalization has developed into anything like an 'irreversible trend' it is still too early to assess to what extent recession is in progress ...

Such relaxation and change as there has been and will be in the foreseeable future is, in the embassy's view, designed solely to perpetuate the régime in power.[2]

No sooner had Gomułka taken his stand than a series of articles articulating his position began to appear in the weekly *Przęglad Kulturalny*. They are written by his friend, the idealistic, yet urbane communist, Władysław Bieńkowski, who had shared Gomułka's disgrace of imprisonment by his own party. Bieńkowski had also worked in the underground during the war

238

when there was little contact with, or help from Moscow. His prose was far more sharp and lucid than Gomułka's, yet no one doubted whose views he represented.

With the help of economists such as Oskar Lange, who had spent the war years as a professor of economics at the University of Chicago in the U.S.A., Gomułka formulated a number of economic measures that he intended to implement as soon as he was back in power. Bieńkowski launched a series of scathing attacks on the existing Polish economy calling it "an economy for the moon." The articles also called for a number of radical political changes—all of them couched in terms of "Polish solutions for Polish problems." Before the month was out, the words "sovereignty" and "democracy," used so frequently in these articles, had become a rallying cry for the nation.[3]

Even before Poznań there had been great interest among Polish workers in the well-publicized "workers' councils" which had emerged in Yugoslavia as a special brand of Yugoslav communism. After Poznań, committees were organized in factories all over Poland to discuss the possibility of establishing such councils.[4] As the confrontation between Gomułka and the liberal faction versus the Natolin Stalinists grew sharper, these factory committees now joined the debate, invariably on Gomułka's side, and resolutions began to be sent to the secretariat of the party's Central Committee in Warsaw urging that Gomułka be restored to the country's leadership.

All of this ferment was reported to Khrushchev rather excitedly by the Kremlin's ambassador to Warsaw, P. K. Ponomarenko. As Khrushchev later reported in his memoirs:

> Shortly after Ochab's return to Warsaw [i.e., early September] we learned from our ambassador that tensions which had been building up had boiled over. Tumultuous demonstrations and general turmoil had broken out at factories in some cities. These outbreaks had distinctly anti-Soviet overtones. Some Poles were ... saying that the treaty signed [after World War II] was unequal and that the Soviet Union was taking unfair advantage of Poland economically ... being forced to supply coal to the Soviet Union with prices lower than ... world market. The demonstrations also demanded the withdrawal of Soviet troops ... Some of the criticisms against us were justified.[5]

As a result, Khrushchev convoked the Soviet politburo to discuss the situation in Poland and within the Polish Communist Party, particularly in the light of Ponomarenko's reporting rumors of Gomułka's possible return to power and an alleged campaign for the removal of Marshal Konstanty Rokossovsky. This Polish-born Red Army marshal Stalin had installed as Polish minister of defense and head of the Polish army in November, 1949.

The rift in the party's Central Committee had become manifest at the hastily convened seventh plenum in July (see Chapter IV) following the Poznań riots. At that time replacements on the politburo were needed for Bierut (the former first party secretary who had died mysteriously in Moscow in March) and Berman, who had resigned, ostensibly for reasons of ill health. One replacement, Adam Rapacki, a former socialist and friend of Cyrankiewicz, was a liberal; but to balance him Edward Gierek and Roman Nowak, linked with neither side, were also added. This meant that it was now possible for the Stalinist Natolin group, which had a clear majority at the beginning of the year, to find itself in a minority in some votes. But First Secretary Ochab—who earlier vacillated and only joined Cyrankiewicz and the liberal wing in September, after he had discovered from Mao Tse-tung himself that China stood behind the Polish position—was deemed by the Soviets to be a "weak" leader, and thus was a major worry for the Russians. One of the marks of his "weak" leadership, in Soviet eyes, was his inability (or disinclination) to head off the demands within the Polish politburo in September for the immediate withdrawal of Soviet "advisers" to the Polish UB (secret police). Though termed "advisers," these KGB men actually controlled the Polish security force. In fact, Ochab seemed to more than acquiesce in this move, so that the Soviets felt they had to comply.[6] The next step, the Soviets rightly feared, would be the demand that all Soviet military "advisers," who actually occupied all the chief positions within the Polish Army—many of them without knowledge of Polish—be recalled.

Indeed, such a demand—particularly the removal of Marshal Konstanty Rokossovsky—was one of Gomułka's conditions to becoming Poland's new leader.

An Eighth Central Committee Plenum had originally been set for November. But the Natolin group, sensing that they could no longer block Gomułka's return to the Central Committee, but desperate to see that he did not become once again head of the party, sought to speed matters up and co-opt him onto the politburo where they felt they could control him before he had enough backing to make good on his most extreme demands. In a series of politburo meetings in early October they managed to get the date moved up to October 17. They were even willing to create a new government post of vice premier for Gomułka, a position which would carry no real power and which would, they hoped, put him in a cul-de-sac. To facilitate this latter move, Hilary Minc—a national symbol of all that had gone wrong with the Polish economy and who was, therefore, expendable—was told he must resign. The communiqué reporting this move "for reasons of ill health," also

240

announced the establishment of the new vice premiership, without adding what everyone suspected, that it would be filled by Gomułka.

Immediately upon Ochab's return from China, the politburo was called together on October first and second to discuss the new situation. It was decided that Gomułka, who had been readmitted to the party on August 4, should become involved in politburo discussions as soon as possible. A week later the politburo drew up four reasons for the present crisis: 1) lack of unity within the politburo itself, 2) "a lack of connection between the party leadership, and the party activists," 3) "a lack of authority among the leadership," and 4) "an unfair situation in the relations between the Polish People's Republic and the U.S.S.R. ..."

Gomułka agreed to attend the politburo meeting two days later, October 12. It was his first since he had been thrown out for "rightist, nationalist deviation" in 1949, and his former colleagues were shocked at his gaunt, even shaky appearance after all those years in prison. At the meeting he argued that "the greatest problem" was "Polish-Soviet relations," which had to be "normalized" in order to "forestall anti-Soviet manifestations." "Today," he added, "no one questions that in the past these relations were unfair."

Gomułka made a strong pitch for unity, implying that he could supply that unity should the politburo decide to bring him back. He concluded his remarks with the following admonition: "Comrades, you have failed to notice the climate prevailing among the working class and in the nation ... Everything that has so far been done ... was wrong ... It is possible to rule a nation without its trust, but such rule can only be maintained with bayonets. Whoever chooses that option also chooses the path of universal calamity. We cannot return to the old methods. Our current difficulties stem from the party's weakness, from our inconsistency."

He followed this warning with the implied threat that if they did not choose him he would "not refrain from political activities ... Until now you have prevented me from doing so, but should you change your minds today I will not say no ... I would like to emphasize that ... I consider my ideas to be correct and I will not retreat. I am a stubborn person ..."[7]

Ochab then agreed to nominate Gomułka along with several of his closest allies for membership on the politburo, at the Eighth Central Committee Plenum, which was now set to begin on October 17.

At the next politburo meeting on October 15, to which Gomułka had *not* been invited, the debate was heated, but Rokossovsky and his three main allies on the politburo were outvoted. It was decided: 1) to postpone the eighth plenum from October 17 to October 19, 2) to accept Gomułka and his three colleagues into the politburo, 3) to elect an entirely new politburo at that meeting, 4) to establish a leadership "search committee" to make these nominations, and 5) to mention, in the press release announcing the postponement of the plenum, that Gomułka was being invited to join the party leadership.[8]

On the same day the press release appeared in the daily newspapers, an article appeared in the only Catholic newspaper in Poland, *Słowo Powszechne* ("The Universal Word"), which sounded a jarring note to all who read or heard about it. This "Catholic" newspaper was allowed to be published because it was run by "peace priests," clergy who had been weaned away from Rome and who owed their positions to the communists. Nothing, of course, was published in this newspaper without authorization from the highest authorities—and sometimes these authorities were not even in Poland. Today's article was by Bolesław Piasecki, head of PAX, the communist-dominated lay Catholic organization and a man widely believed to be in the employ not just of the UB, but the Soviet KGB. "If we fail to restrain discussion within the limits of responsibility," Piasecki warned, "instead of democratization we will provoke a situation where the *raison d'être* will have to be realized in a brutal manner, in circumstances close to those of a state of siege."

Piasecki was not speaking for himself. He had no armed forces at his disposal. Such a menacing statement could only have come from his superiors in Moscow.

If that threat was designed to frighten the Poles, it had, under the circumstances, almost the opposite effect. As word of the article spread, factory and student committees began to check into where they could most quickly obtain arms. There was no official alarm, and in most cases arms were not actually distributed; but arsenals were located and assurances given that, should the need arise, arms would be quickly made available.[9]

"It looked to us," said Nikita Khrushchev in his memoirs, "as though developments in Poland were rushing forward on the crest of a giant anti-Soviet wave. Meetings were being held all over the country and we were afraid Poland might break away from us at any moment."[10]

No hint of what was going on in the Polish leadership, other than the aforementioned press release, was carried in the Polish press. But Swedish, French, British, and American reporters had developed sources reaching into the party leadership. This was particularly true of Philippe Ben of *Le Monde*, who had been born in Poland and had grown up with a number of persons who were now high-ranking members of the party, people he knew on a first-name basis. Ben's highly accurate reports—many sent secretly directly to the Polish desk at Radio Free Europe[11]—were broadcast back into Poland by the

Polish-language broadcasts of Radio Free Europe. So detailed was this information that Poles all over Poland knew what had transpired in the Polish politburo only a day or two before, or even, in some cases, the night before.

But most members of the Polish party hierarchy did not listen to RFE broadcasts—at least they had not yet come to depend on its broadcasts for learning what their superiors were up to. A system of communications had to be set up by the liberals who bypassed party journals and official channels lest Stalinists sabotage their efforts. The key figure in this was Stefan Staszewski, president of the Warsaw city committee and a member of the Central Committee. Staszewski was a journalist and propagandist by training. With his many contacts in the media, he drew up plans for a network, which, in the words of one Western observer, "would send out orders and gather reports with the speed of lightning and the silence of thought."[12] His many journalist friends who had begun to call themselves "the enraged," were eager to help him build this network. In Warsaw alone "he arranged for the mobilization of worker combat groups in sixteen of the largest plants."[13]

On the receiving end of this communist-run network were not only party cadres in the factories, but students in the universities, where information was immediately put up on bulletin boards. At Warsaw University, these bulletin boards were mounted on the iron railings which fenced off the campus from the city, but in such a way that all citizens walking on Nowy Swiat could read them and pass the information on. Party members actually made up a very small minority of workers and students, but as the wave of renewed hopes for more freedom swept through Poland, everyone was eager for any scrap of information about what was going on in the government, and many non-party people added their skills and contacts to this network. Foreign correspondents were also hooked into this network. They were the best means of getting information out into the country at large, for it was certain to come back in the form of radio broadcasts from the West. Information, whether from the network or from foreign broadcasts, was passed on with incredible speed.

All of Poland knew of the cries in Poznań for "Bread and Freedom." Now, at a rally of Warsaw students in mid-October, this slogan was converted to "No bread without freedom, no freedom without bread!"[14]

Most Poles were quite conscious of the role that Tito's Yugoslavia—excluded from the bloc since 1948—was playing in their future. They knew of Khrushchev's "journey to Canossa" the previous year, a trip in which he had flown to Belgrade and had apologized to Tito right at the airport for the Soviet Union's treatment of Yugoslavia up to that time. Ever since, Yugoslav ways, such as a much freer press and Yugoslav "workers' councils," were "studied" by East European communist parties, which had heretofore denounced such things. For if a Yugoslav way to socialism was legitimate, why not a Polish or Hungarian way? They were tired of slavishly—and disastrously—copying the Soviet way.

But after the blowup at Poznań, Khrushchev became acutely aware of the real dangers of "Titoism," and, whether forced by such conservative members of the Soviet presidium as Molotov and Kaganovich, or completely on his own, he had the Soviet Communist Party send the parties in Eastern Europe an official letter on September 3 warning that Tito and the Yugoslav way were *not* to be emulated; that there was, in fact, only one way: the Soviet way to socialism. The note was couched in terms exceedingly disparaging to Tito. Within a few days of its receipt, someone in the Polish party leaked a copy of it to the Yugoslavs. Tito erupted with such righteous fury that Khrushchev, caught slandering Tito behind his back, found it suddenly necessary to "go on vacation" to Yugoslavia to hunt stags with Tito at his vacation retreat on the island of Brioni. And, since his eight-day attempt to pacify Tito was not all that successful, and at the same time he wanted to maneuver the wily Yugoslav leader into a joint communiqué which would somehow imply his return to the bloc, he persuaded Tito to return to the U.S.S.R. with him on September 27. Such a communiqué, he felt, would reduce Tito's attraction for the other East European parties.

Following Tito's reception in Moscow, which included an entourage of his wife, Executive Council President A. Ranković and other high Yugoslav officials, he was persuaded to accompany Khrushchev and many high Soviet officials and generals to the Crimea for the sole purpose, according to the official communiqué, of shooting more innocent stags.

All this was taking place while the Poznań trials and the preparations for the eighth plenum were in progress.

When the Soviet presidium learned that the Polish politburo had postponed the opening of the eighth plenum from October 17 to October 19, they immediately invited the entire Polish politburo to come to Moscow for "discussions." This quite unexpected invitation seemed to the Poles unreasonable and ominous.

They immediately, but politely, declined on the grounds that there was not time for such a visit without postponing the plenum yet again—which they were not about to do. They would be happy to come to Moscow just as soon as the plenum was over; or perhaps the Soviets would like to visit Warsaw as soon as it was over.

The Soviet reaction was instantaneous; since the Poles declined to take the hint, they would immediately descend upon Warsaw before the plenum got underway. Indeed, this contingency must have been planned for well in advance, for a few hours before dawn on Friday, October 19, the most prestigious gathering of high civilian officials and military brass ever to leave the Soviet Union was assembled at Moscow's military airport. Headed by Khrushchev himself, the delegation included presidium members Lazar Kaganovich, Anastas Mikoyan, Vyacheslav Molotov and Defense Minister Marshal Georgi Zhukov. Also in the delegation were Marshal Konev, commander of the Warsaw Pact forces, General Antonov, Soviet chief of staff, and nearly a dozen other generals.

Word of the Soviet determination to come was conveyed to Ochab by Soviet ambassador Ponomarenko in the early evening of Thursday, October 18. Ochab hastily assembled the politburo to meet with Ponomarenko at the Council of State building where the plenum was due to begin the next day. Perhaps the Soviet delegation could come on the second or third day of the plenum, it was suggested. Only Defense Minister Konstanty Rokossovsky was against that idea. Ponomarenko agreed with Rokossovsky that the meeting should take place before the plenum, and, in any case, the Soviet delegation would be departing from Moscow in a matter of hours.

Once Ponomarenko had left them, Ochab not only insisted that all politburo members be present at the airport to greet the Soviet delegation at 7 A.M. the next morning, he called Gomułka and insisted that he be there as well.

◦

Friday, October 19, 1956

The sky is light, but the first rays of the sun have yet to pierce the thin woods surrounding Boernerowo military airport in Babice near Warsaw. A procession of large, black cars—Polish government and Soviet embassy— has arrived in the parking area only moments earlier, their headlights still on, for it had been dark when they left Warsaw. The cars had disgorged several dozen dark-suited officials who had quietly proceeded into the main, single-storey building. For most of the Poles, the scene is entirely new, for they are used to greeting people at Okęcie, the civilian airport. The single-storey, wooden buildings seem more appropriate for a provincial civilian airport than a military one; but soldiers are everywhere in evidence, and guards snap to attention as they enter the building.

A faint, high-pitched scream and then the gathering roar of jet engines flushes the group of dark-suited men out of the building, past the square control tower, and out onto the tarmac. At the far end of the runway the sleek, silver fuselage of a Tupolev-104 glides into view, some five meters above the ground, orange sunlight gleaming off its tall slanting tail. Its speed appears to increase as its wheels near the runway. Then, with a burst of smoke, its tires hit the ground and the roar of reversing engines shakes the air. The giant plane arcs around, comes to a stop, and cuts its engines. Six soldiers push a wheeled metal staircase up to the plane.

The first to emerge through the doorway is Nikita Khrushchev, adjusting his hat as he squints into the first rays of the morning sun. Next come Mikoyan, Molotov, and Kaganovich. Then Marshal Zhukov fills the doorway, his swelling chest resplendent with gleaming medals. He and all the generals who follow him are in full-dress military regalia. There seems to be a full planeload of them. To the Poles, so recently informed of their coming, and only lately having risen from their beds, some without breakfast, it is an appalling, intimidating sight.

A small line of Soviet officers dressed in Polish uniforms forms a line perpendicular to the plane and presents arms smartly. Marshal Rokossovsky and a small color guard take their places in front of it. But there is no martial band, no microphone, no little girl presenting flowers—none of the usual paraphernalia that accompanies visits from heads of state.

First Secretary Ochab and his fellow politburo members are clumped together at the bottom of the mobile staircase, Gomułka, not yet a politburo member, in their midst. A few meters away is another clump, Ambassador Ponomarenko and staff members from the Soviet embassy.

Khrushchev, halfway down the staircase, spots Rokossovsky right away. Ignoring the clump of Poles who are almost at his feet, he calls out in Russian to Rokossovsky: "We shed our blood for this country and now they are trying to sell out to the Americans and the Zionists! But it won't work!" Then looking down at the Poles who had come to welcome him he shakes his finger and shouts, "Traitors! You forget that this territory was liberated by Soviet soldiers and that we lost here hundreds of thousands of men!"[15]

Enraged at this opening insult, Gomułka shouts back in Polish-accented Russian, "We shed more blood than you* and we are not selling out to anyone!"

"*Kto ty takoi?*" ("Who are you?") demands an astounded Khrushchev, using the contemptuous familiar form of address and wheeling around to confront the challenger below him.

---

* He is right. The Poles, who fought on many fronts from 1939 to 1945, lost one out of every five Poles, a far higher percentage that either Nazi Germany or Soviet Russia.

"I am Gomułka whom you put in prison!" says the trembling Gomułka, his voice now lower, but still defiant.

"What is he doing here?" demands a genuinely furious Khrushchev now, recognizing the towering figure of Ochab.

"He is here because he is about to be elected to the politburo," answers Ochab without hesitation.[16]

Khrushchev turns and glares at Gomułka—but says nothing. Then, ignoring Gomułka, he walks up to the other Poles, but refuses to shake hands.[17] He stops in front of Cyrankiewicz, muttering "Hello."

"Why did you come?" asks Cyrankiewicz. "We assured you that we would be perfectly willing to talk to you once the plenum is finished."

Khrushchev gestures wildly at the tall Ochab and diminutive Gomułka. "There has been an act of betrayal," he shouts. "We had to come. It's not just a question of Soviet-Polish relations. You are menacing the whole socialist camp. You are endangering our position in Germany. I insist that you postpone your plenum."[18] His voice carries across the tarmac so that every chauffeur in the parking lot can clearly hear him.[19]

The other Soviet leaders behave much as Khrushchev, refusing to shake hands and shouting insults. Only the Soviet generals stand mute behind them, looking as intimidating as they possibly can.[20] The Poles, appalled at such rude behavior in public, instinctively contain themselves.

Still sputtering—some in barnyard language that reddens the ears of his compatriots—Khrushchev reluctantly allows himself to be stuffed into the black Soviet Zim that heads the long procession of vehicles. Cyrankiewicz, as head of the Polish government, clambers into the seat beside him. Ochab and Gomułka decline the invitation of the Soviet security officer to enter the next car, preferring to take a Polish vehicle. Motors are started up. As soon as the last door slams shut, the motorcade pulls out of the parking lot, shaded by yellow leaves, into the full sunlight and begins its twenty-minute, fifteen-kilometer drive into the city.[21]

Some of the Poles apprehensively catch sight of a line of Soviet bombers coming in low over the horizon, bound, apparently, for Okęcie, the civilian airport. These planes do not, as the Poles fear, contain crack Soviet security troops to secure the airport for a Soviet air invasion, but rather support personnel for this high level visit: secretaries, aides, cooks, and bodyguards, as well as large quantities of food and drink. The Soviets are doing nothing by halves, and are prepared for a long visit.

Polish and Russian security police mounted on motorcycles lead the cavalcade along the flat, but bumpy, highway. As soon as they emerge from the woods, everyone can spot on the horizon in front of them a new (1955) landmark, the Palace of Science and Culture, gift of the Soviet people (read Stalin) to the people of Poland. It is a source of extreme pride for both the Polish and Soviet Communists, though many of the former tend to question, as do most Poles, its taste. It is an almost exact copy of the main building at Moscow State University, which itself is a copy of Robert McCormick's Chicago Tribune building of the 1920s, a Gothic skyscraper Stalin greatly admired when he saw pictures of it.[22]

The Soviets want to go directly to the modern Council of State building where the Central Committee's eighth plenum is to start at 10:00 A.M., but the Polish escort and drivers have been told to take them directly to the Belvedere Palace, former summer palace of royalty, residence of Marshal Piłsudski, home of Bierut, and now guesthouse for foreign dignitaries. It is located in the quiet of Łazienki Park. A serious accident almost results from these conflicting instructions, but at the last minute the Polish motorcyclists manage to divert the procession in the direction of the palace.

While the Russians are shown to their rooms and given time to freshen up, the Poles quickly decide that four of them: Ochab, Cyrankiewicz, Gomułka, and Zawadzki—a squat old communist whom the Russians feel is their man, and who also happens to be president of the Council of Ministers—stay behind and talk with the Russian delegation while the rest of the politburo return to prepare for the opening of the Central Committee meeting.

It is not quite 8:00 A.M. when the refreshed Soviets file into the chandeliered Blue Room, a long French gallery furnished with inlaid tables and satin chairs. The long table in the center has been set with the usual bottles of mineral water, small glasses, coffee cups and pretzels. The Polish side, now reduced to four, seems hopelessly outnumbered, for in addition to the large Soviet delegation, the room now swarms with Soviet secretaries, aides, and interpreters who have arrived less than an hour ago on the converted Soviet bombers.

Before coffee can be offered, Khrushchev opens up. "We have decided to intervene actively in your affairs and we will not allow you to realize your plans," he announces as though he were merely issuing an order. Then, jumping up to his feet, he wags his finger at Ochab and shouts, in the Russian slang he favors: "That number won't pass here!"

He is clearly agitated—whether real or feigned, the Poles cannot tell—and throughout the session he quite neglects his chair and paces up and down behind it.

"We are here to attend your Central Committee meeting," he announces.

"You have not been invited to, at least not the opening meeting," answers Ochab.

248

"We have a right to be heard at your meeting," counters Khrushchev. "We know that you intend to change the politburo. You didn't inform us of this, but we know. You are going to be throwing out good communists, opening up the way for reactionaries and counterrevolutionaries to take over. Your new state will wreck socialism!" Khrushchev now begins to shout almost incoherently, and the only way the Poles can be heard is to out-shout him.

"It's precisely because of what has happened at *previous* Central Committee plenums that you attended that we don't want you at this one," yells Ochab. "Your attendance would not be conducive to improving relations between our two parties."[23]

But Khrushchev is not about to be out-shouted. Pacing up and down and banging his fist into his palm, he launches into a long harangue ending with a list of all the wonderful things the Soviet Union has done for Poland.

The Poles, particularly Gomułka, who is fast assuming the role of leader of the Polish delegation, respond with their own, very specific list of grievances. The are chiefly economic, and center on such matters as the years of forced coal deliveries to the Soviet Union at prices way below the world market, but also include Soviet interference in many Polish domestic matters, by resident Russian "advisers" who do not even bother to learn Polish. Gomułka stubbornly persists in demanding that Khrushchev complete what he began in 1954: namely, the withdrawal of Soviet officer "advisers" from the Polish Army.[24]

Khrushchev begins to respond, but is interrupted by a Polish messenger who rushes up to the Polish delegation. The Poles are clearly shocked by his whispered message. Gomułka gets up and walks over to Khrushchev. "Comrade Khrushchev," he says, his voice quavering with emotion, "I have just received a report that Soviet armored units are moving on Warsaw."

"Is this true?" demands Ochab, equally shaken.

Khrushchev, who, of course, has given the orders for this, shrugs his shoulders and feigns innocence.

"If it is true then I beg of you, no, I demand of you," shouts an excited Gomułka, "to order them to stop and to return to their bases. If you do not, something terrible, something irreversible will happen."

Khrushchev holds up his right hand as if to say, "wait a minute." "There must be some mistake," he protests. "You have received incorrect information."

Gomułka goes to the telephone. In a minute he is back. "No, Comrade Khrushchev, I have just received confirmation that your troops are on the move. Once again I demand that you call them back, or else I cannot answer for the consequences." Gomułka is shaking with rage and Khrushchev notes that foam is forming on his lips.[25]

Khrushchev turns and walks out to where the Soviet generals are congregated in the antechamber. Suddenly the room is filled with muttered Polish, the volume rising the longer Khrushchev remains out of the room.

At length he returns. "Yes, it is true," he says almost triumphantly. "Warsaw is virtually encircled."[26]

Ochab breaks the stunned silence. "If you think you can keep us here while you pull off an armed putsch you are mistaken. We are prepared."

Once more Gomułka steps forward. "Unless you call off the troops—immediately—we will walk out of here and there will be no more negotiations. We will never talk to you while you have a gun on the table." His words are delivered slowly, staccato style, and he is looking Khrushchev in the eye.

Khrushchev begins to equivocate, but Gomułka disdainfully interrupts him. "It is impossible to talk to you people. I see that I will have to go to the radio and tell the Polish people what is going on here and what I think of it."

Gomułka is not bluffing. Nor is Ochab when he says "we are prepared." The Polish radio has already received instructions to prepare a studio and microphone for Gomułka's possible talk.[27]

Stefan Staszewski, the man who had set up the special network, is ready to flash the word. While he is not yet privy to what has been transpiring at Belvedere Palace, he has already sent out a full alert, key workers in every factory in Poland and key students at all the universities know that something big is happening.

For a while Khrushchev is silent and his eyes narrow. If he ignores Gomułka's threat and the excited Pole *does* make such a broadcast, a conflagration could quickly break out and there is no predicting where it will end. But, at the same time he does not want to show hesitation or weakness. At last he says: "All right. We will give the order for the troops to halt." An audible sigh comes from the Poles. Marshal Konev is sent out to pass along the order.

But the Poles refuse to return to the table until they have confirmation from their own sources that the order has been carried out. Yes, they learn ten minutes later by phone, all of the movement has stopped. But, to their dismay, none of the columns have started to withdraw to their bases.

Basically there are three columns of Russian-officered Polish motorized troops which have converged on the city, with some tanks having already entered the working class district of Wola. They are backed by Soviet garrisoned troops which, it now appears, must have left their home bases as much as three days ago. This applies particularly to those from Legnica in southern Poland where the headquarters of the Warsaw Pact is located.

Throughout the day reports of Soviet motorized columns entering the country from East Germany and the Ukraine reach Warsaw. Reports of Soviet warships in Polish waters off Gdańsk are received as well.

But other reports now reach Belvedere Palace. Soviet-officered columns at several points have been intercepted and halted by Polish security forces under General Wacław Komar—one of Gomułka's friends—whom Cyrankiewicz and Ochab had appointed in place of his disgraced predecessor. This they had accomplished while Rokossovsky was out of the country on vacation and had no means of opposing it.[28]

This news means no only that a sizable military force is outside of Rokossovsky's command, but that it is answering to the politburo and Gomułka instead. The Soviets receive the same reports. They have known of the possibility of Komar's opposing them, and now it has come to pass. They have also heard that Polish workers are being supplied arms in their factories.

Neither Gomułka nor Ochab wish to continue—so far as they are concerned the gun is still pointed at their heads—yet even their own people report that all movement has stopped. They feel they must proceed with the talks.

Khrushchev still refuses to speak to Gomułka, calling him an "outsider" who has no business here, and appeals only to the other three. Cyrankiewicz, however, assures him that "Gomułka speaks for the whole party and the whole nation."[29]

Molotov keeps stressing East Germany and the great danger of an eruption there should Poland break away from the bloc. It is an argument no Pole can ignore, and Gomułka softens his earlier demand for total Soviet troop withdrawal from Poland while still demanding that the Soviets cease to interfere in Polish domestic affairs.[30]

After a pause, Khrushchev's tone abruptly changes. "We did not come here to threaten you;" he purrs flashing his famous grin with the shiny steel tooth, "we came to help you." Poland does face enormous economic problems, he concedes, and the Soviet Union is fully prepared to offer Poland a loan of 200 million gold rubles to be used as the Poles see fit.

But the Poles do not bite. They refuse to discuss economic matters until the question of the nation's political leadership is settled.[31]

"Let me come and simply talk informally to the Central Committee if we cannot take part in the actual session," he suggests pleadingly.

"We cannot speak for the Central Committee," says Ochab sensing a trap, "but we will put it to them. They can decide whether or not they want to hear you."

Khrushchev then extracts a promise that the Poles will return to Belvedere as soon as they have launched the scheduled eighth plenum of their Central Committee, for with all the Russians in Warsaw a settlement between them is more important than just going through the mechanics of their Central Committee meeting.

While the four Poles hurry off to the Council of State building a few blocks away, Khrushchev leads his entourage to the Soviet embassy to plot their strategy. Thereafter, most of the military members of the delegation depart for Legnica, the Warsaw Pact headquarters.

The members of the Central Committee have been waiting since 9:00 A.M. and it is now well past 10:00. Rumors have been many, but since only politburo members were informed of the Soviet arrival, and they have been sworn to secrecy for the time being, the real cause of the delay is still unknown to the rank and file members. Everyone is in his seat when Ochab, Cyrankiewicz, Gomułka, and Zawadski enter the chamber.

Ochab announces that he will postpone his prepared report which would normally begin such a plenum, but instead will report on the recent flurry of politburo meetings and the decisions which have been made. These are that an entirely new politburo be elected, that it should be narrowed to only nine members, that Gomułka and three of his colleagues be elected to this new politburo, and that he, Ochab, intends to give up the position of first party secretary in favor of Gomułka occupying that position. Though much of this had been rumored, it is still something of a shock to have it all come out at once, particularly for those who lean toward the Natolin group.

Then Ochab drops the real bomb. Khrushchev and half the Soviet presidium are in Warsaw at this very minute, Soviet troops and Polish troops under Soviet command have been marching on Warsaw and are still threatening the capital. In a short while he and Gomułka and his other two colleagues will have to return to Belvedere Palace to continue the talks they have begun with the Russians and try to complete them. There is not time for a full debate on these proposals, so he asks that the Central Committee at least vote now to bring back Gomułka and his colleagues into the Central Committee, so that when they return to Belvedere, Gomułka will at least be a legitimate Central Committee member.

This seems like buying only half a loaf to committee member Michalina Tartarkowa-Majkowska. She ask permission to speak and stands to propose that Gomułka and his colleagues also be elected to the politburo and that Gomułka be elected first secretary right now.

Cries of "No! No!" arise from the Stalinist delegates who insist that a full debate is necessary. After less than half an hour of discussion the motion to go through with the election now is tabled, but Ochab's proposal that they simply be elected to the Central Committee at this time does carry. Her proposal is still before the committee awaiting action, but the plenum now goes into recess until 3 P.M. by which time it is assumed the talks with the Soviet delegation will be concluded.

The four Poles now return to Belvedere Palace, Gomułka a legitimate Central Committee member, but not yet on the politburo.[32]

News of the Soviet delegation's presence in Warsaw and the movements of armed, motorized troops converging on Warsaw now reaches all end points on the Staszewski communication network and, of course, this includes all foreign news correspondents.

By early afternoon Radio Free Europe is broadcasting it as its lead story.* While life goes on as usual, all of Poland is on tenterhooks.

But it is not just about the Soviet presence that the Staszewski network alerts its "clients," it also is giving a summary of the morning's events, including the new list of nominations for the smaller politburo. Messages urge the recipients of this news to bombard the Central Committee with messages and petitions urging the election of Gomułka and his colleagues and Gomułka's promotion to first secretary. Within hours written petitions from factories all over Poland are pouring into the Council of State building in Warsaw where the Central Committee is meeting.

Party cadres in the factories, who have been alerted in advance, urge workers not to leave the factories but to remain at their workplaces to defend them if necessary. Student meetings at the universities become all-day and night sessions which exchange with other universities and with factories within their vicinity messages of solidarity and information about what actions they are taking. Within a matter of hours the distinction between party member and non-party member disappears; the newly-won freedoms Poles have all been enjoying, and the homeland itself, are threatened. New leaders like Lechosław Góździk, a handsome young party member at the

---

* RFE, through its Paris correspondent, Alan Dreyfuss, had made arrangements with *Le Monde* to receive Philippe Ben's copy as it comes in from Warsaw by phone or wireless. The text is then telexed to RFE in Munich, translated and broadcast in Polish almost as soon—sometimes before—it appears in the newpaper in Paris. (For a more important, direct contact with Ben, see endnote no. 11.)

Żeran automobile factory on the outskirts of Warsaw, emerge to electrify crowds with their oratory. They urge calm and determined vigilence and warn against any precipitous action.[33]

At noon, discussions between the Polish and Soviet delegations resume at Belvedere Palace. While Ochab is still technically first party secretary, it is clear that Gomułka is in charge, and Khrushchev can no longer refuse to address him. Gomułka keeps repeating, "The decisions about the membership of our politburo will be made by Central Committee and by our Central Committee alone. I do not believe that the membership of the leading group of any communist party can be the subject of discussion with any sister party."[34]

Gradually it becomes clear to Khrushchev that Gomułka's election to first party secretary replacing Ochab is not only a foregone conclusion, but probably a good development. At least Gomułka is consistent, and he keeps assuring everyone that it is better relations, not a break, that he wants between the two parties. But Khrushchev has no intention of allowing Marshal Rokossovsky, their Pole with Soviet citizenship, to be dropped from the politburo. As for all of the changes taking place in Poland, "it's not democratization," he says, "it's anarchy. You can't control it. You've got to stop it."

"Our people," replies Gomułka, on a different tack, "date Soviet occupation [of Poland] from the time of Rokossovsky's arrival [1949]. Here he is the symbol of Soviet domination. He cannot remain in the politburo."[35]

"He is deputy commander of the Warsaw Pact forces," responds Khrushchev. "His position is too strategically important. Under no conditions will we take him back. You'll have to put up with him."[36]

The Soviets complain that everything that happens in closed meetings at the top echelons of the Polish party and government is known in the West the next day. Mikoyan reads indignantly from a monitored transcript of a Radio Free Europe broadcast. The embarrassed Poles quickly change the subject, for they are aware that such broadcasts have helped alert the country to the current crisis. In an effort to entrap Gomułka, Mikoyan then begins citing letters and articles written by Gomułka in 1948.

Cyrankiewicz comes to Gomułka's rescue by complaining that Soviet behavior at the airport this morning is contrary to everything decided by the Soviet Central Committee in its July 1955 plenum concerning relations between the two countries. For every complaint from one side comes a countercomplaint from the other, and language frequently become acrimonious.[37]

The Soviets are becoming more consicous of rising opposition throughout the country, for Ambassador Ponomarenko is receving a stream of reports from the embassy. The arrival of each dispatch causes a brief break in the talks.[38]

Now the Poles, conscious of the gathering support developing among their countrymen, begin to string out the discussions until they are in a position to point out to the Soviets' evidence of this support as well as the latest reports from their people as to Soviet armed forces movements.

Molotov accuses the Poles of following the Yugoslav example, and Gomułka responds that no, they are following the Polish way. Cyrankiewicz defends the Polish press; then, probing for some division among the Soviets, turns to Mikoyan, now long silent, and asks him his views. His answer is brief and brutal: "The Soviet Union cannot afford any trouble in Poland. If you start trouble, we will crush you by force, if necessary."[39]

It is now 5 P.M. and the Central Committee has been waiting for two hours for the return of the delegation. Reports come in of further troop movements. Tanks are in the outskirts of Łódź; a Soviet column has been stopped by the Polish tanks of General Komar, and commanders on each side are awaiting orders to open fire.

Rokossovsky is called in. Will he obey the Soviets or the Polish politburo? After some hesitation, he decides to sign an order calling for the withdrawal of all Polish forces under his command that had converged on Warsaw.

Once again the Soviet delegation at Belvedere tries to get the Poles to agree to retain Rokossovsky, this time in return for massive economic aid; but Gomułka refuses to discuss it until the politburo elections have been completed. Moreover, he says, the Central Committee will not reconvene until the Soviets have left the country.

A recess in the talks is then called to allow the Poles to return to the Central Committee and report that the Soviets will soon be leaving and that the plenum can reconvene tomorrow (Saturday) morning.

Back at Belvedere Palace the argument continues. Seeing that the Russian arguments are accomplishing nothing, Khrushchev insists that at least a joint communiqué be issued reaffirming Soviet-Polish friendship. Gomułka demurs, saying that it serves no useful purpose when there are so many outstanding matters to be settled. Khrushchev insists that some sort of communiqué be issued and that it contain the date of the forthcoming visit of the Polish politburo to Moscow. Gomułka agrees that the visit will take place, but refuses to be pinned down to any specific date.

The argument rages back and forth over the whole history of relations during the past ten years. The Soviets are genuinely surprised at the bitterness of their Polish comrades as well as their refusal to give in to the ever-diminishing Soviet demands.

Around 9 P.M. Gomułka receives reports that some Soviet armored columns are still advancing. He begins to shout at Khrushchev, which sets off shouting from both sides.[40] Khrushchev has never seen Gomułka so angry.[41] He assures him the order to pull back has been given and will be carried out.

After several hours of fruitless discussion, a joint communiqué is drafted for release to the press. It reports on the visit of the Soviet delegation, identifies its members, and then simply states: "debates were held in an atmosphere of party-like and friendly sincerity. It was agreed that the delegation of the PUWP (Polish United Workers' Party) politburo will go to Moscow in the nearest future to discuss with the presidium of the CPSU problems of further strengthening the political and economic cooperation" between the two countries and "to further consolidate the fraternal friendship and co-existence of the PUWP and the CPSU." Since it is now 2 A.M., the communiqué is dated October 20, 1956.[42]

The Soviet plane is due to depart at 3 A.M. and their Polish colleagues are eager to see them off. For some unannounced reason, however, the Soviet delegation, which had left Belvedere for the Soviet embassy, does not show up. It is after 6 A.M. before they appear at the airport. The great Tupolev jet finally roars off the runway at 6:40 following goodbyes considerably warmer than had been the greeting almost twenty-four hours earlier.[43]

The haggard Polish politburo members head for their beds; the plenum is due to resume in just four hours. Workers in factories all over Poland are not so lucky. Having received the maximum alert through the Staszewski network in Warsaw, they have remained in their factories at the workplaces waiting for the distribution of weapons, which have been made ready at convenient collective points, but which, in most cases, are never distributed. The workers will remain there all Saturday and Sunday until they receive word that the crisis has passed. Many, like the workers at the Żeran auto factory of Warsaw, vote to work all day Sunday rather than remain idle at their machines. They pledge that the wages they earn for this extra day of production will be donated toward the erection of a memorial honoring the fallen heroes of the Warsaw Uprising of 1944—an event which the Communists have hitherto not allowed to be recognized, much less honored.[44]

When, on Saturday afternoon, Warsaw Radio announces that Soviet columns are withdrawing, some workers in the Żeran auto factory pile into cars just off the assembly line to drive off and see for themselves. Just as they suspect, the Soviet tanks have not budged one inch. In Łódź, workers ask the Soviet tank drivers why they have not returned to their bases. "We have run out of gasoline," comes the cynical reply. Infuriated at this response, the workers ask their colleagues in Warsaw whether they should not immediately go out on strike.[45]

There are still many people in Poland, and still more in the outside world, who are not as yet aware of the sudden Soviet visit to Warsaw and the convergence of Soviet and Polish armored columns on Warsaw. Poles are generally aware of the possibility that a new (to many of them) man named Gomułka, who seems to symbolize all the new changes taking place in the country, may be making a move to take over the government. Indeed, the Western radios, particularly Radio Free Europe, have been talking of little else for some days now. But the official Polish press and radio have said little.

The people who seem to know the most are the Western news correspondents in Warsaw such as Sydney Gruson of *The New York Times*, Flora Lewis of CBS, and Philippe Ben of *Le Monde*. Their dispatches are broadcast almost verbatim back into Poland on the very same day they appear in print in the West.

It is, in fact, a dispatch from Philippe Ben that Jan Nowak, former hero courier of the Polish underground in World War II and now chief of the Polish desk at RFE in Munich, Germany, ponders as he stares out into the darkness of Englischer Garten, which his office window overlooks. Were this a normal Saturday, he would not still be here, but things have been anything but normal in his homeland. Despite his totally bald head and broken nose, he is a handsome man. Suddenly his pale blue eyes narrow in his ruddy face. He wheels around and calls out for his secretary to come in and take a memo. It is brief and addressed to his editors—those who are still in the building—and most of them are. They are to come to his office at once.

Once they are assembled, Nowak breaks the silence. "These people," he says, referring to the Polish Communists in the Ben dispatch he waves in his hand, "they are fighting for their lives, for whatever independence they can get for Poland. We have to help them. That means making a 180-degree turn. We must do everything in our power to see that Gomułka gets the popular support he so desperately needs. From this moment on we are going to scrap all of our scheduled programs and create new ones designed to unite the nation behind Gomułka."[46] Cries of approval come from the group; there is not a dissenting voice. Almost immediately ideas for new programs are excitedly put forward.

Early the next morning (Sunday) Nowak is back in his office, as are most of the important people from the other language desks and the American administration. He summons the American political adviser, William E. Griffith, to his office. Normally it is Griffith who summons the East European exiles to *his* office, but in Nowak's case an exception is made and Griffith does not hesitate. Nowak does not ask Griffith's advice; he merely tells him what the Polish desk has decided to do. He wants to save Griffith the embarrassment of learning about this drastic new policy change only when all of the other desk and department heads, who will be attending the Polish Daily Meeting an hour hence, learn of it. Griffith, who has lost face more than once before when Nowak offered to resign with all of his editors rather than conform to some American policy with which he vehemently disagreed, is quick to go along with Nowak's arguments, particularly the one about making the change with subtlety. It is, in fact, a relief to him to have a language-desk chief who knows so definitely what he his doing.

What Nowak means about making the change with "subtlety" is that RFE's support of "yesterday's enemies [i.e., Poland's ruling Communists] has to be shown in such a way as not to give Moscow arguments confirming the absurd accusations of ties between the 'liberal wing' of the party and American imperialism ... The immediate about-face in our programs [will be] reflected in a change of tone which the listener must pick up right away."[47]

All day Sunday the Voice of Free Poland broadcasts not only the latest developments in Warsaw, but background information on Gomułka, his beliefs and record, and what may be expected of him should he emerge as leader of the Polish Party.

Nowak has actually laid the groundwork for this with his broadcast on Thursday, October 18, in which he had spoken of the Gomułka myth, a myth "based upon the single fact that Gomułka had the courage to oppose Russia during Stalin's lifetime and that because of this he was imprisoned and persecuted ... Peasants are inclined to forgive Gomułka his brutal, bloody methods of combating the Polish Peasant Party," he had continued; "They remember, above all, that [he] opposed collectivization in 1948."[48]

Today Nowak tells his listeners "we have information that a group of Stalinists, headed by Konstanty Rokossovsky and Zenon Nowak, is consciously making toward anarchy and chaos, trying on purpose to increase the boiling atmosphere, in order to justify the necessity of Soviet intervention from outside. It is imperative," he adds, "that the communists not let themselves be provoked and keep the necessary calm. The development of events in the course of the next few days will depend first and foremost on whether the new administration ... will be able to get the situation in hand, calm the atmosphere, and find some immediate means to help the economy.

"There exists another factor on which the final result of the conflict between Warsaw and Moscow will depend. This factor is the behavior of the Polish community." Then, knowing that the great majority of his listeners are strongly opposed to communism, Nowak says: "For those enlightened people who oppose communism, they realize that in its current geographical and political situation Poland cannot risk an attempt at breaking away from the Soviet domain."[49]

All the commentaries are in this vein: no instructions or appeals, just information and suggestion.

At the State Council Building in Warsaw where the plenum is under way, resolutions and signed petitions urging Gomułka's election to first party secretary pour in from factories and universities all over Poland via telex, cable, and physically via cars and motorcycles. During the morning session, steel-helmeted troops from General Komar's security forces take over the offices and transmitters of Radio Warsaw.[50]

As the Central Committee debate proceeds, observers note a remarkable change in attitude as one delegate after another who was thought to be with the Natolin group expresses his or her indignation at the unscheduled Soviet visit and the threats it implied. If Gomułka lacked a majority on Friday, there is no question about his having one now.

Ochab decides not to deliver his prepared report, which normally begins any Central Committee meeting, in favor of taking up the still-tabled motion proposing that Gomułka be elected first party secretary, "I wish Comrade Gomułka much health and strength," he concludes his remarks, "for it takes that to deal with our friends. We thought it could get no worse, but each month it has. The culmination of our ordeal has been the last two days."[51]

A number of scheduled speeches are delivered, and when it becomes clear that most of those thought to be hostile to Gomułka's return to power no longer oppose him, Ochab gives the signal for Gomułka to speak.

Gomułka has not addressed the Central Committee since 1948. Some new members of the Central Committee have never seen him before. But those who remember him well are shocked at what the years in prison have wrought. Instead of the solid figure with taut skin over a ruddy face, a short, wizened figure with slack skin, his once receding hairline reduced to a small fringe around his milk-white pate, mounts the podium. Only the fire in the eyes behind those steel-rimmed glasses remains. He looks like a grandfather of sixty-five. In fact, he is only fifty-one.

His speech, which, in good communist tradition, lasts several hours, is largely a scathing critique of all the wrong things that have been done in Poland during his imprisonment. The arguments and statistics on the ruined economy are not his—they have been compiled by Professor Oskar Lange and his colleagues—but this is the first time the absurdities and appalling wastage of the past eight years have been laid bare by a top party official. The statistics he cites on state-run agriculture versus private peasant farming are devastating. "Why should not the Catholic progressive movement compete with us in ... cooperative farming? It is a poor idea to maintain that only Communists, only people holding materialist views, can build socialism."[52]

As for Poznań, "the workers did not protest against People's Poland" but "against the evil which was widespread in our social system." And "the clumsy attempt to present the Poznań tragedy as the work of imperialist agents ... was very naive ... Agents and provocateurs ... never ... can determine the attitude of the working class." No, "the causes of the Poznań tragedy are to be found in ourselves, in the leadership of the Party, in the government. The inflammable materials had been accumulating for years."[53]

Gomułka then makes a plea for telling only the truth to the working class—including the truth that the treasury is bare; there is no money for the raises they are demanding.

He then outlines economic measures, including material incentives, tax exemptions, abolition of agricultural quota deliveries and even outlines a scheme whereby the coal miners could be given any coal they mine, for their own use or private sale, if it is mined in addition to their required quota. All prices, he says, should be based upon real value and not government decree, as they are now.

He points out that there are different roads to socialism, not just a Soviet way or a Yugoslav way, but ways that are "different still."[54]

But "mutual relations between parties and states of the socialist camp ... should not give cause for any complications ... Each country should have full independence, and the rights of each state to a sovereign government ... should be fully and mutually respected."[55]

The "cult of personality," says Gomułka, which had been "grafted to probably all communist parties" had brought about "tragic events" in Poland "when innocent people were sent to their deaths. Many others were imprisoned, often for many years, although innocent ... many were submitted to bestial torture. We are putting an end to it once and for all!" he declares as loud applause rocks the chamber. He then announces the formation of a commission to investigate and rehabilitate all of the victims.

Now comes the cold water. He condemns anyone trying to exploit that process of democratization in Poland to kindle anti-Soviet "moods." "We shall not allow it," he warns sternly.

The Polish Sejm (parliament), which until now has been a rubber-stamping institution meeting only a few days a year, is to become the most important branch of government and "exercise large-scale control over the work of the government and the state organs." It should be called upon to "evaluate the work of the government," and people will be permitted to "elect, and not only vote" for candidates, for there will be no more one-party slates.[56]

In closing, Gomułka cautions that while "the freedom of criticism in all its forms, including the press" is welcome, "each criticism should be creative and just" and not just negative. And he appeals to "our youth, especially university students, that they should keep their ardor ... within the framework of the decisions which will be adopted by the present plenum."[57]

Despite Gomułka's speech and the trend in his favor, it is clear, once the debate gets under way, that Rokossovsky and his Stalinists are not going to give in without a fight. For most of Saturday they lead a concerted attack on Gomułka and his colleagues. One of the main objects of their assault is Stefan Staszewski, Central Committee member and head of the Warsaw city committee, which is operating the unofficial, nation-wide communications network. It is he, they charge, who is "orchestrating the anti-Soviet campaign."[58] Through innumerable delaying tactics, they succeed in preventing a vote right up to the evening recess.

As the Central Committee members return to their homes or hotel rooms they encounter helmeted security troops stationed outside a number of buildings, some of them private houses. The reason for this, they later discover, is an order issued earlier in the day for the round-up of seven hundred prominent party and government officials, journalists, professors and others—all known to be partial to Gomułka. The preparation of such a list and the issuing of orders for the Polish military to carry out the arrests during the evening of October 20 is what Khrushchev and his colleagues had been up to at the Soviet embassy while the Polish politburo had been waiting to say goodbye to them at the airport. But the Polish military commanders, appalled at what they were being asked to do, insisted that this sort of thing should be carried out by internal security troops, not the regular army, and had thus handed the orders over to the security forces, now headed by General Komar. He, rather than carry out what would amount to his own destruction, sent troops to guard, rather than arrest these individuals. Earlier in the evening most of them had received mysterious telephone calls warning them not to go home. Still later these same mysterious parties had called to say it was now safe to return home.

When, on Sunday morning, word of this becomes public, along with many reports that the Soviet and Polish troops are returning to their bases, people breath more than a sigh of relief. There is a genuine feeling that the crisis is passed.

When the plenum reconvenes Sunday morning it is still dominated by Rokossovsky's struggle to maintain his membership on the politburo, despite the inevitability of Gomułka's accession to the party leadership. Now, finding himself on the defensive, Rokossovsky is asked why he gave orders, as far back as three days ago, for Polish troops to march on Warsaw, orders given without the politburo's knowledge or permission. He stubbornly maintains that these were just "autumn maneuvers," not requiring any clearance with the government. Later, when asked about the movement of a very specific detachment of troops, he maintains they were "simply on their way to help the peasants harvest potatoes"—an explanation so blatantly false that it draws laughter.

At one point Rokossovsky points out that the Central Committee cannot unseat him because he was never elected in the first place. He had simply been appointed head of the army and defense minister by the Soviets (Stalin) and acquired his position on the politburo ex officio.[59]

Gradually all arguments are exhausted, and by 5:30 P.M. the secret balloting on the composition of the new politburo begins. There are 75 members of the Central Committee and it takes 50 votes to elect. Each candidate must be voted on separately, so the process is a slow one. Gomułka gets 74 votes, Cyrankiewicz 73, and Ochab all 75. But Rokossovsky, with only 23, fails to come close. Not surprisingly, there are no Natolin members on the new, nine-man politburo. Gomułka is then elected first secretary by acclamation, replacing Ochab.

Only the wording of the resolution confirming all of these new developments remains, but that, too, is a laborious process, and it is late in the evening before the plenum finally adjourns. The politburo, however, stays on. Over the next few days it will be in almost constant session. First come the all-night telephone conversations with Moscow. Khrushchev, professing to accept the situation—though he has not yet rejected the idea of a military solution—apologizes for his behavior on Friday and wires an official "best wishes" to Gomułka. A new defense minister must be appointed if and when Rokossovsky can be persuaded to depart. By October 28, Khrushchev and his colleagues will have definitely decided against a military solution, so Rokossovsky will fly off "on holiday," and on November 13 will become deputy defense minister of the U.S.S.R.[60]

General Wacław Komar of the Internal Army and General Włodzimierz Mus of the KBW are saying that now is the time to press for complete withdrawal of all Soviet forces from Poland. Quite to the contrary, thinks

Gomułka; this a very dangerous idea and he immediately quashes it. Threats of court martials pass down the ranks.

While the politburo is still meeting Sunday night in Warsaw, the presidium of the U.S.S.R. is also meeting in Moscow. It decides unanimously to "refrain from military intervention" and to "display patience" for the time being.[61]

Meanwhile at Radio Free Europe in Munich, where it is still early evening, a memorandum addressed to the Munich staff from Mucio Delgado, program director of the Free Europe Committee, teletyped from New York earlier in the day, is circulating in many copies around the building. "Once again," it says,

> we stand in anxiety and fearful hope with our Polish confreres in RFE ... The jamming of RFE broadcasts must stop as the surest, quickest , and most convincing evidence which the régime can give this Sunday of its independence from Moscow ...

> We cannot believe the Soviet Union will not, or indeed, has not already changed its attitude about liberalization. It must be plain to them that the desire for independence has gone beyond what they had envisaged as being good for the Soviet scheme ...

> We remember ... the bravery of the men of Poznań who with their bare hands destroyed a jamming radio station ...

> The story from Poland the last two days has had an immense and electric reaction in America. In brief, every radio and television commentator and newscaster has led off with this story all through the day. Press coverage has been tremendous. *The New York Times* alone devotes over 30 full columns to the story today ...[62]

Yesterday Warsaw Radio reported on a nasty page-one article that had appeared in *Pravda* just as Khrushchev and his colleagues were arriving back in Moscow. It accused the Polish press of waging a "filthy, anti-Soviet campaign," and trying to "undermine socialism in Poland."[63] According to communist protocol, this article has to appear in every non-Soviet party daily newspaper the next day.

Meanwhile, the newspaper *Życie Warszawy* ("Warsaw Life") had written "The nation is united as never before—and expects of the men who are sitting in the Central Committee to continue decisive action on behalf of the democratization of life in People's Poland." This, too, had been featured in Radio Warsaw broadcasts.

By way of direct answer to the *Pravda* article, the presidium of the National Council of Polish Students adopts a resolution on Sunday afternoon deploring the *Pravda* article and expressing the hope that *Pravda* will soon publish Polish press opinions and specifically the full text of Zofia Arty-mowska's article entitled "In the name of true friendship" carried in yester-day's *Trybuna Ludu*.[64]

Now, just minutes after the Central Committee plenum ends, Warsaw Radio breaks into its normal broadcasting to announce the results of the election to the nation.[65] It is 10:27 P.M. and many people are already in bed. Nonetheless, lights begin to go on all over the city. For those still dressed, or willing to get dressed again, there is an extra dividend. Extra editions, says the radio, of the daily newspapers, *Trybuna Ludu*, *Życie Warszawy,* and the youth newspaper, *Sztandar Młodych*, none of which usually publish on Sunday, are running off the presses right now.[66]

Soon the sound of volunteer taxis can be heard careening around the empty streets delivering bundles of newspapers to hastily opened kiosks. Student cadres volunteer to drive truckloads of newspapers to provincial cities. Other student volunteers become newsboys, hawking their wares in the streets and the few late night cafés still open. All papers are given out free.[67]

From the top of the Palace of Science and Culture one can see small knots of people gathering under street lights to read the papers, too excited to wait until they get home to read them.[68] Many repair to cafés, whose propri-etors decide to keep them open all night; and it is not long before joyous shouting and not-too-sober singing can be heard in the streets. Most of the papers contain long polemics against the *Pravda* diatribe or recount meetings and resolutions held yesterday around the country. But it is Gomułka's vic-tory and Rokossovsky's ouster from the politburo that they are celebrating.

The name Gomułka is on everyone's lips. Most people do not even know what he looks like, never mind the sound of his voice. But he is the nation's hero. Even Radio Free Europe is praising him for his courageous stand and is warning citizens to remain calm lest any too exuberant action become an excuse to unleash the Soviet onslaught.

In contrast to Sunday's clear skies and sunshine, Warsaw today is shrouded in fog and it is difficult to believe, from the look of the populace shuffling back to work after the weekend, that anything much has been going on.[69]

More details on Soviet troop movements leak out on Monday, including reported clashes between Soviet and Polish troops at the East German border, and clashes between civilians and police. Polish border troops are reported to have opened fire on a Soviet motorized unit trying to enter the country from the German Democratic Republic at Szczecin, and the Soviets, lacking orders to fire, had pulled back. Further to the south quick-witted border guards were reported to have halted a Soviet column by refusing to let anyone pass who did not have a "valid passport" properly stamped with a visitor's entry visa.[70]

Friday, when columns were still converging on Warsaw, the students of Legnica, location of the Warsaw Pact Headquarters in southern Poland, lined the street leading to the Soviet headquarters with posters reading "We wish our Russian friends a good trip home." A number of injuries, but no fatalities, resulted when the Polish police and Soviet soldiers tore them down again amid protesting students on Friday evening and Saturday morning.[71]

Western diplomats report that the rail center at Brest-Litovsk in the Ukraine has been sealed off from all Westerners for five days beginning on Saturday. Reports also circulate among Western diplomats that the Polish politburo has been in close touch with Tito throughout the entire crisis[72] and that Communist China has warned the Soviet Union to refrain from taking any drastic measures against Poland.[73]

"They made the whole thing so easy for us," a prominent Polish party member tells his friend at the British *Manchester Guardian* over the open telephone on Monday, by which he means that Khrushchev's sudden appearance galvanized the country into swinging behind Gomulka.[74]

A student demonstration in Warsaw, meanwhile, parades through the streets bearing banners reading "Polish-Soviet relations must be based on equality" and "The true friend of Poland helps her go on her own way." One banner asks "What's the news?" then answers, "Nothing. Jamming costs 83 million zlotys."[75]

In fact, Polish jamming of RFE and VOA is to end within a few weeks as a result of nationwide pressure from the masses, including many communists, one result of RFE's crucial role in the crisis. For the next twelve years, RFE's Polish broadcasts will still be partially jammed, but only from East Germany and Czechoslovakia, not Poland.[76] Within days, the new régime passes a secret oral message of gratitude to the Polish desk of RFE through circuitous, clandestine means, a fact the Polish desk is careful never to make public.

The demonstrations on Monday occur not only in Warsaw but in Gdańsk, Szczecin and other Polish cities. Even larger demonstrations, involving up to one hundred thousand people, take place the next day in Poznań, Lublin, Bydgoszcz, and Kielce. Resolutions passed at these mass meetings invariably include such demands as: 1) strengthening the alliance with the U.S.S.R. by practicing the principle of full sovereignty, 2) opening of political life, 3) removal of the Natolin group from government and trade unions, 4) removal of all Soviet officers, especially Rokossovsky, 5) release of Cardinal Wyszyński and the imprisoned bishops, 6) return of all Polish prisoners of war still held in the U.S.S.R., and 7) an end to jamming of Western radio stations.[77]

In his broadcast to Poland on October 23, RFE's Jan Nowak asks "How does one explain the astounding change that has taken place [in Poland's Communist leaders]?" It "can be found in the great changes which have taken place in the country within the last few years ... The party could not resist the impact of this wave ...

"This does not mean that society registered its support for the program of the Polish Communist Party. The Communist program will never become our Polish program ... But *any* Pole who speaks in the defense of the independence of his country will meet with the firm support of all the people ..."[78]

On Wednesday, October 24, a crowd of over three hundred thousand assembles in Parade Square to hear Gomułka address the nation for the first time.[79] Excepting the crowds of pilgrims which gather each year at Częstochowa, it is the largest crowd ever assembled in People's Poland; and it will not be surpassed until the Polish pope, John Paul II, visits in June 1979.

The crowd is tightly packed, some youths climbing lampposts for a better look. People are in a boisterous mood chanting "Wies-ław! Wies-ław!" (Gomułka's nickname) and singing "*Sto lat.*" ("May you live for 100 years!")[80] The mood is almost ecstatic—until they hear what Gomułka has to say. He is no orator, nor does he have any gift for language. His origins are humble and his manner straightforward. The most important fact of all, however, is that he is a fanatically self-disciplined, believing communist. Though the changes he pledges draw cheers, the belt-tightening measures and his calls for hard work and for restrained behavior do not. Particularly disappointing are his calls for *stronger* political and military ties with the Soviet Union and his condemnation of those people who would lure Poland away from the Warsaw Pact. Most sobering of all is his urging of everyone to return to their daily work and to stop immediately any more rallies or demonstrations.[81]

The reason for such restraint will become daily more apparent to Poles as they read and hear on October 24 about the intervention of the Soviet army in Hungary.

Their sympathy is totally with their Hungarian brethren, and they show it by flying Hungarian colors from every tram and bus and donating blood and medicines.[82] They know they dare not do more for fear of losing what freedom they have won with Gomułka. It is at this time that a bitter joke circulates, particularly in Western Europe: "Look at the Hungarians; they are behaving like Poles! Look at the Poles; they are behaving like Czechs! And look at the Czechs; they are behaving like swine!"

As all eyes begin to turn to Hungary, Polish prudence carries the day. Many longed-for changes take place over the next few weeks—changes of which the party is not necessarily in favor. Several years will pass before the party, still under Gomułka's control, is able slowly to reverse the gains which have come with what historians will now forever call "The Polish October."

Epilogue

On October 24, 1956, the same day Gomułka addressed the outdoor gathering in Warsaw and full-scale fighting broke out in Budapest, the presidium of the U.S.S.R. met once again in Moscow. On Poland they agreed that "finding a reason for armed conflict now would be very easy [i.e., with fighting going on in Budapest], but finding a way to put an end to such a conflict later on would be very hard."[1] (They might as well have added that letting Poland go its own way for now also freed the U.S.S.R. to concentrate on their problems in Hungary.)

There was also Khrushchev's changing assessment of Gomułka. Nearly two decades later he recalled in his memoirs:

> Here was a man who had come to power on the crest of an anti-Soviet wave, yet who could now speak forcefully about the need to preserve friendship with Soviet Russia and the Soviet Communist Party. Perhaps I didn't appreciate this fact right at the moment, but I came to appreciate it afterwards. He was just the man to take charge ... We believed him when he said he realized we faced a common enemy, Western imperialism. I remember when he almost shrieked with agitation, "Poland needs the friendship of the Soviet Union more than the Soviet Union needs the friendship of Poland!"[2]

Neither Khrushchev nor Gomułka had been in favor of releasing Cardinal Wyszyński, yet both were powerless to prevent it, for even many Polish party members had begun to demand his freedom, and on October 28 the cardinal was freed. Fully aware of the explosive situation into which he is stepping—with the Hungarian revolution's overthrow of communism now seemingly successful—the Cardinal's first words to the nation were: "Pray, because our homeland demands great calm of you now, and great restraint." More than any single individual, Cardinal Wyszyński, kept Poland from boiling over.[3]

Having been so poorly advised by its own embassy in Warsaw, the U.S. Department of State was caught completely off guard by the fast-moving developments in Poland. Secretary of State Dulles was not above stating the obvious—that sending U.S. troops to Poland would start World War III—and taking pot shots: "When practically the whole politburo descended en masse on Warsaw, we got an idea of what they mean by noninterference."[4] But Dulles's policy of offering surplus American food to create stress between the Soviet Union and its satellites now no longer applied to a situation where the stress between Poland and the U.S.S.R. could hardly have been greater. When a group of Polish exiles in the United States suggested that now was the time for the U.S. to offer food to Poland, he merely said he was "sympathetic to the group's proposal." A department spokesman instead said the United States will refrain from offering any aid to Poland "until the Poles themselves request it from us." The Poles, of course, already *had* clandestinely requested aid in the form of a loan in August, which Dulles had dismissed out of hand. The situation now was quite different. U.S. policy makers found it difficult to believe that the Soviets would not react strongly to the rebuff they had received in Warsaw. But the department could not adjust suddenly, or easily, to such unexpected developments. Dulles persuaded President Eisenhower to issue a statement of sympathy to the Poles on October 20, which *Trybuna Ludu* promptly labeled as "crude" interference in Polish affairs. Washington was not even ready to accept that what had happened in Poland had any permanence, much less take any steps to help make it so.[5]

Dulles and the department were wrestling with the problem of whether or not to resume aid to Yugoslavia, which Dulles had righteously suspended as soon as it became clear that Moscow was trying to woo Tito back into the fold. The decision to resume—but hold back the promised fighter planes (which Tito promptly called a "slur" on Yugoslav independence)—was predicated on the possibility that Yugoslavia might well become the center of a new alignment in Eastern Europe and, were this to happen, U.S. fighter planes in Yugoslavia might become a grave provocation to the U.S.S.R.[6]

Moscow had much bigger decisions to make than the composition of an aid package to one of its client nations.

Since March the Kremlin leaders had seen cracks in their East European empire emerge—cracks that they had no idea were there. The ferment catalyzed by de-Stalinization *had* gone much further than intended—certainly much further and faster than in the Soviet Union itself. Not only did it have to be halted, but the origins of the strains had to be eliminated: the countries of Eastern Europe could no longer be treated as Stalin had treated them. An entirely new basis of relations needed to be established if there was to be stability in the area.

To this end a special commission had been set up by the Central Committee to work out and draft a new policy, which, once approved by the committee, could be announced to the world and implemented. Rumors and evidence that such a major Soviet policy shift was in the works came to the attention of the British embassy in Moscow as early as June 4 when the ambassador, Sir William Hayter, cabled to Whitehall that the embassy had "indications that Moscow is preparing to make some special announcement about the satellites."[7] Various statements over the summer that the Central Committee was on the point of announcing Soviet troop reductions in specific East European countries, including East Germany, followed this rumor. Yet, whenever the time seemed ripe, something happened to postpone the announcement.

Not until events in Eastern Europe had seemingly gotten out of hand—an unwanted government in Poland no longer under their full control and a fledgling insurrection in Hungary—did the presidium of the Central Committee agree to instate and announce the new policy which it had been gestating all through the summer and early fall. The formal debate lasted only one day, but by the end full unanimity was achieved.[8] On October 30, with the guns silent in Budapest and the Red Army already withdrawn from the city, the momentous "declaration" was made and broadcast to the world.

"The Soviet government is ready to discuss ..." it proclaimed, "measures insuring ... the strengthening of economic ties between socialist countries in order to remove any possibilities of violating the principle of national sovereignty, mutual advantage, and equality in economic relations ..." (Translation: Stalinist exploitation of the satellites will stop.)

"The Soviet government is ready to examine ... the question of Soviet troops stationed on the territory of [Warsaw Pact] countries." (Translation: We are prepared to negotiate the possible withdrawal of Soviet troops from east-central Europe.)

"The Soviet government has given instructions to its military command to withdraw its units from Budapest as soon as this is considered necessary by the Hungarian government ..."*

"The Soviet government is willing to enter into relevant negotiations with the Hungarian government and other participants of the Warsaw Pact on the question of the presence of Soviet troops in Hungary ..." (Translation: We are willing to consider withdrawing all Soviet troops from Hungary since it is not, like the GDR or Poland, strategically vital to us.)[9]

It had taken eight months—from Khrushchev's secret denunciation of Stalin to this momentous declaration to the world of October 30—for the

---

* The Central Committee doubtless knew this had already taken place, but they left this in the text in order to save face.

Kremlin to come to the full realization that the Stalinist hold on Eastern Europe could not be maintained without Stalin, and that an entirely new relationship had to be forged if Stalin's empire were to be maintained. Unfortunately, Khrushchev's speech had unleashed such chaos in east-central Europe that only a threatened return of Stalin's methods could now save the empire.

The men who made this courageous, albeit tardy, decision to change completely the U.S.S.R.'s relations with its satellites could not have known when they did so that matters were deteriorating too fast in Hungary for the new policy to be carried out. Any possibility of their avoiding a military solution there was obliterated by the French, British and Israeli invasion of Egypt to re-take the Suez Canal, a precipitous operation which began on the very day the declaration was announced.

Thus, on October 31, the new policy, insofar as Hungary was concerned, had to be completely reversed. Britain, France, and Israel were well aware that Soviet troubles in Eastern Europe would prevent the Soviets from coming to the aid of their new client, Nasser; and they fully exploited this Soviet predicament. There is no historical evidence, however, to indicate that the Western allies knew such a major declaration of a Soviet policy change was about to be made, any more than the Soviets knew of the timing, or even the certainty, of the Western attack on Suez. It was purely an accident of history.

Some have claimed that the October 30 declaration was a fake, a front to cover the reinvasion of Hungary by the Red Army. But there is no precedent for such an elaborate deception being carried out by such a large, deliberative body. In fact, many negotiations with the governments and Communist parties of Eastern Europe did ensue in the following years, particularly in the economic sphere. Soviet advisers were withdrawn and in the case of Romania, negotiations took place and Soviet troops were completely withdrawn from that country in May 1958 with reference being made to the October 30 declaration at that time.

What happened in Hungary—and the effect of that revolution within the Communist bloc, and, indeed, throughout the world—is another story.

Appendix A

Faculty[*] of Mathematics and Physics at Charles University, Prague

Resolution adopted by the Faculty Organization of the Czechoslovak Youth Union

In recent days the Youth Union of our Faculty has been holding discussions on the results of the 20th Congress of the Communist Party of the Soviet Union and of the March session of the Central Committee of the Czechoslovak Communist Party. These discussions have been very lively and, thanks to the positive atmosphere generated by the participants, honest and full of constructive criticism. The spirit of the CPSU Party Congress has communicated itself to our own political life.

For a long time it has not been common for our Union to speak so openly about important political questions. This has been the result of incorrect methods of work against which the Party, by condemning the cult of personality and all its consequences, has begun a decisive struggle. Because open discussions were impossible for such a long time, a number of questions were treated that had only a remote connection with the CPSU 20th Congress and, accordingly, certain incorrect or poorly thought out ideas came to the fore.

The participants in the talks, however, consistently presented views whose goal was to remove shortcomings in our political and cultural life, taking advantage of the new opportunities provided by our new Popular Democratic organization.

To confront the most important questions, the Faculty Committee of the Youth Union on April 26, 1956 called a plenary meeting of the Youth Union for the entire faculty which summed up the views of the preceding individual discussions. The reason for the present letter is, on the one hand, to explain the views and needs of the Youth Union Faculty Organization and, on the

---

[*]   The term "faculty" here refers to students rather than teachers of a particular department.

273

other hand, to request answers to certain questions which we ourselves have not been able to answer in a satisfactory way.

1) We consider it necessary that all important measures in individual areas of our national and economic life be discussed in advance with workers, in particular, workers in the areas in question, and that they be submitted for public discussion in the press. Workers' suggestions should be included in any resulting decrees unless there is proper explanation of why they should not be.

Some of the shortcomings in our political and economic life have been caused by failure to observe in practice all of the principles of socialist democracy. We maintain that it is necessary in all cases to invoke as soon as possible the principle that all leading organs and those who work for them bear full responsibility to account for their work and be subject to full scrutiny and control from below. We consider it vital that all citizens be acquainted as thoroughly as possibly[*] with the means they will have to exercise this scrutiny and control over their representatives at the highest echelons and, when necessary, exercise the right to recall them. We regard these measures as necessary to guarantee that past mistakes will not be repeated.

It is also necessary to improve the system of electing candidates to the National Committees and National Assembly, to ensure that candidates will not only have the capability to carry out their duties but also enjoy the confidence of their voters. We consider it necessary to begin to call as soon as possible regular meetings of voters with their representatives in the National Assembly. At these meetings workers could openly express their needs and suggestions for the work of the National Assembly and the government and the other state organs. These meetings would, however, become a mere formality it as it happened frequently in the past, an incorrect criticism (not inciting lawbreaking) would lead to a punishment for the critic. We are convinced that, if Socialist Democratic principles are really observed; that is, if there is a real opportunity for discussion, criticism and presentation of views, all the working masses will enthusiastically join the efforts of the Party and the government of the National Front.

We ask for prompt publication of concrete directives regarding workers' personnel policy. We consider it necessary that all persons be suitably and truthfully informed upon request about the contents of their personnel files and any conclusions a personnel department has come to which are based on them.

---

[*] Possible, perhaps.

We consider it necessary that in working to improve our Parliament the experience of the Polish parliament [Sejm] be taken into full account.

2) We ask that our press, radio and film reporting service inform the public much more promptly, more accurately and with more independence than heretofore. Compared to the Western press and those of the other People's Democratic countries our public was informed about the results of the 20th Congress of the CPSU very late. Certain essential facts in the speeches of the leading representatives of the international workers' movement were simply hushed up. We were thus often forced to confront the paradox that we first learn about Party matters from bourgeois sources.

We consider that the fear of bourgeois views, which can, after all, be objectively rebutted in discussion, is totally unsubstantiated. Removal of this fear would also remove some of its undesirable consequences.

We consider it correct* that foreign currency funds be released for the purchase of scholarly literature and journals from the West so that these publications can be purchased by both individual scholars and students specializing in a given field. We also consider the present situation regarding translation of scholarly literature, and specifically textbooks from the West, to be wholly unacceptable.

In the area of ideological questions we do not consider it necessary to maintain a list of prohibited books, especially in such libraries as the University Library, the Main Library of the Academy of Sciences and libraries of ministries and individual educational institutions.

We also consider it essential to permit the study of Western newspapers and periodicals which represent major political currents.

We do not understand the reasons for jamming Western radio broadcasts or why this practice is necessary at all.

Information about partial successes of the capitalist states (fluctuations in unemployment, increases in production) are still often concealed. At the same time our own failures are also often hushed up, as the example of HUKO [a Slovak steel mill project] shows.

We consider it unnecessary that almost all statistical data are painstakingly concealed from the public. This situation will certainly be resolved by the decision to resume publication of the Statistical Yearbooks.

Given our peaceful coexistence with capitalist countries, we ask that travel to foreign countries be made possible other than through the Czecho-

---

* The Czech phrase (now probably outdated) meant something like 'we would like to see an increase in the foreign currency released'.

slovak State Travel Agency. We urge special emphasis on exchange agreements, particularly those involving students, with minimalization* of foreign currency difficulties. We also consider it necessary that procedures for obtaining permission to travel abroad (which at present require filling out 14 forms) be significantly simplified.

3) The practice of mechanically adopting the Soviet experience has done great harm to our educational system and, in particular, to our economic system. It is, of course, necessary to learn from the USSR as the first socialist state in the world, but it must always be taken into account in what way a Soviet method or approach is better than ours and to apply it in a truly creative manner. Mere copying of the USSR without regard to the differing economic and cultural differences in our two countries should not continue.

Lack of observance of these principles has severely damaged the attitudes of some of our people toward the Soviet Union. The indiscriminate adoption of Soviet works of little value into our cultural life has had a similar effect. Further harm has been done by such "manifestations of love" as the playing of the Soviet national anthem at the end of every broadcast day and the displaying of the Soviet flag at all occasions. We ask that the Soviet national anthem and the Soviet flag be present only on occasions which directly involve the Soviet Union; e.g., the November 7th and May 9th celebrations.

In order to forestall the impression that we only learn from and never teach the USSR and that our relationship with them is not equal, it would be a good idea to demonstrate more often the ways in which the USSR learns from us.

It would [be] a suitable idea for our National Assembly to pass a law regarding the display of state flags, the playing of anthems and the use of state emblems.

4) We do not consider correct the view of Mr. Novotny in his report: "The Central Committee as the collective organ of the Party between the congresses and the center of Party and state activity in our country decides and must decide the most important questions of the Party and state. Its decisions are binding both for the work of the Party as a whole and for state economic and social organs and organizations." The conclusion reflected in this statement does not express the principle that workers must be governed according to their own convictions and thereby distorts the real content and the leading

---

* Perhaps "which will eliminate the problems with foreign currencies."

role of the Party. We ask for an explanation of the role of the non-communist parties of the National Front. They presently seem to us to function in form only.

5) We ask for a public reviewer of the Slansky trial and other political trials. We ask for a guarantee of rightful punishment for persons who tolerated illegal procedures during interrogations for those who directly carried out these procedures. We maintain that it is necessary to publish materials about the actual conduct of the trials and the investigative procedures used, and at the same time about what kind of measures will be taken to guarantee control of the legal apparatus so that such cases will not be repeated.

We ask for amnesty for convicted persons similar to the amnesty recently declared in the Polish People's Republic.

6) University reforms were designed to prepare scholars for the needs of socialism through careful selection of students, better organization of the curriculum and improved economy of university management.

In many cases, however, the results of the reforms show that the productivity of the university student has gone down rather than risen. Let us mention some basic questions:

a) Compulsory attendance. In the past the only check on students was the quality of their performance. The present reform prescribes the way in which they are supposed to work. This constrains individuality in their work.

Most students learn much more from books and from distributed course surveys; listening to lectures which lack value is a waste of time for them. If attendance at lectures is compulsory, then the lecturer has a guaranteed audience, even though his lectures might be poor. Practice has shown that critiquing of lectures in itself rarely improves their quality—whether the fault lies with the choice of material or with the capability of the lecturer. Experience shows that if lecturers are of high quality, students will attend their lectures.

We maintain that things must move in the direction of individual students using their own source materials. If these source materials were sufficient, study programs, particularly in the natural sciences, would be much more efficient.

b) Number of hours. We consider it unacceptable that under the present plan students in their early school years must spend about 36 hours a week in the classroom. How many hours a day do the reformers think a student has to work, given the fact that lectures are supposed to be only a framework and the student's main work lies in individual study?

c) Plan of study. We note a flagrant disproportion between basic, general courses and special courses. For instance, in the first year there are 16 hours of general courses and 18 hours of special courses. Marxism is studied for 4 hours a week for 8 semesters (6 hours a week in the first year). Russian is taught 2 hours a week for 4 semesters, even though students should already know it from secondary schools.

In contrast to this, for example, physical chemistry, which is supposed to prepare graduates for research work in an area which combines physics and chemistry, offers students only 2 or 3 hours a week for 4 semesters.

We ask you to note the following requests:

1) We ask for an immediate review of the whole educational system.

2) We ask that this overall review of the organization of eleven-year schools and universities be publicly discussed in the press.

3) We believe that the introduction of eleven-year schools was a step backwards in our educational system.

4) We reject any action taken that presents teachers and students with a fait accompli.

5) We ask that the public be systematically informed, particularly by the press, about all plans and negotiations concerning school reform.

6) We ask that the review look back to the outstanding traditions of Czechoslovak education and take into account educational expertise worldwide.

7) We ask that the review be carried out by genuine experts and pedagogues who must be given the opportunity to learn about foreign educational systems through actual experience abroad, and not through the bureaucracy of the Ministry of Education.

8) We ask that those officials of the Ministry of Education who implemented the precipitous reforms of the past years be identified and called to account.

9) We ask that Russian courses be limited to 1 semester of scientific terminology and that similar courses in other world languages be established.

10) We ask that Marxism be taught in a way which promotes the development of the students' worldviews without their being bur-

dened with historical details. We believe that six semesters of Marxism-Leninism is enough.

11) We ask that appropriate central organs support an effort to intensify international student contacts—the exchange of publications and reciprocal visits of our students and Western students. We consider it necessary to put an end to the notion and the practice that international contacts are conducted only by officials from the regional level and higher. We ask that the number of student exchanges with the USSR be increased and that study in Western countries be made possible for a specified number of students and, in particular, for young scholars in various fields.

12) With regard to the unsatisfactory state of military training at universities and the difficulties which this causes students, and in the interests of our national defense, we consider it essential that the question of the effective training of reserve officers be discussed at a special meeting with representatives of the Faculty of Military Science and, if need be, on a university-wide scale with representatives of the Ministry of Defense.

7) To improve all of our political work and to increase participation and the interest of people in public life, the mass organizations must work somewhat differently as well. It is not right for them to guarantee fulfillment only of plans from above or to deal only with problems in their workplaces. They must give their members the opportunity to discuss all questions of our life, including foreign policy matters, to discuss everything openly and without fear of ill consequences from superiors. This improvement will come only when these organizations strive not only to win the confidence of the higher organs, but to see to it that their members can trust and rely on their elected organs. These organs must then defend their organizations, explain and endeavor to put through the views of the general rank-and-file, and to help the latter formulate its desires and requests.

Finally, one of the goals of our discussions and of this letter is that the Youth Union itself become such an organization as soon as possible.[*]

---

[*] This 'Princeton' translation of the 1956 resolution was scanned, OCR-ed and reviewed by Ladislav Němec on 12 May, 1996.

Appendix B

Page_____of
Desp. No._____
From_____

OFFICIAL USE ONLY
--(Classification)

Page____1____of
Encl. No.____1____
Desp. No.____425____
From_____Prague

UNIVERSITY

DRAFT RESOLUTION OF THE PLENARY MEETING OF THE HIGH-SCHOOL ORGANIZA-
TION OF THE CZECHOSLOVAK YOUTH UNION AT THE HIGH-SCHOOL OF PEDAGOGICS
IN PRAGUE

At the session of the Central Committee of the Communist Party of Czechoslovakia held March 29 and 30, 1956, it was pointed out that there were many shortcomings and errors in our public and political life, caused for the most part by
disregard of the collective leadership and our laws and the incorrect methods of
work resulting therefrom.

We feel it our duty, both on the basis of our civil rights and on the basis
of the education which our people's democratic State has given us, to express our
views on certain basic questions of our public and political life.

We realize that in the building up of socialism in our country certain mistakes and wrongs are inevitable, but there are mistakes which need not be made
and which could very quickly be rectified if the principle of collective leadership and the voice of the public is observed.

In this resolution we wish to point out the following shortcomings in our
public and political life and to suggest possible ways in which they could be rectified.

I. The Democratization of Public Life

The Press: We consider that the press does not fulfil its basic function of
providing early and accurate information concerning life in our country (for example, Novotny's speech printed 12 days after it was made) and concerning life
abroad (reports published here about western countries are not objective and do
not relate to questions which are characteristic of these countries).

We demand that our press publish factual material instead of extracts and
commentaries which are frequently copied from the Soviet press. For example, as
regards the United Nations Organization, the speeches of the Soviet representatives are published, but only uninformative extracts are given of the speeches
of the Western representatives, or else they are only commented upon. It would
also be proper for the press to publish reports of successes in capitalist countries (especially in the field of technology) and critical comments on mistakes
made in the people's democracies and the Soviet Union.

Mlada Fronta should devote its major attention to the real problems of young
people. The publication by Prague students of their own periodical would also
be worth considering.

In our view, the way to correct these shortcomings would be to lighten the
censorship (for example, the contribution to the debate at the Second Authors'
Congress made by Eva Vrchlicka was not published) and to lift restrictions on
the circulation of individual newspapers so that people may read those papers
which provide quick, accurate and interesting information.

We demand

Appendix B

Page_____of
Desp. No._____
From_____

OFFICIAL USE ONLY
(Classification)

Page 2 of
Encl. No. 1
Desp. No. 425
From Prague

We demand that foreign newspapers and periodicals should be made available to a greater extent, at least in libraries, if it is not possible to buy more.

Radio: We consider that the jamming of foreign broadcasts (even in the case of such a station as "Radio Free Europe") is beneath the dignity of our State. It would be more to the advantage of our press and radio if they published news before these stations, and if they refuted the unfounded reports of these stations with facts. Then it would not happen that people only learn of certain aspects of our internal affairs through the transmissions of these stations and the appropriate "explanation", or that they learn of them before they are reported on our stations (the dismissal of Cepicka, the secret speech of Mr. Khrushchev). Another shortcoming of our radio lies in the fact that all our stations broadcast the minimum number of programs. The level of the programs transmitted is also not high enough ("Moscow Calling", etc.) and very often there is a lack of proportion in the programs broadcast (for example, very little attention is paid to youth problems).

Regular and timely information about events in this country and the rest of the world would be the best weapon against unfriendly propaganda. Radio should become an instrument for open discussion directed towards correcting the mistakes which occur in our country.

The National Assembly: Press reports on the activities of the National Assembly give the impression that its work is merely formal. The press publishes only reports of unanimous voting and never any news of the course of a debate or of critical comments. We demand that reports should be published in the press on the preliminary debates of the National Assembly; this would make it possible at meetings of voters and members of Parliament for citizens to be informed of the matters debated and for the members of Parliament to learn the views of their supporters.

Cadre Work: We are aware of the importance of cadre work in a people's democracy. Owing to irresponsible workers, bad methods of cadre work and an overgrown cadre apparatus mutual confidence has been undermined and the settlement of personal grievances made possible, and thus the main object of cadre work - the constructive side - has not been achieved. In assessing qualifications too much emphasis was placed on political maturity (measured on the basis of subscription to the press, membership in organizations and non-critical attitude to contemporary events) at the expense of specialist qualifications.

Therefore, we demand (1) that a reduction be made in the size of the cadre apparatus; (2) that unsuitable methods in cadre work be ended (for example, non-objective methods of obtaining references); (3) that directives be issued concerning public assessment of qualifications and that the documents on which assessments are based be open to inspection in accordance with the proposals made by Comrade Novotny.

The Judiciary: Since in the past the principles of the socialist rule of law were not observed, we demand that all political cases be re-tried. The new

trials must

Page_____of.
Dep. No._____
From_____

. OFFICIAL USE ONLY
(Classification)

Page___3___of .
End. No. 1
Dep. No. 425
From   Prague

trials must be conducted by persons who were not present in the original proceedings. We demand that all persons who permitted violation of these principles be
strictly punished. The general public should be informed of the results of the
re-trials by press and radio.

II. Relations with the Soviet Union

The fraternal relations with the Soviet Union which were formed and strength-
ened after the liberation in 1945 were considerably impaired in the course of the
following years. In our opinion this state of affairs was caused by badly conducted educational work and propaganda. In propaganda the influence of the Soviet Union on our history, our political and cultural life and on the development
of our industries is exaggerated. It has reached such a stage that it would seem
that everything our nation has achieved was due to the example of the Soviet
Union. The slogan "The Soviet Union – Our Model" is being mechanically applied
in all sectors of our activities (all branches of industry, education and art)
and even in those sectors in which we were, and are, the model for the Soviet
Union to follow. Soviet experts themselves draw attention to this state of affairs with disapproval.— On the other hand in many respects in which we could
learn from Soviet experience we fail to do so. Arbitrarily and uncritically we
accept everything they have in the Soviet Union (in education, the title PPOV,
"pripraven k obrane vlasti", for the Soviet GTO). We forcibly introduce into our
national life traditions which are characteristic of and peculiar to the Soviet
Union (Father Frost).

As regards culture we see the following mistakes: the uncritical importation of inartistic Soviet films, so that the popularity of Soviet films in general suffers, and distrust and antipathy is aroused towards Soviet films in general; the translation into Czech of unsuitable literature; the disproportion in
the size of the editions of classics by Czechoslovak, Soviet and Western authors;
reports on the Soviet Union which are frequently incomplete and distorted and
give an idealized picture — people who visit the Soviet Union as tourists are
disillusioned and consequently true reports are not believed; the playing of the
Soviet national anthem and the flying of the Soviet flag even on those occasions
which have nothing to do with the Soviet Union (1st May, graduation ceremonies,
the signing off of radio stations).

III. Cultural Life

1. In the interests of obtaining a true and clear picture of the Western
countries we consider it essential that the importation and translation of the
literature and periodicals of these countries be facilitated and promoted (this
applies not only to technical works but also to philosophical and political
literature and fiction).

2. All students must be allowed access to literature such as, for example,
that classified in the University Library as "Libri prohibiti".

3. The

OFFICIAL USE ONLY
(Classification)

3. The Marxist world theory must be developed in competition with abstract philosophy. For this purpose we consider it necessary that students be fully informed of non-Marxist philosophical trends.

4. Facilities should be provided for the importation of Western films of artistic merit on a wider scale.

5. Visits to foreign countries by students should be made possible and facilitated (both from the organizational and material aspects).

6. (The publications plan should be revised with regard to the demand for good literature (for example, Capek, Seifert). In view of this the extravagant use of paper for unnecessary printed matter and various propaganda material of doubtful value should be considerably curtailed.

7. We consider it wrong and undignified to make changes other than minor corrections from the linguistic point of view in published literary works (for example, the omission of parts of Capek's "War of the Newts").

IV. Education

The present course of study for university students does not meet their needs for adequate preparation for future callings. The basic shortcoming is overloading the course with an excessive number of subjects, making it impossible to study individually and direct from sources. We are of the opinion that it is only the university student's individual study which leads to genuine knowledge, and is a guarantee of good preparation for his future calling.

In view of these shortcomings and their consequences we demand:

1. A revision of the secondary school reform because eleven years of study is not adequate preparation for study at a university. Inadequate preparation is the result of shortening the time for secondary school studies, and a poor selection of subjects and curriculum.

2. A reform of the existing system of secondary school studies, and the submission of a draft of the reform for thorough discussion by students and teachers.

3. This reform should include the following:

(a) Abolish obligatory attendance at all lectures but maintain obligatory attendance at seminaries and practical training courses. Voluntary attendance at lectures will be an indicator of their standard.

(b) Within the framework of non-obligatory lectures, we demand that in the final years some of the lectures be considered as selective, which would serve to deepen technical knowledge and interest.

(c) Improve

P ge_____of
Desp. No._____
From_____

| OFFICIAL USE ONLY |
(Classification)

Page___5___of
Bnd. No. 1_____
Desp. No. 425
From____Prague

(c) Improve the mutual relation between lectures of approved groups and other subjects in favor of subjects of approved groups. Abolish certain seminary courses on secondary subjects (e.g. seminary course on the history of pedagogics).

(d) Take up seriously the question of university textbooks (duplicated lectures) which, in certain sectors, practically do not exist. Textbooks and especially duplicated lectures are too expensive and are printed on bad paper.

(e) We demand that September be reserved for individual studies (for instance the collection of materials to be used in study throughout the year). We demand, therefore, that in this month no lectures be given.

(f) We demand the abolition of fees for re-examination in subjects in which the student has failed.

(g) We demand the establishment of additional students' colleges and the return to the students of those buildings which belong to them, so that all the students will be assured of accommodation.

The existing overburdening of students by the number of lectures results in their not being able to devote themselves to independent studies or participate in public work (leaders of Pioneer Organization) or cultural and physical training activities. For these reasons we demand that our demands be met without delay.

V. Physical Training

1. We move that experts and sportsmen participate in a public discussion published in the periodical "Czechoslovak Sport", on the draft statutes for a uniform physical training organization.

2. That the new voluntary physical training organization be named "Sokol", because that was the name of an organization in the national spirit which had a good name abroad.

3. That the voluntary physical training be carried out by volunteers under the leadership of a minimum number of paid workers with technical training.

4. That the services of the former volunteer trainers be secured for work in this organization.

5. That material support be secured for the university volunteer physical training centers (playgrounds and gymnasia).

VI. Questions

Certain things are not clear to us in our public life, and therefore we demand that the following questions be answered:

1. We

Page_____of
Desp. No._____
From_____

OFFICIAL USE ONLY
(Classification)

Page____6____of
Encl. No._1_
Desp. No. 425
From____Prague____

1. We assume from their present activities that the function of the other parties of the National Front is purely formal.

2. We are not clear regarding the ownership and management of the Jachymov mines and the uranium resources, a question we often encounter.

3. The privileged position of Soviet citizens in the Jachymov mines and elsewhere (Soviet School in Prague XIV):

We demand that our resolution with its comments and questions be discussed, and that we be informed in writing of the results of the proceedings.

At the Plenary Meeting it was resolved to send the full text of this resolution for discussion to the Central Committee of the Czechoslovak Communist Party, the Central Committee of the Czechoslovak Youth Union, and the Ministry of Education.

We demand that the Central Committee of the Czechoslovak Youth Union support our demand for the publication of the full text of our resolution in Mlada Fronta, because the report published in Mlada Fronta on May 9, 1956, distorted the actual course of the meeting. Because we are of the opinion that all these questions should be discussed by the National Assembly, we are sending the full text of the resolution also to the Presidium of the National Assembly and our Deputy.

- - - - - - - - - - -

Note (not contained in the resolution): This draft Resolution was approved at a plenary meeting of the Czechoslovak Youth Union at the High School of Pedagogics. Analogous resolutions were prepared at other faculties. This is an exact copy of the resolution.

                    Informer.

A Note on Sources

My sources have been primary—actual participants in the depicted events whom I have been fortunate to have interviewed—and secondary— books, newspaper articles, and documents found in official archives of five countries. Since I am not fluent in any of the languages of Eastern Europe, I have had to depend upon translations for many of these books and documents.

Because I have written what I call "historical journalism" primarily for the general reader and not a scholarly book for professional historians, I have tried to use, wherever possible, actual words the participants are purported to have said. This means using tertiary sources, for in most cases the authors of these books and articles were not actually present when these words were spoken, but were later told them by people who were. Such quotations help to dramatize the events and bring the reader closer to what actually happened than a mere recitation of the events can accomplish. Wherever such quotations appear to have a real basis in fact, I have made use of them.

In the course of pursuing such quotations I have made use of one particular source, who has, since I selected the passages, been exposed not only as an anti-Semite, but a "holocaust denier," the English scholar/journalist, David Irving. It was obvious to me when I read his book *Uprising*, that David Irving was anti-Semitic, and I have been careful not to include any passage that reflected that extreme bias. I was not aware, until his public unmasking, what an unsavoury character he is or that some of his scholarly judgments, heretofore held in high esteem by many of his peers, are now called into question.

Irving's book was the first book—and for a long time the only book—in English attempting to tell the story of, and not simply document, that revolution. Because he researched it in Hungary a little over two decades after the events, he was able to interview many of the primary participants on both sides—most of those arrested having long since been released from prison. The events themselves and the dramatic comments spoken at public meetings in 1956 were still relatively fresh in their minds. There was no reason for Irving to misquote or elaborate on what they told him.

I happen to have known for many years the Hungarian lady who acted as Irving's official translator. She attests that the persons whom Irving quotes in his book said what he says they said and that his accounts are wholly acurate recordings of her translations. In the end I decided to retain a few colorful Irving quotations.

Use of his book in no way reflects my opinion of Irving as a person, whom I find both infuriating and despicable.

Notes

Notes to Chapter I: Stalin Denounced

1. Lenin scholars, who later looked up the quotation, found it referred to something written by Lenin in 1916, before he even called his Bolshevik faction the Communist Party. The examples of "peaceful transition to socialism" Khrushchev was referring to came later in the speech. These were: Czechoslovakia, Estonia, Latvia, Lithuania, Bulgaria, Romania, Albania, Yugoslavia and … China! See *Khrushchev and Stalin's Ghosts,* Bertram D. Wolfe, Praeger, N.Y., 1957, pp. 56, 60-61.

2. *Khrushchev: A Political Portrait*, Konrad Kellen, Praeger, N.Y., 1961, p. 154.

3. *Izvestia*, December 21, 1955.

4. Khrushchev here refers to 10 million peasant households (over 20 million people) branded "*kulaks*" (bourgeois, capitalist farmers) who had been "liquidated" by killing, starving or being forced into state collectives in the early to middle 1930s (see *Khrushchev and Stalin's Ghosts*, pp. 165-67).

5. This commission, known as the Pospelov Commission, for the man who headed it, went far beyond the investigation of the party congresses, investigating all of Stalin's crimes and was the basis for the text of the secret speech.

6. Ironically, this directive was still operative in 1953 when Khrushchev and his colleagues arrested, tried, and shot Beria.

7. Probably because he, as wartime party leader in the Ukraine, was directly involved in the administration of both expulsions.

8. *Khrushchev and Stalin's Ghosts*, p. 80.

9. *Khrushchev Remembers*, translated by Strobe Talbott, Little, Brown & Company, Boston, 1970, p. 343.

10. The "virgin lands" scheme was one of Khrushchev's early successes. Soviet agriculture had been in a very bad way ever since the "liquidation" of the kulaks and the forced collectivization of the remaining peasants. To give a dramatic increase in wheat production, Khrushchev proposed that vast tracts of virgin land in Siberia, which had never been under cultivation, be brought under cultivation, and he inspired young people from all over the Soviet Union—much as John F. Kennedy inspired young Americans to go into the Peace Corps—to

sign up as young volunteers in this pioneering enterprise. Soviet wheat production soared for several years as a result. Then came a few years of drought, and the whole enterprise collapsed and had to be abandoned. But by that time, Khrushchev was in a far more powerful position as head of the party than when he had first proposed it.

11. *Khrushchev Remembers.* This and all subsequent quotations come from pp. 347-49.

Notes to Chapter II: Cold War Synopsis

1. *Sovetskaya Kultura*, Oct. 1, 1988, SOBSEDNIK, no. 49, pp. 67-68.

2. *Invitation to Moscow*, Zygmunt Stypulkowski, Thomas and Hudson, London, 1951, pp. 211-214.

3. For a fascinating, up-to-date account of this Soviet intelligence gathering, see *The Sword and the Shield, the Mitrokhin Archives and the Soviet History of the KGB*, Christopher Andrew and Vasili Mitrokhin, Basic Books, N.Y. 1999.

4. For a full account of Hall and his accomplices, see *Bombshell: The Secret Story of America's Unknown Atom Spy Conspiracy,* Joseph Albright and Marcia Kunstel, Times Books, Random House, N.Y., 1997.

5. *The Sword and Shield*, pp. 132-134. See also *Whittaker Chambers*, Sam Tanenhaus, Random House, N.Y., 1997, pp. 519-20.

6. *The Great Terror: A Reassessment*, Robert Conquest, The University of Alberta Press, 1990, p. 486.

7. Box 23, Folder 47, Moscow via War Department, Feb 20, 1946, Papers of George F. Kennan, Seeley G. Mudd Manuscript Library, Princeton University, Princeton, N.J. Articles and pronouns not carried in the original have been added by the author to make the text immediately comprehensible to the reader.

8. *Foreign Policy*, Vol. 25, no. 4, July 1947, "The Sources of Soviet Conduct," George F. Kennan, p. 515.

9. *Cold War*, Jeremy Isaacs and Taylor Downing, Transworld Publications, Ltd., London, 1998, p. 55.

10. The aid was not just food and machinery. In Greece, where the soil was rocky and farming primitive, the Americans sent not tractors but Missouri-bred mules. These were far bigger and more powerful than the local donkeys and soon became the major source of pride for each farmer who was lucky enough to acquire one.

11. See *Cold War International History Project Bulletin*, issue 5, Spring 1995, Woodrow Wilson International Center for Scholars, Washington, D.C., "Korea, 1949-50," Katheryn Weatherly.

12. *Khrushchev Remembers*, translated by Strobe Talbott, Little Brown & Co., Boston, 1970, pp. 100-101.

13. U.S. General Curtis LeMay had secretly lobbied for just such a pre-emptive strike when he was in command of SAC (Strategic Air Command). For an account of just how close America came to unleashing such an atomic bomb attack on the U.S.S.R., see "Annals of the Cold War: The General and World War III," Richard Rhodes, p. 47, *The New Yorker*, June 19, 1995.

14. *Cold War*, p. 126.

15. Ibid., p. 127.

16. *Inside the Kremlin's Cold War: From Stalin to Khrushchev*, Vladislav Zubok and Constantine Pleshakov, Harvard University Press, Cambridge, Mass. 1996, p. 156.

17. Ibid., p. 161.

18. Ibid., p. 162.

19. *We Now Know: Re-thinking Cold War History*, John Lewis Gaddis, Clarendon Press, Oxford, 1997.

20. "The Early Post-Stalin Succession Struggle (Part 3)," Mark Kramer, *Journal of Cold War Studies*, Vol. 1, no. 3, (Autumn 1999) p. 28, Davis Center of Russian Studies, Harvard University.

21. *The Soviet Sea Around Us: A Message from Berlin*, Graphische Gesellschaft Gruenewald GmbH, Berlin, Gruenewald 1959, pp. 11-15.

22. *The United States, the East German Uprising of 1953, and the Limits of Rollback*, Christian F. Ostermann, Working Paper 11, p. 40, Cold War International History Project, Woodrow Wilson International Center for Scholars, Washington, D.C.

23. "The Early Post-Stalin Succession Struggle (Part 3)," Mark Kramer p. 25.

24. Ibid., p. 27.

25. Cable from Conant to Dulles, August 8, 1953, *Foreign Relations of the United States*, Department of State, Washington D.C., 1952-54, vol. VII, p. 1640.

26. "The Early Post-Stalin Succession Struggle," Mark Kramer, pp. 19-20.

27. Christian F. Ostermann, Working Paper 11, p. 38.

Notes to Chapter III: Majáles

1. This chapter is based in part upon documents turned up during four visits to Prague—two to Budapest and one in Bratislava, and from Foreign Office and State Department documents recently made available in London and Washington and other written sources from the time. Most importantly, it is based on hours of interviews in Prague, Bratislava, and Princeton with seven of the movement's leaders, one of them being the prime mover and key author of probably the first of the many Czechoslovak student resolutions. Other than brief accounts in the Western and Czechoslovak press of the time, the author has been unable to find any comprehensive treatment of this student revolt. Even Professor Gordon Skilling's *East Europe after Stalin,* University of Toronto Press, 1964, and *Czecho-*

Notes

slovakia's *Interruptes Revolution*, Princeton University Press, 1976, devotes only a few paragraphs to the subject.

2. A student carnival, which for hundreds of years featured a parade through Prague at the beginning of May. The students dress up in costumes and carry symbols and slogans lampooning their studies, their professors, and anything else they wish to barb with their wit. The populace of Prague and other university towns in Czechoslovakia where it takes place usually turn out in great numbers to observe it.

3. Confidential "S" Dispatch no. 48, March 14 1956, British Embassy, Prague, to Foreign Office, FO371/122 1441 Ref. 7277, Public Records Office, London.

4. Ibid.

5. Confidential "S" Dispatch no. 61, April 11, 1956, British Embassy, Prague, to Foreign Office, p. 4 FO371/122141, Ref. 7277, Public Records Office, London.

6. Priority Dispatch no. 276, March 14, 1956, Sir William Hayter, British Embassy, Moscow to Foreign Office, FO371/122588, Ref 7333, Public Records Office, London.

7. Confidential "S" Dispatch no. 61, April 11, 1956, British Embassy, Prague, to Foreign Office, p. 4 FO371/122141, Ref 7277, Public Records Office, London.

8. Author's interview with Prof. Jiří Skopec, Geology Faculty, Charles University, Prague, March 1996.

9. Author's interview with Dr. Ladislav Němec, Princeton, N.J., April 13, 1996.

10. Author's interview with Prof. Jan Havránek, Asst. Dir., Historic Archives, Charles University, Prague, March 6, 1996.

11. Author's interview with Ladislav Němec.

12. Confidential "S" Dispatch no. 61, British Embassy, Prague, to Foreign Office, FO371/122141 Ref. 7277, Public Records Office, London.

13. Resolution adopted by the School Organization of the Czechoslovak Youth Union, School of Mathematics and Physics, Charles University, Prague, April 26, 1956. Translated by Prof. Charles E. Townsend, Princeton University (See Appendix A for full text).

14. "We Lift Our Visors," *Mladá Frontá*, April 28, 1956, translated by Prof. Townsend.

15. Author's interview with Dr. Michael Heyrovský, Institute of Physical Chemistry, Czech Academy of Sciences, Prague, March 5, 1996.

16. Author's interview with Dr. Ladislav Němec.

17. Ibid.

18. Author's interview with Dr. Michael Heyrovský.

19. *News from Behind the Iron Curtain* (NFBIC) (Free Europe Committee, Inc.) November issue, 1956, p. 22.

20. Author's interview with Dr. Michael Heyrovský, March 14, 1996.

21. Author's interview with Dr. Ladislav Němec.

22. Author's interview by phone with Dr. Saša Mangel, June 12, 1996.

23. Confidential "S" Dispatch no. 69, May 15, 1956, British Embassy, Prague, to F. O, FO371/122141 Ref. 7277, Public Records Office, London.

24. Radio Free Europe (RFE) internal document "Student Demonstrations Interpretive," Central Newsroom (CNR) D-26, May 30, 1956, Open Society Archives, Budapest.

25. Confidential "S" Dispatch, no. 69, May 15, 1956, British Embassy, Prague, to Foreign Office, FO371/122141, Public Records Office, London.

26. Limited Official Use Telegram no. 528, May 22, 1956, U.S. Embassy, Prague, to State Department, 4900/5-2256, National Archives, College Park, Maryland.

27. Ibid.

28. An RFE Czech language five-page analysis of the CSM (Czechoslovak Youth Union) published internally as 8909 on September 27, 1956, points out that the student May festivals "were planned precisely by the lowest departmental CSM organizations. The planning of student demonstrations was more than the higher organs could handle and thus escaped their control. So the students, against which the few fanatics from the committee of the district were absolutely powerless, did what they wanted. The May festival was something that convincingly demonstrated the utterly embarrassing position and role of the CSM among the students." Open Society Archives, Budapest.

29. Author's interview with Mgr. Juraj Marušiak, Bratislava, June 13, 1966.

30. In February 1956 when Slovak students discovered that Defense Minister Alexej Čepička planned to abolish military departments at universities and require students, upon graduation, to be subject to two years of compulsory military service in place of a concentrated two-month training period during their course of study, 3 to 400 students in their pajamas gathered in their dormitory cafeteria—later referred to as "the pajama rebellion." "During the stormy discussions the students hissed down Comenius University secretary, Jaroslav Fill, as he threatened to report them to their personnel sections ... Some participants called on their colleagues to go out into the streets to demonstrate, but they received no support from the rest. Finally the students approved a resolution demanding that the order be rescinded." From "The Pajama Rebellion—Slovak Students in the Year 1956," by Mgr. Juraj Marušiak, in *Historická Revue*, Cislo 8, Ročnik V, p. 19. Translated by Prof. Charles E. Townsend.

31. "The Pajama Rebellion: Slovak Students in the Year 1956" translated by Prof. Charles E. Townsend.

32. *NFBIC*, November 1956, p. 24.

33. RFE item no. 6297/56 "Bratislava University Students Ridicule Regime in 'Majáles' Parade." Open Society Archives, Budapest.

34. Limited Official Use Telegram no 325, June 6, 1956, U.S. Embassy, Prague, to State Department, 749.00/6-1356, National Archives, College Park, Maryland.

35. *NFBIC*, November 1956, p. 22.

36. Author's interview with Mgr. Juraj Marušiak, Bratislava, June 13, 1996.

37. Author's interview with Prof. Jozef Jablonický, Dir., Politological (*sic*) Institute, Slovak Academy of Sciences, Bratislava, June 14, 1996.

38. RFE item no. 5742/56, p. 2 ref. *Kulturný Život,* May 26, 1956, Open Society Archives, Budapest.

39. *NFBIC*, November 1956, p. 21.

40. Author's interview with Prof. J. Jablonický.

41. Ibid., and author's interview with Mr. Juraj Marušiak.

42. According to RFE item no 9173/56, "during the first week of June 1956 the Slovak Ministry of Education arranged several meetings at student dormitories in Bratislava. Subsource participated in one of these meetings. Communist agitators attempted to explain how the freedom of students is to be understood in a state ruled by the proletariat, and to whom the students' demands are to be presented, i.e., to communist or communist-sponsored organizations only. The Slovak minister of education, Ernest Sykora, while repeating the statements of the agitators, was booed by the students," Open Society Archives, Budapest.

43. Author's interview with Dr. Michael Heyrovský, March 14, 1996.

44. Central Archive of the Czechoslovak Communist Party Central Committee, Fond 02/2, Volume 102, Archive no. 118, Item 30, Prague.

45. Hand-written notes (presumably by person recording meeting), Central Archive of the Czechoslovak Communist Party's Central Committee, Fond 02/2, Volume 102, Archive no. 118, Prague.

46. Limited Official Use Telegram no. 528, May 22, 1956, U.S. Embassy, Prague, to State Department. 749.00/5-2256, National Archive, College Park, Maryland.

47. Author's interview with Prof. Jiří Skopec.

48. Ibid.

49. RFE item 5721/56, June 7, 1956, Open Society Archives, Budapest.

50. Author's interview with Dr. Michael Heyrovský, March 5, 1956.

51. Sydney Gruson. *The New York Times* dispatch from Prague, May 21, 1956.

52. RFE item no. 912/56, p. 2, Open Society Archives, Budapest.

53. *NFBIC*, November 1956, p. 24.

54. Ibid.

55. RFE item no 7912/56 p. 2, Open Society Archives, Budapest.

56. Ibid.

57. Limited Official Use Telegram no. 528, May 22, 1956, U.S. Embassy, Prague, to State Department, 749.00/6-656, National Archives, College Park, Maryland.

58. Author's interview with Prof. Jiří Skopec.

59. Limited Official Use Telegram no. 425, U.S. Embassy, Prague, to State Department, 749.00/6-1356, National Archives, College Park, Maryland.

60. United Press dispatch datelined Vienna, September 28, 1956.

61. Author's interview with Dr. Ladislav Němec and a letter sent from Dr. Michael Heyrovský, June 26, 1996.

62. Ibid.

63. Author's interview with Dr. Ladislav Němec and Dr. Herovsky.

64. CETEKA (Czechoslovak Communist news agency) transmission no. 27, September 26, 1956, 19:15 hours transmission.

65. According to RFE item no. 7057/56 of July 20, 1956, "The Ministry of Education and Culture, which controls the preparatory work for this congress recently recalled nine of the 15 members of the students' committee which is working on the preparations, and the Ministry of the Interior replaced them with its 'trustees.'" Open Society Archives, Budapest.

66. Author's interview by telephone with Dr. Saša Mangel, Prague June 12, 1996.

67. Limited Official Use Telegram, no. 576, June 17, 1956, U.S. Embassy, Prague, to State Department, 749.00/6-1756, National Archives, College Park, Maryland.

68. *NFBIC*, November 1956, p. 26.

69. In fact, Kahuda himself had more recently relaxed requirements for entrance into the universities. RFE item no. 6145/56 published by the Czechoslovak desk on June 22, 1956 states: "An acute shortage of academically trained technical personnel is being felt in Czechoslovakia, a well-informed recent refugee reports. Therefore in the autumn of 1955, the authorities quietly decided to authorize students previously fired from the universities for political reasons to re-enlist and continue their studies. Among the 'rehabilitated' were students who had been expelled after the 1948 coup d'état and had even been temporarily arrested." Open Society Archives, Budapest.

70. *NFBIC*, November 1956, p. 26.

71. Author's interview with Dr. Michael Heyrovský, March 5, 1956.

72. RFE item no. 10135/56, p. 2, Open Society.

Notes to Chapter IV: Poznań Uprising

1. *Breaking the Barrier: The Rise of Solidarity in Poland*, by Lawrence Goodwyn, Oxford University Press, 1991, p. 53.

2. Many of the facts in this section preliminary to the strike and uprising are taken from *A Case History of Hope* by Flora Lewis, Doubleday, New York, 1958.

3. Most of the facts in this section on the build-up to the strike were taken from *Breaking the Barrier: The Rise of Solidarity in Poland* by Lawrence Goodwyn, Oxford University Press, 1991.

4. Unless otherwise indicated, the facts in the following pages are taken from *Poznański Czerwiec 1956* by Jaroslaw Maciejeński and Zofia Trojanowiczowa, Poznań, 1986, sections of which were translated for the author by Kasia and Stephen Jerzak-Larsen.

5. *Poznański Czerwiec w Świadomości i Historii*, Wydawnictwo WiS, Poznań, 1996, translated for the author by Katarzyna Hegemajer, p. 111.

6. From pictures purchased by the author in July 1956 from German business-men who had taken them.

7. Foreign Service dispatch no 21, July 11, 1956 from Oslo to Department of State quoting a returning eyewitness. 748.00/7-2856, National Archives, College Park, Maryland.

8. *Poznański Czerwiec w Świadomości i Historii*, Wydawnictwo, WiS, Poznań 1996, translated for the author by Katarzyna Hegemajer, p. 113.

9. Author's interview with Aleksandra Banasiak, Poznań, Oct. 5, 1996.

10. Author's interview with Andrzej Górny, Poznań, October 4, 1996.

11. Author's interview with Andrzej Górny, Poznań, April 1998.

12. Author's interview with Aleksandra Banasiak, Poznań, Oct. 5, 1996.

13. Ibid.

14. Ibid.

15. Author's interview with Andrzej Górny, Poznań Oct. 4, 1996

16. U.S. Dept. of State, Office of the Secretary, Memorandum of Conversation, June 28, 1956, National Security Archive, Record 66091, George Washington University, Washington, D.C.

17. From an RFE Polish language broadcast at 21:00 hours, Aug. 4, 1956 quoting Kaczmarek who had fled to West Germany via Sweden three weeks after the events.

18. From a Polish language broadcast by the chief of RFE's Polish desk, Jan Nowak, on June 29, 1956, translated for the author by Katarzyna Hegemajer.

19. Author's interview with Jan Wieczorek, Poznań, Oct. 5, 1996

20. From a Polish-language broadcast by the popular writer Tadeusz Nowa-kowski, June 29, 1956, translated for the author by Katarzyna Hegemajer.

21. Author's interview with Aleksandra Banasiak, Poznań, Oct. 5, 1996.

22. Unless otherwise indicated, all incidents and quotations are taken from the chapter "Krajobraz po Czerwcu" by Zofia Trojanowiczowa, pp. 35-56 in *Poznański Czerwiec w Świadomości i Historii.*

23. Author's interview with Pawel Machcewicz, Warsaw, June 1997.

24. *A Case History of Hope*, Flora Lewis, Doubleday, N.Y, 1958, p. 168.

25. Ibid., p. 170.

26. British Warsaw Embassy dispatch no. 153, July 31, 1956 from Ambassador A.N. Noble to Foreign Office, Public Records Office, Kew Gardens, London

27. *A Case History of Hope,* p. 173.

Notes to Chapter V: The Petőfi Circle

1. *The European Right,* Hans Rogger and Eugene Weber, eds., "Hungary" by István Deák, University of California Press, 1965, p. 372.

2. *Hungary and the Soviet Bloc* by Charles Gati, chap. 4, Duke University Press, Durham 1965.

3. *The European Right,* pp. 267-68.

4. *Hungary and the Soviet Bloc*, Table 3.1, Communist Party Membership in Eastern Europe, 1944 to 1948, p. 82.

5. *Hungary and the Soviet Bloc*, p. 132.

6. Ibid., pp. 135-36.

7. *The Petőfi Circle: Forum of Reform in 1956* by András B. Hegedűs, *The Journal of Communist Studies and Transition Politics*, Vol.13, June 1987, #2, Frank Cass, London.

8. *Uprising*, David Irving, Veritas Publishing Co., Bullbrook, Western Australia, 1981, p. 169.

9. Ibid., p. 170.

10. Ibid., p. 171.

11. Unless otherwise indicated, all quotations and exchanges are taken from the official minutes of the June 27 meeting by András B. Hegedűs and translated for the author by Ms. Rita DiFiore-Czipczer.

12. *Uprising*, p. 173.

13. *The Petőfi Circle: The Forum of Reform in 1956*, pp. 124-27.

14. From a special briefing given to Radio Free Europe officials on July 5 1956 by *TIME* correspondent Simon Bourgin, Open Society Archive, Budapest.

15. Ibid.

16. *Uprising*, p. 174.

Notes to Chapter VI: Chronology

1. *Balloon Leaflets: Operations of Free Europe Press, 1954–1956* by Howard S. Weaver, Free Europe Press, April 1958.

2. *Foreign Relations of the United States* (FRUS) 1956, pp. 119, 120.

3. *FRUS*, 1956, pp. 124-25.

4. Harrison Salisbury dispatch to *The New York. Times,* Moscow, March 17, 1956.

5. Confidential Telegram no. 341, U.S. Legation, Budapest, to Department of State, March 15, 1956, 764.00/3 – 1556, National Archives, College Park, Maryland.

6. Department of State Press Release no. 140, March 16, 1956.

7. "The Truth about Overflights: Military Reconnaisance Missions over Russia before the U-2, One of the Cold War's Best Kept Secrets," by B. Cargill Hall, *Military History Quarterly* 9 (3), Spring 1997, p. 36.

8. Summary of Discussion, March 23, 1956, 280th meeting of the NSC (National Security Council) March 22, 1956 A.W.F. NSC Series, Dwight D. Eisenhower Papers as President, Box 7, Eisenhower Library, Abilene, Kansas

9. RFE/FEP Special Guidance 26: XXth Congress CPSU, March 24, 1956, Stalin, Joseph, Allen W. Dulles Papers, Box 72, Seeley Mudd Library, Princeton University.

10. "S" Restricted Dispatch, British Embassy, Warsaw, to Foreign Office, April 24, 1956, FO371/122589, Public Records Office, Kew Gardens, London.

11. Confidential Dispatch 372, U.S. Embassy, Warsaw, to Department of State, April 13, 1956, National Archives.

12. *News from Behind the Iron Curtain (NFBIC)* May 1956, p. 43.

13. *FRUS*, 1956, p. 132.

14. *NFBIC,* May 1956 p. 48.

15. Ibid., p. 42.

16. Confidential Telegram 383, U.S. Legation, Budapest, to Department of State, April 26, 1956, National Archives.

17. Reuters dispatch from Prague, April 2, 1956, author's private collection.

18. *NFBIC,* May 1956, p. 48.

19. MTI (Hungarian Press Agency) dispatch from Budapest in English, April 4, 1956, author's private collection.

20. *NFBIC,* May, 1956, p. 48.

21. *The New York Times*, London, April 8, 1956.

22. *NFBIC*, May 1956, p. 17.

23. Dispatch no 2448, U.S. Embassy, Bonn to Department of State, June 5, 1956, National Archives.

24. *FRUS*, 1956, p. 141.

25. Ibid., p. 147.

26. U.S. CIA "Purge of Stalinism," a speech given by Allen W. Dulles before the Los Angeles World Affairs Council, April 13, 1956.

27. Confidential Foreign Service dispatch 378, U.S. Embassy, Warsaw, to Dept. of State, April 17, 1956, National Archives, College Park, MD.

28. Confidential "S" telegram no. 1072/56 British Embassy, Prague, to Foreign Office, April 25, 1956 FO371/ 122141, Public Records Office.

29. *NFBIC,* May 1956, pp. 50-51.

30. *The New York Times*, Moscow, April 14, 1956.

31. Ibid., April 15, 1956.

32. *NFBIC*, May 1956, p. 48.

33. Ibid., p. 42.

34. *The New York Times*, London, April 18, 1956.

35. *FRUS,* 1956, p. 151.

36. Confidential "S" no. 64, British Embassy, Prague, to Foreign Office, April 18, 1956, Public Records Office.

37. Confidential Telegram 884, U.S. Embassy, Warsaw, to Dept. of State, May 28, 1956, National Archives.

38. *NFBIC,* June 1956 p. 44.

39. Confidential Dispatch 379, U.S. Embassy, Prague, to Dept. of State, April 26, 1956, National Archives.

40. *The New York Times,* London, April 28, 1956.

41. *FRUS*, 1956, p. 155.

42. *NFBIC,* June 1956, p. 44.

43. *Mladá Frontá*, April 28, 1956.

44. Coded Message #13/XXII from Soviet Embassy, Budapest, to Soviet Central Committee in Moscow, April 29, 1956, Presidential Archives of the Russian Federation, Moscow.

45. *NFBIC,* June 1956, p. 55.

46. *FRUS*, 1956, p. 161.

47. Limited Official Use Dispatch 498, U.S. Embassy Prague to Dept. of State, May 5, 1956, National Archives.

48. Sydney Gruson, *The New York Times*, Warsaw, May 6, 1956.

49. Confidential "S" Dispatch 93, British Embassy, Warsaw, to Foreign Office, May 8, 1956 FO371/122588, Public Records Office.

50. "The Truth about Overflights: Military Reconnaissance Missions over Russia before the U-2, One of the Cold War's Best Secrets," p. 37.

51. *NFBIC,* June 1956, p. 52.

52. Confidential Dispatch 506, U.S. Embassy, Prague, to Dept. of State. 10, 1956, National Archives.

53. *NFBIC,* June 1956, p. 55.

54. Ibid., p. 56.

55. *Szabad Nép*, May 11, 1956.

56. *NFBIC*, July 1956 p. 40.

57. Ibid., p. 49.

58. Dispatch from Moscow to *The New York Times,* May 15, 1956.

59. Limited Official Use Telegram 515, U.S. Embassy, Prague, to Dept. of State, May 14, 1956, National Archives.

60. Cypher/OTP 621, British Embassy, Moscow to Foreign Office, May 14, 1956, FOP371/122068, Public Records Office.

61. Cypher/OTP 624, British Embassy, Moscow to Foreign Office, May 15, 1956, Public Records Office.

62. *NFBIC,* June, 1956, p. 46.

63. *Béke és Szabadság*, May 16, 1956.

64. *FRUS*, 1956, p. 154; *NFBIC,* June 1956, p. 54.

65. *FRUS*, 1956, p. 163.

66. Confidential Dispatch 1012, British Embassy, Warsaw, to Foreign Office, May 18, 1956 FO371/1222589, Public Records Office.

67. *NFBIC*, July 1956, p. 45.

68. *FRUS*, 1956 pp. 168-69.

69. "The Truth about Overflights," p. 38.

70. *FRUS*, 1956, pp. 172-74.

71. *The New York Times*, Moscow, June 2, 1956.

72. *NFBIC,* July 1956, p. 47.

73. *Gentleman Spy: The Life of Allen Dulles*, Peter Grose, Houghton Mifflin, N.Y. 1994, p. 424.

74. U.S. Department of State Information Memorandum, Secret Staff Summary, "Soviet Flashpoints" Seeley G. Mudd Manuscript Library, Princeton University.

75. U.S. Department of State Information Memorandum, June 5, 1956, National Security Archive record 65309, George Washington University, Washington, D.C.

76. Foreign Office Confidential Memorandum, June 5, 1956, FO371/122068, Public Records Office.

77. FSO Dispatch 424, U.S. Embassy, Prague, to Dept. of State, June 7, 1956, National Archives.

78. *Radio Free Europe*, Robert T. Holt, University of Minnesota Press, Minneapolis, 1958, p. 94.

79. *NFBIC,* July 1956, pp. 46-47.

80. Department of State Press Release 314, June 12, 1956.

81. Limited Official Use Telegram 571, U.S. Embassy, Prague, to Dept. of State, June 15, 1956, also Limited Official Use Telegram 576 of June 17, 1956, National Archives.

82. Limited Official Use Telegram 576, U.S. Embassy, Prague, to Department of State, June 17, 1956, National Archives.

83. Confidential "S" (1012/19/6) British Embassy, Warsaw, to Foreign Office, June 19, 1956, Public Records Office.

84. *NFBIC,* Aug 1956, pp. 45, 47.

85. Ibid., p. 46.

86. Ibid., p. 46.

87. *FRUS*, Eastern Europe, 1956, p. 176.

88. *Executive Sessions of the Senate Foreign Relations Committee*, 1956 p. 503.

89. Dept. of State Memorandum of Conversation, June 28, 1956, Secretary of State, John Foster Dulles, National Security Archive, record 66091, George Washingon University, Washington, D.C.

90. Memo of Conversation, Dept, of State, Office of the Secretary, June 29, 1956, National Security Archive, record 66089.

91. *FRUS*, 1956, p. 184.

92. Confidential Telegram to the Secretary of State, 22, U.S. Embassy, Prague, July 12, 1956 511.49/7/1256, National Archives.

93. U.S. National Security Council, "East-West Cultural Exchange," Memo of conversation, William H. Jackson, June 29, 1956, record 64537, National Security Archive, George Washington University, Washington, D.C.

94. *NFBIC,* August 1956, p. 44.

95. 84th Congress, 2nd Session, House Resolution 574, July 3, 1956.

96. NSC 5608; *FRUS*, pp. 191-194.

97. *FRUS*, 1956, p. 195.

98. Confidential Letter, British Embassy, Belgrade, to Foreign Office, July 7, 1956, FO 371/122676, Public Records Office, London.

99. Annex to NSC 5608; *FRUS*, pp. 198-209.

100. *NFBIC,* August, 1956, p. 42.

101. Limited Official Use Telegram 17, U.S. Embassy, Prague, to Dept. of State, July 10, 1956, National Archives.

102. Confidential "S" Dispatch 148, British Embassy, Warsaw, to Foreign Office, July 24, 1956, FO371/122589, Public Records Office, London.

103. Memo of Conversation, 5:26 P.M., Office of the Secretary, U.S. Department of State, July 10, 1956, National Security Archive.

104. *NFBIC,* Sept. 1956, p. 40.

105. Minutes of the National Security Council July 12, 1956 meeting, National Security Archive record 66035, George Washington University, Washington, D.C.

106. Telegram 52, U.S, Embassy, Prague, to Dept. of State, July 14, 1956, National Archives.

107. *NFBIC,* Sept. 1956, p. 47.

108. *Wiener Wochenliche* 29, July 19, 1956.

109. Foreign Service Dispatch 23, U.S. Embassy, Prague, to Department of State, July 17, 1956, National Archives.

110. Confidential Dispatch 1338/10/56, British Embassy, Washington, to Foreign Office, July 27, 1956, Public Records Office.

111. Limited Official Use Priority Telegram 31, U.S. Legation, Budapest, to Dept, of State, July 19, 1956 National Archives, also *FRUS*, 1956, p. 223.

112. Auswertiges Amt (For. Office) "Note Verbale" U.S. Telegram 87, U.S. Embassy, Prague, to Dept. of State, July 19, 1956, National Archives.

113. Confidential telegram (via pouch) no 336, U.S. Embassy, Paris to Dept. of State, July 19, 1956, National Archives.

114. *FRUS*, 1956, pp. 225-26.

115. Confidential "S" Dispatch 1051/56, British Embassy, Prague, to Foreign Office, July 24, 1956, FO371/122145, Public Records Office.

116. Limited Official Use Telegram 31, U.S. Legation, Budapest, to Dept. of State, July 19, 1956, National Archives.

117. Limited Official Telegram no 93, U.S. Embassy, Warsaw, to Dept. of State, July 27, 1956, National Archives.

118. *Szabad Nép*, July 23, 1956.

119. *NFBIC,* September 1956, p. 40.

120. Senate Joint Resolution 201, July 23, 1956.

121. *NFBIC,* Sept. 1956, p. 54.

122. Limited Official Use Telegram 99, U.S. Embassy, Warsaw, to Dept. of State, July 24, 1956, National Archives.

123. NSC Operations Coordinating Board memorandum, July 27, 1956, National Security Archive, record no 64490, George Washington University, Washington, D.C.

124. *NFBIC,* Sept. 1956, p. 43.

125. Official Use Only Telegram 46 U.S. Embassy, Prague, to Dept. of State, July 31, 1956, National Archives.

126. *NFBIC,* Sept. 1956, p. 46.

127. White House Memorandum of Record, President–Senator Bush Appointment, Aug. 1, 1956, Dwight D. Eisenhower Library, Abilene, Kansas.

128. *NFBIC,* September 1956, p. 49.

129. Confidential Dispatch 164, British Embassy, Warsaw, to Foreign Office, Aug. 5, 1956, Public Records Office.

130. Official Use Only Telegram 166, U.S. Embassy, Warsaw, to Dept. of State, Aug. 9, 1956, National Archives.

131. *FRUS*, 1956, p. 230.

132. *Trybuna Opolska*, Aug. 9, 1956, also *Times* of London, Aug. 27, 1956.

133. *Gentleman Spy,* p. 429.

134. Ibid., p. 430.

135. Confidential Telegram 200, U.S. Embassy, Warsaw, to Dept. of State, Aug. 14, 1956, National Archives.

136. *NFBIC,* Oct. 1956, p. 54.

137. Ibid., p. 51.

138. Ibid., p. 49.

139. *Gentelman Spy,* p. 430.

140. *NFBIC,* Oct. 1956, p. 56.

141. Ibid., p. 50.

142. Limited Official Use Telegram 237, U.S. Embassy, Warsaw, to Dept. of State, Aug. 25, 1956, National Archives.

143. *Trybuna Ludu.* Aug. 25, 1956.

144. *NFBIC,* Oct. 1956, p. 44.

145. *FRUS,* 1956, p. 232.

146. Ibid., p. 242.

147. RFE Stockholm correspondent, Items C-83 & C-84, Central Newsroom, Sept. 4, 1956, author's private collection.

148. PAP (Polish Press Agency) via radio teletype, Warsaw, Sept. 6, 1956, author's private collection.

149. *FRUS,* 1956, p. 243.

150. *NFBIC,* Oct. 1956, pp. 44-45.

151. Reuters Dispatch, Warsaw, Sept. 6, 1956, author's private collection.

152. *The Daily Worker* (NYC), Warsaw, Sept. 11, 1956.

153. *NFBIC,* Nov. 1956, p. 44.

154. Dept. of State, Secret Staff Summary, Sept 14, 1956, CIA and Embassy, National Security Archive Record 65217, also *NFBIC,* Oct. 1956, p.52.

155. *Trybuna Ludu,* Sept. 13, 1956.

156. Air Force Memorandum, Folder 15, Box 121, Series 7 (Memorabilia) Papers of Allen W. Dulles, Seeley Mudd Library, Princeton University.

157. *The New York Times*, Sept. 17, 1956.

158. RFE Analysis based on Hungarian Press Summary, Central Newsroom items C-160 & D-31, Sept. 17, 1956, author's private collection.

159. *NFBIC,* Nov. 1956, p. 36.

160. *NFBIC,* Oct. 1956, p. 56.

161. RFE Polish language monitoring, Sept. 20, 1956, author's private collection.

162. Foreign Service Dispatch 533, U.S. Embassy, Bonn, to Dept. of State, Sept 14, 1956, National Archives.

163. Form letter from Secretary of U.S. Delegation to North Atlantic Council, Melvin L. Mansfull, Sept. 21, 1956, FO371/122141, Public Records Office.

164. TASS dispatch, Moscow, Sept. 22, 1956, author's private collection.

165. Reuters dispatch, Copenhagen, Sept. 22, 1956, author's private collection.

166. Reuters dispatch, London, Sept. 23, 1956, author's private collection.

167. United Press dispatch, Passau, Bavaria, Sept. 23, 1956, author's private collection.

168. Associated Press dispatch, Moscow, Sept. 23, 1956, author's private collection.

169. United States Information Service (USIS), Vienna, Sept. 23, 1956, author's private collection.

170. Reuters dispatch, Warsaw, Sept. 24, 1956, author's private collection.

171. Agence France Presse, Budapest, Sept. 24, 1956, author's private collection.

172. USIS, Bonn, Sept. 24, 1956, author's private collection.

173. Reuters dispatch, Moscow, Sept. 24, 1956, author's private collection.

174. Various wire service reports from Warsaw, Sept. 25, 1956, author's private collection.

175. MTI (Hungarian Press Agency), Budapest, Sept. 25, 1956, author's private collection.

176. Various wire service reports from Copenhagen, Sept. 25, 1956, author's private collection.

177. RFE Special Dispatch from Eric Gedye in Vienna (in German), Sept. 25, 1956, author's private collection.

178. Reuters dispatch, Berlin, Sept. 25, 1956, author's private collection.

179. *New York Herald Tribune*, New York, Sept. 25, 1956.

180. Reuters dispatch from Stockholm, Sept 25, 1956, author's private collection.

181. (NYC) *The Daily Worker*, dispatch from Warsaw, Sept. 24, 1956.

182. TASS dispatch from Budapest, Sept. 26, 1956, author's private collection.

183. CETEKA radio teletype dispatch in English from Prague, Sept. 26, 1956, author's private collection.

184. British Foreign Office, Sept. 26, 1956, 371/122587, Public Records Office.

185. Religious News Service, Geneva, October 1956, author's private collection.

Notes to Chapter VII: Rajk Reburial

1. RFE Central News Room item C-140, Oct. 6, 1956, Open Society Archives, Budapest.

2. *Szabad Nép*, September 20, 1956, translated for the author by Ms. Rita DiFiore-Czipczer.

3. Own Correspondent, *Times*, London, Vienna, October 7, 1956.

4. Associated Press, Budapest, as carried in the *The New York Times*, October 7, 1956.

5. Author's interview with László Rajk, Jr., October 28, 1999.

6. Ibid.

7. Author's interview with Dr. György Litván, October 30, 1999.

8. Gavro Altman in *Borba,* Belgrade, October 6, 1956, RFE translation, October 11, 1956, Gen. Desk item C-94, Open Society Archives, Budapest.

9. Author's interview with László Rajk, Jr.

10. RFE Research and Evaluation Section, Background Report, p. 1, October 12, 1956, Open Society Archives, Budapest.

11. Author's interview with György Litván.

12. RFE Research and Evaluation section, Background Report, pp. 6-8, October 12, 1956, Open Society Archives, Budapest.

13. Gavro Altman, Borba, Belgrade, October 8, 1956.

Notes to Chapter VIII: Poznań Trials

1. Foreign Service Dispatch 288 from U.S. Embassy, Warsaw, to Department of State, Sept. 11, 1956 748. 00/9 – 1156, National Archives, College Park, Maryland.

2. Restricted Dispatch (1641/28/9) from British Embassy, Warsaw, to Foreign Office, Sept. 28, 1956, FO371/122567, Public Records Office, Kew Gardens, London.

3. Inward Saving Telegram 662, British Embassy, Washington, to Foreign Office, Sept 28, 1956 748.00/ 9 – 2856, Public Records Office, Kew Gardens, London.

4. *A Case History of Hope*, Flora Lewis, Doubleday, N.Y., 1958, pp. 175-176.

5. Confidential Dispatch 175 (NP. 1015/8) British Embassy, Warsaw, to Foreign Office, July 30, 1956 FO371/12287, Public Records Office, Kew Gardens, London.

6. Confidential Dispatch 517 (NP 1015/8) British Embassy, Warsaw, to Foreign Office, August 1, 1956, FO371/122587, Public Records Office, Kew Gardens, London.

7. Confidential Telegram 274, U.S. Embassy, Warsaw, to Dept. of State, Sept. 6, 1956, 748.00/9 – 0656, National Archives, College Park, Maryland.

8. White House press release by James C. Hagerty, Sept. 26, 1956 371/ 122587, National Archives, College Park, Maryland.

9. Reuter's news dispatch, New York, Oct. 7, 1956.

10. *A Case History of Hope*, p. 174.

11. Ibid., p. 182.

12. Ibid., p. 187.

13. Reuter's dispatch from Poznań, Sept. 26, 1956.

14. *Trybuna Ludu*, 285, Oct. 12, 1956 (translated by British Embassy).

15. Confidential Telegram (NP 1015/14) Foreign Office re F.O. telegram 457 to British Embassy, Warsaw, Sept. 19, 1956 FO371/122587, Public Records Office, London.

16. RFE monitoring of Radio Warsaw II, Oct. 4, 1956, RFE Central Newsroom item C-181, Oct. 5, 1956, author's private collection.

17. Confidential "S" Telegram (1641/9/10) British Embassy, Warsaw, to Foreign Office, Oct. 9, 1956, p. 1, FO371/122587 Public Records Office, London.

18. Sidney Gruson report to *The New York Times* from Poznań, Oct. 4, 1956, and Philippe Ben report from Poznań to *Le Monde*, Oct. 4, 1956, author's private collection.

19. Philippe Ben report to *Le Monde*, Oct. 3, 1956, author's private collection.

20. Sidney Gruson report to *The New York Times* from Poznań, Oct. 4, 1956, author's private collection, and Confidential "S" telegram (1641/9/10) British Embassy to Foreign Office, Oct. 9, 1956, FO371/122587, Public Records Office, London.

21. Confidential "S" telegram (1641/9/10) British Embassy to Foreign Office, Oct. 9, 1956, FO371/122587, Public Records Office, London, p. 2.

22. Sidney Gruson report to *The New York Times* from Poznań, Oct. 4, 1956.

23. Confidential "S" telegram, p. 3.

24. *A Case History of Hope*, pp. 190-191.

25. Gordon Cruickshank report to the London *Daily Worker*, Oct. 4, 1956, author's private collection.

26. *A Case History of Hope*, pp. 192-193.

27. Ibid., p. 192.

28. Confidential "S" telegram, p. 4.

29. Ibid.

30. Philippe Ben report from Poznań to *Le Monde,* Oct. 3, 1956, author's private collection.

31. *A Case History of Hope*, p. 191.

32. Confidential "S" telegram, p. 4.

33. Ibid., p. 5.

34. Dept. of Air Force memo, April 17, 1956, Series 7, "Memorabilia," Box 121, Folder 15, Allen W. Dulles Papers, Mudd Library, Princeton University. Also, *Gentleman Spy*, p. 433.

35. *Poznański Czerwiec 1956* by Jaroslaw Maciejewski and Zofia Trojanowiczowa, Wydawnictwo Poznańskie, Poznań, 1990, excerpts from pp. 391-396, translated for the author by Katarzyna Hagemajer.

36. Ibid., excerpts from pp. 396-404.

37. Confidential "S" telegram, p. 5.

38. *A Case History of Hope*, p. 190.

39. British Foreign Office Northern Department's "Report on Poznań Trials" (NP1015/27) Oct. 16, 1956 FO371/122587, Public Documents Office, London.

40. Confidential "S" telegram (1641/4/12) British Embassy to Foreign Office, Dec. 4, 1956 FO371/122587, Public Documents Office, London.

41. For a heartrending account of one mother of one of the prisoners still held in late October, 1956, see "Appendix to Chapter VIII."

Notes to Chapter IX: The Polish October

1. *A Case History of Hope*, Flora Lewis, Doubleday, N.Y., 1958, p. 193.

2. *Foreign Relations of the United States*, Vol. XXV, Eastern Europe, pp. 247-249.

3. *A Case History of Hope*, p. 199.

4. Ibid., p. 198.

5. *Khrushchev Remembers: The Last Testament*, translated and edited by Strobe Talbott, Little Brown, Boston, 1974, p. 198.

6. *Cold War International History Project Bulletin*, issues 8-9, Winter 1996-97, Mark Kramer, "New Evidence on Soviet Decision-Making and the 1956 Polish and Hungarian Crises," p. 360.

7. *Cold War International History Project Bulletin*, issue 5, Spring 1995, "Khrushchev, Gomułka and the Polish October," by L. W. Głuchowski, pp. 38-39.

8. Ibid., p. 39.

9. *A Case History of Hope*, p. 200.

10. *Khrushchev Remembers*, pp. 119-200.

11. *War on the Airways*, Jan Nowak, unpublished, 2001, pp. 513-14:

> Before Ben was sent to Warsaw by *Le Monde* in June 1956, he often visited us in Munich to take advantage of our information, assessments, and materials in the Research Department.
>
> Even before the October crisis, I made a secret agreement with Ben. It was clear to me that, in addition to the whole array of sources, he must have had a close contact from prewar years in the highest rungs of the ruling elite. This person was probably a member of the Central Committee, perhaps one of the secretaries of the Central Committee representing the 'liberals.' Ben knew about everything that was going on within the party leadership, as well as between Moscow and Warsaw. Of course, he could not publish everything that reached him under his own name because he would have gotten booted out of Poland. My secret agreement with Ben was that every day he would call the private number of our London office secretary between 10:00 and 11:00 in the evening. He would dictate to her in English. She would then pass on the first part by teletype to the editorial desk of *Maariv* in Tel Aviv. The second, much longer part she would pass on the same way to our newsroom. Besides me and one of my Polish asistants, absolutely no one else knew who sent the telegrams.

12. *A Case History of Hope*, p. 203.

13. *War on the Airways*, p. 520.

14. *A Case History of Hope*, p. 203.

15. Philippe Ben dispatch from Warsaw to *Le Monde*, Oct. 20, 1956, Central Newsroom (CNR) item C-216, author's private collection.

16. *A Case History of Hope,* p. 210.

17. Philippe Ben Dispatch from Warsaw to *Le Monde*, Oct. 20, 1956, RFE CNR item C-216, author's private collection.

18. *A Case History of Hope* p. 210.

19. Głuchowski, p. 40.

20. Philippe Ben dispatch to *Maariv*, Israel, from Warsaw, Oct. 21, 1956, RFE CNR item C-47, author's private collection.

21. *A Case History of Hope*, pp. 209-10.

22. To this day Warsovians will advise you that you will get the very best view of Warsaw from the top of the Palace of Science and Culture, not because it is the tallest building and is in the center of Warsaw, but because it is the *only* place in Warsaw where you *cannot* see the Palace of Science and Culture.

Shortly after the palace's completion in 1955, the following joke swept Poland:

> A man goes to his tailor to have a suit made. The tailor's shop is shut with only a note saying: "Gone away for an indefinite period." When he tries his friends' tailors he finds the same thing has happened. When he complains to a friend the friend says, "Sh–sh–sh—Haven't you heard?"
>
> "Haven't I heard what?"
>
> "An emergency has been declared. All the tailors of Warsaw have been drafted into a secret project. They are all out at some secret place in the countryside."
>
> "Why?" asks the man. "What are they doing?"
>
> "They are making a giant SLIPCOVER for the Palace of Science and Culture!"

23. *A Case History of Hope*, p. 211.

24. Głuchowski, p. 38.

25. *Khrushchev Remembers*, pp. 203-4.

26. Ibid., p. 204.

27. *War on the Airways*, pp. 525-26.

28. *A Case History of Hope*, p. 201.

29. Ibid., p. 214.

30. Ibid., p. 213.

31. Ibid., p. 214.

32. Głuchowski, pp. 40-41.

33. *A Case History of Hope*, pp. 215-16.

34. Philippe Ben dispatch from Warsaw to *Le Monde*, October 22, 1956, RFE CNR item D-71, author's private collection.

35. *A Case History of Hope*, p. 216.

36. Ibid., p. 217.

37. Głuchowski, 42.

38. *War on the Airways*, p. 526.

39. *A Case History of Hope*, 217.

40. Głuchowski, p. 43.

41. *Khrushchev Remembers*, p. 204.

42. Głuchowski, p. 45.

43. *A Case History of Hope*, p. 218.

44. Philippe Ben dispatch from Warsaw to *The Daily Mail*, London, Oct. 22, 1956, RFE CNR item C-49, author's private archive.

45. *A Case History of Hope*, p. 219.

46. Author's telephone conversation with Jan Nowak, January 20, 2001.

47. *War on the Airways*, pp. 529-30.

48. J. Nowak, RFE script, Oct. 18, 1956, RFE CNR item B-99, author's private collection.

49. J. Nowak, RFE script, October 20, 1956, RFE CNR items D-85 and D-87, author's private collection.

50. United Press dispatch from Warsaw, October 20, 1956, RFE CNR item D-14, author's private collection.

51. *A Case History of Hope*, p. 220.

52. *National Communism and Popular Revolt in Eastern Europe*, edited by Paul E. Zinner, Columbia University Press, 1956, p. 221.

53. Ibid., p. 208.

54. Ibid., p. 226.

55. Ibid., p. 227.

56. Ibid., pp. 236-37.

57. Ibid., p. 238.

58. Philippe Ben dispatch from Warsaw to *Le Monde*, October 22, 1956, RFE CNR item D-73, author's private collection.

59. "Before appointing Rokossovsky we told the Poles we would give them one of our experienced generals as Minister of Defense. And we decided to give them one of the best—Rokossovsky. True, he spoke Polish badly, stressing the wrong syllables. He wasn't happy about going there, but it was very important for us that he be there, that he put everything in order. After all, we knew nothing about them." (Vasili Molotov, in *Molotov Remembers, Inside Kremlin Politics, Conversations with Felix Chuev*, edited by Alfred Resis, University of Chicago Press, Ivan R. Dee, 1993, p. 54.)

60. *A Case History of Hope*, pp. 223-29.

61. Kramer, p. 361.

62. Delgado Message, marked "FYI Not for Broadcast." RFE CNR item P and P1, October 21, 1956, author's private collection.

63. *Pravda*, Oct. 19, 1956, p. 1.

64. RFE Polish Language Monitoring, CNR item B-50, October 21, 1956, author's private collection.

65. Głuchowski, p. 45.

66. RFE Polish Language Monitoring, CNR item B-57, October 21, 1956, author's private collection.

67. *A Case History of Hope,* p. 224.

68. Philippe Ben dispatch from Warsaw to *The Daily Mail*, London October 22, 1956, RFE CNR item C-48, author's private collection.

69. Philippe Ben dispatch from Warsaw to *The Daily Mail,* London, October 22, 1956, RFE CNR item D-74, author's private collection.

70. *A Case History of Hope*, p. 213.

71. United Press dispatch from Vienna, October 20, 1956, author's private collection.

72. Reuters dispatch from Stockholm, October 20, 1956, author's private collection.

73. International New Service dispatch from Berlin, October 22, 1956, author's private collection.

74. Reuters dispatch from Manchester, England, October 22, 1956, author's private collection.

75. Sidney Gruson dispatch from Warsaw to *The New York Times*, Otober 22, 1956, RFE CNR items D-54 & D-57, author's private collection.

76. *War on the Airways*, pp. 552-53.

77. Ibid., p. 537.

78. Ibid., p. 534.

79. RFE CNR item D-44, October 2, 1956, author's private collection.

80. *War on the Airways*, p. 539.

81. Kramer, p. 361.

82. *A Case History of Hope,* p.229.

Notes to the Epilogue

1. Kramer, p. 361.

2. *Khrushchev Remembers*, p. 205.

3. *War on the Airways*, p. 543.

4. Associated Press dispatch from Washington, October 22, 1956, RFE CNR item D-12, author's private collection.

5. Joseph Harsch's dispatch from Washington to *The Christian Science Monitor*, October 21. 1956, RFE CNR item D-44 (on October 22) author's private collection.

6. Ibid., D-42.

7. Restricted dispatch from British ambassador, Sir William Hayter, British Embassy, Moscow, to Foreign Office, June 4, 1956, FO371/122068, Public Records Office, Kew Gardens, London. Also confidential minutes by G. G. Brown of a Foreign Office meeting, June 5, 1956, Public Records Office.

8. Kramer, p. 368.

9. *East Europe* magazine 6 (3), March 1957, pp. 52-53.

Bibliography

Albright, Joseph and Marcia Kunstel, *Bombshell: The Secret Story of America's Unknown Atom Spy Conspiracy* (New York: Times Books, Random House, 1997).

Andrew, Christopher, and Vasili Mitrokhin, *The Sword and Shield: The Mitrokhin Archives and the History of the KGB* (New York: Basic Books, 1999).

Bain, Leslie B., *The Reluctant Satellites* (New York: Macmillan, 1960).

Cold War International History Project Bulletin (Washington, D.C.: Woodrow Wilson International Center for Scholars).

Conquest, Robert, *Stalin: The Breaker of Nations* (New York: Viking, 1991).

——— *The Great Terror: A Reassessment* (University of Alberta Press, 1990).

Foreign Relations of the United States (Washington, D.C.: Department of State, 1957).

Gaddis, John Lewis, *We Now Know: Re-Thinking Cold War History* (Oxford: Claredon Press, 1997).

Gati, Charles, *Hungary and the Soviet Bloc* (Durham, N.C.: Duke University Press, 1965).

Goodwyn, Lawrence, *Breaking the Barrier: The Rise of Solidarity in Poland* (Oxford: Oxford University Press, 1991).

Grose, Peter, *Gentleman Spy: The Life of Allen Dulles* (New York: Houghton-Mifflin, 1994).

Hegedűs, András B., *The Petőfi Circle: Forum of Reform in 1956*, The Journal of Communist Studies, Frank Cass, London 1987.

Held, Joseph, *The Columbia History of Eastern Europe in the Twentieth Century* (New York: Columbia University Press, 1992).

Holt, Robert T., *Radio Free Europe* (Minneapolis: University of Minnesota Press, 1958).

Irving, David, *Uprising* (Bullbrook, W. Australia: Veritas, 1981).

Isaacs, Jeremy and Taylor Downing, *Cold War* (London: Transworld Publications, Ltd., 1998).

Bibliography

Kellen, Konrad, *Khrushchev: A Political Portrait* (New York: Praeger, 1961).

Khrushchev, Nikita, *Khrushchev Remembers*, trans. Strobe Talbott (Boston: Little, Brown and Company, 1970).

———— *Khrushchev Remembers: The Last Testament*, trans. Strobe Talbott (Boston: Little, Brown and Company, 1974).

Kramer, Mark, "The Early Post-Stalin Succession Struggle," *Journal of Cold War Studies* (Cambridge, Mass., Autumn 1999).

Lewis, Flora, *A Case History of Hope* (New York: Doubleday, 1958).

Marchio, James David, "Rhetoric and Reality: The Eisenhower Administration and Unrest in Eastern Europe, 1953-1959," unpublished dissertation, UMI Dissertation Services, 1990.

Medvedov, Roy, *Khrushchev: A Biography* (New York: Anchor Press, Doubleday, 1984).

Nowak (Jezioranski), Jan, *War on the Airways*, unpublished book, 2001.

Osterman, Christian F., "The United States, the East German Uprising of 1953, and the Limits of Rollback," working paper 11, Cold War International History Project (Washington, D.C.: Woodrow Wilson International Center for Scholars).

Poznański Czerwiec w Świadomości i Historii, Wydawnictwo, WiS (Poznań, 1996).

Puddington, Arch, *Broadcasting Freedom: The Cold War Triumph of Radio Free Europe and Radio Liberty* (University of Kentucky Press, 2000).

Roggeer, Hans and Eugene Weber, *The European Right* (University of California Press, 1956).

Sosin, Gene, *Sparks of Liberty: An Insider's Memoir of Radio Liberty* (Pennsylvania State University Press, 1999).

Stonor-Saunders, Frances, *The Cultural Cold War: The CIA and the World of Arts and Letters*, (London: The New Press, 2000).

Stypulkowski, Zygmunt, *Invitation to Moscow* (London: Thomas and Hudson, 1951).

Tanenhaus, Sam, *Whittaker Chambers* (New York: Random House, 1997).

The Soviet Sea Around Us (Berlin: Graphische Gesellschaft Gruenewald, GmbH, 1959).

Trojanowiczowa, Zofia and Jaroslav Maciejeński, *Poznański Czerwiec 1956* (Poznań, 1986).

Urban, George R., *Radio Free Europe and the Pursuit of Democracy* (Yale Universisty Press, 1997).

Weaver, Howard S., *Balloon Leaflets: Operations of Free Europe Press, 1954-1956* (New York: Free Europe Press, April 1958).

Wolfe, Bertram D., *Khrushchev and Stalin's Ghosts* (New York: Praeger, 1957).

Zinner, Paul E., *National Communism and Popular Revolt in Eastern Europe* (Columbia University Press, 1956).

Zubok, Vladimir and Constantine Pleshakov, *Inside the Kremlin's Cold War: From Stalin to Khrushchev* (Cambridge, Mass.: Harvard University Press, 1996).

INDEX

A

Academy of Sciences (Czechoslovakia), 275
Acheson, Dean, 45
Aczél, Tamás, 178
Adam Mickiewicz University, 126
Adenauer, Konrad, 51
"Affair of the Doctor-Plotters," 15, 47
Air Force, U.S., 44, 169, 191-92
A.K. *See* Home Army (Armia Krajowa) (Poland)
Albrecht, Jerzy, 135
ALES (Hiss code name), 31
Allied Control Commision (Hungary), 143
Allied Control Council (Berlin), 41
Alsop, Joseph and Stewart, 150
Anders, Władysław, 90
Andics, Erzsébet, 147
Andropov, Yuri, 175
Animal Farm (Orwell), 52, 167
Anti-Semitism, 139-41, 143, 196
Antonov, General, 245
Apró, Antal, 210-11
Armia Krajowa. *See* Polish Home Army
Army Security Corps (Poland), 112, 114
Arrow Cross Party (Hungary), 140-41, 203
Artymowska, Zofia, 264
Ash, Timothy Garton, 2n
Association of Polish Lawyers, 177
Association of Working Youth (DISZ) (Hungary),
    145-46
Attlee, Clement, 32
Auschwitz (death camp), 32
ÁVH (Office of State Security) (Hungarian secret
    police), 147
ÁVO (Division of State Security) (Hungarian secret
    police), 142, 144, 147n, 189, 203, 210n

B

Bacílek, Karol, 69-70
Banasiak, Aleksandra, 113, 120-22, 126, 131
Barák, Rudolf, 71
Barnes, Tracy, 193
Batthyány, Lajos, 211
BBC (British Broadcasting Corporation), 37, 47, 56,
    166, 222
Béke és Szabadság (publication), 178
Belvedere Palace (Warsaw), 248, 250-56
Ben, Philippe, 222-23, 228, 242, 253, 257
Bentley, Elizabeth, 44

Beria, Lavrenty, 14, 15, 21, 48-49, 51-52, 144
Berlin, Germany, 26, 41-42, 44-45, 51
Berlin Assembly, 43
Berlin blockade, 25, 44
Berman, Jakub, 176, 195, 240
Bessenyei, György, 145
Bessenyei Circle. *See* Petőfi Circle
Betlen, Oszkár, 151
Bevin, Ernest, 37
Bible, 157
Bidault, Georges, 37
Bieniek, Tadeusz, 101, 104, 106
Bieńkowski, Władysław, 238-39
Bierut, Bolesław, 4, 57, 88, 90, 176, 240, 248
Big Four Foreign Ministers. *See* Council of Foreign
    Ministers
Biliczek group (Poznań defendants), 231
Black Madonna of Częstochowa (Poland), 193, 266
Blunt, Anthony, 29n
Board of Metal Workers Trade Unions (Poland), 95
Bognár, József, 198
Bolshoi Ballet, 197-98
Borba (newspaper), 212
Bratislava, 3
Bratislava Majáles (traditional student parade),
    66-72, 79, 177
Breda, Knut, 101
British Broadcasting Corporation. *See* BBC
British Council (arts organization), 198
British Foreign Office, 38, 172-73, 180, 222n
British Socialist Party, 160
British-Soviet Friendship Society, 197
Budapest demonstration, 201-13
Budapest University, 147
Budenz, Louis, 44
Bulczyński (Poznań defendant), 231-32
Bulganin, Nikolai, 8, 17, 53, 134-36, 171, 173,
    189-90, 197, 237
Bulgarian Communist Party, 172
Bunker, Ellsworth, 199
Burgess, Guy, 29n
Bush, Prescott, 191
Butchery Company, 100, 106
Byrnes, James (Jimmy), 36, 39

C

Cairncross, John, 29n
"Cambridge five," 29-30
Čáslavská, Vera, 83
Catholic Church. *See* Roman Catholic Church
CBS (Columbia Broadcasting System), 222, 257

Index

Index

Máté, György, 150, 157
Matyja, Stanisław, 97, 107, 118, 130
Matyjas, Bogdan, 97
Mazhiask Highway (Soviet), 13
Mazur, Franciszek, 193
Mazurkiewicz, Władysław, 218
McCarthy, Joseph, 45
McCloy, John J., 42
McCormick, Robert, 248
Mechanical Equipment Factory, 100
Mechanical Equipment Production Enterprise, 100
Méray, Tibor, 159
Mikolajczik, Stanisław, 39
Mikoyan, Anastas, 7, 8, 9, 14, 18, 20, 144n, 162,
    188-89, 218-19, 245-46, 254-55
Military Collegium of the Supreme Court (Soviet),
    13
Minc, Hilary, 176, 240
Mindszenty, József, 46, 144, 177
Ministry of Culture (Soviet), 198
Ministry of Defense (Czechoslovakia), 279
Ministry of Education (Czechoslovakia), 60, 278
Ministry of Justice (Hungary), 202, 206
Ministry of Machine Industry (Poland), 95, 97
Ministry of Produce Collection (Hungary), 184
Ministry of the Interior (Hungary), 141-43
Ministry of the Interior (Poland), 112, 122
Mladá Frontá (newspaper), 59, 62-65, 69, 79, 175
Mladá Garda (student dormitory), 68-71
Mlynska Prison, 109-10, 112, 117, 121, 123, 125,
    130, 228
MO (Civic Militia) (Poland), 234-35
Mocsár, Gábor, 153
Molnár, Erik, 186
Molotov, Vyacheslav, 7, 8, 18, 23, 27, 36, 38, 41,
    43, 48-49, 179-80, 244-46, 251, 255
Molotov-Ribbentrop Pact (1939), 27
Monde, Le (newspaper), 193, 223, 227-28, 242, 253,
    257
Morawski, Jerzy, 134, 186
Morgenthau Plan, 32
Moscow State University, 248
"Mr. X." (Kennan pseudonym), 37
Mulicz, Sergeant (Hungarian policeman), 181
Münnich, Ferenc, 211
Murphy, Robert D., 171
Mus, Włodzimierz, 262
Mussolini, Benito, 27
MVD (Soviet secret police), 48, 52

N

Nagy, Ferenc, 39, 142-43

Nagy, Imre, 52-53, 57, 141, 144-46, 150, 153,
    159-63, 175, 196, 203, 205, 208, 210
Nagy, Péter, 151
Nándorfehérvár (Belgrade), Battle of, 181
Nasser, Gamal Abdul, 1, 272
National Assembly (Czechoslovakia), 274, 276
National Committees (Czechoslovakia), 274
National Council of Polish Students, 264
National Front (Czechoslovakia), 274, 277
National Peasant Party (Hungary), 140
National Security Council (U.S.), 40, 167, 169, 178,
    184-85, 187, 190
NATO (North Atlantic Treaty Organization), 42,
    44, 53, 217
Natolin group, 237, 239-40, 252, 259, 262, 265
Nazi Germany, 27-28, 92, 140, 203, 234
Němec, Ladislav, 57-60, 62-65, 68, 71, 81-82, 279n
Nemes, György, 158-59
Népszava ("People's Word") (newspaper), 179,
    195, 212
"New Course" (Hungary), 52, 53, 144-46, 147n,
    205
New York Stock Exchange, 199
New York Times (newspaper), 66-67, 136, 180, 192,
    195, 197, 222, 257, 263
Nikolaev (Kirov's assassin), 12
Nineteenth Party Congress (Soviet), 18
NKVD (Soviet secret police), 12, 31
Nobel Prizes, 82
Noble, Andrew, 135n, 176, 178, 191, 216-17
Nógrádi, Sándor, 150, 157
Non, György, 191
North Atlantic Council, 196
North Atlantic Treaty Organization. *See* NATO
Novotný, Antonín, 4, 57, 61, 63-64, 70-71, 172,
    181, 184, 276
Nowak, Jan, 129, 257-59, 266
Nowak, Roman, 127, 240
Nowak, Zenon, 90, 135n, 190, 258
Nowakowski, Tadeusz, 131
Nowa Kultura (magazine), 92, 136
Nowe Drogi (journal), 177
Nuremberg Trials, 222
Nyugat (West) (periodical), 202

O

Ochab, Edward, 57, 91, 98, 101, 104, 107, 109, 126,
    132, 135n, 136, 171, 182, 218-19, 223, 232,
    239-41, 245-54, 259, 262
Office of Strategic Services (OSS), 40
Officers School of Army Armored and Mechanized
    Forces (Poland), 107, 119, 125

Index

Index

U.S. Air Force, 44, 169, 191-92
U.S. Congress, 37-38, 168, 184, 187, 189
U.S. Democratic Party, 194, 218
U.S. Department of State, 20, 31, 35, 38, 48, 170, 172-73, 179-80, 188, 269
U.S. National Security Council, 40, 167, 169, 178, 184-85, 187, 190
U.S. Republican Party, 191, 194
U.S. State Department, 20, 31, 35, 38, 48, 170, 172-73, 179-80, 188, 269

V

Valouch, Miloslav, 83
Vas, Zoltán, 159
Vásárhelyi, Miklós, 208
Vavřička, Stanislav, 58
Večerni Praha ("Evening Prague") (newspaper), 63, 66
Vilsvader, F., 70
Vince, Ivan, 197
Vistula River, 28, 92
Vjesnik (newspaper), 201
Vlasov, Andrei, 32
VOA (Voice of America), 4, 5, 47, 166, 172, 174, 185, 218, 222, 265
Voice of Free Poland, 258
Volek, Mrna, 68
"Volunteer Freedom Corps," 175
Voroshilov, Kliment, 21, 22, 177
Vrbican, M., 70
Vyshinsky, Andrei, 3, 31

W

W-3 (factory section), 94-97
Wachowiak, Emilia, 233n, 234-35
Wachowiak, Jacek, 233
Warsaw Council of State Building, 245, 248, 252-53, 259
Warsaw Pact, 53, 251-52, 254, 265-66, 271
Warsaw Radio. *See* Radio Warsaw
Warsaw State Council Building
Warsaw University, 243
Warsaw Uprising, 28-29, 92, 190, 256
Warta River, 93, 100
Wasilkowska, Zofia, 174
Wasylik, Lucyna, 125
Wasylik, Pawel, 125
Wasylik, Piotruś, 125
Ważyk, Adam, 92, 180
Wehrmacht (German Army), 32, 92
Wenckheim, counts of, 202

We Now Know: Rethinking Cold War History (Gaddis), 49
West Berlin, 42-43
"White Terror" (Hungary), 139-40
Wieczorek, Jan, 130
Wilson, Woodrow, 37
Witkiewicz, Jan, 124
Wolfe, Bertram D., 24
"Workers' councils," 239, 243
World Affairs Council (Los Angeles), 172
World War I, 33, 139
World War II, 25-26, 28, 87, 93, 166, 199, 221, 239, 257
World War III fears, 44, 45, 91, 269
World Youth Festival, 92
Writers' Association (Hungary), 53, 150, 154, 162, 195
Writers' Association Congress (Hungary), 145, 170-71, 185, 196
Writers' Congress (Czechoslovakia), 176, 185
Writers' Congress (Poland), 185
Writers' Union (Poland), 53, 92
Wyszyński, Stefan, 89, 266, 269

Y

Yalta Conference (1945), 25, 29, 30, 31, 39
Yalu River, Korea/Manchuria, 46
Yenukidze (Soviet official), 12
Youth Union (Slovakia), 68, 71
"Yugoslav Affair," 15
Yugoslav Communist Party, 56
Yugoslav way, 244, 260
Yugov, Anton, 173

Z

Zalenka, Jan, 63
Zambrowski, Roman, 90
Zapotocký, Antonín, 63, 181
Zawadzki (Polish communist), 248, 252
Zelmanović, Đorđe, 201-2, 205
Żeran auto factory, 254, 256
Zhivkov, Todor, 80
Zhukov, Georgy, 29, 52, 189, 245-46
ZISPO. *See* Cegielski plant
ZNIK. *See* Poznań Rolling Stock Repair Factory
Żurek, Kazimierz, 225
Życie Warszawy ("Warsaw Life") (newspaper), 263-64

About the Author

John P. C. Matthews retired in 1994 from the presidency of his own company, East Europe Trade Associates, to conduct research on the year 1956 in east-central Europe. The first product of his research, "Majáles: The Abortive Student Revolt in Czechoslovakia in 1956," was published by the Cold War International History Project of the Woodrow Wilson International Center for Scholars in 1998. He is currently beginning research for a book on the Hungarian revolution of 1956.

In 1968 he helped to found the International Research and Exchanges Board (IREX) and until 1981 was in charge of its East European operations. Prior to that he helped to administer international programs at his alma mater, Princeton University, from which he had graduated in 1951. Three years as Director of Programs at the World Affairs Center of the Foreign Policy Association in New York followed his ten years with the Free Europe Committee, which he served in both Munich and New York. After four and a half years with Radio Free Europe (RFE) he joined Free Europe Press and eventually became head of European operations for that branch of the committee. Relevant articles include: "Renewal in Poland," *Worldview*, June 1981," "Hungary Remembered, 1956-1981," *Worldview*, Nov. 1981, and "RFE's Role in the Hungarian Revolution," *Budapest Sun*, Nov. 4-10, 1993.

Matthews resides in Princeton, New Jersey, and summers in Middletown, Rhode Island.

Printed in the United States
879400002B